Knowing God's Word

Knowing God's Word

Stanley A. Ellisen

Thomas Nelson Publishers
Nashville • Camden • New York

Published in Nashville, Tennessee, by Thomas Nelson, Inc., Published and distributed in Canada by Lawson Falle, Ltd., Cambridge, Ontario.

Library of Congress Cataloging in Publication Data
Ellisen, Stanley A.
 Knowing God's Word.

 1. Bible. O.T.—Outlines, syllabi, etc. I. Title.
BS1193.E44 1984   221.6′1   84-14795
ISBN 0-8407-5886-3

Printed in the United States of America.
1 2 3 4 5 6 7 8 9 10 11 12 13 14 15—88 87 86 85 84

Contents

Contents

Contents

vii

Contents

Preface

How well do you know the Old Testament? This was the Bible of Jesus and the Apostles and is the foundation of the New Testament. Though it is almost a closed book for many of our modern generation, it speaks with great illustrations to the problems of our day. The purpose of these Interpretive Charts and Outlines is to help open those pages and unlock their treasures with the help of graphic overviews. Knowing God's Word in the Old Testament has the explicit promise of true success in life (Josh. 1:8).

Though many fine "introductions" and "surveys" of the Old Testament are available dealing with technical matters of backgrounds and apologetics, simple guides to the content, movements and personal applications of these books are not so plentiful. This is quickly discovered by anyone seeking to study or teach the Old Testament books. That was my experience some twenty-five years ago as I prepared for the teaching task. To fill this need, much of my doctoral work was done in this area of research and organization. Since then it has been my delight to teach and refine these materials by developing workbooks on all books of the Bible. The seminary classroom has proved a most wholesome "crucible of fire" for both teacher and workbooks. This present volume is an attempt to summarize the basic substance of those materials on the Old Testament, using graphs to display the contents, movements, and relationships.

Several essential features have been highlighted. Each of the four Old Testament divisions has been introduced to help one appreciate the various types of literature. The individual books are then introduced and sketched with a symmetrical and interpretive outline. This outline is given in a single-page display to show its symmetry and relationship to the central theme, making it easy to grasp and recall. Many chronologies and historic listings have been included. These serve to set the people and events in more clear perspective and to show the drama between biblical and historical settings and events. A final feature included is a section of "Unique Contributions" for each book to show the individual importance of that book and how it harmonizes and contributes to the whole of the Bible.

Numerous acknowledgments and debts clamor for mention. Suffice it to say that I claim no originality in the effort, having consulted and gleaned from a vast array of biblical craftsmen and women over the years. Patient teachers and more patient students have contributed much by way of input and encouragement. Speaking of patience, my wife, Evelyn, has without doubt contributed the most. I would finally express my great appreciation to the editors of Thomas Nelson for their interest and "faith" in the project. The encouragement and suggestions of Ronald E. Pitkin, Executive Editor, Academic and Reference Books, have been most invaluable, and the meticulous copyediting of Marlene Patterson so essential to the completion of the work. Their patience with my heavy classroom schedule while refining the materials has been grace itself.

Solomon said: "*It is* the glory of God to conceal a matter, But the glory of kings *is* to search out a matter" (Prov. 25:2). The Lord delights to "play hide-and-seek" with us in our quest for truth to mature us with the joy of its discovery. Our sincere hope is that these charts and outlines will enhance that search in the Old Testament and provide many fruitful applications to life.

Stanley A. Ellisen
Portland, Oregon

Guiding Principles for Bible Interpretation

Problem	Principle
How much of the Bible is actually true?	1. Recognize all the Bible as the inerrant Word of God by virtue of its being "God-breathed" as God's Word. "Thy Word is truth." This quality of "truth" extends to all its recorded data.
Which translation should we use for Bible study?	2. It is helpful to use various translations for reading and study purposes. The final ground of appeal for any doctrine or interpretation, however, should be the Hebrew and Greek texts of the two Testaments.
How literally should we interpret the Bible?	3. Seek the meaning most normally understood by the people addressed. This is done by interpreting the grammar in its historical setting. As with all literature, recognize the occasional use of figures of speech to convey and impress literal truths.
	4. Be sure the interpretation fits the historic context and answers the specific problem involved. This is inductive Bible study. Beware of claiming promises or applying charges out of their contexts.
How can we check whether we have the correct interpretation?	5. Check doubtful interpretations by referring to other clear passages on the subject. This is the deductive principle of the "analogy of faith" which recognizes the overall harmony of the Bible.
	6. Recognize the principle of "progressive revelation." This reminds us that God gave the Word in a gradual, progressive stream of truth that was adequate for each generation, and yet only complete in the whole.
How should we understand human descriptions of divine truths?	7. Recognize the principle of "divine accommodation." This means that God appropriated human language, not as a "faulty instrument," but as a prepared vehicle to convey His truth. Divine truths are often taught by the use of human analogies.
How should we make applications for Christian living today?	8. Learn to draw principles from the historic lessons and doctrinal truths of a text. Study of the text is really aborted without this careful application of principles for Christian living today.

The Hebrew Calendar
and Time Reckoning

THE HEBREW YEAR. Israel developed a lunisolar calendar, fixing all their annual festivals by the new moon. The sacred year began with the new moon of the vernal equinox, which became Abib 1 ("Nisan" after 600 B.C.) Modern Jews use a "civil" calendar that begins with the new moon of the autumnal equinox, Tishri 1. Their year had twelve months of 30 or 29 days alternately. This made a lunar year of 354 days, approximately 11¼ days short of the solar year (365 days, 5 hrs., 48 min., 46 sec.). This shortage was made up by adding an intercalary month after the last month every three years (or every 3rd, 6th, 8th, 11th, 14th, 17th, and 19th year of a 19 year cycle). Adding these "leap year" months preserved the regularity of harvests and restored the solar year. The Hebrew calendar dates from the "year of creation," 3760 BCE (B.C.), as determined by Rabbi Jose ben Halafta, c. A.D. 125 (Louis Finkelstein, *The Jews,* Vol. II, p. 1786).

THE HEBREW MONTH. Israel's months always began with the new moon, and trumpets were blown to announce them. They were called by numerical order in ancient Israel, only four having names: Abib and Ziff, the first two in the spring, and Ethanim and Bul, the 7th and 8th (first two of fall). In Babylonian or post-exilic times, Abib became Nisan and six others were named or renamed: Sivan (3rd), Elul (6th), Tishri (7th), Kislev (9th), Shebat (11th), and Adar (12th). The Talmud later made the following changes and additions: Iyyar (2nd), Tammuz (4th), Av (5th), Marheshvan or Heshvan (8th), and Tebet (10th). The intercalary month was called Ve-Adar or Adar II.

THE HEBREW CALENDAR CORRELATED WITH THE GREGORIAN. Our calendar is solar, called "Gregorian" after Pope Gregory who in 1582 revised the Julian calendar which was instituted by Julius Caesar in 45 B.C. The Gregorian adjustment simply cancelled the leap-year day of each hundredth year, except for the fourth hundred, to shorten the Julian year by twelve minutes. Because the lunar year is 11¼ days shorter than the solar, the new moon on our calendar drops back 11¼ days (or jumps ahead 19) each year, continually changing the relation of Hebrew months to the Gregorian. This continual change may be observed from the following correlation for the years 1983-1987 (*American Jewish Year Book,* 1983).

THE DIFFICULTY OF TRANSLATING EXACT HEBREW DATES. The chart on page 4 demonstrates the impossibility of expressing Bible dates on our calendar with accurate equivalency. The common method is to identify Hebrew months within two of our months (e.g., Nisan = Mar./Apr.; Iyyar = Apr./May, etc.). This points to the general time-frame, but lacks the preciseness expressed in the Hebrew texts. In these charts and outlines we have chosen to simply place the Hebrew dates on our calendar months in their numerical order. This admittedly sacrifices astronomical accuracy, but it serves our purpose of making the biblical dates both specific and easily remembered.

Hebrew Months	(Days)		Sample Correlation of Hebrew Months With Gregorian Months					
Pre-exile	Post-exile		New Moon	1983	1984	1985	1986	1987
1st Abib	Nisan	(30)	Nisan 1 — Mar. 15	Apr. 3	Mar. 23	Apr. 10	Mar. 31
2nd Ziff	Iyyar	(29)	Iyyar 1 — Apr. 13	May 2	Apr. 21	May 9	Apr. 29
3rd	Sivan	(30)	Sivan 1 — May 13	June 1	May 21	June 8	May 29
4th	Tammuz	(29)	Tammuz 1 — June 11	June 30	June 19	July 7	June 27
5th	Av	(30)	Av 1 — July 11	July 30	July 19	Aug. 6	July 27
6th	Elul	(29)	Elul 1 — Aug. 9	Aug. 28	Aug. 17	Sept. 4	Aug. 25
7th Ethanim	Tishri	(30)	Tishri 1 — Sept. 8	Sept. 27	Sept. 16	Oct. 4	Sept. 24
8th Bul	Heshvan	(29)	Heshvan 1 — Oct. 7	Oct. 26	Oct. 15	Nov. 2	Oct. 23
9th	Kislev	(30)	Kislev 1 — Nov. 6	Nov. 25	Nov. 14	Dec. 2	Nov. 22
10th	Tebet	(29)	Tebet 1 — Dec. 6	Dec. 24	Dec. 13	Jan. 1	Dec. 22
11th	Shebat	(30)	Shebat 1 — Jan. 5	Jan. 23	Jan. 11	Jan. 31	Jan. 21
12th	Adar	(29)	Adar 1 — Feb. 3	Feb. 21	Feb. 9	Mar. 1	Feb. 20
	Adar II		Adar II 1 — Mar. 4	—	Mar. 11	—	—

The Books of the Old Testament

The Greek and English Arrangement—39

THE HISTORICAL BOOKS	(17)	Pentateuch	(5)	Genesis through Deuteronomy
		Later History	(12)	Joshua through Esther
THE POETIC BOOKS	(5)	Wisdom	(3)	Job; Proverbs; Ecclesiastes
		Hymnic	(2)	Psalms; Song of Solomon
THE PROPHETIC BOOKS	(17)	Major	(5)	Isaiah through Daniel
		Minor	(12)	Hosea through Malachi

Chronological Structure
of the Old Testament

The Old Testament contains a history framed in a broad chronological structure. The Book of Genesis begins with primeval history where no secular events can be related. It gives both the genealogical line and a careful dating of births and deaths. Each member from Adam to

The Hebrew Arrangement—24

THE LAW —"Torah"	(5)	Books of Moses	Genesis —"In the beginning" Exodus —"Now these *are* the names" Leviticus —"Now the LORD called" Numbers —"Now the LORD spoke" Deuteronomy —"These *are* the words"
THE PROPHETS —"Neviim"	(8)	Former Prophets	Joshua Judges Samuels Kings
		Latter Prophets	Isaiah Jeremiah Ezekiel The Twelve (Minors)
THE WRITINGS —"Kethubim"	(11)	Poetic Books	Job Psalms "Book of Praises" Proverbs
		Scrolls (Rolls) (Read at Feasts)	Song of Solomon (Read at Passover) Ruth (At Pentecost) Lamentations (Announcement of Destruction at Jerusalem) Ecclesiastes (At Tabernacles) Esther (At Purim)
		Histories	Daniel Ezra–Nehemiah Chronicles (1 and 2) "Words of Days"

Catholic and Anglican Bibles also include Apocryphal books (from Greek LXX), calling them "Deutero-canonical." These are *1 Esdras, Tobit, Judith, Wisdom of Solomon, Ecclesiasticus* (Sirach), *Baruch, The Prayer of Manasseh, 1 and 2 Maccabees,* plus various additions to Esther and Daniel, and *2 Esdras* (which is not in the *Septuagint,* LXX).

Joseph is precisely related to his father to preserve the exact time sequence. The period from Joseph to Moses is also described in Exodus 12:41 in exactness, "on that very same day." This precision in chronology is continued to the reign of Solomon in 1 Kings 6:1.

VARYING SYSTEMS OF CHRONOLOGY

There are, however, a variety of Bible dating systems, the most familiar being that of Archbishop James Ussher (1650) who dated creation at 4004 B.C. This variety stems from several exegetical problems, the major one being Exodus 12:40 which gives the length of the Egyptian sojourn. The *Samaritan Pentateuch* and the Greek LXX resolve the problem by including patriarchal history in the 430 years of the sojourn. Chronologists subtract that period of 215 years from the 430 to make 215 years to be the Egyptian sojourn. This happily dates creation at 4004 B.C. precisely 4000 years before Christ's birth (some also suggesting His return after 6000 years in 1996).

The Hebrew text, however, precisely gives "the time that the sons of Israel lived in Egypt" as 430 years. This also conforms with the approximations of Genesis 15:13, 16 and Acts 7:6, and the precise dating of Galatians 3:17 (recalling that God re-confirmed the covenant to Jacob in Gen. 46:3). Based on this more reliable text, we have structured the Old Testament chronology in strict accord with the precise datings of the various Bible texts. The purpose is not to rule out other interpretations such as dynasties or vast age gaps (as in *Sumerian Kings List*), but to clearly unfold the normal rendering of the text as a whole. To interpret a text, one must first know what it says, and justify any divergence from this on other contextual grounds.

CHRONOLOGICAL TIME–SPANS OR KEY DATES:

			An. Hom.	B.C.
1. Creation of Adam (Anno Hominis = year of man)			0	4173
2. Creation to Jacob's descent into Egypt (Gen. 5; 11; 47:9)	— 2298 years		2298	1875
3. Jacob's descent to Moses' Exodus (Ex. 12:40)	— 430 years		2728	1445
4. Exodus to Solomon's temple building	— 480 years		3208	966
5. David's reign begun	—		3163	1010
6. Division of the kingdom	—		3242	931
7. Purge of both kingdoms by Jehu	—		3332	841
8. Fall of Samaria	—		3451	722
9. Judean exile begun (606; 597; 586)	—		3567	606
10. Return under Zerubbabel to rebuild temple	—		3636	537
11. Return of Nehemiah to rebuild city wall	—		3729	444
12. Return edict to Messiah being cut off (See Daniel note for lunar conversions)	— 476 years		4210	A.D. 33
13. Birth of Messiah (Several months before death of Herod who died shortly after moon eclipse March 12, 4 B.C.)	—		4169	A.D. 5

For further study see Martin Anstey, *Romance of Bible Chronology* (traditional classic); Jack Finegan, *Handbook of Biblical Chronology;* Harold Hoehner, "Genealogy," in *Wycliffe Bible Encyclopedia;* Phillip Mauro, *The Chronology of the Bible;* Kenneth Kitchen, *Ancient Orient and The Old Testament.*

Introduction
to the Pentateuch

I   *Title.* The name "Pentateuch" (Gr. *Pente*–Five; *teuchos*–tool or sheath) is a Greek term applied to the five books of Moses. Ancient books were written on scrolls, usually 30 feet long, about the right length to accommodate Genesis through Deuteronomy. They are referred to in the Bible as "The Law," "The book of the Law of Moses," "The book of the Law of God," and sometimes as the "Torah" (teaching).

II   *Authorship.* That these five books were written by Moses is the traditional view of both the Jewish community and the church. Since Baruch Spinoza began to question this in 1671, however, it has been the common practice of critical scholars to deny the Mosaic authorship on various textual and linguistic grounds. In spite of these challenges, the authorship by Moses is strongly confirmed by both internal and external evidences from the Old and New Testaments. The fact that he used other documents, as well as direct words from God, is certainly consistent with divine inspiration in which God superintends the selection of such materials. To reject the Mosaic authorship is to reject the universal testimony of the Bible writers and to undercut the credibility of both the Pentateuch and the rest of the Bible. The authorship is Mosaic, not a mere "mosaic" from different authors. (See The Book of Genesis Introduction for further discussion.)

III   *The Importance of the Pentateuch*

The importance of these ancient books is incalculable. This may be seen by reflection on five broad areas in which they are foundational:

A. *Cosmically,* they explain the cosmos by giving the only ancient account identifying the "First Cause." "The unifying principle of the universe, blindly sought by philosophers and ancients, is grasped in the opening phrase."

B. *Ethnically,* the Pentateuch describes the beginning and spread of the world's three racial divisions, Oriental, Negroid, and Occidental.

C. *Historically,* these books are alone in tracing the origin of man in a continuous line back to Adam. They do not purport to present a complete history of all races, but give a highly specialized history of God's theocratic kingdom and plan of redemption. In the process the history of Israel is traced back to Abraham through whom redemption was promised.

D. *Religiously,* these books are most foundational. They portray the Person and character of God, the creation of man and his fall in sin, and the covenants or promises of God to bring redemption through a divine Redeemer.

E. *Prophetically,* the Pentateuch is the seed-plot of the major prophetic themes of the Bible. It is Messiah-centered history combined with Messiah-centered prophecy.

Together they present a symmetrical philosophy of history, its prophecies fulfilling the demands of its histories throughout the rest of revelation.

IV   The Divisions of the Pentateuch

A. EMPHASIZING THE PERSON OF GOD

GENESIS	God's sovereignty over creation, man and nations.
EXODUS	God's power to judge sin and redeem His people.
LEVITICUS	God's holiness and provisions for holy living.
NUMBERS	God's goodness and severity in disciplining His people.
DEUTERONOMY	God's faithfulness to fulfill His promises.

B. EMPHASIZING THE PROGRAM OF GOD IN ESTABLISHING HIS KINGDOM

GENESIS	The need and preparation for God's kingdom rule.
EXODUS	The inauguration and legislation of the kingdom.
LEVITICUS	The spiritual organization of the kingdom.
NUMBERS	The political organization of the kingdom.
DEUTERONOMY	The renewed organization of the kingdom for life in Canaan.

The Book of Genesis

Introduction

AUTHORSHIP

A. THE TITLE
1. The Hebrews called it "Bereshith," by the opening phrase, "In the beginning."
2. The Greek Septuagint (LXX) translators named it "Genesis" (Origins) after its general content which traces the origins of the universe and man to the creative work of God.

B. THE MOSAIC AUTHORSHIP CHALLENGED
1. Until the seventeenth century the authorship of the five Pentateuchal books was universally attributed to Moses by the Jewish and Christian communities.
2. Following the claim of Baruch Spinoza in 1671 that the author may have been

Ezra, many theories of authorship have been propounded. Critical scholars have extrapolated various original documents because of the different names of God employed, different literary styles, and different stages of the development of worship. Several prominent men are associated with the growth of these "documentary hypotheses":

  a. Jean Astruc (1753) assumed a dual authorship on the basis of the names of God used, Elohim (E) and Yahweh (J), (German, Jahweh).
  b. Johann Eichhorn (1780) also distinguished literary styles with the two names of God, maintaining two authors.
  c. Alexander Geddes (and popularized by W. M. de Wette, 1792) assumed many authors but one redactor who assembled the fragments on the basis of the more primitive and diverse institutions to the more unified.
  d. Hermann Hupfeld, Karl Graf, and Abraham Kuenen (1853–69) further divided E to discern a Priestly Code (P) and determined Deuteronomy to be the latest document (D).
  e. Julius Wellhausen (1876) gave the classic organization of the Documentary Theory, setting the order as JEDP.

3. The Wellhausen Documentary theory with its extremely late dates for the Pentateuch (exile or later) is no longer widely held, but the four documentary theory is.

The four principal sources are generally seen in the following sequence:
  a. J or Yahwist wrote in the southern kingdom about 950 B.C.
  b. E or Elohist wrote in the northern kingdom about 850 B.C.
  c. D or Deuteronomist composed Deuteronomy about 650 B.C., just before Josiah.
  d. P or the Priestly Code was composed from ancient Mosaic traditions after the exile, about 525 B.C.

4. The denial of Mosaic authorship inevitably results in the erosion of other related doctrines as well:
  a. Divine inspiration came into question since the books appeared to be the product of religious machinations, rather than the direct words of Moses, the prophet of God.
  b. The historical trustworthiness of the narratives and legislation also were challenged, inasmuch as an aura of fraudulence pervades the whole. Thus the histories are often seen as pious myths in the development of religion, rather than authentic, factual history.

C. THE MOSAIC AUTHORSHIP CONFIRMED

1. Moses is acknowledged as the most learned man of antiquity and one who claimed to write under command of God (Ex. 17:14; 34:27; Deut. 31:9, 24; cf. Acts 7:22). No other such author of antiquity has been identified.
2. The unity of content, antiquated style, and character of words distinguish the Pentateuchal books from all other Old Testament writings. There is an obvious continuity of content and style that runs throughout these five books.

3. The testimony of Christ and New Testament writers affirm Moses as the author of the five books known as "The Law" (John 1:17; 5:47; 7:19; Rom. 10:5, 19).
4. Substantial archaeological evidences today confirm that intense literary activity pre-dated Moses at least to the time of Abraham.
5. Jewish traditions almost universally recognized the authorship by Moses until modern times.
6. The recognition that Moses used various available ancient documents in his selection process is entirely consistent with divine inspiration, for many other Bible writers acknowledge this practice (e.g., Luke 1:1-3).

Outline of Genesis

THEME: God's Handiwork in Creation and Initiating Salvation.

HISTORICAL SETTING

A. *DATE OF WRITING*—c. 1443 B.C.

1. Though Moses had the ability to write this history during his forty years exile in Midian, it is doubtful he had either the human motivation or the divine inspiration at that time to compose this monumental literary work. A time subsequent to his divine commission at the burning bush to be God's prophet is more likely.

2. The writing of Genesis probably took place during the early part of the wilderness wandering as he sought to instruct Israel in the foundational truths of God's world and His covenant program for the nation.

B. *THE HISTORICAL SPAN OF GENESIS*—2369 years

1. The Genesis story runs from God's initial creation of the universe and man to the death of Joseph, last of the Patriarchs of Israel.

2. This time span is specifically delineated within its narrative as 2369 years, accepting the normal rendering of the Hebrew Masoretic text. (See Chronology of the Book of Genesis.)

C. *THE GEOGRAPHICAL SPAN OF GENESIS*

1. The geographical movement of the book is from the Mesopotamian Valley, known as the "cradle" of the human race, to the Nile Valley in Egypt, the cradle of the Hebrew race.

2. This area with a crescent configuration is called the "Fertile Crescent." Three continents converge at its center making it in many ways the "center of the earth."

D. *THE RELIGIOUS SETTING*

1. Religion or a person's relation to God figures prominently in Genesis. Prior to the great flood, monotheism evidently prevailed quite universally. The judgments of the flood and at Babel were for insolence and rebellion. In the time of Abraham a condition of general idolatry had developed both in the Chaldees and Egypt. The later judgment of Egypt was specifically directed at idolatry.

2. The religious movement of Genesis 1–11 graphically portrays the inevitable results of sin in the world, gradually overpowering and corrupting all that it touches. Beginning with independence and selfish desires it is seen moving from the heart and will to the home, family, descendants, and to society in general. At the flood judgment God had to nearly destroy the race to save it.

3. In the story of Abraham and his covenant line God's redemptive program is traced as God's answer to man's dilemma in sin. Out of a world enmeshed in idolatry (Josh. 24:2), God selected Abraham as a man of faith to be the recipient of His grace and covenants through which His redemptive program would be developed.

THE PURPOSE OF THE BOOK OF GENESIS

A. Its historical purpose was to provide an authentic history of man's noble beginning as created by God, his ignoble fall into sin with its consequences of corruption and judgment, and the introduction of God's kingdom and redemptive programs in the earth. The history is specific rather than general, constantly setting aside collateral lines to trace the redemptive and covenant programs.

B. Its theological purpose is to set in bold relief the sovereignty of God over all His creation and to emphasize the responsibility of man to that sovereign God. Responding positively by obedience brings God's grace and deliverance, while negative responses of rejection and rebellion bring God's hand of judgment.

Chronology of the Book of Genesis*

NAME	DATE OF BIRTH		AGE AT BIRTH OF SON	YEARS LIVED AFTER	AGE AT DEATH	DATE OF DEATH	
	An. Hom.	B.C.				An. Hom.	B.C.
1. Adam	0	4173	130	800	930	930	3243
2. Seth	130	4043	105	807	912	1042	3131
3. Enosh	235	3938	90	815	905	1140	3033
4. Cainan	325	3848	70	840	910	1235	2938
5. Mahalalel	395	3778	65	830	895	1290	2883
6. Jared	460	3713	162	800	962	1422	2751
7. Enoch	622	3551	65	300	365	987	3186
8. Methuselah	687	3486	187	782	969	1656	2517
9. Lamech	874	3299	182	595	777	1651	2522
10. Noah	1056	3117	500	450	950	2006	2167
GREAT FLOOD	1656	2517					
Japheth							
11. Shem	1558	2615	100	500	600	2158	2015
Ham							
12. Arphaxad	1658	2515	35	403	438	2096	2077
13. Shelah	1693	2480	30	403	433	2126	2047
14. Eber	1723	2450	34	430	464	2187	1986
15. Peleg	1757	2416	30	209	239	1996	2177
16. Reu	1787	2386	32	207	239	2026	2147
17. Serug	1819	2354	30	200	230	2049	2124
18. Nahor	1849	2324	29	119	148	1997	2176
19. Terah	1878	2295	70	135	205	2083	2090
Haran	1948	2225					
Nahor							
20. Abraham	2008	2165	100	75	175	2183	1990

GENEALOGICAL OUTLINE OF GENESIS ("These are the generations," Heb. *Toledoth*)*

1. The Generations of the Heavens and earth.   2:4 (From 1:1)
2. The Generations of Adam.   5:1
3. The Generations of Noah.   6:9
4. The Generations of the Sons of Noah.   10:1
5. The Generations of Shem.   11:10
6. The Generations of Terah.   11:27
7. The Generations of Ishmael.   25:12
8. The Generations of Isaac.   25:19
9. The Generations of Esau.   36:1, 9
10. The Generations of Jacob.   37:2

*Note the movement from the collateral lines to the redemptive line.

Unique Contributions of Genesis

1. **THE SOVEREIGNTY OF GOD.** The Bible's initial statement introduces God as the sovereign "First Cause" of all things. His existence is assumed as the axiomatic foundation of all truth. No proof is offered for His existence, for no other authority can judge Him. To do so is to pronounce oneself a fool (Ps. 14). As Sovereign Creator, He

CALL OF ABRAHAM	2083	2090					
21. Isaac	2108	2065	60	120	180	2288	1885
22. Jacob	2168	2005	91	56	147	2315	1858
23. Joseph	2259	1914	?	?	110	2369	1804
(Note: Covenant line goes through Judah, not Joseph)							

DESCENT OF JACOB   2298   1875
TO EGYPT
(Note: The 430 years "in Egypt" was reckoned either from Abram first receiving the covenant in 2090 or its being confirmed to Jacob in 1875 B.C. See Gen. 12:1-3; 15:13; 46:2-4; Ex. 12:40; Acts 7:6, and Gal. 3:17.)

Moses	2648	1525	—	—	—	2768	1405

*1) Dates based on 1445 B.C. date of exodus (John Garstang *Foundations of Bible History*; Gleason Archer, *A Survey of Old Testament Introduction* and 967 B.C. date of beginning of temple (Edwin R. Thiele, *The Mysterious Numbers of the Hebrew Kings*; J. Barton Payne, *An Outline of Hebrew History*) plus or minus one year, and 430 years sojourn in Egypt from descent to the exodus.

2) The genealogies of Genesis are apparently unique among Bible genealogies in that each link is dated by relating the person to his father's age. This compilation is thus intended to present a chronology based on a literal reading of the text of Genesis. It is recognized that very few modern scholars would date the birth of Adam in 4173 B.C.; these dates are presented in the present format as a beginning point for interpreting the text.

answers to no one, but commands respect and obedience of all His subjects. He reveals nothing of His origin or past, but simply appears out of the mysterious eternity past to commence His work of creation. As Creator, He is designated as "Elohim" in Chapter 1, emphasizing His greatness or plenitude (by the plural), as well as suggesting the Trinity. His sovereignty is the great keynote of the book.

2. *THE ONLY AUTHENTIC RECORD OF BEGINNINGS.* Though several ancient documents have been found giving vague accounts of man's beginning, none compares even remotely with the simple and majestic, specific record of Genesis 1–2. Israel's first lawgiver and historian here gives specific instruction with available documents and divine inspiration concerning the origin of all things essential to life. Without this record we would have no objective word on how the world began, how the various forms of life began, the true origin of man, how sin entered the world, how the various races formed, and why languages diversified rather than became unified. This oldest book known to man provides these essentials truths.

3. *THE ENTRANCE OF SIN.* Without this record, the origin of sin or evil would be difficult to determine. Genesis clearly shows that sin or evil is one thing that the Creator did not create. It arose internally within the hearts of the first couple. Its cause was not a bad environment, nor the serpent or fruit tree. These were not the causes, but the occasion. The cause lay in the selfish use of their wills to reject God's sovereign will in disobedience.

At the entrance of sin, it immediately began to multiply. This movement is described in Genesis 4–6, progressing from the heart to the home, to children, and thence to all society. The result is described in 6:11-12 where "the earth was filled with violence," and "all flesh had corrupted their way."

It was not possible for sin to lie dormant or remain as merely a "minor defect."

4. *THE BOOK OF GREAT SUPERNATURAL JUDGMENTS.* Like Revelation at the end of the Bible, Genesis highlights several supernatural judgments from heaven. These were 1) the curse brought on at the fall; 2) the great flood; 3) the confusion of tongues at Babel; and 4) the fire and brimstone on Sodom and Gomorrah. Each of these was for a concerted rebellion against God's will bringing corruption. The judgments graphically portray God's intolerance of sin and rebellion. Attendant with each, however, was God's offer of mercy and grace for responding. It should also be noted that the Lord has preserved the consequence or "wreckage" of each of these judgments to remind the earth of His wrath against sin, even in this day of grace.

5. *THE PROTO-EVANGEL OR "FIRST GOSPEL."* Besides judgment, the entrance of sin also brought God's promise of redemption (3:15). He promised that the woman's "seed" would crush the serpent's head as the serpent crushed His heel (referring to Christ and the devil, John 12:31-32; Rev. 12:9). This is a thumbnail sketch of God's kingdom and redemptive programs. Christ's death potentially destroyed Satan and his kingdom as He provided redemption for Adam and Eve's children. This first promise

from God was the "John 3:16" of the Old Testament, appealing to faith shown by the shedding of animal blood.

6. *THE ABRAHAMIC COVENANT.* The story of Abraham and the covenant is central to Genesis. The first eleven chapters portray "man's dilemma," or the progress of sin, and the last thirty-nine portray "God's deliverance," or the promise of salvation. This promise with its four elements is called the Abrahamic covenant, and it is foundational to all God's future program with mankind. To Abraham God promised to bring

The Bible Covenants: God Outlines His Program

THE SEMINAL COVENANTS	*ADAMIC COVENANT*—Promise of redemption through the Seed of the Woman. (Gen. 3:15)
	NOAHIC COVENANT—Promise of no more great flood for suppressing evil by society. (Gen. 9:1-17)
THE CENTRAL COVENANT	*ABRAHAMIC*—Fourfold promise of blessing to and through Abraham. (Gen. 12:1-7) 1. Personal Blessing — Great Name promised to Abraham. 2. Territorial Blessing — Great Land promised to "seed." 3. National Blessing — Great Nation promised. 4. Spiritual Blessing — Grace promised to all nations through Abraham's Seed.
THE SPECIALIZED COVENANTS	1. *MOSAIC COVENANT*—Personal blessings promised to Israel on condition of obedience. (Ex. 20–23)
	2. *PALESTINIC COVENANT*—Land of Palestine promised to Israel forever— but tenancy conditioned on obedience. (Deut. 28–30)
	3. *DAVIDIC COVENANT*—National throne of Israel promised to David forever. (2 Sam. 7:10-16)
	4. *SPIRITUAL COVENANT*—"Justification by faith" offered all through Seed of Abraham (Gal. 3:8).
THE SECONDARY COVENANT	*JEREMIAH'S NEW COVENANT*—To replace Mosaic Covenant for personal blessing in Israel's new economy. (Jer. 31:31-34)

personal, national, territorial, and spiritual blessings through His "Seed." Abraham's life is a story of the giving of the covenant. In a series of six meetings with Abraham, "Yahweh" (covenant God) 1) stated the covenant (12:1-3); 2) confirmed it (12:7); 3) enlarged it (13:14-17); 4) ratified it in a rite (15:8-18); 5) "sign"ified it (17:10); and 6) added His oath (22:16-18). Guaranteed by God alone, it could not be nullified by Abraham's failures or the failures of any of his seed.

Though partially fulfilled in Israel's history, and spiritually fulfilled in Christ's first coming, the complete fulfillment of all its elements awaits the second coming of Christ, Who is Abraham's "Seed" (Gal. 3:16).

7. **CHRISTOLOGY IN GENESIS.** This book of beginnings also anticipates the coming of Christ. Though veiled to the secular mind, these subtle references alert the faithful to One Who would fulfill their final promise or expectation.

These Christological references may be seen as specific prophecies or veiled types.

Specific Prophecies.
   a. The "seed" of the woman in the proto-evangel (3:15). A coming Son of Eve (or Mary) would fatally crush and be temporarily crushed by the "serpent" or Satan (Gal. 4:4).
   b. The "seed" of Abraham in the Abrahamic covenant (12:3). A coming descendent of Abraham would bless all nations with the offer of justification by faith (Acts 3:25; Gal. 3:7-9).
   c. A "Lion" of the tribe of Judah would arise as world Ruler (Gen. 49:9-10; Rev. 5:5).

Veiled Types.
   As prophecies were designed for Old Testament foresight, types are mainly for New Testament hindsight—more retrospective (1 Cor. 10:6, 11).
   a. *Adam* typified Christ as head of the race whose one act affected all the race. As all

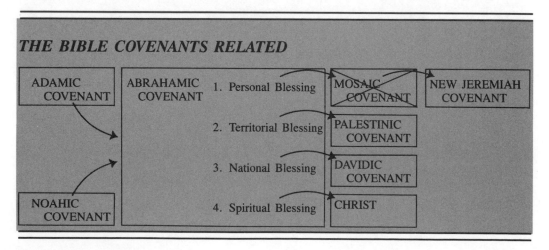

THE BIBLE COVENANTS RELATED

ADAMIC COVENANT	ABRAHAMIC COVENANT	1. Personal Blessing	MOSAIC COVENANT	NEW JEREMIAH COVENANT
		2. Territorial Blessing	PALESTINIC COVENANT	
		3. National Blessing	DAVIDIC COVENANT	
NOAHIC COVENANT		4. Spiritual Blessing	CHRIST	

"in Adam" die, so "in Christ all shall be made alive" (Rom. 5:12; 1 Cor. 15:21-22).

b. *Abel* typified Christ by his "more excellent sacrifice" of blood (Gen. 4:4; Heb. 11:4).
c. *Melchizedek* typified Christ as God's specially appointed High Priest, being also a King-Priest (Gen. 14:18-20; Heb. 7:1).
d. *Isaac* typified Christ as the long-awaited "seed," his submission to altar sacrifice, and his receiving a bride from a far country (Gen. 21, 22, 24). (Inferred by the New Testament, rather than directly stated.)
e. *Joseph* portrayed Christ in many ways by his resisting evil, being betrayed by his brothers, loved of his father, suffering for the sins of others, taking a Gentile bride while in exile, and finally becoming a world ruler after which he restored his brothers (Acts 7:9-13).

The Book of Exodus

Introduction

AUTHORSHIP

A. *THE TITLE*
  1. The Hebrews called it "We'elleh Shemoth," from the opening phrase, "Now these are the names."
  2. The Septuagint translators called it "Exodus" (departure) from the central theme with its redemptive actions.

B. *THE AUTHOR*
As with Genesis, the Mosaic authorship of Exodus is confirmed by its close connection and unity with the rest of the Pentateuch. In this book, however, Moses names himself as being central to all its actions (17:14; 24:4; 25:9; 36:1).

HISTORICAL SETTING

A. *THE TIME OF WRITING*—c. 1440 B.C.
If Moses undertook the writing of Genesis c. 1443, the date of 1440 would allow ample time for the writing of this history of Israel during this first part of the wilderness wanderings at Kadesh Barnea.

B. *THE DATE OF THE EXODUS*—1445 B.C.
Two dates are usually defended by different parties, 1445 B.C. and 1290 B.C.

1. The "late date" supposed. The 1290 date is often posited on the theory that Rameses II (1292–1234) built the Delta cities of Pithom and Ramses. This view denies that Jericho and Canaan could have been occupied in the late fifteenth century. (See Leon Wood's *A Survey of Israel's History,* or Gleason Archer's *A Survey of Old Testament Introduction* for cogent refutations of this view.)

Outline of Exodus

THEME: Israel's Redemption and Organization as a Covenant People.

I *THE EXODUS—EMPHASIZING GOD'S POWER* ....1—18
    A. *Israel's Affliction in Egypt* 1–11
        1. Their bondage and Moses' preparation ....(1–4)
        2. The plagues and Pharaoh's hardening ....(5–11)
    B. *Israel's Deliverance from Egypt* 12–15
        1. The Passover instituted ....(12)
        2. The departure in haste ....(13–14)
        3. The song of praise in jubilation ....(15)
    C. *Israel's Journey to Mt. Sinai* 16–18
        1. The Lord's power to provide ....(16–17)
        2. The Lord's power to protect ....(17)
        3. Jethro's counsel to delegate duties ....(18)

II *THE LAW—EMPHASIZING GOD'S PRINCIPLES* ....19—24
    A. *The Covenant Proposed by the Lord* 19
    B. *The Spiritual and Moral Commandments* 20
        1. Man's prior relations with God.
        2. Man's proper relations with his neighbor.
        3. Moses' priestly relations as mediator.
    C. *The Social and Civil Ordinances* 21–23
        1. To show mercy and justice ....(21)
        2. To respect property rights ....(22)
        3. To provide for the poor and God's servants ....(23)
    D. *The Covenant Accepted by Israel.* 24

III *THE TABERNACLE—EMPHASIZING GOD'S PRESENCE* ....25—40
    A. *God's Plan for the Tabernacle Design* 25–31
        1. Design of the inside furniture ....(25)
        2. Design of the outside parts ....(26–27)
        3. Design for the priests and service ....(28–31)
    B. *God's Punishment on the People's Idolatry* 32–34
        1. Israel's idolatry and judgment ....(32)
        2. Moses' intercession and God's mercy ....(33)
        3. The Lord's injunction in renewing the Covenant ....(34)
    C. *God's Presence at the Tabernacle's Completion* 35–40
        1. The congregation supplies abundantly ....(35)
        2. The craftsmen build superbly..(36–39)
        3. The Lord descends in a cloud of glory ....(40)

2. The "early date" supported. The early date of 1445 is preferred for a number of textual reasons:
   a. 1 Kings 6:1 places the exodus 480 years before Solomon began to build the temple, which is established at 967 B.C.
   b. Judges 11:26 places the conquest of the Trans-Jordan at 300 years before the time of Jephthah (who lived c. 1100 B.C.).
   c. Acts 13:17-20 approximates the time from the exodus to Samuel as 450 years. Samuel died c. 1020 B.C.
   d. Archeologist John Garstang's dating of the fall of Jericho is still the best supported, though doubted by Kathleen Kenyon (e.g. no burials in Jericho could be dated later than 1375 B.C.).
   e. The late date reasoning would require the exodus to be no sooner than 1210, for the affliction and building of these cities began before Moses was

The Pharaohs of Egypt Especially Related to Israel

I THE OLD KINGDOM—Dynasties I–VI—c. 2850–2200 B.C.
   1. *Menes* was Egypt's first king (c. 2850), reigning at Thebes in Upper Egypt, according to Manetho, the priest historian of Egypt in 280 B.C.
   2. *Zoser* (c. 2700) of the third dynasty, reigned at Memphis and built there the Step Pyramid, the first of about sixty pyramids to be built from 2700 to 2200 B.C.
   3. *Khufu* (c. 2400) of the fourth dynasty, built the greatest of the pyramids (nearly 500 feet high), and his successor, *Khafre*, built the great Sphinx.

II THE INTERMEDIATE KINGDOM—Dynasties VII–XI—2200–1900 B.C.

III THE STRONG MIDDLE KINGDOM—Dynasty XII—1900–1750 B.C.
   4. *Amenemhet I* (c. 1900) began the twelfth dynasty as the Theban, but reigned at Memphis. This was a period rich in literature and commerce, and Syria and Palestine were partially under Egypt at this time.
   5. *Senusert II* (1894–1878) and Senusert III (1878–1871) were reigning at the time Joseph came to Egypt, one of which made Joseph prime minister and welcomed Jacob and family to live in Goshen. They built the first canal between the Red Sea and the Nile at the Delta.

IV THE SECOND INTERMEDIATE KINGDOM—Dynasties XIII–XVII—c. 1750–1570 B.C.
   6. *Hyksos'* rule in dynasties XV–XVI (1720–1550) constituted the rule of Egypt by foreign Asiatic shepherd kings. Ruling from Avaris in the Delta, they had to rule by force, introducing the horse and chariot to Egyptian warfare.

V THE NEW KINGDOM—Dynasty XVIII–XX—c. 1570–1150 B.C.
   7. *Amosis I* of previous dynasty (1580–1558) ruling from Thebes, drove out the

(Chart continued on page 20)

born, eighty years before the exodus. This would be an impossible date, even for the "late daters."

f. The name "Rameses" derived from the sun god, "Ra," and could have been used long before this strong and popular Pharaoh.

C. *THE LIFE OF MOSES SKETCHED*—Three periods of forty years each.

    1. His first forty years in Egypt at Pharaoh's palace and his parent's home. Born in Goshen c. 1525 B.C., he was the second son of Amram and Jochebed who were of the tribe of Levi. Here he received his religious, intellectual, and military and political training.

The Pharaohs of Egypt Especially Related to Israel

(continued from page 19)

Hyksos. Though Israel's oppression probably began with the Hyksos, it was greatly increased by these new native rulers who feared foreign conquest.

8. *Thutmose I* (1539–1514) greatly enlarged Egypt's borders. It was probably he who issued the order to slay all Israeli male babies, fearing their growth.

9. *Queen Hatshepsut* (1504–1482) was Pharaoh Thutmose I's daughter. She usurped the throne when her half-brother and husband, *Thutmose II*, died, and had a strong rule. She was evidently the Pharaoh's daughter that adopted Moses.

10. *Thutmose III* (1504–1450, though not ruling till 1482) was perhaps Egypt's strongest ruler, conqueror, and builder. Strongly resenting Hatshepsut's usurpation, he tried to obliterate her memory. Defeating the Hittites in Megiddo in 1482, he ruled from the fourth cataract south to the Euphrates. He was probably the Pharaoh from whom Moses fled in 1585, though Queen Hatshepsut was still living.

11. *Amenophis II* (1450–1426) followed his father Thutmose II to the throne at age 18 and was a successful warrior ruler. He was evidently the Pharaoh at the time of Israel's exodus upon whom the plagues fell. The next Pharaoh was not his heir apparent, but a later son, suggesting his first born had died.

12. *Rameses II* (1290–1224) was one of the strongest Pharaohs, conquering even the Hittites in Palestine. He was one of ten Rameses that ruled for two centuries. Many suppose him to be the Pharaoh of the exodus.

VI *THE DECLINING KINGDOM—Dynasties XXI–XXX—*c. 1150–332 B.C.

13. *Shishak (Sheshonk I)* (945–924) began dynasty XXIII which lasted two centuries. He was the first of several Lybian rulers, establishing his capital in the East Delta. It was he that sacked Jerusalem in 925 B.C.

14. *Necho II* (609–593) of dynasty XXVI was the Pharaoh who killed King Josiah at Megiddo when Josiah opposed him in his pursuit to aid Assyria at Carchemish. Soon after Nebuchadnezzar dispossessed Egypt of all her Asiatic possessions.

15. *Ptolemy I* (323) began the Ptolemaic era in Egypt when he received Egypt as one of Alexander's generals who divided up the Greek Empire.

---

2. His second forty years in Midian as an exile from Pharaoh meditating as a shepherd. Here he married Zipporah, daughter of Jethro the priest, and raised two sons, Gershom and Eliezer (Ex. 18:3-4).

3. His last forty years in Egypt and the Wilderness as Israel's first leader. Here he served the Lord as prophet, priest, and king before these offices were established in Israel. He taught them as a prophet, interceded for them in their idolatries, and provided leadership in leading them out of their place of bondage and organizing them as a covenant people of God.

D. *THE GEOGRAPHY OF EGYPT*

Ancient Egypt consisted of two parts, Lower Egypt with its wide delta region, and Upper Egypt with its narrow ribbon of land (c. 12 miles wide) running along the Nile River c. 600 miles south. This land was naturally isolated from other countries by the deserts, the sea, and the upper river cataracts. Having almost no rainfall, it was entirely dependent on the Nile which flowed from several rivers and lakes deep in Africa. Each September the Nile overflowed to irrigate and fertilize the Nile valley with its rich alluvial waters and deposits, making Egypt the "bread-basket" of the Middle East. Its isolated position also made for tranquility and peaceful progress in many periods of its history.

E. *THE POLITICS OF EGYPT*

1. Egypt's politics was greatly affected by its geography. Egypt was made up, as noted, of two sections north and south, and in their history the capital shifted quite often between the two centers of Thebes (No Amon) in southern Upper Egypt, and Memphis (Noph or Rameses) or Avaris in the delta of Lower Egypt. The Bible name for Egypt was "Mizraim," meaning the "two Egypts."

2. Manetho, a priest-historian during the reign of Ptolemy II, Philadelphus (285–247 B.C.), was appointed to write a history of Egypt as part of the literary-science pursuits of this monarch. In so doing he became the main source for information on ancient Egypt. Many other documents and tablets from various tells and tombs have been used by modern Egyptologists to reconstruct that history, but all admit that the datings are yet subject to great impreciseness, especially the most ancient.

3. The Pharaohs of Moses' time might be briefly noted:
   Amosis I (1580–1558) not only continued the oppression of the militant Hyksos, but increased it, probably because of Israel's foreign background and great numerical growth.
   Thutmose I (1539–1514) was the one slaying infants at Moses' birth.
   Queen Hatshepsut (1504–1482) was the daughter of Thutmose I and the wife of Thutmose II, reigning by usurpation herself after the death of Thutmose II (1520–1504) was very likely the Pharaoh's daughter who adopted Moses in 1525.
   Thutmose III (1504–1450) was the Pharaoh from whom Moses fled to the wilderness of Midian, (though Hatshepsut was yet living).

Amenophis II (1450–1426) was the Pharaoh whom Moses confronted and on whom God brought the plagues. The following Pharaoh (Thutmose IV) was not the heir apparent, but a later son, suggesting his firstborn had died.

F. *THE RELIGIOUS SETTING OF EGYPT*
1. The Religions of Egypt.
   a. The ancient Egyptians were very religious, worshiping myriads of gods. They had national gods, local gods, and fetishes related to all parts of nature. Some of their chief deities were: Ra and Amun-Ra, their sun gods; Osiris the god of the Nile was worshiped as the god of fertility or life; Horus was also a sun god, represented by a hawk; Ptah was the god of Memphis and artists. Every object of nature was conceived to be indwelt by a spirit that had chosen that form to express itself. This idea led to the worship of such animals as the bull, cow, cat, and crocodile.
   b. The chief deities had immense temples built for them, and their priests wielded great power over the people and the politics of Egypt. Circumcision was one of their outstanding rites.
   c. A prominent feature of their religions was the belief in life after death. This inspired great concern and preparations for death and burial, and the rich and rulers built great tombs and monuments to preserve their material possessions to go with them into the afterlife.
2. The Religion of Israel in Egypt.
   a. Joseph's spiritual influence on Israel was no doubt great until his death in 1804 B.C., having been their leader for fifty-one years. Their isolation in Goshen also contributed to their protection from the idolatry of Egypt.
   b. At some point, however, the nation fell into the idolatry of Egypt and most of the people were affected by its corruption. This fact is revealed, not by Moses, but by Ezekiel in Ezekiel 20:6-10. For this idolatry and its corruption, the Lord resolved to "pour out My fury on them . . ." and preserved them only for the sake of His Name and His covenant. This perhaps answers the question as to why Israel was so severely oppressed in Egypt, aside from the political reasons. God used their politics as His tool in bringing His wrath on their idolatrous practices.
   c. The coffin of Joseph, however, was a continual reminder to Israel of God's covenant to bring them out of Egypt, back to Canaan.

THE PURPOSE OF THE BOOK OF EXODUS

The primary purpose of Exodus is to describe Israel's redemption from her bondage and idolatry in Egypt to her place of prominence as the Lord's peculiar people in covenant relations with their theocratic God. Moses preserves for the people a record of their ignominious background and God's redemption and deliverance of them through His mighty arm and the blood of a lamb. This purpose is carried out by describing three grand events: the exodus from Egypt, the giving of the Law, and the building of the tabernacle.

Unique Contributions of Exodus

1. *THE BIRTH OF THE NATION ISRAEL.* This book gives the only ancient record of the birth and organization of Israel. It describes her ignominious beginning in a foreign land in cruel bondage, her divine deliverance from her reluctant captors, and her almost instant organization as a nation with a set of spiritual, social, and civil laws to govern her corporate life. Her beginning itself was miraculous.

2. *THE FIRST MIRACLES OF THE BIBLE.* Aside from the supernatural judgments of Genesis, the plagues in Egypt were the first display of miracles or supernatural signs performed by men. These plagues and the Lord's routing the Egyptian army at the Red Sea portray Israel's God, Yahweh (Jehovah) as a "Warrior" (Ex. 14:14; 15:3). This was an altogether unique turn in God's manifesting Himself to the world or to His people, except for the unusual victory given Abraham in rescuing Lot. This first display of Bible miracles also suggests the primary purpose for which miracles were given. They were almost always given to confirm God's Word through a messenger. Moses, being the first Bible writer, was also the first to perform miraculous works as he gave God's Word. God confirmed His Word by His works.

3. *THE PASSOVER SUPPER INSTITUTED.* Though Israel kept many feasts or memorials, none was quite so important as Passover. It was their first holy festival of the religious year (middle of first month). We may discern a threefold purpose in this Passover Supper: 1) It commemorated the physical redemption and rescue of their firstborn sons by the death of a substitute lamb. 2) It also reminded each one of his need for spiritual redemption from sin by substituting a slain lamb, thus pointing to a future provision by God promised in the Abrahamic covenant. 3) Its purpose was also to teach us the significance of Christ's death who fulfilled this type as the "Lamb of God" (John 1:29). As the Passover Supper was a type that looked forward to Christ's death, so the Lord's Supper

---

The Lord Reveals Himself in Exodus

1. The "I Am" at the burning bush	(Ex. 3)—A Covenant-keeping God.
2. The Plagues	(8–12)—A God of Judgment.
3. The Passover	(12)—A God of Redemption.
4. The Red Sea Crossing	(14)—A God of Power.
5. The Journey to Sinai (hunger, thirst, and warfare)	(16–17)—A God of Provision.
6. The Law given	(19–24)—A God of Holiness.
7. The tabernacle, priests, offerings	(25–30)—A God of Fellowship.
8. The judgment for the golden calf	(32)—A God of Discipline.
9. The Renewal of the Covenant	(33)—A God of Grace.
10. The Descent of the Glory	(40)—A God of Glory.

is a memorial that looks back to that central offering for the sin of the world. The Passover Lamb was the greatest type of redemption in the Old Testament.

4. ***THE MOSAIC LAW AND COVENANT INSTITUTED.*** No written document has had more influence on the moral and judicial laws of society than the Law of Moses. Since it was both eternal and temporary, we should note its two basic purposes.

   a. It was given to reveal *God's spiritual and moral principles* for His people as a way of life. It was not intended as a way of salvation, but as a way of life (Gal. 2:21). These principles underlying the Law were given to reveal God's holiness and His intention that His people should likewise be holy. (Matt. 5:17; Rom. 3:31).

   b. It was also given as *a covenant system* or agreement between the covenant Lord and His covenant people. As such it was conditional and temporary, being a test of their faithfulness to respond to Him as their covenant Lord (Ex. 19). It was given to motivate them to holiness by providing a basis for blessing or chastisement as they grew into a theocractic nation (Deut. 5:32-33). As a "covenant system" of blessing and judgment, the Mosaic Law came to an end at the cross when Jesus became High Priest, ending the Aaronic priesthood and Law that went with it (Heb. 7:12). Jeremiah announced that the Lord would make a new covenant with Israel and Judah after the nation has passed through their great time of affliction and are restored to fellowship with Him (Jer. 31:31-34; 32:37-41).

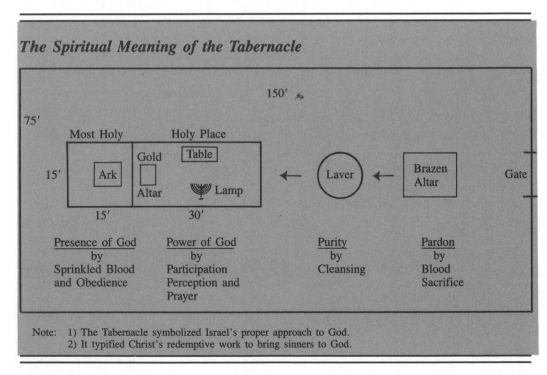

The Spiritual Meaning of the Tabernacle

Presence of God by Sprinkled Blood and Obedience	**Power of God** by Participation Perception and Prayer	**Purity** by Cleansing	**Pardon** by Blood Sacrifice

Note: 1) The Tabernacle symbolized Israel's proper approach to God.
   2) It typified Christ's redemptive work to bring sinners to God.

5. **THE INSTITUTION OF THE SABBATH.** The Sabbath observance for Israel was first instituted in connection with the eating of manna in Exodus 16:23-30. It was later restated as part of the covenant Law in chapter 20:8, and was declared to be a "sign" or signature of the covenant between Israel and the Lord in 31:13, 17 (cf. Ezek. 20:12, 20). As a covenant "sign" or requirement, it was to continue "throughout your generations," expressing their continued response to His covenant leadership. In this sense, the Mosaic Law ended at the cross when the priesthood of the Law ended and the new priesthood of Christ began (Gal. 3:19; Eph. 2:15; Heb. 7:12). As an eternal principle, however, the sabbath requirements continue to remind God's people that the Lord has a claim on their time. One cannot worship and serve God without giving amply of his time to Him. Though grace does not legally demand the keeping of a sabbath, it lovingly suggests that giving time to the Lord is absolutely essential for fellowship with Him and to receive His blessing (Heb. 10:25).

6. **THE BUILDING OF THE TABERNACLE.** Israel remained at Mount Sinai until the end of their first year primarily occupied with the construction of this divinely designed tabernacle. Its primary purpose was to represent a place of God's dwelling among His people. As the Law portrayed God's holiness and man's estrangement because of disobedience, so the tabernacle portrayed God's grace in providing a place of meeting and fellowship by the sacrifice of blood. For Israel it simply symbolized their one and only approach to God through the pattern of sacrifice, cleansing, and walking in His light. Typically, the tabernacle pictures Christ as man's only approach to God. The various pieces of furniture describe in visual form the many purposes that were fulfilled in His life and death to enable persons to approach and have fellowship with Him (Heb. 9:1-14).

7. **FOREGLEAMS OF CHRIST IN EXODUS.** Though Exodus gives no express prophecies of Christ, it is rich in types that foreshadow His Person and work.
   a. Moses typified Christ in several ways; he sacrificed his royal position to seek to deliver his people (Phil. 2:5-10; Heb. 11:24-26); he was rejected by his people at first, but was later received as their deliverer and ruler (Acts 7:35); he had the unique position of prophet, priest, and king (Deut. 18:15; Ex. 24:6-8; Deut. 33:4-5, respectively).
   b. Aaron the high priest typified Christ in many areas of his priestly work (Heb. 5, 7).
   c. The Passover lamb was an outstanding Old Testament type of Christ as the Lamb of God, its blood being both shed and applied for salvation (John 1:29; 1 Cor. 5:7).
   d. The manna was declared by Christ to be a type of Himself, freely given from heaven to be received by the people for their spiritual life and sustenance (John 6:32-33, 58).
   e. The tabernacle and its furniture vividly typify Christ's work of providing a person's only approach to God, as previously noted.

(In applying Old Testament types, it is a good general rule that whereas symbolisms often teach by their structures, the point of significance of types is best drawn from their intended functions or purposes. This serves to restrict subjectivism in their application.)

The Book of Leviticus

Introduction

AUTHORSHIP

A. *THE TITLE*
  1. The Hebrews called this book "Wayyiqra," from the opening phrase, "Now the LORD called." This emphasized God speaking out of the sanctuary. It was also referred to as "The Law of the Priests."
  2. The Greek Septuagint named it "Leviticus" (Leuitikon), because of its emphasis on the Levitical priesthood (though Levites are mentioned in only one passage, 25:32-33). It was a Levitical handbook for priestly service.

B. *THE AUTHOR*
  1. The Mosaic authorship is strongly confirmed internally by the fact that the text declares fifty-six times that "the LORD spoke to Moses." No other Bible book has such strong internal attestation of its authorship.
  2. It is also one of the books that Jesus confirmed as being by Moses, as noted in Matthew 8:4.
  3. The opening phrase, "Now the LORD called," also shows a strong connection between Exodus and Leviticus. The Lord, in Exodus 40, begins to instruct the nation from the sanctuary.

HISTORICAL SETTING

A. *DATE OF WRITING*—c. 1440 B.C.
  This book was probably composed by Moses shortly after writing Exodus during the years of wandering and comparative leisure at Kadesh Barnea. Though much of its content was received directly from the Lord, its organization in this form probably was done after the rebellion and the Lord's judgment of forty years of wandering.

B. *THE TIME-SPAN INVOLVED*—c. 30 days
  1. This legislation was evidently given to Moses just after the tabernacle was erected on April 1, 1444, B.C., and before their march began on May 20. (Ex. 40:17; Num. 10:11). Since the last twenty days were taken up with the census (Num.

1:1), the events of Leviticus probably occurred in the thirty days of April 1-30 (Abib).

2. During this time the first anniversary of the Passover and the Exodus were celebrated for seven days (Num. 9:1-12). Those defiled by touching a dead body were allowed to keep the Passover one month late.

C. *THE RELIGIOUS SETTING*

1. Fresh out of Egypt with its idolatry, these 2,500,000 Israelis spent their first year in the mountainous wilderness of Sinai. Theologians call this their "theological year," for they were given an immense body of religious truths during this time. Instead of going directly into Canaan, they were led by the pillar of fire and cloud south to Sinai. Before encountering the enemy in warfare, they needed a special rendezvous with the Lord. For this the Lord made all provision

---

Outline of Leviticus

THEME: The Need for Cleansing and Holiness to Approach God.

---

of food, water, clothing and health, that He might wean them from idolatry and teach them the ways and character of the One Living God.

2. Having received the Law and the tabernacle, they needed instruction on how to worship and serve at the sanctuary and how to live this life of holiness. This book provides that instruction, especially for the ministration of the priests. This involved proper atonement for sin and separation for service. The word ''holy'' occurs ninety-three times in this book, and the word ''atonement,'' fifty-one times.

D. *THE RELATION OF LEVITICUS TO THE OTHER BOOKS OF MOSES*

1. Whereas the other books deal with much history, Leviticus is almost wholly legislative (with the exception of chapters 8–10). Its legislation is primarily religious ritual. It deals with the spiritual organization of the people, as Exodus and Numbers deal with their civil, social, and military organization. Its key phrase is, ''You shall be holy, for I the LORD your God *am* holy'' (19:2). The word ''holy'' means ''set apart'' to the Lord.

2. Leviticus is central to the Pentateuch in its emphasis as well as in its location. Genesis and Exodus portray man's ruin and redemption from idolatry, bondage, and death: Numbers and Deuteronomy prepare the nation for service and conquest; but Leviticus emphasizes the need for worship and fellowship with the Lord. Between the pardon of Exodus and the power of Numbers must come the purity of Leviticus. Worship and fellowship are shown to bridge the gap so that redemption can be properly expressed and service properly executed.

THE PURPOSE OF THE BOOK OF LEVITICUS

Leviticus has the singular purpose to call God's people to personal holiness. The many rituals are used as visual aids to portray the Lord as a Holy God and to emphasize that fellowship with Him must be on the basis of atonement for sin and obedient living.

Unique Contributions of Leviticus

1. *THE LORD'S DIRECT MESSAGE TO ISRAEL.* Leviticus differs from the rest of the Pentateuch in being almost completely dictated by the Lord to Moses for Israel. The Lord identifies Himself by the phrase, ''I *am* the LORD,'' in Leviticus more than in any other Bible book. Speaking out of the just completed tabernacle, the Lord's first lesson to Israel was on the theme of ''Holiness.'' In doing so He constantly identified Himself as the covenant Lord or ''Yahweh.''

2. *THE LORD'S PRINCIPLES OF HOLINESS.* The word ''holy'' (qodesh) is used in Leviticus, more than in any other book. It simply means ''set apart,'' but is here used in a technical sense as being ''set apart unto the Lord.'' The term is used more of things

and places in Leviticus, but it is also used to describe the Lord (11:44ff.), and often the Lord's people are commanded to "be holy" (11:44ff.). Interestingly, the Holy Spirit is not mentioned in this book, perhaps to impress the objective work of Christ in the offerings that is the basis of holiness. The holiness described is not a mind-set of piety, but simply being set apart to God. The emphasis is both on separation "from" the profane and "unto" God. It is when the Lord warns them to separate themselves from the immorality of the Canaanites in chapter 18 that He first stresses His identity in the book (18:2-3). He had sanctified His covenant Name (Yahweh) for them, and they were to sanctify themselves unto Him.

3. **THE LORD'S INSTRUCTION FOR WORSHIP AND FELLOWSHIP.** The Lord's instruction in Leviticus is not the way of salvation, but the "way of fellowship." Redemption was typified in the Passover lamb as they left Egypt, not in these Levitical offerings. These offerings teach God's people how to worship and give thanks in fellowship and how to restore that fellowship when it is broken by sin. Fellowship is seen as a love relation which involves two things in making a sacrifice: The giving of a worthy animal and the shedding of blood. The first speaks of the believer's gift to God and the second speaks of the Gift of God in atoning for the sin that separates man from God's fellowship. As love always involves the giving of oneself, so fellowship with God must always be sacrificial. The worshiper does not come to God empty-handed, as does the sinner for salvation. Thanksgiving cannot be spelled—or offered—without "giving."

4. **THE BLOOD-SHEDDING BOOK OF THE BIBLE.** Leviticus speaks of "blood" ninety three times, even more times than "holy." We don't usually put these two together, for slaughter is gruesome and removed from our concept of piety today. In Bible times slaying an animal was commonplace for both domestic use and religion. Saving religion by its nature must involve "bloodshed," for "it *is* the blood *that* makes atonement for the soul" (17:11). This truth was first introduced in God's first lesson to Adam and Eve after they sinned. It is here in Leviticus that this truth is first systematized to define the various meanings of those typical offerings. The various offerings symbolized truths for Israel of what worship and fellowship involve, and they typify for us many aspects of Christ's offering as He became the anti-type for all offerings. Without these explanations in Leviticus, New Testament believers could not fully grasp the meaning of Christ's death on the cross. Every believer should familiarize himself with his wealth in Leviticus.

5. **LOVE YOUR NEIGHBOR; LOVE YOUR ENEMY** (19:18, 34). Leviticus 19 is often called the Old Testament "Sermon On the Mount." It could easily have been Jesus' text, if He needed one. This is the high point of love in the Old Testament, never again commanded in such terse terms. Each command is followed by, "I *am* the LORD." Jesus saw this as the second great commandment of God's law (Matt. 22:39).

6. ***ISRAEL'S GREAT DAY OF ATONEMENT—"YOM KIPPUR"*** (16). The ritual of Yom Kippur, occurring on the tenth day of each new year (Zichri 10), was regarded as the holiest day of the year. It was a day of personal mourning for any unconfessed sins of the past year, highlighted by a national ritual that symbolized that confession and God's removal of those sins in the offering of two goats. The preparation for this required the offering of a bull for the ceremonial cleansing of the high priest to perform this holy duty of entering God's presence in the Holy of Holies. One goat was chosen by lot for Yahweh, to be slain; the other was for "Azazel" (or destruction), to be the "scapegoat." The slain goat symbolized the "means of atonement," a proper substitute; the scapegoat

The Sacrificial Offering System in the Old Testament

I   *The Origin and History of Old Testament Offerings:*
   A. God slew animals to clothe Adam and Eve as He gave His redemptive covenant (Gen. 3:15-21).
   B. Abel's blood offering was accepted as "by faith" (Gen. 4:4; Heb. 11:4).
   C. Noah worshiped God by offering clean animals in the new world (Gen. 8:20).
   D. Abram, Isaac, and Jacob worshiped the Lord with offerings (Gen. 12:7; 26:25).
   E. Making offerings was an almost universal practice of ancient peoples.
   F. The Lord gave a systematic pattern of offerings as part of Israel's covenant.

II   *The Significance of Old Testament Offerings:*
   A. Blood offerings symbolized the substitutionary principle of atoning for sin through the giving of life.
   B. They represented repentance, faith, worship, and thanksgiving to God.
   C. They constituted religion in action (Heb. 11:4, "By faith Abel offered. . . .")
   D. They acknowledged and confessed God's right to man's life and property.
   E. They typified various aspects of Christ's "once-for-all" offering.

III   *The Meaning of the Levitical Offerings:*

The Offering	The Symbol for Israel	The Type of Christ
THE ONE REDEMPTIVE OFFERING (Ex. 12:1-13)		
Passover Lamb	Redemption from sin and death through the blood of a lamb.	Christ's offering for sin as the Lamb of God. (John 1:29)

symbolized the "effect of atonement," the removal of sins. Only on this annual day did the high priest enter the Holy of Holies in the sanctuary, once for himself and once for the people.

The word "atonement," used only in the Old Testament, literally meant "to cover" (*kaphar*) and is used fifty-two times in Leviticus. Since the effect of this "covering" was to bring reconciliation, it is called "at-one-ment." In Christ's death on the cross the

THE WORSHIP OFFERINGS (Lev. 1–3)		
Burnt Offering	The dedication of one's life to God.	Christ's complete dedication of Himself to God (Heb. 10:5-7)
Grain Offering	The consecration of one's produce to God.	Christ's body presented to God as a perfect life. (Heb. 10:5)
Peace Offering	The expression of thanks to God by sharing with Him and others.	Christ's offering provides for peace with God. (Eph. 2:14)
THE RESTORATION OFFERINGS (Lev. 4–7)		
Sin Offering	Restoration to fellowship by the blood of a substitute	Christ's offering provides for continual renewal by confession. (Heb. 9:12, 26; 1 John 1:9)
Trespass Offerings	Restitution for damage of sins both to God and to man.	Christ's offering compensates God for damage of sin. (2 Cor. 5:19)
THE CEREMONIAL CLEANSING OFFERINGS (Lev. 14; Num. 19)		
Two birds	Spiritual cleansing from defilements of physical diseases.	Christ's offering cleanses the defilements of diseases. (Heb. 9:22)
Red heifer	Spiritual cleansing from accidental defilements.	Christ's offering cleanses also accidental defilements. (Heb. 9:13-14)

types of the two goats was fulfilled: as the "slain goat," His blood became the propitiation (satisfaction) to God for our sins, opening the way to God's presence; as the "scapegoat," He became the "Lamb of God" bearing away the sins of the world (John 1:29). This twofold work is graphically portrayed in Isaiah 53. Jews today still highly regard this day as their major "fast" day. (Louis Finkelstein, *The Jews: Their History, Culture, and Religion,* Vol. II, p. 1783), but strongly emphasize the removal of

The Hebrew Calendar of Sacred Feasts

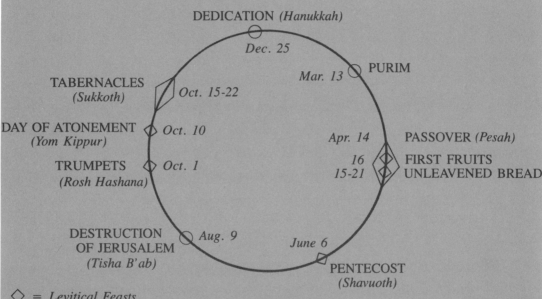

◇ = *Levitical Feasts*
○ = *Later Jewish Commemorations*

Note the Historical Purposes of the Feasts
   1. *Politically* —To keep the nation united by regular convocations.
   2. *Socially*   —To renew friendships at the harvest festivals.
   3. *Religiously* —To worship the covenant God and to remember their covenant
            relations with Him.

Note the Typical Fulfillments of the Feasts
   1. *The Spring Feasts were fulfilled* typically in Christ's death and resurrection and
      in the birth of the Church as the early harvest of Pentecost.
   2. *The Fall Feasts are·yet to be fulfilled* typically when Israel regathers at the
      beginning of her "new year," has her time of spiritual mourning and cleansing,
      and begins her millennial age of blessing.

social animosities to renew bonds of friendship. That of course emphasizes the result of atonement rather than the process.

7. *ISRAEL'S SACRED CALENDAR OF "SABBATHS"* (Lev. 23). Since Israel's redemption from Egypt symbolized her birth as a nation, the month of that event (Nisan) became the first month of their sacred year. In this calendar the number seven stands out in several ways:
   a. The weekly Sabbath —7th day
   b. The Feast of Passover and Unleavened Bread —7 days in length
   c. The Feast of Pentecost (or "Weeks") —7th week (after First Fruits)
   d. The Feast of Trumpets, Atonement, and Tabernacles —7th month (as sacred)

The Sacred Feasts of Israel and Their Significance

The divine purpose of the Feasts of Israel was to bring the element of time into the circle of worship. These were the Lord's "appointments" with Israel for fellowship, instruction, and reflecting on their covenant relations and responsibilities. The following is a summarization of their specific dates and functions.

---

1. *The Weekly Sabbath*—Noted in Leviticus 23:3 to introduce the annual feasts.
   Purpose: To give rest to both man and animals and to provide a special time to remember Israel's covenant-keeping Lord.
   Ritual: To cease from all labor; the priests to make double the daily offerings and to present fresh loaves in the tabernacle.
   Type Of: Typified believers resting in Christ's finished work (Heb. 4:1-10).

2. *Feast of Passover and Unleavened Bread*—14th and 15–22 Abib.
   Purpose: To recall their deliverance from bondage and death in Egypt and the Lord's purchase of them as His "firstborn."
   Ritual: All men gather at tabernacle, houses cleaned of leaven, and an unblemished lamb slain and eaten by the family.
   Type Of: Slain lamb typified Christ's vicarious death for sin; unleavened bread, His sinless life on which believers feed in reflection.

3. *Feast of Firstfruits*—16th Abib (second day of Unleavened Bread; originally Sunday).
   Purpose: To dedicate the whole harvest to God on whose land they were tenants.
   Ritual: Stalks of new grain were selected (on 10th), then were waved as given to the Lord on 16th. (Later the grains were also harvested.)
   Type Of: The new grain typified Christ's resurrection as the firstfruits of the believers' resurrection (1 Cor. 15:20, 23).

(Sacred Feasts continued on page 34)

e. The Sabbatical Year (of rest)   —7th year

f. The Sabbatical Year of Jubilee (50th)   —7th week of years just before Jubilee

Though these Sabbaths had physical and social purposes, their main design was to stress their covenant relations by meeting with the covenant Lord and reflecting on His covenant law and promises.

8. ***TYPES OF CHRIST IN LEVITICUS.*** This priestly book obviously foreshadows Christ in His priestly work. As Melchizedek typified His Person, Aaron typified His work. This work is portrayed by two emphases in Leviticus.

The Sacred Feasts of Israel and Their Significance

(Continued from page 33)

4. ***Feast of Pentecost*** (Weeks)—6th Abib (Sunday).

   Purpose: To give thanks for barley harvest, dedicate the coming wheat harvest, and to recall their deliverance from slavery in Egypt.

   Ritual: All men gather at tabernacle; two leavened loaves (as daily food) presented to the Lord; and liberality shown to the poor.

   Type Of: The two loaves typified the Spirit's two-fold harvest of firstfruits of the church and later of Israel (James 1:18; Rev. 14:4).

5. ***Feast of Trumpets***—1st Tishri (c. October).

   Purpose: To mark beginning of civil year and to alert the nation to the beginning of the sacred month with its important activities.

   Ritual: Trumpets were blown longer and louder on this day than on the usual new moons.

   Type Of: Israel's regathering prior to their day of mourning and millennial joy.

6. ***Day of Atonement***—10th Tishri (c. October; originally Friday).

   Purpose: To atone for any unatoned sins and to symbolize God's removal of them thus cleansing the nation ceremonially for another year.

   Ritual: To mourn and afflict their souls; the high priest to offer a bull and two goats, symbolizing expiating and carrying away their sins.

   Type Of: Typified Christ making atonement for all sins by both paying their penalty and bearing them away (Heb. 10:23-26).

7. ***Feast of Tabernacles***—15–22 Tishri (October, originally two Wednesdays inclusive).

   Purpose: To commemorate Israel's wilderness wanderings and God's care; to rejoice in the past year's harvest; and to fulfill vows of freewill offerings and thanksgiving made during the year.

   Ritual: To dwell in palm booths; to keep year-end vows; to rejoice with fruit and palm waving; priests to offer special offerings seven days.

   Type Of: Typified Israel's millennial joy and peace after cleansing (Zech. 14).

---

a. Aaron's official functions: Aaron's primary work was twofold: to make offerings for sin and to make intercession for sinners. So Christ offered Himself on the cross for sin and then entered God's presence to make intercession for His people (Is. 53:12).

b. Aaron's offerings. These are seen to be of three kinds in Leviticus:

    1) The Passover lamb typified Christ as the unblemished substitute to provide redemption or deliverance from death.

    2) The five worship and restoration offerings typified Christ's offering of Himself in life and death to provide perfect fellowship with the Father, as well as peace and joy among His people.

    3) The two goats of the Day of Atonement portray His complete resolution of the sin issue, both paying the price of sin's judgment and removing or bearing those sins into a place of destruction.

The Book of Numbers

Introduction

AUTHORSHIP

A. *THE TITLE*

    1. The Hebrews called it "Wayyedabber," ("And He said") or more often "Bemidbarh" "In the Wilderness," from the first and fifth words respectively.

    2. The Greek translators named it "Numbers" (Arithmoi) after the numbering or censuses recorded in chapters 1–3 and 26.

B. *THE AUTHOR*

    1. The Mosaic authorship is confirmed internally by its close connection with Leviticus and Deuteronomy, the numerous assertions that "the LORD spoke to Moses," and the fact that the Lord commanded Moses to write (Num. 33:2).

    2. Externally, Jesus and the apostles related Moses to the events of Numbers on many occasions (John 3:14; 1 Cor. 10; Heb. 3; 4; 10:26) and Jesus spoke of Moses as the author of these books (John 5:46).

HISTORICAL SETTING

A. *DATE OF WRITING*—Completed 1405 B.C.

B. *THE TIME-SPAN INVOLVED*—1444–1405 B.C.

    1. The contents of Numbers begins with the Lord's command on May 1, 1444 B.C.

to take a census, and it ends with the assembly on the banks of the Jordan, shortly before Moses' death. The recording of the second Passover on April 14, 1444 is given in retrospect to explain the optional date for keeping the Passover late (Num. 9).

2. The total time in Numbers is 38 years, 9 months, in four periods:
   a. Taking the census and preparing to march   (1–10) — 20 days.
   b. Journeying to Kadesh Barnea; spying mission (11–14) — 70 days.
   c. Wandering in Wilderness around Kadesh   (15–20) — 38 years, 1 month.
   d. Journeying around Edom to Plains of Moab (21–36) — 5 months.
3. See Chronology of Israel's Wilderness Journeys for specific dating of events.

Outline of Numbers

THEME: Preparation for Service Enroute from Sinai to the Jordan.

C. *THE RELIGIOUS SETTING*

1. Two distinct generations of Israel are involved in this book, the first generation coming out of Egypt and the second that was to enter Canaan. The first had seen great miracles performed by Moses and received the Law also in a miraculous way, yet they were destroyed for disobedience and rebellion. The second generation grew up on the Law and on daily manna and were used of God to destroy the whole East Jordan population whom God had ordered destroyed for corruption.

2. As the first generation began to march from Sinai, the mood of the people steadily worsened. It began with dietary complaints about the manna and their lack of thankfulness for God's supply. Even in Moses' own family jealousy and bickering showed up which God had to judge. Following the great rebellion at Kadesh Barnea, many of the leaders and congregation continued in rebellion until the first generation died. Moses also was found a rebel at the end of the period, and was denied entrance into Canaan.

3. The two great sins of the whole assembly in the Wilderness occurred at Sinai and at Kadesh, both by the first generation. The first was idolatry and the second rebellion. Both occurred on August, in 1445 and 1444. Both also preceded the Lord's giving them great gifts, the Mosaic Law and the land of Canaan. Following each God's wrath was shown and His resolve to destroy them was expressed. In each the Lord showed His wrath and His mercy, pardoning them on the basis of His covenant with Abraham and His lovingkindness for them.

4. Following Aaron's burial, a new era began with a new high priest, Eleazar. The new generation had to be retaught many of the lessons of the first, of murmuring, unbelief, and idolatry. This new era commenced with the Lord showing them great victories in Trans-Jordan.

5. Though they were given the Law and the levitical system, it is doubtful they kept all those regulations in the Wilderness, for they did not keep the circumcision requirement until after they crossed the Jordan (Josh. 5:5).

THE PURPOSE OF NUMBERS

The purpose of Moses in this book was to preserve a record of God's long-suffering with the people He had chosen and to show that His redemptive mercy did not preclude His strong punishment for their sins. Though He had redeemed them in grace, He did not save them to a life of ease, permissiveness, and independence. Rather, He saved them for training, service, and warfare. The key phrase (fourteen times in chapter one) is, "All who *were able to* go to war." In this preparation the Lord showed them that no enemy can stand against them when they trust His power and respond to His word. The theme then is, "Preparation for service Enroute from Sinai to the Jordan."

Chronology of Israel's Wilderness Journeys

Book	Event	Date B.C.	Reference
EXODUS (eleven and one-half months)	Passover instituted in Egypt.	April 14, 1445	Ex. 12:6
	Departure from Rameses, Egypt.	April 15, 1445	Ex. 12:18; Num. 33:3
	Crossing the Red Sea.	April 18, 1445	Num. 33:8
	Arrival at Wilderness of Sin.	May 15, 1445	Ex. 16:1
	Arrival at Mount Sinai.	June 1, 1445	Ex. 19:1
	Theological Year at Sinai.		
	Completion of tabernacle and descent of the Glory.	April 1, 1444	Ex. 40:17
LEVITICUS (one-half month)	Leviticus legislation given by the Lord from the tabernacle.	April 1-14, 1444	Lev. 1:1
NUMBERS (thirty-eight years, eight and one-half months)	Second Passover kept—at Sinai.	April 14, 1444	Num. 9:1
	First census of Israel taken. Tribes arranged in camps.	May 1, 1444	Num. 1–3
	Departure from Mount Sinai.	May 20, 1444	Num. 10:11
	Arrival at Kadesh Barnea after twenty-one stops. Delayed seven days at Hazeroth for Miriam's leprosy.	June 20, 1444	Num. 12; 33 Deut. 1:2
	Rebellion at Kadesh Barnea and death promised that generation. (thirty-eight years wandering in wilderness)	August 1, 1444	Num. 14
	Re-assembly at Kadesh Barnea. Death of Miriam. Disobedience of Moses and Aaron.	April 1, 1406	Num. 20:1-13
	Death of Aaron at Mount Hor.	August 1, 1406	Num. 33:38
	March from Mount Hor to Jordan River. Great victories over Canaanites, Amorites, Bashan, and Midianites.	September 1, 1406	Num. 20:29
DEUTERONOMY (two months)	Moses receives Deuteronomic code and instructs people for life in Canaan.	February 1, 1405	Deut. 1:3
	Death of Moses at Mount Nebo followed by thirty days mourning.	March 1, 1405	Deut. 34:8
JOSHUA (one-half month)	Joshua leads Israel across Jordan.	April 10, 1405	Josh. 4:19
	Passover kept at Gilgal.	April 14, 1405	Josh. 5:10

1. *ISRAEL'S MILITARY CENSUSES AND ORGANIZATION* (1–3; 26). As Leviticus gives Israel's organization for worship, Numbers records her organization for work and warfare. Under God's command, Moses numbered both the first and second generations of fighting men for warfare. Though the large number of over 600,000 is sometimes

Arrangement of the Tribes of Israel in the Wilderness *

		Camp of Dan		
	DAN	ASHER	NAPHTHALI	

BENJAMIN				JUDAH
		Merarites		
MANASSEH	Camp of Ephraim	Gershonites	TABERNACLE	Moses and Priests	Camp of Judah	ISSACHAR
		Kohathites		
EPHRAIM				ZEBULUN

		Camp of Reuben		
	GAD	SIMEON	REUBEN	

Note: 1) The camp was always set up with the tabernacle facing east.
2) The camp arrangement emphasized the centrality of worship and the Lord's presence in a theocratic society.
3) Their order of march also emphasized this by the tabernacle and Levites in middle rank, preceded by the camps of Judah and Reuben, and followed by the camps of Ephraim and Dan.

*See Numbers 2

questioned by critics, it harmonizes with other numberings (Ex. 12:37; 38:26), and other biblical references to Israel's great size (Ex. 1:9; Num. 22:11). As Moses had proclaimed in Exodus 15:3, ''The Lord *is* a man of war,'' in Numbers He is seen preparing them for battle. He numbers them, teaches them how to camp and march, feeds them rations, disciplines them to obey His delegated authorities, and leads them into battle. He even shows them how to divide the booty (31; 34–35). Numbers 1–20 constitutes their painful ''boot camp'' experience, and 21–36 their battles, successes, and reassessments for further engagements.

2. ***THE NAZIRITE VOW FOR SPECIAL SERVICE*** (Num. 6). This book of service made special allowance for a lay person to participate in sacred service. The Nazirite vow was available for anyone, man or woman, who desired to give this special service to the Lord. Rather than being paid, however, they were required to make a special offering and were restricted from several normal activities: 1) eating or drinking any fruit of the vine; 2) shaving with a razor; or 3) touching any dead person. These stringencies emphasized the high privilege of serving the Lord.

3. ***ISRAEL'S REBELLIONS AND WANDERINGS*** (13–14). The great rebellion at Kadesh Barnea was preceded by dissatisfaction by both laity and leaders. The laity were judged for complaining about the food, and Miriam and Aaron were judged for jealousy of Moses. Following the mutiny at Kadesh, other leaders rebelled at Moses leadership and were judged. Even Moses himself rebelled momentarily (20:12; 27:14), and was denied entrance into Canaan. The second generation also learned about judgment for idolatry and immorality (25). These many occasions of sin and rebellion demonstrate

Arrangement of the Tribes on the March*

DAN	EPHRAIM		REUBEN		JUDAH	
		Kohath LEVITES carry tabernacle furniture		Gershom and Merari LEVITES pull wagons carrying tabernacle structure and coverings		
ASHER	MANASSEH		SIMEON		ISSACHAR	ARK
NAPHTALI	BENJAMIN		GAD		ZEBULUN	

*See Numbers 2; 10:11-28.

Moses, Aaron and his sons accompanied the Ark as led by the Pillar of Cloud.

They marched by camps and tribes, not abreast but in succession; not in ''lockstep'' but loosely, each family with its members and livestock.

that they were not a chosen people because of their righteousness, but only because of the Lord's covenant mercy.

4. *THE LORD'S GREAT JUDGMENT ON REBELLION.* Many judgments of the Lord are recorded in Numbers, especially on the sin of rebellion. The rebellion of the Levite leaders brought immediate destruction of their families. The grumbling of the people at their food brought a great plague. The rebellion at Kadesh brought judgment on the whole generation, denying them entrance into Canaan. Though Moses was not part of that rebellion, he later shared that judgment because of a quick-tempered rebellion in bringing water from the rock. Rebellion was a willful sin that brought immediate judgment for which no reprieve was allowed (Heb. 10:26).

5. *INTENTIONAL AND UNINTENTIONAL SINS DISTINGUISHED* (15:22-36). Though unintentional sins could be atoned for by various offerings, intentional or defiant sins could not be; these required payment, whether one's life or other required payment. Intentional sins were not necessarily vicious crimes, but sins for which they had been warned. The man picking up sticks on the Sabbath was stoned, not because he was so vile, but because the penalty had been fixed by the Lord (Ex. 21:14; 35:2-3). The penalties of death, however, did not deprive them of eternal life, but of physical life. Moses was one that received this judgment (27:14).

6. *THE PROPHET BALAAM AND HIS "TALKING DONKEY"* (22–24). Balaam was a self-serving prophet from Mesopotamia who was hired by King Balak of Moab to curse Israel. As with his "talking donkey," God used this perverse, heathen prophet to inform Balak and the Moabites of His plan to bless Israel in spite of her enemies.
   a. God here showed His omnipotence over all so-called gods and His irrevocable purpose to bless Israel. Their cursing Israel could only become blessing.
   b. He impressed His continued love for Israel in spite of her impudence, not finding iniquity in her that would revoke His blessing on her (23:20-21).
   c. From Israel would come a "star" or King who would rule over the Middle East. This was one of the first specific prophecies of Messiah's coming, one that the Magi from the East knew as they followed the star to Bethlehem.
   d. Balaam later deceived Israel in idolatry and adultery with the Moabites, for which he himself was slain (25; 31:8). The New Testament warns against his way, error, and doctrine as using the prophetic office for personal gain and seducing God's people by lustful attractions (2 Pet. 2:15; Jude 11).

7. *THE EAST JORDAN SETTLEMENT OF REUBEN, GAD, AND HALF-MANASSEH* (32). The settlement of these two and a half tribes short of Canaan is questionable as to their motivation. Moses saw it as a kind of rebellion and desertion, though he later allowed it after their agreement to send troops into Canaan. Their admitted motivation, however, was that East Jordan was "a land for livestock, and your servants have livestock" (32:4). They appeared to be led by their cattle. In the future, these tribes

Israel's Population in the Wilderness*

	Tribe	Census 1444	Census 1405
Leah's Sons	Reuben	46,500	43,730
	Simeon	59,300	22,200
	(Levi)	(8,580)	
	Judah	74,600	76,500
	Issachar	54,400	64,300
	Zebulun	57,400	60,500
Rachel's	Ephraim	40,500	32,500
	Manasseh	32,200	52,700
	Benjamin	35,400	45,600
Bilhah's	Dan	62,700	64,400
	Naphtali	53,400	45,400
Zilpah's	Gad	45,650	40,500
	Asher	41,500	53,400
	Totals—	603,550	601,730

Note:
1) The tribes of Simeon and Levi (Moses' tribe) were greatly reduced at the second census. (24,000 lost in plague, 25:9)
2) The firstborn of Israel (22,273) were also greatly reduced. With a total of 612,130 adult males, this would mean twenty-seven sons to a family.
   Possible solution: Many firstborn males were slain by Pharaoh and some may have been lost to the death angel in Egypt.
3) The census of 612,130 adult males suggests a total population of at least 2,500,000.

The Levites	Total Males	Service Age 30–50	Duties (Num. 3–4)
Gershonites	7,500	2,630	Carried internal tabernacle furnishings.
Kohathites	8,300	2,750	Carried external coverings.
(8600 = copiest error) Merarites	6,200	3,200	Carried structural parts.
Totals—	22,000	8,580	

*See Numbers 1 for 1444 census, Numbers 26 for 1405 census.

were always the brunt of attack by Israel's enemies. They were the first to go into captivity into Assyria. This at least suggests the danger of settling for short-term attractions rather than pressing on to long-term commitments.

8. **TYPES OF CHRISTIAN EXPERIENCE IN NUMBERS** (1 Cor. 10; Heb. 3–4). New Testament writers saw this wilderness experience of Israel as lessons for Christians to observe, calling them ''types'' or examples. Paul used them as a warning to believers not to displease the Lord by grumbling and making idols of our desires. The Hebrews writer warned of the danger of becoming hardened after receiving so much from the Lord by failing to respond. This, he declared, denies believers of the rest and satisfaction of effective service (Heb. 3:12–4:8).

9. **ISRAEL'S GRAND INVOCATION AND BENEDICTION** (6:24-26). The high priest's benediction as given by Moses to Aaron invoked a threefold blessing on Israel of the Lord's protection, grace, and peace. Meant for those in covenant relations with the covenant Lord, it is most fitting also for New Testament believers. It concludes with Israel's adopted greeting, ''Peace'' (Shalom).

10. **TYPES OF CHRIST IN NUMBERS.**
   a. Redemption money (five shekels) (3:40-51). The shortage of Levites to replace Israel's firstborn males required five shekels compensation per family. The historic lesson was that God required full payment for their lack of Levites to fulfill the service of the firstborn whom God claimed. The type lesson is that Christ paid in full the redemptive payment and service for our sins. His work on the cross was not a mere ''token'' payment, but complete.
   b. Ashes of the red heifer (19). Historically, this symbolized the need to be cleansed from accidental sins; typically, it portrayed Christ's death as including these also, but requiring confession and appropriation (1 John 1:9).
   c. The bronze serpent lifted up (21:9). As Moses required the sinner to look to the instrument of God's judgment, so sinners today are saved by looking to Christ's cross and accepting His substitutionary work for us (John 3:14).
   d. Aaron's rod that budded (17). As the budding of Aaron's rod demonstrated that he was Israel's only high priest or mediator, so Christ's resurrection demonstrated that He was the only Mediator between God and man (1 Tim. 2:5). Note: that demonstration was designed to end all ''murmurings'' or complaining (17:10).

The Book of Deuteronomy

Introduction

AUTHORSHIP

A. THE TITLE

1. The Hebrews called it "Elleh Haddevarim," "These are the Words," or simply "Devarim," (words), characteristically using the introductory words.
2. The Greek Septuagint gave it the name, "Deuteronomion," meaning "Second Law" or repetition of the Law, which the Latin Vulgate also adopted.

B. THE AUTHOR

1. Until recently documentary critics assigned this book to the time of Josiah (621 B.C.), but have discarded that theory now with little agreement as to the date or author of the book.
2. The Mosaic authorship has strong internal and external confirmation. Like most Scripture writers, Moses wrote in the third person, referring to himself thirty-eight times in this book. Just before his death he declared he had written this Law before giving it to the priests (Deut. 31:9, 24–26).
3. Besides many Old Testament references to Deuteronomy as "Moses' Law," there are many confirmations by Jesus and the apostles (Matt. 19:8; Mark 10:3; John 1:17; 5:46; Acts 3:22; Rom. 10:5; 1 Cor. 9:9).
4. The last chapter on Moses' death is an appendix added later, perhaps by Joshua, Eleazar, or Samuel.
5. The differing statements of the Law in Exodus and Deuteronomy do not deny Mosaic authorship, but rather confirm it. Whereas a later, pseudo-Moses would not have deviated from Exodus, Moses himself would hardly have merely repeated the original. The differences are naturally accounted for by the new circumstances which necessitated this further elaboration of the Sinaitic code for the new conditions of Canaan.

HISTORICAL SETTING

A. DATE OF WRITING—1405 B.C.

1. A specific date of February 1, 1405 B.C. is given when Moses gathered the nation for this final series of messages (1:3). Though several sessions may have been involved in its delivery, the term "this day" is repeated sixty-seven times in the book.
2. Since Moses' death took place thirty days later, the speaking and writing of these messages evidently occurred quite close together (34:8).

B. *THE CIRCUMSTANCE*
   1. Geographically, Israel was poised near the banks of the Jordan, eager for the new adventure in Canaan. Having conquered a vast area of East Jordan with almost no casualties under the Lord's direction, they were ready for the challenge of Canaan.
   2. Religiously, this new Israel was different in many ways from the first generation that came out of Egypt. They had not known the idolatry of Egypt, but had been under Moses' leadership for forty years in the wilderness. They had also learned the power and victory of trusting the Lord in battle. They were, however, prone to self-righteousness and idolatry and had many family and social problems that needed resolving. Having learned warfare, they needed to be reminded of the sacredness of innocent life and how justice should be maintained in their life in Canaan.

THE PURPOSE OF THE BOOK OF DEUTERONOMY

Moses' purpose in writing this book or giving these addresses was *to prepare the new generation of Israel for life in Canaan* by a restatement of the Sinaitic Law. Since the original Law was rather brief and pointed, Moses here puts the basic parts of that Law into sermonic form, elaborating on basic principles and making hortatory applications. This he does by reminding them of the past, exhorting them concerning the present, and encouraging them with God's promises for the future. While reminding them of God's Law, he seeks to motivate them by God's love. He stresses the certainty of God's Word and covenant promises, but constantly reminds them of their own responsibility of obedience to bring those promises to pass.

Unique Contributions of Deuteronomy

1. *SUPPLEMENTARY TO EXODUS: WHY A SECOND LAW?* Though Deuteronomy supplements all the four preceding books, it especially elaborates the Sinaitic Law of Exodus 20–23.
   a. Deuteronomy 5:7-21 repeats the Decalogue of Exodus 20 almost verbatim, only giving a different reason for Sabbath keeping, her redemption from slavery.
   b. Deuteronomy emphasizes love: God's love for Israel (five times); man's need to love God (twelve times); and Israel's need to love the alien (one time).
      "Love" is seen as the eleventh command or the underlying motivation of all the commands.
   c. Deuteronomy stresses the personal profit of keeping God's commands: "that it may go well with you" (e.g., 4:40; 5:16). Most of the commands are given with a rationale, as if appealing to one's sense of rightness. In restating the death penalty for capital crimes, it adds the reason: "so you shall put away the evil *person* from among you" emphasizing its deterrent effect (13:5; 17:7; 19:19; 22:21, etc.).
   d. Deuteronomy is more impassioned and hortatory than Exodus, given as a sermon

from a preacher, rather than a summons from a policeman. Moses here addresses especially the conscience and heart, rather than just the intellect.

e. Deuteronomy emphasizes the inevitable relation between obedience and blessing and of disobedience and cursing, not mentioned in Exodus.

f. Deuteronomy expresses a strong concern for the needy, orphans, widows, and strangers, only briefly noted by Exodus.
It includes a special section on human rights (23–25).

g. Deuteronomy has much to say on family life, marriage, divorce, remarriage, and women's rights in general.

h. Deuteronomy stresses the responsibilities of various leaders (16–18).

i. Deuteronomy includes many warnings of the danger of prosperity (6:10ff., 8:10ff. 11:14ff.).

j. Deuteronomy emphasizes God's loving choice of Israel and their need to make a loving choice of Him (4:37; 7:7-8; 30:19-20).

2. *ISRAEL'S "SHEMA" OR "CONFESSION OF FAITH"* (6:4-9). "Hear, O Israel: The LORD our God, the LORD is one!" followed by the command to love God and teach His Word is the central doctrine of Hebrew theology. Though emphasis is usually put on the unity of God, Jesus stressed the command to love God and man (Matt. 22:37). The Hebrew word, "one" *(echad)*, however, means a unit with possible divisions rather than an absolute singularity (as the word "yakeed" would express). In Genesis 2:24 the man and woman are joined to be "one flesh" *(echad)*. The word "one" (echad) insists on the oneness or unity of God, but allows for the later revelation of the three Persons, Father, Son, and Holy Spirit as being the One God.

This Shema confession has been the hallmark of Israel's religion throughout her history, though they have distorted the significance of "one," (echad).

3. *THE CENTRAL THEOLOGICAL BOOK OF THE OLD TESTAMENT.* Most of the strands of Old Testament theology are found in Deuteronomy. It contains 259 references to Moses' previous four books and presents a beautiful blend of the love, holiness, and justice of God. It adverts to Israel's past, present, and future and alludes to the four Old Testament covenants made with Israel. This book treats more varied areas of human relations than any other book of the Bible.

4. *MOST QUOTED OLD TESTAMENT BOOK.* Deuteronomy is quoted 356 times by later Old Testament writers and is quoted over 190 times in the New Testament. It was one of Jesus' favorite books, for He too quoted this book more than any other. In refuting the devil, for instance, He met each challenge with a quote from Deuteronomy, devastating him with its simple power. The devil, in Matthew 4:6, used Psalm 91, quoting it out of context.

5. *ISRAEL'S FOUR SPIRITUAL LAWS* (10:12-13). Moses' answer to "What does the

LORD your God require of you?'' summarizes the Law and the essence of true religion in four points:

a. To fear or reverence the Lord your God;

b. To walk in all His ways and love Him;

c. To serve Him with all your heart and soul;

Outline of Deuteronomy

THEME: Moses Expounds the Covenant Laws for Life in Canaan.

*Note the structure of four addresses by Moses:
 First address, 1–4; Second, 5–26; Third, 27–28; Fourth, 29–30.

*Note the similarity to ancient suzerain-vassal treaties of fifteenth century B.C.
 1. Preamble (1:1–5)
 2. Historical prologue (1:6–4:49)
 3. Stipulations, general and specific (5–26)
 4. Curses and blessings attached (27–30)
 5. Witnesses and succession arrangements (31–34)

d. To keep the Lord's commandments (which are given "for your good").
Micah later answered this same question as a summary of the prophets' message in Micah 6:8.

6. *THE RESPONSIBILITY OF PUBLIC LEADERS* (16–17). Three classes of Israel's leaders are envisioned in these two chapters, judges, priest-judges, and kings. Their primary responsibilities were to administer justice without partiality. Two safeguards were required to insure their impartial judgment: 1) they were to guard against the taking of any kind of bribes, and 2) they were to constantly seek counsel at God's Word.

7. *ISRAEL'S "LEX TALIONIS" Or "Law of Retaliation"* (19:21). First stated in Exodus 21:23-24 and Leviticus 24:20, it is here repeated and declared to be a basic deterrent to crime in Israel (19:20-21). The principle underlies the justice system expounded in Deuteronomy. It was designed as a humanitarian principle of equal justice for all, not as a legalistic "hound of heaven" to gnash at every offender. Its purpose was to restrict punishment to the limit of the offense, and it was never to be done with malice or vengeance. Jesus' reference to it in Matthew 5:38 was to correct their misapplication of it to exact "the last pound of flesh" in personal disputes. It was a judicial principle of the courts, certainly not a personal principle to "get even."

8. *ISRAEL'S RIGHTEOUS WARFARE AND INNOCENT BLOODSHED* (20–21). Israel was called to be God's executioner of the corrupt society of Canaan. This was not to be done as the heathen, however. Special instructions were given to guard against becoming a violent society herself. To accomplish this mission in the proper way, two basic principles were enunciated in these two chapters:
   a. At God's command, they were to slay the wicked as a solemn responsibility, not as an option.
   b. Extreme caution was to be taken in the home society that no innocent person be slain for whatever reason. God would hold the whole city accountable for the slaying of innocent blood. Violence in any form was to be guarded against.

9. *THE PALESTINIC COVENANT WITH ISRAEL* (28–30). Israel was to be God's guest in Palestine and was promised immense blessing or cursing on the basis of obedience. For disobedience the nation would be chastened and finally scattered "from one end of the earth to the other" (28:64). There they would "find no rest," "a trembling heart, failing eyes, and anguish of soul" (28:65). Following that scattering, "in the latter days" (4:30), the Lord would restore them and regather them to the land (30:1-5), when they "return to the LORD . . . and obey His voice." The covenant may be summarized in three points:
   a. The land of Canaan belonged to the Lord, and He had promised it to Abraham's children for an everlasting possession.
   b. Its occupancy, however, was dependent on their obedience to the covenant Lord.

    c. Ultimately, the Lord would restore and regather the nation when they "return to the Lord and obey Him."

10. *THE GREAT PERIL OF IDOLATRY.* Almost unremitting is Moses' warning of idolatry in these discourses (over thirty references, e.g., 4:16-19; 5:7-9; 6:14-15; 7:4-5; 8:19-20). They had come from a land of much idolatry, had reverted to idolatry several times in the wilderness, and were about to invade a land with people that worshiped a whole pantheon of idols. The land of Canaan was rich in many ways, but wicked and corrupt in their idolatry. The tendency would be to adopt their idolatry since this appeared to enrich the Canaanites. They were about to enter a spiritual battle as well as a military one. Moses here discusses the various schemes by which the devil might lead them into idolatry.

11. *THE MESSIANIC PROPHECY OF DEUTERONOMY:* "A PROPHET LIKE UNTO MOSES" (18:18-19). Christ's coming as a Prophet is first mentioned in this Deuteronomy passage. The mission of a prophet was to speak the words of God to the people for which God would hold them responsible. Moses was a mighty prophet in works and words, in mighty miracles and in the mighty words of the Law. His works demonstrated he spoke the true words of God, as did Elijah after him. Likewise, Jesus' great miracles demonstrated His messiahship and the truth of His words. Though most of Moses' miracles were works of judgment, most of Jesus' were works of mercy. In giving this prophecy, Moses stressed the absolute accuracy and prophetic certainty of the words Messiah would speak (18:22).

Select Commentaries on the Pentateuch*

GENERAL INTRODUCTORY WORKS

*Adams, J.M. (Revised by J. A. Calloway). *Biblical Backgrounds*. Nashville: Broadman Press, 1965.
*Aharoni, Yohanan. *The Land of the Bible: A Historical Geography*. Revised. Translated by A. F. Rainey. Philadelphia: Westminster Press, 1979.
————. *The Macmillan Bible Atlas*. Revised. New York: Macmillan, 1977.
  Albright, William F. *The Archaeology of Palestine*. Revised. Baltimore: Penguin Books, 1960.
*Archer, Gleason. *A Survey of Old Testament Introduction*. Chicago: Moody Press, 1964.
  Bright, John. *A History of Israel*. Philadelphia: Westminster Press, 1952.
  Bruce, F. F. *Israel and the Nations*. Grand Rapids: Eerdmans, 1963.
  Finkelstein, Louis. *The Jews: Their History, Culture and Religion*. New York: Schocken Books, 1960.
  Graetz, Heinrich. *History of the Jews*. 5 vols. Philadelphia: Jewish Publication Society, 1891.
*Harrison, R. K. *Introduction to the Old Testament*. Grand Rapids: Eerdmans, 1969.
————. *Old Testament Times*. Grand Rapids: Eerdmans, 1970.
  Josephus, Flavius. *The Works of Flavius Josephus*. 4 vols. Grand Rapids: Baker, 1974.
  Kitchen, K. A. *The Bible in Its World: The Bible and Archaeology Today*. Downers Grove, Ill.: InterVarsity Press, 1978.

LaSor, William S., David A. Hubbard, and F. W. Bush. *Old Testament Survey*. Grand Rapids: Eerdmans, 1982.

*Mansoor, Menahem. *The Dead Sea Scrolls*. Grand Rapids: Eerdmans, 1964.

Schultz, S. J. *The Old Testament Speaks*. San Francisco: Harper and Row, 1980.

Thiele, Edwin R. *The Mysterious Numbers of the Hebrew Kings*. Revised. Grand Rapids: Eerdmans, 1965.

*Unger, Merrill F. *Archaeology and the Old Testament*. Grand Rapids: Zondervan, 1954.

———. *Introductory Guide to the Old Testament*. Grand Rapids: Zondervan, 1951.

Wilson, R. *A Scientific Investigation of the Old Testament*. Revised. Chicago: Moody Press, 1959.

*Wood, Leon. *A Survey of Israel's History*. Grand Rapids: Zondervan, 1970.

———. *Israel's United Monarchy*. Grand Rapids: Baker, 1979.

Young, E. J. *Introduction to the Old Testament*. Grand Rapids: Eerdmans, 1960.

THE PENTATEUCH

GENESIS

Allis, O. T. *The Five Books of Moses*. Philadelphia: Presbyterian and Reformed Press, 1949.

Custance, A. C. *The Flood: Local or Global?* (Doorway Papers) Grand Rapids: Zondervan, 1979.

*Davis, John J. *Paradise to Prison: Studies in Genesis*. Grand Rapids: Baker, 1975.

Kidner, F. Derek. *Genesis: An Introduction and Commentary*. Chicago: InterVarsity Press, 1967.

*Leupold, H. C. *Exposition of Genesis*. 2 vols. Grand Rapids: Baker, 1959.

Morris, Henry M. *The Genesis Record: A Scientific and Devotional Commentary on the Book of Beginnings*. Grand Rapids: Baker, 1976.

Pieters, Albertus. *Notes on Genesis*. Grand Rapids: Eerdmans, 1954.

Schaeffer, Francis A. *Genesis in Space and Time*. Downers Grove, Ill.: InterVarsity Press, 1972.

*Thomas, W. H. G. *Genesis: A Devotional Commentary*. Grand Rapids: Eerdmans, 1946.

*Whitcomb, J. C. and H. M. Morris. *The Genesis Flood*. Philadelphia: Presbyterian and Reformed Press, 1964.

Young, E. J. *Studies in Genesis One*. Philadelphia: Presbyterian and Reformed Press, 1964.

*Zimmerman, P. A., ed. *Darwin, Evolution, and Creation*. St. Louis: Concordia, 1959.

EXODUS

*Bush, George. *Notes On Exodus*. 2 vols. Minneapolis: James and Klock, 1976. (Reprint)

*Cassuto, Umberto. *Commentary on the Book of Exodus*. Jerusalem: Magnus Press, 1967.

Cole, R. A. *Exodus: An Introduction and Commentary*. Downers Grove, Ill.: InterVarsity Press, 1973.

Dale, R. W. *The Ten Commandments*. New York: Hodder and Stoughton, n.d.

*Davis, John J. *Moses and the Gods of Egypt*. Grand Rapids: Baker, 1972.

Finegan, Jack. *Let My People Go*. New York: Harper and Row, 1963.

*Keil, C. F. and F. Delitzsch. *The Pentateuch*. Grand Rapids: Eerdmans, 1951.

Levine, Moshe. *The Tabernacle, Its Structure and Utensils*. New York: Soncino Press, 1969.

*Meyer, F. B. *Devotional Commentary on Exodus*. 2 vols. Grand Rapids: Zondervan, n.d.

*Moorehead, W. G. *Studies in the Mosaic Institutions*. New York: Revell, 1957.

Morgan, G. Campbell. *The Ten Commandments*. New York: Revell, 1901.

Pfeiffer, Charles F. *Egypt and the Exodus*. Grand Rapids: Baker, 1964.

Pieters, Albertus. *Notes on Old Testament History*. 2 vols. Grand Rapids: Eerdmans, 1950.

Tatford, F. A. *The Message of Sinai*. London: Victory Press, 1957.

*Wallace, R. S. *The Ten Commandments: A Study of Ethical Freedom*. Grand Rapids: Eerdmans, 1965.

LEVITICUS

*Bonar, Andrew. *Commentary on the Book of Leviticus*. Grand Rapids: Zondervan, 1959.

*Bush, George. *Notes Critical and Practical on Leviticus*. Boston: Henry Young, 1870.

*Harrison, R. K. *Leviticus: An Introduction and Commentary*. (Tyndale series) Downers Grove, Ill.: InterVarsity Press, 1980.

 Jukes, Andrew. *The Law of the Offerings*. Fincastle, Va.: Scripture Truth, 1954.

*Kurtz, J. H. *Sacrificial Worship of the Old Testament*. Minneapolis: Klock, 1980.

*Moorehead, W. G. (See under Exodus)

 Pfeiffer, Charles F. *The Book of Leviticus*. Grand Rapids: Baker, 1963.

 Porter, J. R. *Leviticus* (Cambridge Bible series). Cambridge: Cambridge Press, 1976.

 Ritchie, John. *The Feasts of Jehovah*. Kilmarnock, Scotland, 1895.

 Seiss, Joseph A. *The Gospel in Leviticus*. Grand Rapids: Zondervan, 1972.

*Wenham, G. J. *The Book of Leviticus*. (NICOT) Grand Rapids: Eerdmans, 1979.

NUMBERS

*Bush, George. *Notes on Numbers*. Minneapolis: Klock, 1976. (Reprint)

 Coates, C. A. *An Outline of the Book of Numbers*. London: Stow Hill, n.d.

 Gabelin, Arno C. *The Annotated Bible*. Vol. I. New York: Our Hope Press, 1913.

*Greenstone, J. H. *The Holy Scripture with Commentary: Numbers*. Philadelphia: Jewish Publication Society, 1939.

 Jensen, Irving. *Numbers: Journey to God's Rest-Land*. Chicago: Moody, 1964.

*Wenham, G. J. *Numbers: An Introduction and Commentary* (Tyndale series) Downers Grove, Ill.: InterVarsity Press, 1981.

DEUTERONOMY

*Craigie, Peter C. *The Book of Deuteronomy*. Grand Rapids: Eerdmans, 1976.

 Keil, C. F. and F. Delitzsch. (See under Exodus)

 Kline, Meredith G. *Treaty of the Great King*. Grand Rapids: Eerdmans, 1961.

*Manley, G. T. *The Book of the Law*. Grand Rapids: Eerdmans, 1957.

*Reider, Joseph. *The Holy Scripture with Commentary: Deuteronomy*. Philadelphia: Jewish Publication Society, 1937.

 Schultz, Samuel J. *Deuteronomy: The Gospel of Love*. Chicago: Moody Press, 1971.

*Thompson, J. A. *Deuteronomy: An Introduction and Commentary*. Downers Grove, Ill.: InterVarsity Press, 1971.

---

*Though all entries are recommended, the asterisks identify those of first priority.

Introduction
to the Historical Books

I **Titles.** "Former Prophets." The Hebrews called six of these books the "Former Prophets" (Joshua, Judges, 1 and 2 Samuel, 1 and 2 Kings), considering them as four books. These are contrasted with the "Latter Prophets" (Isaiah, Jeremiah, Ezekiel, and The Twelve Minor Prophets), also considered four books. The terms "Former" and "Latter" do not refer to their historical chronology necessarily, but to the first and second groups of books. The Former Prophets furnish the historical background for the Latter Prophets. The designation of these history books as "Prophets" emphasizes the fact that they present a religious history, or history with a religious purpose. The Former Prophets are historical; the Latter Prophets are hortatory.

"Historical Books." This group name is a general classification of the twelve books, Joshua through Esther. They differ from the books of Moses, which were also historical, primarily in their basic emphasis. The Pentateuch traced redemptive history from creation to the death of Moses, but its emphasis was on the covenant and legislative foundations of Israel. The Historical Books, on the other hand, dramatize the historical movement of the nation during its whole history in Palestine. Though they certainly do have religious motives and hortatory interludes (by various judge and prophet cycles), their main thrust is on the historical developments in Israel throughout the period.

II **Authorship.** The twelve Historical Books are all anonymous (in contrast to the Latter Prophets which are all identified). They were evidently written or compiled by various individuals with the prophetic gift, recognized as God's spokesmen. Four such men are generally considered the primary authors, Joshua, Samuel, Jeremiah, and Ezra, with editorial help from Eleazar the high priest and Nathan and Gad the prophets. Jeremiah was doubtlessly assisted in the compiling of Kings by his secretary, Baruch. Most of these books admit the use of various documents and chronicles which the authors or compilers used under the superintendence of the Holy Spirit.

III **Historical Movement.** These books trace the history of Israel from her occupation of Palestine under Joshua through the apostasies that led to her expulsions by Assyria and Babylon and to her partial restoration by the Persians. The time period covers nearly 1000 years, 1405 B.C. to c. 425 B.C. They provide the historical framework for the rest of the Old Testament period to the time of Nehemiah and Malachi. They move from the time of Moses the Law-giver to that of Ezra the Law-teacher.

The final words of Moses in Deuteronomy 28–30 constitute an excellent introduction to these Historical Books. Or, conversely, these books demonstrate precisely what Moses said in those chapters the covenant Lord would do for them in the event of either obedience or disobedience. The blessings he promised for obedience are seen in the victorious conquest of Joshua and the glorious reigns of David and Solomon; the curses for disobedience are demonstrated in the apostasies of the judges and the later idolatries and captivities of the two kingdoms. The promises of final restoration await the future "latter days" (Deut. 4:30), of course, but their partial fulfillment is seen in the returns of Zerubbabel, Ezra, and Nehemiah.

IV The Geography and Political Setting of Palestine

A. *THE GEOGRAPHY.* The name "Palestine" was not used in Bible times but was later derived from the term "Philistines," which the Greeks called "Palaistine" and the Romans named "Palestina." The Bible name for this area was "Canaan," the land in which Canaan the son of Ham settled and which the Lord promised to Abram (Gen. 9:25; 10:6; 12:5-7). The land of Canaan (with a curse) was to be given to Abram (with a blessing). Though Canaan originally designated the land west of the Jordan River, Palestine later came to identify the land both east and west of the Jordan.

The land of Palestine stretches from lofty Mount Hermon in the north to the desert region south of the Dead Sea. Its dimensions are 150 miles from Dan to Beersheba, with an average width of 70 miles from the Mediterranean coast to the eastern highlands. Its geography is often described as four parallel strips running north and south: 1) the Coastal Plain along the Mediterranean; 2) the Central Highlands with mountainous peaks over 3000 feet; 3) the Jordan Valley with the Dead Sea at the level of 1290 feet below sea level; and 4) Eastern Palestine or Trans-Jordan, a vast fertile plateau at heights of over 3000 feet. It is a small land of great contrasts in topography, encompassing some 11,000 square miles.

Geologically, the Jordan Valley is a most unique formation of nature being a part of the great geological rift extending from Syria in the north to south of the Dead Sea. This valley was supposedly once filled with water, making a lake of two hundred miles long from northern Galilee to 50 miles south of the Dead Sea. In Bible times this area had three great bodies of water: 1) Lake Huleh in northern Galilee which was 230 feet above sea level (now drained); 2) the Sea of Galilee (Chinnereth) at 685 feet below sea level; and 3) the Dead Sea at 1290 feet below sea level. Joining these is the Jordan River which descends rapidly and snakes some 160 miles to travel the 65 miles from Galilee to the Dead Sea (Salt Sea). The Yarmuk River also joins the Jordan 10 miles below Galilee, carrying a similar volume of water as the Jordan from the eastern highlands. The Mediterranean sea coast in ancient times had no ports for shipping, requiring Solomon to establish shipping at Ezion Geber at the north end of the Gulf of Aqabah. Only recently were the ports of Haifa and Ashdod developed for commercial use.

Perhaps the greatest distinction of Palestine's geography is that it forms a bridge

The Three Divisions of the Historical Books

BOOK	DATE	COVENANT RELATIONSHIP	SECULAR RELATIONSHIP
PRIOR TO THE KINGDOM—1405–1075 B.C.			
JOSHUA	1405–1375	The promised land occupied by faith and courage.	Egypt had withdrawn from Palestine (internal problems). Seven nations of Canaan ripe for promised judgment.
JUDGES	1375–1075	Demonstrations of blessing for obedience and judgment for apostasy as promised.	Small local kingdoms harass the various tribes. The Philistines immigrate from Crete to challenge Israel.
RUTH	c. 1330	True faith attracts a woman of neighboring Moab. The Davidic line is traced to Moab through Ruth.	Israel's peaceful relations with Moab.
THE RISE AND FALL OF THE KINGDOM—1070–586			
SAMUELS	1100–970	The establishing of a faith-king to rule the kingdom for God.	The powerful Philistine invaders nearly take over the land of Canaan.
KINGS	970–586	The kingdom challenged by Canaanite idolatry and is divided and finally taken to a land of idolatry.	Israel is harrassed by Egypt and Syria and is finally exiled by Assyria and Babylon.
CHRONICLES	Creation of Adam–586	The Davidic line of kings traced, and the rise and fall of Solomon's temple.	Surrounding kingdoms and empires are seen rising and falling to serve God's design for the Davidic kingdom.

between three continents and historically constituted the necessary crossing from Egypt to Mesopotamia. As such it was inevitably destined to see much history as the hub of world civilizations and the "center of the earth." This was the plot the Lord chose as His covenant land for His covenant people.

B. *THE POLITICAL SETTING*. Being so strategically located, the land of Palestine was often a prize fought over by world conquerors. Prior to Israel's occupation, it had been taken by the Mesopotamian conquerors from the east, the Hittites from the northwest, and the Egyptians from the southwest. During Israel's occupation, they were often harassed or attacked by these, as well as a variety of small local kingdoms. These marauding neighbors kept them constantly on the defensive.

The biblical view of these political and military problems, however, is always given from the prophetic or divine perspective. Those neighboring nations and world empires were unwittingly serving God's purposes for His people Israel. When Israel was obedient and responsive to the Lord, those other nations were weak or easily held in check. When Israel apostatized, the Lord raised up a foreign power to serve His purpose in chastising, exiling, or returning them from exile. This was so, for instance, when Joshua invaded Canaan at a time Egypt had just withdrawn after strong dominance; when Israel's idolatry increased in the time of the judges, the powerful Philistines from Crete invaded southern Palestine. Likewise with the Syrians, Assyrians, Babylonians, and Persians. In this sense, Bible history is certainly history, but with the prophetic perspective as "His Story."

BOOK	DATE	COVENANT RELATIONSHIP	SECULAR RELATIONSHIP
THE REMNANT'S CARE IN THE TIMES OF THE GENTILES—537–432			
EZRA	537–458	The return from exile to rebuild the temple and to restore proper worship.	The new Persian Empire begins policy of returning captured people and their gods to their native countries.
NEHEMIAH	445–430	The return from exile to rebuild Jerusalem's wall and establish a limited governorship in the land.	The Persian rulers' continued goodwill allows the remnant to rebuild for protection against local adversaries.
ESTHER	483–473	The divine care of the covenant people while out of the covenant land.	Persia rules from India to the Hellespont. The Jewish Prime Minister, Mordecai, brings peace and power to world Jewry.

The Book
of Joshua

Introduction

AUTHORSHIP

A. *THE TITLE*

The name "Joshua" derives from the principal figure of the book, whose name means "salvation of the Lord" (Yehoshua, Deut. 3:21; Hoshea, Deut. 32:44). The Greeks translated it "Iesous" or Jesus, as used also in the Latin Vulgate.

B. *THE AUTHOR*

1. The book is anonymous and its authorship has been hotly debated, especially by those who hold the documentary theory for the Pentateuch. The bulk of this book could well have been written by Joshua himself who knew the facts first-hand and was also a writer (24:26). A later editor obviously added the last five verses on the deaths of Joshua and Eleazar. This could have been Phinehas or one of the elders.
2. The fact that this book is the first of the "Former Prophets" suggests it was written by someone with the prophetic gift or office. That, of course, would suggest Joshua as the most likely author.
3. Since the content of this book is limited to Joshua's leadership, the book was probably authored by him rather than by a later writer who might have continued the story of faith to the time of Othniel in Judges.
4. Joshua was perhaps the most outstanding son of Joseph and was of the tribe that Jacob especially blessed (Gen. 48:19). As Joseph was the "savior" of his brothers in Egypt, Joshua led them to deliverance and rest in Canaan.

HISTORICAL SETTING

A. *THE DATES INVOLVED*—1405–1375 B.C.

1. Assuming Joshua was the same age as Caleb (who was forty years at the spying of Canaan, Josh. 14:7), Joshua began his command of Israel at age seventy-nine. Since he died at age 110, his leadership extended thirty-one years (24:29). We also know that the initial conquest took seven years to complete (14:7, 10).
2. The calendar dates can then be estimated as 1405 to 1375 (by adding the 480 years of 1 Kings 6:1 to the year 965, beginning of the temple building, and subtracting the 40 years wilderness period).
3. John Garstang's archaeological digs have ascertained the date of the fall of Jericho as c. 1400 B.C. (*Foundations of Bible History,* Garstang, p. 145ff.). Findings at Tel el Amarna in Egypt and Ugarit in West Syria seem to confirm the 1400 date in royal correspondences of that period that speak of the "Habiru" in Canaan. (See also Gleason Archer, *A Survey of Old Testament Introduction,* p. 253ff.)

B. *THE STATE OF THE NATION*
1. Leadership of the nation had just passed over to Joshua at the death of Moses 30 days before, March 1, 1405 B.C. The Jordan crossing took place just before Passover, a time when the Jordan overflowed its banks.
2. The entire population (c. two and one-half million) were all in high spirits to invade Canaan after their successful conquest of East Jordan. Though two and one-half tribes negotiated with Moses to remain in Trans-Jordan, they sent 40,000 troops to participate in the conquest of Canaan.

Outline of Joshua

THEME: Israel's Venture and Victory of Faith.

The Tribal Divisions of Israel and the Cities of Refuge

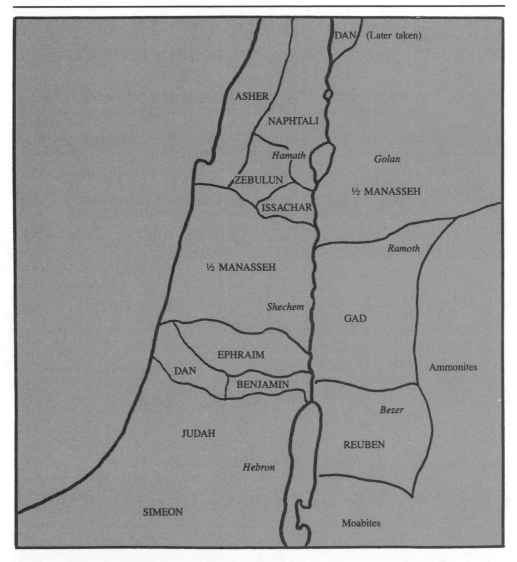

Note: 1) The coastal plains were largely unpossessed.
2) Three Cities of Refuge were provided on each side of the Jordan River.
3) The Levites were also given forty-eight cities in Israel, with suburbs.

C. *THE CONDITION OF CANAAN*
  1. Geographically, the land of "Canaan" constituted the entire western strip from Sidon in the north to Gaza and Sodom in the south (Gen. 10:19). The name "Canaan" was a general designation for the whole area, being the land where the children of Canaan settled. The land was later dubbed "Palestine" by the Romans (following Herodotus) which is the Greek form of "Philistia" (Palaistine). They called the natives the "Philistines."
  2. Racially, the land was populated by a mixed group who appear to be descendants of Canaan the son of Ham and Noah (Gen. 10:15-20). Many Bible listings are given of them (Gen. 10; Deut. 7:1; Josh. 3:10). They may be further identified by their localities:
     a. Hittites   —from the sons of Heth who settled in Asia Minor.
     b. Girgashites—from the region west of the Sea of Galilee.
     c. Amorites   —a mountain people in the highlands west and east of the Dead Sea.
     d. Canaanites—technically, from the northern section.
     e. Perizzites   —associated with the Canaanites in the north.
     f. Hivites   —the peaceful Gibeonites near Jerusalem.
     g. Jebusites   —the warlike tribe settled around Jerusalem.
  3. Politically, Canaan had been dominated by Egypt since 1468 B.C. They established garrisons and royal cities throughout the land and set up native princes, educated in Egypt, to rule as puppet monarchs. In 1400, however, Egypt's foreign power had deteriorated, making the land ripe for invasion. Canaan's cities, however, were well-fortified. Jericho, for instance, was on a high mound, surrounded by two brick walls, one 12 feet thick and the other 6 feet thick.
  4. Religiously and morally, the land was infested with completely debased idolatry. This may be seen by recalling the pantheon of gods worshiped:
     a. *El* was the supreme deity. Ugaritic poems describe him as a bloody and cruel tyrant, of uncontrolled lust.
     b. *Baal* was the son of El and his successor. Baal dominated the Canaanite group and was considered the "Lord of heaven." He was the god of rain and vegetation.
     c. *Anath* was sister of Baal and one of three goddesses who were patronesses of sex and war. Concomitant with her cult of sacred prostitution was child slaughter.
     d. *Ashtoreth (Astarte)* and *Asherah* were also consorts of Baal and goddesses of sex and war.
     e. *Molech* and *Milcom* were Ammonite gods of orgy as *Chemosh* was the national deity of the Moabites.
     These gods of sexual perversion and violence reflect the cruelty and corruption of the people who made gods like themselves (Ps. 115:8).

THE PURPOSE OF THE BOOK OF JOSHUA

The purpose of Joshua is to preserve a history of the conquest of Canaan and the division of the land among the tribes. This history demonstrates the Lord's faithfulness as a covenant-keeping God (Josh. 1:2-6). It also demonstrates for Israel's posterity the great victory that can be theirs if they will simply respond to the theocratic leadership of the Lord, rather than resort to the arm of the flesh. Its theme is the venture and victory of faith.

Unique Contributions of Joshua

1. *FULFILLING GOD'S PROMISE TO ABRAHAM.* Joshua's invasion fulfilled the second aspect of the Lord's covenant with Abraham, the giving of the land of Canaan. As the first promise of a "seed" took twenty-five years to fulfill, the second took nearly 700 years. The promise of a kingdom with a king would take yet 400 years, and the coming of the universal Blessor, another 1400 years. In the Lord's last words to Moses,

A Moral Review of Joshua's Conquest of Canaan

This book highlights a crucial, moral question—how God's chosen people could be justified in taking Canaan, slaughtering its population, and expropriating its land and wealth as their own. We face that moral issue in other books such as Numbers and Samuels where Israel wields the sword on the heathen rather than preaches the Word. Why were they not sent into Canaan as evangelists rather than executioners? Several significant reasons should be noted from the historic background:

1. *Because of Canaan's Debased Religion.* The cultic religion of Canaan had become especially abhorrent in its views of God and of morality itself. Ugaritic excavations have shown the extreme lewdness of their whole religion with its pantheon of gods, e.g., El the head deity is pictured proudly as being completely sensual, sordid, and bloodthirsty even with his own. The three Canaanite goddesses are shown with serpents wrapped about them in vile, sexual postures. The system gave homage to serpents, was totally debased, and was due for extinction.

2. *Because of Their Degenerate Culture.* This worship of demonic sex and war idols reflected a society with the grossest kinds of immorality and violence. Archeological digs reveal their temples were centers of vice with Sodomite priests and prostitute priestesses. Burning children alive on their altars had become a common ritual. The wretchedness of this idolatry may be contrasted with that of Egypt and Mesopotamia whose morality had not sunk to such depths of vulgarity and brutality. The whole culture was due for destruction (Lev. 18:25).

3. *Because of God's Warnings and Patience.* The text many times declares that the Lord was the real landowner of Canaan and could give or deny it to whom He would for reasons

He emphasized the literal certainty of His Word in fulfilling the promise of giving Canaan to Jacob's tribes (Deut. 34:4).

2. *CROSSING THE JORDAN* (4). Why another miraculous water crossing? This one was obviously a repeat of the Red Sea crossing to impress the new generation (who may not have believed reports of the former). Several other purposes were served: 1) it confirmed Joshua's leadership as God-ordained (3:7); 2) it was a sign from the Lord that He was the one dispossessing the Canaanite nations and giving the land to Israel (3:10); and 3) it uniquely demonstrated the power of the ark with God's Law as the ark led the procession into the waters and the waters parted.

3. *THE REDEMPTION OF RAHAB THE HARLOT* (2:12-21; 6:22-25). Though this Canaanite woman is portrayed as both a harlot and a liar, the New Testament judges her actions as works of faith (Heb. 11:31; James 2:25). Did God approve her actions? Certainly not her harlotry or her deception to her countrymen, but her active faith and response to the God of Israel, though it was shown in a crude way. Not having a high

not always apparent to men. His plan of giving and probation is several times noted long before Moses and Joshua:

a. Through Noah God predicted judgment on the Canaanites for their lewdness (Gen. 9:22-27).
b. To Abram and his children the Lord promised the land of Canaan which they would receive after the sins of the Amorites were full (Gen. 15:13-16).
c. As with the Sodomites before its destruction, the Lord doubtless gave the Canaanites ample opportunities to respond by repentance (Gen. 18:25; Rom. 1:18-22). God waited 400 years for that response.

4. *Because of Israel's Divine Commission.* Israel was not called to be a religious organization only, but a civil government with covenant obligations to the Lord. As such, its first commission was to execute judgment on a corrupt and violent society in compliance with the Noahic covenant (Gen. 9:6). Though continually reticent to perform this sordid duty, Israel was under specific command of the Lord to take the land, destroy the Canaanites, and receive its wealth (Num. 31:7; Deut. 9:3; 7:16; Josh. 1:1-7). Israel's attacks, in fact, were often responses to the Canaanites initial attacks (Num. 21:1, 23-24, 33; Josh. 9:1-2; 10:1-4; 11:1-5).

5. *Because of God's Covenant Promises.* As declared to Abraham and Israel by the Lord, the final occupation of Palestine by Israel will extend from Egypt to the Euphrates (Gen. 15:8; Deut. 1:7-8; 30:5). Before that future, final occupation, however, the Lord will again purge the land of vile idolatry and brutality brought in by a Satan-inspired religious system (Rev. 14:16f.; 19:15).

ethical standard, she desperately demonstrated her faith in this God whom she saw coming to cleanse the land of its idolatry. Her harlotry perhaps characterized the moral state of the city and may have been imposed on her, rather than chosen. The enormity of her redemption is seen in the fact that she was to become a maternal ancestor to David and to the Messiah. Rahab thus brought into the messianic line the heritage of Moab which traces back even to the incest of Lot and his daughter. Maternally, Jesus came from many nations (Canaanites, Moabites, Ammonites, etc.), though His paternal line was strictly Hebrew.

4. *JOSHUA MEETS HIS "COMMANDER"* (5:14). As with Moses at the burning bush (Ex. 3:5), Joshua was given a special meeting with the Lord before beginning his work. In this meeting he was dramatically told that the Lord was "commander" and Joshua was His lieutenant. The strategies and logistics of each battle were to be given by the Lord. To demonstrate this the "commander" immediately outlined for Joshua His plan for taking Jericho, an obviously ridiculous maneuver. Purposely illogical by human standards, it nevertheless brought an easy victory by simple obedience. This meeting stressed a principle all subsequent leaders were not to forget—a theocratic leader must get his orders from the Lord.

5. *THE SIN OF ACHAN* (7). What was so horrendous about this sin as to deserve his destruction and that of his family and possessions? Did not Moses promise them the spoils of Canaan as their booty (Deut. 20:14)? Achan's theft from Jericho was wrong in two ways, it violated a direct command, and it was stealing from the Lord (6:17-19). Since Jericho was the firstfruits, or first city of Canaan to be taken, the Lord declared its spoils to be "under the ban" (Lev. 27:29), reserved for His treasury. In later campaigns the people were allowed to help themselves (8:2). This judgment and lesson was most important for Israel at the beginning of their life in Canaan, for they were always to remember that the land belonged to the Lord and He required they always bring Him the firstfruits of their harvests. Cheating on the Lord was the reason they were finally exiled, as noted in 2 Chronicles 36:21.

6. *JOSHUA'S CAMPAIGN OF ANNIHILATION.* This mission of slaughter is hard to reconcile with God's redemptive purposes. Some have assumed from this that the God of the Old Testament was more primitive and judgmental than the God of the New Testament who is merciful and compassionate. (See accompanying chart on p. 60 for reconciliation.)

7. *RECITING THE LAW AT SHECHEM* (8:30-35). After taking Ai, Joshua led the twelve tribes 20 miles north to Shechem to recite the Law between two mountains. Six tribes stood on Mount Gerizim and six on Mount Ebal, antiphonally repeating "amens" to the pronounced blessings and curses. Strangely, the six responding to the curses were the children of Jacob's handmaids (tribes of Gad, Asher, Dan, and Naphtali), plus the tribes of Reuben and Zebulun, the first and last sons of Leah.

This meeting at Shechem was significant for several reasons. It was at Shechem that Abram first received the covenant (Gen. 12:6-7). It was here also that Jacob first came in returning from Haran, purchasing the ground later given to Joseph (John 4:5). The purpose of this pilgrimage of Joshua and Israel to Shechem was to remind them of God's promise to Abraham and of His Law to Moses. The blessings of Abraham would continue with them if they were careful to keep the Law of Moses.

8. *"THE SUN STOOD STILL"* (10:13). Two supernatural interventions aided the southern campaign against the Amorites: 1) The Lord threw large hailstones that destroyed more than the troops; 2) the Lord lengthened a day of battle in which Joshua's army was able to overtake the enemies before they escaped. Though this miracle is often seen as a poetical expression and scientifically impossible, it makes no sense as mere poetry and the text says that day was unique in all history (10:14). Space scientists have recently claimed to have discovered by computer calculations a one-day time lapse in ancient history. Recognizing Israel's Lord as the God of creation, however, makes the problem to be exegetical, certainly not scientific, and the language gives evidence of a divine miracle.

9. *ASSIGNMENT OF THE LAND TO THE TWELVE TRIBES* (13–21). The unevenness of the land distribution is rather surprising. Why the giant share for Judah, Ephraim, and Manasseh and the small share for others? This decision was made by "lots," revealing the Lord's will (Josh. 18:6; Prov. 16:33). We might note several factors involved in this distribution: 1) Judah received the large southern section because Caleb was of this tribe and Moses had promised him the land he had spied; 2) Since Joseph was given the birthright (1 Chr. 5:1), his two sons Ephraim and Manasseh were given the large central section. Also, Joshua was both a faithful spy and of the tribe of Ephraim, entitling him to a special choice. (For some strange reason the four tribes that came from Jacob's handmaids, Bilhah and Zilpah, all ended up in the far north, i.e., Asher, Naphtali, Zebulun, and later Dan.) In accord with Jacob's prophecy, Simeon and Levi received no special area, but were scattered in Israel.

10. *"CHOOSE FOR YOURSELVES THIS DAY WHOM YOU WILL SERVE"* (24:15). This classic challenge was given by Joshua at Shechem as he gathered the tribes at the end of his life. Seeing their tendency to idolatry, he warned of the dangers of presuming to serve the Lord and failing to do so. To this solemn call to consecration and austerity the people responded positively, giving a happy ending to this book of faith and victory.

11. *SEEING CHRIST IN JOSHUA.* Though no prophecies of Christ are given in Joshua, several types may be seen. Rahab's "scarlet cord in the window" (2:18, 21) is often seen as an inferred type of Christ's work of redemption. As blood on the doorposts in Egypt delivered those in the house from the death angel, so the scarlet cord in Jericho identified those of faith in Rahab's house (Heb. 9:19-22). Also the "Commander of the

army'' is doubtless a Christophany (Josh. 5:14). Joshua himself, however, is the outstanding type of Christ in this book, his name being ''Jesus'' (or ''salvation'' of the Lord), and his work being that of bringing the people into rest (Heb. 4:6-10). The Christian life is also portrayed by Paul in Ephesians 6, as a battle that can be won by the use of the full armor of God.

The Book of Judges

Introduction

AUTHORSHIP

A. *THE TITLE*

The title, ''Judges'' (Shophetim), is obviously derived from the divinely appointed leaders who were raised up intermittently to provide leadership in times of emergency during the period from Joshua to the kingdom under Saul. The name ''Judge'' describes two functions of these leaders:

a. To deliver the people from their oppressors as a military leader.

b. To settle disputes and maintain justice as a civil leader.

B. *THE AUTHOR*

This author is also anonymous, but Jewish tradition attributes it to Samuel for several reasons. He was a writer and an educator (1 Sam. 10:25). The emphasis on the tribe of Benjamin suggests the time of King Saul when Samuel still judged, before the name of Jebus had been changed to ''Jerusalem'' (Judg. 1:21; 19:10).

HISTORICAL SETTING

A. *THE DATES INVOLVED*—1375–1075 B.C.

1. This book gives the only account of a long period of Israel's history. It describes three civil wars, seven oppressions by five enemies, seven wars of liberation, a number of peaceful judgeships, and a final unsuccessful judgeship by Samson that ended in a near takeover by the Philistines.

2. Though the total time periods of rest and oppression add up to 410 years, the actual time involved was approximately 300 years to the death of Samson. This difference is accounted for by overlapping and provincial judgeships.

B. *THE STATE OF THE NATION*

1. Following the death of Joshua, Israel had no national leader for over 300 years. The tribes were independent and every man was a law unto himself. During this

time the Lord raised up judges primarily for emergencies, to deliver them from invading enemies and to maintain civil justice.

2. This period was a time of the Lord's testing the nation to see how they would keep His covenant in a heathen environment of idolatry (3:1-5). A chronic condition of apostasy developed as they would enthusiastically accept the Lord's deliverances, and then quickly revert to heathen practices about them when they were without strong righteous leadership.

3. The spiritual state of the nation is in sharp contrast to that in Joshua's time. The Book of Joshua presents a story of faith, obedience, and victory under the theocratic leadership of Joshua; Judges presents a history of continued failure as "everyone did *what* was right in his own eyes," (17:6). Except for the Lord's

Outline of Judges

THEME: Israel's Cycles of Failure and Apostasy Without a National Leader.

merciful rescue operations during this period, the nation would have sunk into irretrievable, heathen idolatry.

THE PURPOSE OF THE BOOK OF JUDGES

The primary purpose of Judges is to preserve a record of Israel's character during the time she was without a national leader, emphasizing her need for a theocratic king. The many cycles of failure and judgment repeatedly emphasize the Deuteronomic truth that apostasy from the Lord inevitably brings the judgment of slavery and chaos.

*Chronology of the Period of the Judges**

DATE	OPPRESSOR	JUDGE	TRIBE	REFERENCE	SIGNIFICANCE
1382–1374 B.C. 1374–1334	Mesopotamia (8)	Othniel (40)	Judah	Judges 3:7-11	Baal worship soon after Joshua. Oppression by a distant, ancient enemy.
1370	Tribe of Dan migrates to north because of failure to drive out Philistines in southwest.			17–18	Cowardice, independence, and idolatry shown as Dan moves north. Grandson of Moses as priest.
1365	Tribe of Benjamin's immorality brings civil war with Israel. Phinehas was still high priest.			19–21	The baby tribe of Benjamin fails to discipline its youth and is nearly destroyed by brethren.
1340	Probable time of Ruth of Moab who married Boaz, son of Rahab. (See Introduction to Ruth)			Book of Ruth	Relations with Moab still good. A Moabitess becomes ancestor of David and Messiah.
1334–1316 1316–1235	Moabites (18)	Ehud (80)	Benjamin	3:12-30	Kindred neighbor disciplines Israel. Benjamin is again strong. Followed by longest peace period.
1230	Philistines	Shamgar	Judah	3:31	Rampant crime in streets of Israel. An early Philistine oppression. Use of ox goad—iron scarcity.
1235–1216 1216–1176	Canaanites (20)	Deborah (40)	Ephraim	4–5	Fearful male leaders suggested. Two valiant women deliver Israel (Jael and Deborah).

---

1. *THE JUDGMENT MOTIF.* As the Book of Joshua demonstrates the blessings of the covenant through faith and obedience, Judges portrays the curses of disobedience. Joshua was full of victory; Judges is full of defeat. Though the longest periods in the book are times of rest and peace following repentance, the emphasis is on the inevitable consequences of idolatry as Moses so strongly warned them. As the cycles of idolatry progress, the times of oppression become longer and of rest, shorter. At the end of the period the Philistines are in control, even seducing and destroying Israel's strongman, Samson.

1176–1169 1169–1129	Midianites (7)	Gideon (40)	Manasseh	6–8	Baal worship and fear drives Israel into caves. Pillages by Bedouins. A humble farmer is empowered.
1129–1126	Usurper king (3)		Manasseh	9	An evil son of a great leader attempts to become Israel's first king by violent ursurpation.
1120–1097	Peaceful era	Tola (23) Jair (22)	Issachar Gilead	10:1–2	Judges as "Justices of the Peace," rather than as deliverers.
1103–1085 1085–1079	Ammonites (18)	Jephthah (6)	Manasseh (Gilead)	10–12	Israel serves many foreign gods. An outcast Israeli is empowered to deliver, then rebuke Ephraim.
1100–1085	Peaceful era	Ibzan (7) Elon (10) Abdon (8)	Judah Zebulun Ephraim	12:8–15	North, south, and middle tribes experience peace.
1103–1063 1095–1075	Philistines (40)	Samson (20)	Dan	13–16	Philistines occupy western Israel. A gifted Nazirite without morals is the only judge that failed.
1095–1055 1070–1020	Philistines (40)	Samuel (50)	Levi	1 Sam. 7–16	First of the prophets and first leader to unite all Israel since Joshua (over 300 years).

*Chronologists vary greatly in dating the judges for lack of secular pinpoints or overall time-spans given. Two essential references are Judges 11:26 and 1 Kings 6:1. Overlaps and provincial judgeships explain the 410 total years in 300 actual years. The dates adopted are similar to those of Gleason Archer in *The Expositor's Bible Commentary* (Frank E. Gaebelein, Ed.), pp. 367-68.

The appendix stories of Dan and Benjamin conclude the book with this judgment motif. Failing to obey the Lord and conquer their enemies within, they are conquered by them and judged of God.

2. *ISRAEL'S NEED FOR A KING* (17:6; 18:1; 19:1; 21:25). This need is obviously portrayed in chapters 1–16, and is stated four times in the appendix. Without a king they were in a state of anarchy. Why did the Lord leave them without a central leader or not immediately give them a king as promised in Deuteronomy 17–18? The purpose of this waiting period apparently was to help them see their need of a king. It was also a testing period to let them demonstrate their choice of the covenant Lord as their theocratic King, as Moses had said (Deut. 12:2, 5). They were allowed to choose the Lord's leadership without any coercion of a monarch. Their failures only intensified the need for such leadership.

3. *THE RESETTLEMENT AND APOSTASY OF DAN* (17–18). Rather than conquering the hill country of the Philistines with God's help, this half tribe sought an easy life in the far north with their "valiant men." In doing so, their valiance turned to violence and the whole tribe turned to homemade idolatry. Taking Moses' grandson (Jonathan) as priest with Micah's idols, they showed their rejection of God's one place of worship at the tabernacle. This tendency to idolatry continued through most of the Old Testament period until the Assyrians took them to their ancient home of idolatry. It might be noted that both Samson (a Danite at the end of this period) and the Danites at the beginning lived for their appetites, employed violence to fulfill them, and failed to conquer what God had given them.

4. *BENJAMIN: THE BABY TRIBE NEARLY LOST* (19–21). Shortly after Joshua's time, a "holocaust" of immense proportions took place, the near decimation of Joseph's little brother tribe. The tragedy teaches several lessons: 1) Their refusal to discipline their youth very quickly brought this central city of Gibeah to the condition of sodomy, the reason for Sodom's destruction. Not even a favorite son was spared when that condition set in. 2) It showed the danger of being self-defensive concerning wickedness, rather than facing it with repentance. 3) It later showed God's redemptive grace to the fallen in allowing a new beginning. From this fallen remnant came such leaders as Ehud the judge, Saul the first king, and Paul of Tarsus, the great apostle of grace to the Gentiles.

These twin disasters in Dan and Benjamin have some striking similarities: 1) Both stories begin with a Levite coming from Bethlehem. 2) One involves a grandson of Moses (Jonathan) and the other a grandson of Aaron (Phinehas). 3) In both stories a group of 600 men start anew. 4) Both show the quick growth of violence arising in Israel shortly after they were without a leader. 5) Note also God's grace in allowing a mighty hero to arise from each of these tribes at the end of the period to deliver the land from the Philistines. Both, however, failed because they were led by passions rather than principles (Samson and Saul). Saul of Tarsus evidently tried to make up for them, constantly crucifying his passions to live by principles.

5. *GIDEON'S FLEECE* (6:37-40). Like Joshua (and Jephthah later), Gideon was a great son of Joseph. His victory over the Midianites was perhaps the most spectacular of the judges. More is also said of his preparation, his special meeting with the Lord, his great humility, his having many miracles performed (6:13-21). He was more like Moses than any of the judges. What significance should we draw from his famous fleece? 1) For Gideon who was suddenly made commander of an army and faced an innumerable horde of Bedouin pillagers, this fleece-test was important. Living in idolatry he knew little of "biblical principles," though he had heard of the exodus miracles. Commanded to perform miracles himself in facing this vast foe, he needed this sign of the Lord's presence. 2) Faith-actions today, however, are not confirmed by physical manifestations, but by biblical principles already confirmed in the Old and New Testaments. We may, however, draw a principle from Gideon's fleece that any new course of action that involves a large step of faith in a new direction should be thoroughly checked to make sure it is the Lord's leading and not just some egotistical reaction to the status quo.

6. *JEPHTHAH'S FOOLISH VOW* (11:29-40). Of four judges it is said that the Spirit of the Lord came upon them (Othniel, Gideon, Jephthah, and Samson). Jephthah's story is important for three things: His appointment as an outcast; his argument with the Ammonites, claiming Trans-Jordan as a gift from the Lord; and his vow of an offering to God. Did he actually offer his daughter as a "burnt offering" (11:31)? It should be noted that his vow allowed for two options: Whatever came out of his house when he returned from Ammon, 1) it "shall surely be the LORD's," or 2) "I will offer it up as a burnt offering. The fact that she wept two months because of "her virginity" and that "she knew no man," strongly implies Jephthah used the first option—giving her to the Lord for temple service. Since Jephthah had no other child to continue his family name, it was a great sacrifice. Human sacrifices were never actually condoned by the Lord (including Isaac).

7. *THE TRAGIC ROMANCE OF SAMSON* (13-16). Samson was the most uniquely gifted of the judges and was the only Nazirite identified in the Old Testament. Like Isaac, Samuel, John the Baptist, and Jesus, his birth was predicted by an angel. His great gift of strength was specifically given to deliver Israel from the Philistines who had overrun Israel. This one with the greatest personal power was the only judge who failed in his mission and who came to a tragic end. This failure is attributed to two things: 1) He lived by his passions rather than by his Nazirite principles. He was seduced by three Philistine women. 2) He evidently lost sight of his real mission for the Lord in his lustful exploits. Though he by faith "stopped the mouths of lions" (Heb. 11:32-33), he only annoyed the Philistines as they interfered with his sexual pleasures.

8. *CHRIST IN JUDGES*. If Jesus included Judges in His Old Testament survey concerning Himself in Luke 24:27, two things might have been discussed: 1) Israel's lack of a king or national leader to unify them as an effective, theocratic nation. The Book of Judges is a preparation for the coming of David, but also for the coming of Messiah Himself. 2) The judges themselves upon whom the Spirit came might adumbrate the Lord's coming,

especially in His future role as the righteous Judge when He judges His people, destroys their enemies, and brings righteousness to the nation.

The Book of Ruth

Introduction

AUTHORSHIP

A. *THE TITLE*

The name "Ruth" means "friendship," a true characteristic of the one for whom the book is named. The book is one of six historical books that take the name of one of the principal figures described (Joshua, Ruth, Samuel, Ezra, Nehemiah, and Esther). It is one of two books of the Bible named after women:

1. Ruth, a Gentile woman who married a wealthy Jew of royal promise.
2. Esther, a Jewess who married a wealthy Gentile of royal power.

B. *THE AUTHOR*

Samuel who is the probable author of Judges, may have written Ruth as well. Many have seen Ruth as a third appendix to Judges 1–16, providing a welcome relief of faith and love in a time of infidelity, idolatry, and violence. Since the genealogy in chapter 4 is traced to David, but not to Solomon, it was probably written after David was anointed as God's choice for king, but before he came to the throne or Solomon was in view. Samuel was still alive and is the most likely one to have written this, while David's parents were in Moab.

HISTORICAL SETTING

A. *THE DATE OF THE EVENTS*—1340 B.C.

Although the events of Ruth are often dated c. 1100 B.C. to make Boaz the great-grandfather of David, the following data suggest an earlier date:

1. Five generations are given from Salmon to David (1405–1040). All the biblical genealogies record these (Ruth 4:21-22; 1 Chr. 2:11-15; Matt. 1:5-6; and Luke 3:32).

    But four births in 365 years suggests a gap may be involved.
2. The only gap possibility appears to be *between Obed and Jesse:*
    a. There can be no gap between Salmon and Boaz (Matt. 1:5).
    b. There can be no gap between Boaz and Obed (Ruth 4:17).
    c. There can be no gap between Jesse and David (1 Sam. 16:1ff.).
3. Since some obvious gaps are involved in Matthew's genealogy (Matt. 1:8, 11), a

gap may occur where no father's age at the son's birth is given.

4. Assuming Boaz to have been born to Salmon and Rahab c. 1390 B.C., the latest probable date for the birth of Obed to Ruth and Boaz would be 1340 B.C.

B. *THE CIRCUMSTANCE*

1. The book begins with the unusual circumstance of a famine in Bethlehem (which name means "house of bread"). As with Joseph in Egypt, the Lord used a famine to bring salvation and spiritual blessing through the faithful.

2. The story presents the ironic twist of a virtuous woman, who came from a people born of incest (of Lot and his daughter) and had lured Israel into idolatry and immorality (Gen. 19:37; Num. 25:1ff.), now inspiring Israel with her love and virtue.

THE PURPOSE OF THE BOOK OF RUTH

The purpose of this book appears to be twofold: 1) To portray the godly courage and love of

---

Outline of Ruth

THEME: The Love of Ruth for Naomi and Her Inclusion in the Davidic Line.

two women of different countries at a time of interracial strife, violence, and idolatry. 2) To remind them of David's genealogical relation to Moab, perhaps during his sojourn with his parents in Moab. It incidentally shows the strong Gentile strain in Messiah's line, coming through Rahab the Canaanite and Ruth the Moabite, maternally.

Unique Contributions of Ruth

1. *A BOOK HONORING WOMEN.* Two Old Testament books are named after women, Ruth at the beginning of Israel's history in Canaan, and Esther at the conclusion of Israel's history in the Old Testament. Ruth was one of many prominent women in the early period of the judges. Others were Deborah, Jael, the unnamed woman who slew the usurping king Abimelech, Jephthah's daughter, and Samson's mother. In the Book of Ruth, the attractiveness of Naomi in difficult trials is seen to have drawn Ruth to Israel's God, the love of Ruth is seen to transcend racial ties, and the two virtuous women are seen fulfilling Israel's law and in the process bringing about the birth of David, Israel's great king. Samuel, who himself had a very godly mother, Hannah, saw this story of two noble women as deserving a place in Israel's history among all the stories of Israel's great men.

2. *A PICTURE OF GENTILE FAITH IN THE OLD TESTAMENT* (1:16). Ruth's declaration of faith is a classic in the Old Testament: "Your people *shall be* my people, and your God, my God." Though certainly not the first Gentile conversion recorded in the Old Testament, this conversion of Ruth is the most detailed and famous. It also presents an interesting contrast with the conversions of her mother-in-law, Rahab. Whereas Rahab's is presented as a response to the fear of coming judgment, Ruth's is especially a response to love (Josh. 2:9-13; Ruth 1:16). The Lord uses both love and fear to activate faith in both the Old Testament and the New.

3. *THE UNIQUE STORY OF A FAMILY TRIAL AND TRAGEDY.* Ruth is the only book of the Bible that focuses on the trials and difficulties of a single family, rather than on the larger perspective of a tribe or nation. More specifically, it deals with a single widow in Israel whom tragedy struck three times after famine had driven her and her family from Bethlehem. Like the Book of Esther, this story portrays how God works within the shadows to care for His own in the most difficult of times and how He used these trials to sovereignly bring about the birth of David and eventually, the coming of Messiah. The emphasis of the book is on "the offspring . . . from this young woman" (4:12), through whom the Lord promised His program would be fulfilled.

4. *MOAB'S RELATION TO DAVID AND MESSIAH* (4:18-22). Though the Moabites were the children of Lot and his daughter (by incest) and were therefore cousins of Israel,

they were denied entrance to Israel's assembly "to the tenth generation" for their hostility toward Israel coming from Egypt (Deut. 23:3-6). Why then was Ruth welcomed to Israel within two or three generations? That law evidently applied to Moabite men rather than women, similar to the regulation for receiving a captive woman as a bride in Deuteronomy 21:10-13. This Moabite connection stresses the fact that, though the line of David and Messiah was made up of only Hebrew fathers, it included many Gentile women. Tamar and Rahab were of the Canaanites, Ruth was of the Moabites, and Naamah

Significance of the Levirate Marriage in Ruth

MEANING: A "levirate marriage" was the marriage of a brother-in-law to his widowed sister-in-law, living at the father's house (i.e., the younger brother not having yet married).

PURPOSE: To preserve the name and family line of the deceased brother and to make provision for his widow.

PASSAGES: Gen. 38:8 —The original principle stated and illustrated.
Deut. 25:5-6 —The Mosaic principle as divinely sanctioned.
Lev. 25:25-28 —The kinsman-redeemer relationship stated.

RESPONSIBILITIES OF KINSMAN-REDEEMER BRIDEGROOM:
1) To be qualified as a kinsman—a legitimate, close kinsman.
2) To be qualified as a redeemer—capable to redeem from the debts and poverty of the indebted deceased.
3) To be a willing defender, protector, and go-between.
4) To be a willing bridegroom and provider for those he redeems.

THE APPLICATIONS IN THE BOOK OF RUTH:
1) Naomi and Ruth were widows needing redemption and protection to preserve the line of Elimelech and Mahlon.
2) Boaz alone qualified as kinsman-redeemer by virtue of his kinsman relationship and his ability to adequately redeem.
3) The marriage of Boaz to Ruth preserved the line of Elimelech, but also produced the royal line of kingship in Israel.
4) The tracing of the genealogy back to Perez also emphasizes the levirate relationship in Ruth. It was just prior to the birth of Perez (who was born of incest) that the levirate responsibility was first pronounced to Onan at the death of Er (Gen. 38:8).

THE TYPICAL APPLICATION TO CHRIST AND THE CHURCH:
1) Christ became one of the race as a qualified Kinsman.
2) Christ provided full redemption by his payment of man's debt and His provision for man's happiness. (All that man lost in Adam's death, Christ more than supplied.)
3) Christ became man's able Defender and Go-between.
4) Christ fulfills this type as the heavenly Bridegroom taking a Gentile bride whom He warmly welcomes and richly endows.

the mother of Rehoboam was of the Ammonites. Messiah actually came from a wide background of nationalities in His maternal line.

5. *RUTH: ISRAEL'S MEDITATION FOR PENTECOST.* This book was annually read by the nation in a public reading as they gathered for the summer feast of Pentecost. Its harvest scene reminded them of the early barley harvest which the Lord gave and the rewards of loving service which were yet to come. As Pentecost celebrated the harvest of the first crop, the reading of Ruth also spoke of a firstfruits harvest of the Gentiles. We recall also that the New Testament Pentecost event celebrates the firstfruits of God's harvest in the Church, many of whom are Gentiles.

6. *CHRISTOLOGY IN RUTH.* There are two basic references to Christ in the Book of Ruth, both relating to Boaz.
   a. Boaz is an inferred type of Christ as a kinsman-redeemer who is both qualified and willing to redeem his people. This is an aspect of Christ's work illustrated nowhere else in the Bible (though Jer. 32:6-25 uses it for another purpose). The term ''redeem'' (gaal) is used eight times in Ruth. As the believer's Kinsman-Redeemer, Christ becomes his Redeemer to repay all his debts, his Avenger to defend against all adversaries, his Mediator to achieve reconciliation, and his Bridegroom for perpetual union and fellowship.
   b. Boaz is noted in all the genealogies of Jesus (see the Introduction), but only in Matthew 1:5 is Ruth mentioned as well. In that genealogy Matthew purposely mentions Ruth and three other foreign-related women. The christological point seems to be to impress the wide international background of Messiah who was to bring salvation to all nations. He did not come as a mere ''provincial'' Savior.

The Books of Samuel

Introduction

AUTHORSHIP

A. *THE TITLE*

The books of Samuel take their title from the first prominent figure, Samuel, whose name means ''name of God,'' or possibly a short form of ''asked of God.'' The two were originally one book in the Hebrew canon, ''The Book of Samuel,'' but were divided into two by the Greek translators (LXX) who called them ''1 and 2 Kings.'' The books we call 1 and 2 Kings they called 3 and 4 Kings.

B. *THE AUTHOR*

These books, like most of the historical books, are anonymous. The prophet Samuel is generally considered the author of 1 Samuel 1–24 and Nathan and Gad the authors of the remainder. The detailed descriptions and exactitudes suggest the authors were eyewitnesses of the events. As the Hebrew Talmud suggests, the declaration of 1 Chronicles 29:29 probably provides the best clues: they are "the book of Samuel the seer," the "book of Nathan the prophet," and the "book of Gad the seer."

HISTORICAL SETTING

A. *THE DATES INVOLVED*—c. 1100–970 B.C.

1. The events described in the two books cover the period from the birth of Samuel to the end of David's reign. Assuming Samuel was c. 30 when he began his leadership in 1070 B.C. (five years after the death of Eli), Samuel must have been born c. 1100 B.C. Inasmuch as David's reign extended from 1010 to 970, the time span for the books of Samuel is c. 130 years.

2. Just prior to Samuel's judgeship, several other judges ruled in Israel. Samson judged in the southwest over Judah, and Dan, Jephthah ruled over Manasseh and eastern Ephraim, and Ibzan, Elon, and Abdon judged in other sections as Samuel was growing up at Shiloh.

3. Several overlapping time periods are involved in this history:

   40 years—Philistine oppression   —1095–1055 (Judg. 13:1)
   40 years—judgeship of Eli the priest —1115–1075 (1 Sam. 4:18)
   75 years—ark at Kirjath Jearim   —1075–1000 (1 Sam. 7:2; 1 Chr. 15:25)
   40 years—judgeship of Samuel   —1055–1015 (1 Sam. 7:14-16)
   40 years—reign of Saul   —1050–1010 (Acts 13:21)
   40 years—reign of David   —1010– 970 (2 Sam. 5:4)

B. *THE RELIGIOUS STATE OF THE NATION*

1. This period began with idolatry and immorality still prevalent in Israel (1 Sam. 7:3). Though Eli the priest was faithful as a priest, he failed to honor God by disciplining his sons (1 Sam. 2:29) who served at the tabernacle at Shiloh in gross immorality and greed. For this the Lord pronounced judgment on Eli's house, saying they would be cut off from the priesthood (1 Sam. 2:33). This condition of perfunctory religion and immoral practices was evidently general throughout Israel, provoking the Lord to allow the Philistine's invasion for their discipline.

2. The tabernacle and ark had been located at Shiloh (9 miles north of Bethel) from the time of Joshua to the time of Eli. When the ark was stolen at the time of Eli's death, these two main articles of Israel's religious system were separated and remained apart for 75 years until David returned the ark in 1000 B.C. Note the various locations of the tabernacle and ark from Joshua's time:

Tabernacle		Ark	
At Gilgal	—1405–1398	At Gilgal (with tabernacle)	—1405–1398
At Shiloh	—1398–1075	At Shiloh (with tabernacle)	—1398–1075
At Nob	—1075–1015	At Philisia	—1075

Outline of 1 Samuel

THEME: The Establishing of Israel as a Theocratic Kingdom.

Tabernacle	Ark
At Gibeon —1015–1000	At Kirjath Jearim —1075–1000
At Jerusalem —1000– 960	At Jerusalem (in tabernacle)—1000 – 960
(Temple completed, 960)	At Jerusalem (in temple) — 960 – 586

C. *THE POLITICAL STATE OF THE UNION*
    1. Internal divisions. At the beginning of the eleventh century Israel's low spiritual

Outline of 2 Samuel

THEME: The Establishing of David as a Theocratic King.

Chronology of Events in the Books of Samuel

DATE	EVENT	PASSAGE	SIGNIFICANCE
DURING THE JUDGESHIPS OF ELI AND SAMUEL			
1115–1075 B.C.	Eli's judgeship (40 years)	1 Sam. 4:18	Corruption even in the priesthood.
1100	Samuel's birth	1 Sam. 1	A godly mother prepares a leader.
1103–1055	Philistine oppression	Judges 13:1	Israel's longest bondage to the Philistine invaders.
1075	Eli's death after the Philistines take ark	1 Sam. 4	Losing the ark to the Philistines a time of Israel's lowest point.
1055	Samuel's judgeship begins	1 Sam. 7:2-3	Samuel's revival unites Israel.
DURING THE REIGN OF SAUL			
1050	Saul is anointed king	1 Sam. 9–10	God gives Israel a ''big'' king, according to their desires.
1045	Saul's first battle unites the nation with Saul	1 Sam. 11	Saul's humble start gives promise of godly leadership.
1030	Saul's impatience to await Samuel's blessing	1 Sam. 13	Saul shows independence of Samuel before going to battle.
1025	Saul's incomplete obedience with Amalekites	1 Sam. 15	Saul shows incomplete obedience after victory in battle.
1024	Samuel anoints David	1 Sam. 16	God chooses a shepherd boy to be the shepherd of Israel.
1023	David slays Goliath	1 Sam. 17	God demonstrates His power through faith and obedience.
1018	David flees from Saul	1 Sam. 19	Saul's rebellion against the Lord expressed in jealousy of David.
1016	Saul destroys 85 priests of Nob (Eli's family)	1 Sam. 22	Saul's independence of God turns to warfare against God's priests.
1015	Samuel dies at Ramah	1 Sam. 25:1	His long ministry led the nation from anarchy to the monarchy.

state was matched by her low political state. It was a time of divided leadership and general anarchy. The nation had had no central leadership since the time of Joshua, but the tribes were judged by divinely appointed judges in emergencies and at times by the ruling priest (Phinehas and Eli).

2. External oppressions. The Philistines from the southwest constituted Israel's greatest external opposition during this time, though they were sporadically attacked by their kindred neighbors to the east and Syria in the north. Not only was the ark lost to the Philistines, but the whole of west Jordan was almost taken over by them at various times. Many campaigns of war were waged against the Philistines during this eleventh century. (See Outline of 1 Samuel)

3. Under David's reign the problems of internal anarchy and external oppression were progressively resolved. The nation grew from a group of rivaling tribes to a united political force respected by all nations in the area. Under his leadership the Philistines were driven out, the countries of Edom, Moab, Ammon, and Syria were made vassals to Israel, and a peace treaty was made with Phoenicia.

THE PURPOSE OF THE BOOKS OF SAMUEL

The unified purpose of the books of Samuel is to present a history of Israel's development from a state of anarchy to a state of theocratic monarchy. It gives a religious portrayal of the nation's growth, showing the futility of attempting unification and national growth by hu-

DURING THE REIGN OF DAVID			
1010	Saul is slain and David becomes king over Judah	2 Sam. 1–2	Israel's great king begins his reign of righteousness.
1003	David becomes king over all Israel at Jerusalem	2 Sam. 5:5	Awaiting God's timing, David is given the whole kingdom.
1002	David defeats Philistia	2 Sam. 5	Philistine opposition shattered.
1000	David restores the ark	2 Sam. 6	The ark and tabernacle are again united at Jerusalem.
1000	David is given covenant	2 Sam. 7	His dynasty to last forever.
999–992	David defeats all his enemies	2 Sam. 8–12	The Davidic kingdom is extended throughout Palestine.
995	David's sin with Bathsheba	2 Sam. 11–12	David's time of trouble begins.
993	Solomon is born to David and Bathsheba	2 Sam. 12	David's repentance brings God's grace with His judgment.
987	Absalom's revolt	2 Sam. 13–14	David's insensitivity judged.
985	David's sin in census	2 Sam. 24	Temple site purchased after sin.

man strength and leadership and the great power and prestige of a nation founded on theocratic principles under a God-appointed king. Its overriding motif is the glory and power that comes to a nation that responds to the sovereign Lord.

Israel's Battles in Consolidating the Kingdom

The eleventh century was a time of many battles for Israel as the kingdom was formed and consolidated. While the large empires of Egypt and Mesopotamia were weak and unaggressive, the smaller nations surrounding Israel made many assaults on the land seeking to annex it as their own. Israel was challenged from four directions: Syria and Zobah in the north; Ammon and Moab in the east; Edom in the south; and Philistia in the southwest. Under David's rule these enemy-provoked battles were exploited to extend Israel's borders and put her enemies under vassalage. Her key battles during this period were the following:

DATE	ENEMY	LOCATION	LEADER	PASSAGE	RESULT
BATTLES PRIOR TO THE KINGDOM					
1106 B.C.	Ammon	Gilead	Jephthah	Judg. 10:7	Deliverance from Ammonite bondage.
1080–1060	Philistia	West Judah	Samson	Judg. 14–16	Samson only annoyed the Philistia.
1075	Philistia	Aphek	Eli and sons	1 Sam. 4	Philistines occupied central Palestine, took the ark, and destroyed Shiloh.
1055	Philistia	Mizpah	Samuel	1 Sam. 7	Israel unites in Samuel's revival and Israel's first defeat of Philistia.
BATTLES UNDER KING SAUL—Israel's Choice for King					
1045	Ammon	Jabesh	Saul	1 Sam. 11	Israel unites under new king, Saul.
1030	Philistia	Michmash	Saul	1 Sam 13	Philistines overrun Israel: Saul's impatience costs him the kingdom.
1027	Philistia	Michmash	Saul and Jonathan	1 Sam. 14	Jonathan's great victory in spite of Saul's foolish vow.
1025	Amalek	Southwest Judah	Saul	1 Sam. 15	Saul's incomplete obedience brings judgment of rejection by the Lord.
1023	Philistia	Elah	Saul and David	1 Sam. 17	David slays Goliath and routs the Philistines.
1010	Philistia	Gilboa (Jezreel)	Saul	1 Sam. 31	Saul and Jonathan are slain as the Philistines take North Israel.

Unique Contributions of 1 and 2 Samuel

1. **SAMUEL THE KINGMAKER.** Old Testament history introduces us to three oustanding Levites which stood at the beginning, middle, and end of the national period of Israel: Moses, Samuel, and Ezra. Each was also vitally involved in the giving of God's Word. Moses wrote the first five books, Ezra wrote the last four or five historical books and organized the canon, and Samuel is the probable author of three of the middle books. Samuel's greatness, however, inheres in the fact that he became the Lord's kingmaker, anointing the first two kings of Israel. This role of kingmaker continued to be a special function of the prophets of Israel even to the time of John the Baptist's presentation of Jesus. The prophets were called as men of deep spiritual character to represent God in the selection of kings.

2. **HANNAH'S CLASSIC PRAYER AND INSIGHTS** (1 Sam. 2:1-10). This prayer of the mother of Samuel is regarded as one of the most outstanding prayers of the Bible. In it she especially exulted in the greatness of God and His grace in raising up the humble and insignificant to confound the wise and mighty. This very appropriately set the tone and emphasis of the books of Samuel where this principle is constantly stressed. Her prayers also introduced the use of two significant names of the Lord: 1) The first is "the LORD of hosts" (1 Sam. 1:3, 11), a designation used nearly 300 times in the rest of the Old Testament. As Moses sang of the Lord as a "man of war" and Joshua saw Him as a "Commander of the army of the LORD," (Ex. 15:3; Josh. 5:14), Hannah's prayer states, "The LORD kills and makes alive" (1 Sam. 2:6), adverting to His almightiness. 2) Hannah also referred to God's king as "His anointed," (1 Sam. 2:10), a term interpreted as "Messiah" in Daniel 9:25-26 and the derivation of the name "Christ" in

BATTLES UNDER KING DAVID—God's Choice for King					
1002	Philistia	Rephaim Southwest Judah	David	2 Sam. 5	In two battles David decisively ended Philistine domination.
1000	Moab	Moab	David	2 Sam. 8	David made Moab and Syria vassals.
998	Ammon and Syria	Helam (Gilead)	David	2 Sam. 10	David routs the combined forces and the Syrians become servants.
995	Ammon	Rabbah	Joab and David	2 Sam. 11–12	David allows faithful Uriah to be slain; Ammonites made servants.
992	Edom	Valley of Salt	David	1 Chr. 18: 12–13	Edomites made servants of David. Kingdom extended to Valley of Salt.

the New Testament. This anointing spoke of the Spirit's power by which men of God and even Messiah performed God's service. The two designations, "LORD of hosts" and "His anointed," nicely introduce the books of Samuel where David is anointed with the Spirit's power to serve the Lord of hosts in destroying the enemies of the Lord and setting up His kingdom.

3. *THE TRAGIC FIGURE OF ELI* (1 Sam. 2:12-36). Eli the high priest symbolized the condition of Israel at that time—having a form of godliness without power or personal discipline. This ruling priest lost the priesthood for two reasons, involving God's sovereignty and man's responsibility. 1) Sovereignly speaking, the Lord had given the high priesthood to Phinehas the son of Eleazar as a perpetual priesthood, not to the house of Ithamar to which Eli belonged (Num. 25:11-13). 2) The human reason, however, was the failure of Eli to discipline his sons (1 Sam. 3:13). They had made merchandise of the priestly office for their own gain, and the Lord assigned part of the blame to Eli (1 Sam. 2:29). In their place the Lord would raise up a faithful priest who would have an enduring house. This was evidently Zadok (in the line of Phinehas). Though Abiathar (of Eli's house) did serve under David, for personal reasons, along with Zadok, Solomon retired him and left the high priesthood to Zadok's line.

4. *THE LOST ARK: "ICHABOD"* (1 Sam. 4–6). Eli and his sons brought Israel to her lowest point of shame by their superstitious use of the ark in battle. Not only was the battle of Aphek lost to the Philistines, but the ark was lost as well. The name given Eli's grandson, "Ichabod" ("The glory has departed" 1 Sam. 4:21), appropriately characterized the nation. For seventy-five years the ark was separated from the tabernacle. During the seven months the ark was in Philistia, however, it was used to teach the Philistines some profound lessons about the God of Israel. When it was put in the temple of Dagon, the Philistine god twice fell down before it, nearly destroying itself the second time. When they sent it to the five cities of Philistia, disease ravaged the people, striking fear in the nation, as if giving a seminar on the awesome power of God's Word in the ark. These warlike people were made to ponder the great power of the God of Israel, which message Israel had failed to properly proclaim to them.

5. *SAUL, ISRAEL'S CHOICE OF A "BIG" KING* (1 Sam. 9–15). As the folly of Eli is contrasted with Zadok, God's choice of a faithful priest, so the folly of Saul is contrasted with David, God's choice of a faithful king. Saul's appointment as king was an interesting twist or acquiescence of the Lord in that Saul's city and tribe (Gibeah of Benjamin) were nearly completely destroyed three centuries earlier for their immorality. The people's choice of Saul, however, reflected their trust in physical greatness rather than spiritual strength. Likewise, Saul's failures were due to spiritual weaknesses, as evident in several highlights of his downfall: 1) In facing the powerful Philistine invaders, he became impatient with Samuel and brazenly usurped the priestly function of sacrifice; 2) hungry for victory, he became egotistical in his demands of the troops; 3) after a partial victory over the Amalekites, he failed to obey God's commands to destroy them

all (assuming a later sacrifice would compensate his disobedience); 4) when David succeeded where he failed, he became jealous; 5) when chastened by the Lord for his errors, he became bitter rather than humble. Saul's tragic end in suicide demonstrated the futility of mere bigness in accomplishing God's work.

6. *DAVID AND GOLIATH* (1 Sam. 16–17). The great contrast with "big" Saul is seen in the Lord's choice of the young lad, David, whom his own family wouldn't consider as a candidate for king (1 Sam. 16). That point is again emphasized in the following chapter where the young shepherd defeated the towering giant who held Israel's entire army at bay. This he did without sword or armor, but in the name of "the LORD of hosts" (17:45). So great was David's faith in this venture that he retorted to Goliath's challenge that he would give the whole army of the Philistines to the birds and beasts (v. 46). In sharp contrast to Saul's pursuing his own desires in battle, David is later described as constantly inquiring of the Lord before going into battle (1 Sam. 22:10; 23:2, 4, 10; 30:8; 2 Sam. 2:1; 5:19, 23). In defeating Goliath, David's greatest problem was not with Goliath or the Philistines, but with the doubt and unbelief in the camp of Israel. Breaking free from that camp of unbelief, he was ready to take on the whole Philistine army. His contagious faith was used to ignite the faith and action of Saul and his fearful troops.

7. *INCOMPARABLE DAVID.* Perhaps no man of the Bible is so highly esteemed by both God and man as David. He set the standard by which God measured all later kings of Israel. He was used of God not only to establish the kingdom, but also to instruct the nation in worship and praise to God. His psalms have probably inspired more people than any other literary compositions of men. What were some of the keys to David's greatness? 1) He had a profound love of God and was dedicated to doing His service. 2) He had the courage of his convictions that was undaunted by the unbelief and negativism about him. 3) David assumed the kingly throne as a "servant of the people," rather than as their master (as had Saul). 4) In his long period of trial, he learned to wait on the Lord and commit any personal vengeance to the requiting of the Lord. 5) He learned to delegate responsibilities and to give credit to those serving well. 6) Though David was not perfect in many ways, he showed a remarkable ability to accept the blame for problems and to respond positively to the Lord's chastening. Whereas chastening embittered Saul and drove him to egotistical violence, it produced in David a mellowness and enlargement of heart.

8. *THE DAVIDIC COVENANT* (2 Sam. 7). As the Abrahamic covenant outlined the personal, territorial, national, and spiritual blessings to Israel, the Davidic covenant was given to elaborate on the national aspect regarding the king. This covenant promised David that his sons would have the throne rights to Israel forever, and that that line was to go through Solomon, the temple builder. The New Testament significance of this is that Matthew proved Jesus' rights to be King of Israel by virtue of His genealogy through Joseph (legally) and back to Solomon and David. He made no mention of Mary's line

in this connection, for her line came through Nathan, not Solomon. As Jeremiah later affirmed even after Israel's great idolatry and judgment, the right of David's line through Solomon was based on God's faithfulness, not man's.

9. *DAVID'S SIN WITH BATHSHEBA* (2 Sam. 11–12). This "casual affair" at the height of David's reign became a watershed event in his life. It is the dividing point between his triumphs and his troubles. The sin itself developed almost accidentally. His casual look at his neighbor's wife led to covetousness, which led to adultery, which led to the deception and coverup, which led to stealing his neighbor's wife, which led to the slaying of his neighbor in a conspiracy against one of the most noble men in his army. This he neatly covered up as the sad consequence of war. The powerful parable of the prophet, however, laid open the whole sordid affair. In the aftermath four results of this sin may be seen, two judgmental and two merciful. 1) The immediate result was judgment—in David's heart and in his loss of the newborn son. 2) The second was his immediate forgiveness from the Lord when he confessed his sin (2 Sam. 12:13). 3) The third was the harvest of judgment that David reaped in his family. He reaped the harvest of his adultery in his oldest son Amnon and his daughter Tamar; he reaped his murder in two of his sons being slain by two of his other sons; he reaped his stealing another man's wife in his son Absalom stealing the kingdom and shaming his concubines in public. Though he received immediate forgiveness upon confession, he paid dearly in the human consequences of the crimes the rest of his life. 4) The fourth result was the grace God showed David after his deep pentitence in that Bathsheba was allowed to have another son by David to whom the throne would be given. Psalms 32 and 51 reveal David's greatness in confession and humiliation and the greatness of his restoration to effective service for the Lord.

10. *THE TRAGEDY OF DAVID'S SONS*. David had a dozen wives (eight are named) and at least ten concubines, twenty-one sons, and one daughter (2 Sam. 3:2-5; 5:13-16; 1 Chr. 3:1-9; 14:3-7; 2 Chr. 11:18). To three of his older sons moral tragedy struck in their violent deaths (Amnon, Absalom, and Adonijah), when each was an heir apparent to the throne. The Lord attributed part of this blame to David (1 Kin. 1:6). These tragedies in the godly home of David are difficult to explain, but they remind us of a strange anomaly in the families of the four prominent men in 1 and 2 Samuels. The three prominent men of God (Eli, Samuel, and David) are said to have failed to discipline their sons for which they lost the kingdom (David temporarily). The one ungodly king, Saul, however, had one of the most noble and godly men in the book, Jonathan. That strange anomaly will also be seen many times in later kings.

11. *DAVID'S PURCHASE OF THE TEMPLE SITE* (2 Sam. 24). Second Samuel highlights two great sins of David, his adultery and his egotistical numbering of the people. Following his repentance and the Lord's judgment, David was shown God's grace in a remarkable way in each case. After repenting for his sin with Bathsheba and Uriah, David was given another son by her who would be the temple builder, Solomon. After

his sin and judgment for the census, David was allowed to procure the temple site, Mount Moriah. Though the Lord struck with awesome judgment, He also demonstrated that His grace can overwhelm the tragedy, when the chastening is responded to in a penitent and positive way.

12. *CHRISTOLOGY IN SAMUELS.* Two references to Christ may be noted in these books, both related to David. (Samuel is sometimes seen as a type of Christ, as prophet, priest, and ruler, though the relation is never suggested in the New Testament. He is better regarded as a type of John the Baptist, the prophet-priest who officiated at the anointing of Jesus.) In David we see both *a type of Christ as King and a prediction of Christ as the covenant seed promised David.* Many typical relations between David and Christ are seen in both his first anointing and days of humiliation and his later taking the throne to establish the kingdom.

The one specific prediction of Christ in Samuels is the promised seed of David Who would come through Solomon and establish His Kingdom forever. (2 Sam. 7:16; Lk. 1:32-33)

The Books of Kings

Introduction

AUTHORSHIP

A. *THE TITLE*

These two books take their name from the first Hebrew words, "Wehammelek" ("And the king"), which nicely fits the subject matter of the reigns of the kings of the two kingdoms. The Hebrews considered them as one book, since they obviously constitute one continuous story. The Greek translators divided them into two, calling them 3 and 4 Kings, perhaps because the Greek translation (having more letters) required two scrolls (as with Samuels).

B. *THE AUTHOR*

1. Though the books are anonymous, Jeremiah is traditionally held to be the author, assisted by his secretary, Baruch (Jer. 45). It is evident that the author was at least contemporary with Jeremiah and the emphasis of the books strongly suggests the viewpoint of the prophets. Thus Jeremiah the prophet who lived at the time of the exile (described in the final chapters) could well have been the author.

2. The author, of course, made use of many historical records of the time, referring

to some ten or more such documents many times in the two books. The records that were evidently available to him were:

a. The Book of Jasher (2 Sam. 1:18).
b. The Book of The Acts of Solomon (1 Kings 11:41).
c. The Book of The Chronicles of the Kings of Judah (1 Kings 14:19, noted eighteen times in the two books).
d. The Book of the Chronicles of the Kings of Judah (1 Kings 14:29, noted fifteen times in the two books).
e. The Book of Isaiah (2 Kings 18–20—relate Isaiah 36–39).
f. The Chronicles of King David (1 Chr. 27:24).
g. The Chronicles of Samuel the Seer (1 Chr. 29:29).
h. The Chronicles of Nathan the Prophet (1 Chr. 29:29).
i. The Chronicles of Gad the Seer (1 Chr. 29:29).
j. The Prophecy of Ahijah the Shilonite (2 Chr. 9:29).
k. The Visions of Iddo the Seer (2 Chr. 9:29).

Outline of 1 Kings

THEME: The Glory of Solomon's Kingdom and the Great Challenge of Idolatry.

HISTORICAL SETTING

A. *THE DATES INVOLVED*—970–560 B.C.

1. The events of 1 and 2 Kings extend from the death of David, the first covenant king, to the captivity of Zedekiah the last king of Judah. An appendix reference is made in the last chapter to the release of Jehoiachin in Babylon at the accession of Evil-Merodach in 560 B.C.

2. This period from Solomon to Zedekiah is known as the Solomonic Temple Era, extending from the building of the temple by Solomon to its destruction by Nebuchadnezzar.

Outline of 2 Kings

THEME: The Lord's Great Judgment on Israel and Judah for Their Idolatry.

B. THE POLITICAL SETTING

1. Nationally, these books cover the period of Israel's greatest political influence in the time of Solomon to her complete political eclipse when the southern kingdom was destroyed and the remnant was exiled in Babylon. The seeds of that fall were planted early in the harsh domestic policy of Solomon which led to national unrest. After the fall of the North in 722, the southern kingdom had only sporadic periods of political greatness before her similar destruction in 586 B.C.

2. Internationally, this period began with no great world empire exerting much influ-

Chronology of the Kings of the Divided Kingdom

JUDAH				ISRAEL		
DATES	KING	1 KINGS	2 CHRON-ICLES	DATE	KING	1 KINGS
In 931 B.C. the ten northern tribes revolted from Rehoboam and formed the kingdom of Israel.						
931–913	Rehoboam (17)	14:21	12:1	931–910	Jeroboam I (22)	14:20
913–911	Abijam (3) (Abijah)	15:1-2	13:1			
911–870	Asa (41)	15:9-10	16:13	910–909	Nadab (2)	15:25
				909–886	Baasha (24)	15:28-33
				886–885	Elah (2)	16:8
				885	Zimri (1 week)	16:10, 15
				885–874	Omri (12)**	16:23
873–848	Jehoshaphat* (25)	22:41-42 2 Kings	20:31	874–853	Ahab (22)	16:29
853–841	Jehoram (8)*	8:16-17	21:5, 20	853–852	Ahaziah (2)	22:51
841	Ahaziah (1)	8:25-26	22:2	852–841	Jehoram (12)	2 Kings 3:1
In 841 B.C. army captain Jehu slew both Ahaziah and Joram, seized the throne of Israel, and destroyed all the house of Ahab and Jezebel as well as all Baal worshipers in the north.						
841–835	Queen Athaliah	11:3-4	22:12	841–814	Jehu (28)	10:36
835–796	Jehoash (40) (Joash)	12:1	24:1			
				814–798	Jehoahaz (17)	13:1
796–767	Amaziah (29)	14:1-2	25:1	798–782	Jehoash (16)	13:10
792–740	Azariah (52)* (Uzziah)	15:1-2	26:3	793–753	Jeroboam II* (41)	14:23
750–732	Jotham (16)*	15:32-33	27:1-8	753–752	Zachariah (6 months)	15:8
				752	Shallum (1 month)	15:13
				752–742	Menahem (10)	15:17
				742–740	Pekahiah (2)	15:23
743–728	Ahaz (16)*	16:1-2	28:1	752–732	Pekah (20)***	15:27
728–698	Hezekiah (29)	18:1-2	29:1	732–722	Hoshea (9)	15:30; 17:1

ence or showing prominence on the world scene. As if geared to Israel's spiritual condition, however, the world empires came to power and prominence as Israel's spiritual condition began to deteriorate. The new Assyrian Empire, for instance, came to world dominance just before the captivity of the North. Right on time a century later the new Babylonian Empire arose just before the time for God's judgment on the southern kingdom. This prophetic viewpoint of Israel's fortunes permeates the two books.

C. THE RELIGIOUS SETTING

1. The building of Solomon's temple at the beginning of this period constituted a high point in Israel's religious history. Solomon also instituted the highly organized worship system and, at first, inspired strong religious sentiment by his dedicatory ceremonies and address. That good beginning, however, did not last, and idolatry again inundated the nation, led by the accommodating practices of Solomon who built shrines for his heathen wives. After the division of the kingdom, Jeroboam immediately introduced calf-worship in the North at the two shrines of Bethel and Dan. To this was added the Canaanite Baal worship system by Ahab and Jezebel in the North and by their daughter, Athaliah, in the South. In spite of the Baal purge by Jehu in 841 B.C., idolatry continued to pervade both kingdoms until their destructions in 722 and 586 B.C.

2. The religious temperament of the period may be seen in the character of the various kings who reigned over each kingdom. Following Solomon, Judah had nineteen kings and one queen, only eight of which were nominally righteous accord-

DATES	KING	1 KINGS	2 CHRON- ICLES	DATE	KING	1 KINGS
In 722 B.C. Samaria was destroyed by Assyria after a three year siege and northern Israel was deported to Assyria. Judah was evidently spared judgment at this time by the hurried reformation and purge of idolatry by Hezekiah (even holding an emergency Passover).						
698–643	Manasseh (55)	21:1	33:1			
643–641	Amon (2)	21:19	33:21			
641–609	Josiah (31)	22:1	34:1			
609	Jehoahaz (3 months)	23:31	36:2	(Also called Shallum, 1 Chr. 3:15; Jer. 22:11)		
609–598	Jehoiakim (11)	23:36	36:5			
598–597	Jehoiachin (3 months)	24:8	36:9	(Also called Jeconiah, 1 Chr. 3:16; Matt. 1:11; and Coniah, Jer. 22:24, 28)		
597–586	Zedekiah (11)	24:18	36:11			
In 586 B.C. Nebuchadnezzar destroyed Jerusalem and the temple and exiled all but the poor to Babylon. Three deportations constituted this exile to Babylon—in 606, 597, and 586 B.C.						

Datings are basically those of Edwin R. Thiele (see Select Commentaries) with several deviations.
  *Co-regency with father included in total reign.
  **Omri's twelve years include four years while Tibni had a rival reign (1 Kin. 16:23, 29).
***Pekah's twenty years evidently include a twelve-year reign in Gilead as a rival to Menahem and Pekahiah (see Thiele, pp. 122–125).

ing to God's standard. The northern kingdom of Israel also had nineteen kings, but every one was designated "evil." Thus the religious heritage of Abraham, Moses, and David was often more of a shell than an inner reality in Israel.

THE PURPOSE OF THE BOOKS OF KINGS

The two books have an obvious twofold purpose, one literary and the other religious.

A. *The literary purpose* of the author was to complete the history of David's kingdom which was begun in the books of Samuel some 400 years earlier. As 2 Samuel ended with David's purchase of the temple site, so 1 Kings begins with Solomon's preparation to build the temple, and 2 Kings continues the story to the destruction of the temple as the period ends.

B. *The religious purpose* of relating this history to the keeping of the covenant also pervades the books. The devout author seeks to emphasize to the nation as they went into captivity in 586 the inseparable connection between obedience and blessing and between disobedience and cursing. In contrast to the later books of Chronicles which were given to encourage the humble, the books of Kings have a strong emphasis on the need for repentance and response to the covenant God that restoration might be effected and the covenant purposes fulfilled.

Crucial Events in Israel from Solomon to Zedekiah

JUDAH	ISRAEL	EVENT	REFERENCE
967–960 B.C.		*Solomon's temple built* with unprecedented splendor to symbolize the greatness of Israel's God to the nations.	1 Kings 5–8
931	931	The *kingdom divided* after Solomon's death into "Israel" (North) and "Judah" (South).	12:1–20
	931	*Calf-worship instituted* by Jeroboam I at Bethel and Dan.	12:27ff.
927		*Shishak of Egypt ransacks the temple* as his southern alliance captures much of Judah.	14:25ff.
	879	*Omri builds Samaria* and moves northern capital from Tirzah.	16:24
	874	*Baal worship is instituted* in Samaria by Ahab and Jezebel.	16:31ff.
873		*Jehoshaphat promotes great revival* in Judah through Bible conferences, resulting in most prosperous reign since Solomon.	1 Chr. 17
870–841	870–841	Unique *period of friendship* between Judah and Israel through the alliance of Jehoshaphat and Ahab.	1 Kings 22– 2 Kings 8
	870–850	*Elijah* the first great miracle-working prophet has a twenty year ministry of rebuking Baal-worship after instituted by Ahab.	1 Kings 17–22
841	841	*Jehu slays kings of North and South*, takes Israel's throne and purges the house of Ahab and Baal worship in the North.	2 Kings 9ff.
790	790	*Civil war* between Judah and Israel nearly destroys Jerusalem and temple after Amaziah of Judah foolishly attacks the North.	14

1. *THE GREATNESS OF SOLOMON* (1 Kings 1–11). Solomon's prominence lay in three areas; his wisdom, temple building, and reign of peace and splendor. His wisdom is seen in the three books attributed to him (Proverbs, Ecclesiastes, and Song); his temple building produced a work of art and splendor unprecedented in the ancient world; and his reign of peace and glory brought him world acclaim. This greatness briefly portrayed the blessings promised David's kingdom built on covenant obedience and theocratic principles, displaying the Lord's intention for His people if they would respond to His leadership. Solomon, however, failed to practice what he so grandly preached.

2. *SOLOMON'S TEMPLE OF GOLD* (1 Kings 5–8). This was Israel's contribution to the "seven wonders of the world." In materials and workmanship, it outclassed anything of its time. The Illinois Society of Architects has estimated its total value at $87 billion, according to present day values (gold then at $35/ounce). Later temples were larger (Zerubbabel's and Herod's), but not nearly so ornate or carefully constructed (no ham-

770–750	770–750	*Golden age* of prosperity for both kingdoms during strong kingdoms of Azariah (Uzziah) of Judah and Jeroboam II of Israel	2 Kings 14:21ff.
	752	Chaos and *disintegration in North* after "golden age," involving four dynasties and four assassinations in thirty years.	15:8ff.
	743	Assyrian *Tiglath-Pileser begins series of invasions* of Israel, taking Galilee and Trans-jordan in 733 and deporting the people.	15:29ff.
728		*Hezekiah instituted immediate reform* in Judah following his wicked father Ahaz, seeking to stem tide of anticipated judgment.	18ff. 2 Chr. 29:1
	722	*Assyria captured Samaria* after three-year siege and deported the total population to Assyria, attributed to Israel's idolatry.	2 Kings 17
714–701		*Assyrian invasion of western Palestine* by Sargon and Sennacherib, taking Ashdod and many cities, isolating Jerusalem as an island.	18:9ff.
701		Miraculous *judgment of Assyrian army of 185,000* as Hezekiah turned fully to the Lord under counsel of Isaiah.	19:35
650		*Manasseh was bound and taken captive* to Babylon by Assyria where he later repented and was restored to seek to undo his evil.	2 Chr. 33:11
629		*Josiah's reformation* was the most thorough of Judah's history, spurred on by finding the lost "Book of the Law" in the temple, and making a determined effort to stem the tide of judgment.	2 Kings 22
606–586		*Jerusalem and the temple are destroyed* by Babylon in 586 after their refusal to bow to Babylonian rule. Three deportations to Babylon took place in 606, 597, and 586, leaving only the poor.	24–25

mering or iron tools on site, 1 Kings 6:7), nor so costly. Its sanctuary including walls and floor were covered with pure gold. The plans for this structure were given by the Lord, and the gold and silver were mostly collected by David (1 Chr. 28:19; 29:1-9). Why such an ornate house of God when many of the people were poor? This temple was to reflect the glory and greatness of Israel's God and symbolize that glory for the nations (2 Chr. 2:5-12).

3. *THE DIVIDED KINGDOM—931 B.C.* (1 Kings 12). After eighty years of building and establishing the kingdom under David and Solomon, it was permanently divided into two kingdoms just after the death of Solomon. Ten tribes amalgamated under Jeroboam and two under Rehoboam, called Israel and Judah. (Actually most of Simeon and Levi also came to Judah.) Why would such a splendid kingdom split so quickly? Three reasons stand out; spiritual, economic, and political.
   a. Spiritually, it occurred as the Lord had predicted, because of Solomon's idolatry brought on by his taking many wives, a violation itself (1 Kings 11:11).
   b. Economically, it resulted from Solomon's tyranny and heavy taxation program. He had built a rich throne, but left the people poor and oppressed (1 Kings 12).
   c. Politically, an ancient rivalry between Judah and Ephraim persisted and was exploited by Jeroboam who was an Ephraimite. Ephraim was often reluctant to bow to Judah's leadership, being the tribe of Joshua and Joseph, Israel's great leaders.

4. *ISRAEL'S CALF– WORSHIP SYSTEM* (1 Kings 12:25ff.). This institution was obviously a political expedient of Jeroboam to keep the people from Jerusalem and its temple. In doing this, he guarded against the worship of heathen gods (11:33), but began a false, substitute system of worshiping Yahweh (12:28). As with Aaron before him, he broke the second command to make worship convenient. It also required a new priest system, using laity rather than Levites who had gone to Judah (2 Chr. 11:14). This sin of Jeroboam was what condemned every future king of the North.

5. *BAAL WORSHIP INSTITUTED BY AHAB AND JEZEBEL* (1 Kings 16:29ff.). Israel's acceptance of calf-worship made her easy prey also to Canaanite Baal worship sixty years later. Calf-worship violated the second command, but Baal worship violated the first. Baal was the chief god worshiped in the Canaanite pantheon of gods. His special appeal as the god of agriculture, rain, and fertility was attractive to Israel. The entire system was without morals and was diametrically opposed to the holy God of the Hebrews. Jezebel, Ahab's wife from Phoenicia, was the instigator of this religion in Israel and hired an entourage of 850 prophets of Baal and Asherah (1 Kings 18:19). The Baal system constituted a direct challenge to Yahweh the God of Israel who laid claim to the land of Canaan as His special land.

6. *ELIJAH AND ELISHA, THE MIRACLE-WORKING PROPHETS* (1 Kings 17–2 Kings 9). Elijah came on the scene of Israel with his miraculous powers quite suddenly when Baal worship was instituted in Israel by Ahab and Jezebel. His one purpose was to

denounce the Baal system and call attention to the greater power of Israel's God. His first miracle of shutting the heavens for over three years was a challenge to the central power of Baal as god of agriculture and rain. Elisha's ministry with a double portion of Elijah's spirit brought the issue even more to a head by his more numerous miracles (fourteen rather than seven) and his cool boldness that defied many of the kings who followed the Baal system. This team of miracle-workers came to northern Israel as the nation was about to adopt the very system of idolatry the Lord had brought them to Canaan to destroy. Elisha's last act was to anoint Jehu to destroy the house of Ahab and the whole Baal-worshiping system in Israel (2 Kings 9:6-10).

7. *THE FALL OF SAMARIA, 722 B.C.* (2 Kings 17). Political chaos characterized Israel's last thirty years with five dynasties and four assassinations in its twilight years. The last king, Hoshea, was imprisoned by Shalmaneser during his last two years before the collapse of the city in 722. Samaria had been built by Omri, the king who brought in Jezebel through a marriage alliance, and it was appropriate that the end of the kingdom should also occur here. The fall of the north was designed as a warning to Judah that the Lord would not long stand for idolatry in His land (Ezek. 23:11).

8. *HEZEKIAH'S REFORMATION IN JUDAH* (2 Kings 18–20; 2 Chr. 29–32). King Hezekiah conducted one of the most significant reformations in Judah. The point of its significance, however, is tied to the dating of his reign, which is a much debated question among chronologists. Whereas 728–698 is the traditionally held date, the current prevailing date is 715–686 with co-regencies involved on both ends. The later view is supported by the fact that Sennacherib withdrew in 701, according to the Assyrian Taylor prism, and seems to relate to the fourteenth year of Hezekiah in 2 Kings 18:13. The reasoning is that that chapter dates the events by two regencies of Hezekiah, his co-regency with Ahaz and his full regency (2 Kings 18:1, 9, 10, 13). The traditional view dating his full regency in 728, however, appears to be more consistent and true to the text for several reasons:

   a. The author pegs Hezekiah's reign to the third year of Hoshea's reign three times (2 Kings 18:1, 9, 10), and he gives no hint of changing that pinpoint when referring to Sennacherib in v. 13.

   b. The text gives no suggestion that Ahaz still reigned as a co-regent when Hezekiah began his reformation in 728. Both were strong-willed men with diametrically opposed religious purposes. It rather emphasizes that he hurriedly began his reformation the first month of his twenty-nine year reign, as if driven by coming judgment.

   c. Hezekiah's invitation to the northern tribes makes sense only if that great Passover took place before those tribes were taken captive to Assyria in 722, for "none was left" to be invited after that captivity (2 Kings 17:6, 18). The young reformer would not have invited the new mongrel race of people brought in from Assyria to that strictly kosher Passover event.

   d. The text does not say Sennacherib came against Judah the same year the 185,000 Assyrians were destroyed (2 Kings 18:13). An extended time lapse was obviously involved for traveling, taking many difficult cities in Philistia, encountering the Egyptian army, taking forty-six cities of Judah, which required building huge dirt causeways to the wall tops, and seizing numerous villages. Hezekiah also made long preparations for Assyria's coming (2 Chr. 32:1-8). Besides building great military fortifications, he redirected the city's water supply by building a huge tunnel 1777 feet long through solid rock, a monumental feat (2 Kings 20:20). Rather, the indication of Isaiah 20:1 is that Sargon sent his son Sennacherib against the cities of Philistia and Judah much earlier, before the fall of Ashdod in 711, for the whole west was surging with unrest against Assyria in those years.

If these confirmations for an early date of his reformation beginning in 728 are valid, that reformation apparently served to postpone Judah's judgment by a massive purge of idolatry which had been more corrupt than the north under Hezekiah's father, Ahaz. That hurried reformation postponed Judah's final judgment 136 years.

9. **REFORMERS IN JUDAH.** Though northern Israel had only evil kings by God's standard, Judah had nine good kings (of the total nineteen). Five of these engaged in reformations: Asa, Jehoshaphat, Joash, Hezekiah, and Josiah. Two of the reformers, however, apostatized in old age (Asa and Joash), and the other three reformers had wicked sons following them that destroyed nearly all the good they had done (Jehoshaphat, Hezekiah, and Josiah). Strangely, four of these reformers came from wicked fathers, but only one raised a godly son (Asa, the father of Jehoshaphat). The point is often made that when they became "great" or wealthy, they turned from the Lord (2 Chr. 18:1; 26:16).

10. **JOSIAH'S GREAT BUT FUTILE REFORMATION** (2 Kings 22–23; 2 Chr. 34–35). Judah's last reformation was perhaps its greatest, but it was too late. No more dedicated effort was made than that of young Josiah who almost single-handedly turned the nation from idolatry and political chaos to a time of purging and prosperity the likes of which the nation had not seen since Samuel. He was no doubt counseled by such prophets as Jeremiah and Zephaniah and the prophetess Huldah. No death in Israel was so greatly mourned as his untimely death when he unwisely tried to stop Pharaoh Neco from going to the aid of Assyria against Babylon at Carchemish. He failed, however, to raise godly sons, and for this failure all the worthy prospects of his reformation were quickly lost, for his wicked sons each had a hand in leading the nation to destruction.

11. **THE DESTRUCTION OF JERUSALEM AND THE TEMPLE, 586 B.C.** (2 Kings 25; 2 Chr. 36). The calamity of Jerusalem's fall and the temple's destruction was an epochal event in the history of Israel. Its fall on August 9 (Tisha B'Ab) in the 380th year of the temple was memorialized by Jeremiah in his Lamentations, and it is remembered annually by world Jewry. Three deportations to Babylon took place in 606 (Dan. 1:1), 597 (2 Kings 24:11-12), and 586 (2 Kings 25:8-11). That event abrogated many of their rituals and customs which have never been fully restored. Though the city and temple have been rebuilt several times and new Israel is now independent, they have

never had all three together since. The reasons for this destruction and their captivity may be summarized in three points:

a. They refused to keep the covenant Law and resorted to all the idolatry and abominations of the heathen (Deut. 28:58; 2 Chr. 36:14).

b. They refused to respond to the corrections of God's prophets and the chastisements of the Lord (Lev. 26:14-33; 2 Chr. 25:4; 36:15-16).

c. They refused to keep God's sabbaths and the sabbatical years (Lev. 26:33-35; 2 Chr. 36:21). They shortchanged the Lord seventy years. Since the Lord required seven sabbaticals and one jubilee year every fifty years, the total time they had neglected this requirement was 437 years (going back to 1023). The indication is that they very rarely kept the sabbath and jubilee years of rest for the land. This divine reckoning stressed the fact that the land belonged to the Lord, and they were His tenants on the land if they kept the covenant code.

12. *CHRISTOLOGY IN KINGS.* These books have no messianic predictions, but King Solomon is the outstanding type of Christ in his office as king. As the son promised David who would build the temple and inherit his kingdom, Solomon typifies Christ especially in His coming in glory to bring peace, prosperity, and equity throughout the earth (Matt. 12:42). The miracle ministries of Elijah and Elisha are also an adumbration of the prophetic ministry of Christ, confirming His word by numerous miracles.

The Books of Chronicles

Introduction

AUTHORSHIP

A. *THE TITLE*

1. The name "Chronicles" is a Christian name given these books by Jerome in the fourth century A.D. The title is well chosen, suggesting their purpose to give a chronological record of sacred history.

2. The Hebrews regarded them as one book, calling them "Journals" or "Words of Days," and placed them at the end of the Canon as an annalistic review of divine dealings with the nation.

3. The Greek translators called them "Omissions," regarding them as supplements to the books of Samuels and Kings.

B. *THE AUTHOR*

1. Though anonymous, these books are evidently the work of Ezra the priest, as

Hebrew tradition avers. The literary style, priestly viewpoint, and obvious purpose relate well with other works by Ezra. The last verses of Chronicles, it should be noted, are the same as the first verses of Ezra, suggesting a continuation.

2. The author functions here as more of a compiler than a composer. Besides his use of the Pentateuch, Samuels, and Kings, he makes reference to about twelve other documents extant at that time (1 Chr. 9:1; 29:29; 2 Chr. 9:29; 12:15; 13:22; 20:34; 26:22; 27:7; 32:32; and 33:19).

HISTORICAL SETTING

A. *THE TIME SPAN*—From Adam's creation to Cyrus the Persian (538 B.C.).

Outline of 1 Chronicles

THEME: The Sovereignty of God in Establishing David's Throne.

Outline of 2 Chronicles

THEME: The Faithfulness of God to Discipline David's Dynasty.

1. The writing evidently took place following the return from exile to provide a theocratic background for the exhortations in Ezra–Nehemiah. About 430 B.C. would be a likely date of its writing.
2. The events or chronologies of the books, however, cover the whole of Old Testament history from Adam to the grandsons of Zerubbabel, Pelatiah and Jeshaiah in 1 Chronicles 1–3, who were contemporaries of Ezra (Keil). Thus its chronological reach is the greatest of any Bible book, from Genesis 1 to Malachi.

B. *THE POLITICAL SETTING*
1. When these Chronicles were compiled, Judah was no longer a monarchy, but a small group of exiles returned from Babylon under vassalage of the Persian Empire. The "times of the Gentiles" (Luke 21:24) had begun in 606 B.C. commencing the time in which Israel is ruled by Gentile nations.
2. The Jews, however, were not without influence in the Empire at this time. Daniel had risen to the position of prime minister in both the Babylonian Empire of Nebuchadnezzar and the Persian Empire of Cyrus (Dan. 2; 6). Esther and Mordecai had risen to queen and prime minister in the Persian Empire in the time of Ahasuerus, father of Artaxerxes I Longimanus who reigned in Ezra's time. They had exerted great influence for the Jews in the Empire.

C. *THE RELIGIOUS SETTING*
1. Though the events of 2 Chronicles concerns the Solomonic Temple Era, the writing of them took place in the Zerubbabel Temple Era (536-?). That new temple was completed some eighty-five years before and the city wall was recently rebuilt, but not much else had happened. The promised Messianic age had not materialized and religious stagnation was setting in. Their return to these rather barren hills reminded them of their great insignificance in the vast area of the Persian Empire. The tendency was to dismiss the covenant promises of a great Davidic kingdom in Palestine as mere religious fantasies of a bygone era.
2. This religious stagnation is seen in all of the six post-exilic books (Ezra, Nehemiah, Esther, Haggai, Zechariah, and Malachi). The probability is that they expected the Lord to quickly institute the Messianic kingdom following their return from exile, and He seemed to have let them down. With defection and spiritual lethargy setting in, they needed to be reminded of the overall program and purposes for Israel as seen from the divine perspective and how God was sovereign and faithful in all His dealings. These Chronicles then were compiled by Ezra, the priest, to emphasize God's sovereignty over the nation and His concern for proper worship and obedience to bring about the blessings of the covenants (2 Chr. 7:14).

THE PURPOSE OF THE BOOKS OF CHRONICLES

A twofold purpose may be discerned in this survey by Ezra of the Old Testament period:
A. The *historic purpose* of these books was not to continue the history of Israel where

2 Kings left off, but to succinctly present the whole story from the divine perspective. Rather than starting with Samuel or Abraham, he starts with Adam. In this restatement he omits much of the content of Samuels and Kings that deal with wars, politics, and even many sins of the people. The emphasis is rather on provisions for worship in the temple and Levites, the positive blessings of repentance, and God's sovereignty to restore them and to fulfill His promises if they will respond to Him.

B. A *canonical purpose* is also suggested by the setting of these books at the end of the Hebrew Canon. Ezra (who is thought to have arranged the Hebrew Canon with the Great Synagogue) did not place them at the end for mere modesty, but to give them a place of special importance. They constitute a unique kind of repetition in the Old Testament, summarizing the whole of sacred history to remind all future generations of the centrality of God in the midst of His people. Though much of Israel was in dispersion, His program for them remains intact; though He raises up world empires to discipline them, He will yet sovereignly fulfill all His covenant promises to them. This appears to be the point with which Ezra desired to close the Old Testament.

Unique Contributions of 1 and 2 Chronicles

1. *THE DIVINE PERSPECTIVE.* Chronicles' presentation is not a repetition, but a divine overview of Israel's history. The books emphasize the sovereignty of God overruling in the affairs of His people to fulfill His purposes in spite of the whims of men. This divine perspective is everywhere evident. We read constantly of "My people," the "anointed of the LORD," the "ark," "covenant," "temple," "anger," "sword," "kingdom," "eyes," and even of the "LORD sitting on His throne." (1 Chr. 6:10-11; 11:2; 13.2, 10; 21:12). As the final books of the Hebrew canon, they finish the Old Testament by viewing God's covenant nation from above.

2. *SPECIFIC CONTRASTS OF CHRONICLES WITH SAMUELS AND KINGS.* The purpose of these books may be seen by contrasting their special emphases with those of Samuels and Kings.
   a. Chronicles gives the priestly viewpoint, rather than the prophetic. Much is said of the priest and Levites, while the ministries of the great prophets Elijah and Elisha are hardly mentioned. The temple is more central than the throne.
   b. The national focus is on Judah in Chronicles, rather than on all Israel. Little is said of the northern kingdom, except as it relates to Judah. Only the kingly line of David is traced, hardly mentioning the kings of Israel.
   c. The basic plot is more ecclesiastical in Chronicles than political or military. The writer is not so concerned with military campaigns as he is with reformations. Much of David's life is seen to be concerned with preparation to build the temple. Military successes are always determined by relations to the Lord.

d. The style of Chronicles is more statistical than biographical. David seems to come out of a long line of genealogical statistics, with little mention of his shepherd and courtier background. Careful attention is given to David's organization of the priesthood, the Levites and singers, and his administration.

e. The purpose of Chronicles is more to encourage than to castigate, more to incite to loyalty than to indict for guilt. The evil dynasties of the north are only incidental here. The great sins of David and Solomon are not even mentioned. Even the evil kings of Judah are seen to have pursued reforms to emphasize the positive rather than the negative (e.g., Rehoboam and Manasseh). He sought to impress the depressed remnant with God's sovereignty and the fact that He will yet restore the nation to greatness if they will respond to Him.

f. The problem stressed in Chronicles was not idolatry, but spiritual indifference. Jeroboam's sin of calf-worship, mentioned four times in Kings, is not even noted in Chronicles. Solomon's destructive sin of idolatry is passed over. In describing the captivity of 586, the reason is not given as idolatry but failure to heed the Lord. When Chronicles was compiled by Ezra, the remnant was quite cured of its idolatry, but it was indifferent to the covenant purposes and had developed a tendency to adopt the commercial ways of the world.

3. *"SEEK THE LORD."* This admonition which occurs often in the Psalms and Prophets is not used in the previous historical books of Samuels and Kings; but it is stressed eleven times in Chronicles. The insightful author juxtaposes the two basic concepts of God's sovereignty and man's responsibility in the fulfilling of His purposes for His people. Second Chronicles 7:14 could well be the key verse, strongly impressing the need for personal repentance and turning to God that the covenant blessings might be fulfilled.

4. *THE GENEALOGICAL TABLES* (1 Chr. 1–9). These are the classic genealogical chapters of the Old Testament. Special stress in these tables is given to the genealogies of Judah and David to trace the throne rights, and to the genealogies of Levi and Aaron to trace the priestly rights. The basic biblical sources used to compile the Davidic line were Genesis 4; 5; 10; 11; 25; 35; 36; 46; Exodus 1; 6; Ruth 4; 2 Samuel 3; 5; and 1 and 2 Kings. Other non-extant sources are noted by the Chronicler (besides those noted in Kings) they are the following:

a. The History of Shemaiah the Prophet (2 Chr. 12:15).
b. The Works of Iddo the Prophet on Genealogies (2 Chr. 12:15).
c. A Midrash of Iddo the Prophet (2 Chr. 13:22).
d. The History of Jehu, son of Hanani (2 Chr. 20:34).
e. The Acts of Uzziah, by Isaiah the Prophet (2 Chr. 26:22).
f. The Midrash of the Books of the Kings (2 Chr. 24:27).
g. The History of the Hozai (seers) (2 Chr. 33:19).

The following is a composite of the fifty-three generations from Adam to Zerubbabel:

Adam	Shem	Isaac	Obed	Joash	Jeconiah
Seth	Arphaxad	Jacob	Jesse	Amaziah	Pedaiah (Or Shealtiel)
Enosh	Shelah	Judah	David	Azariah	Zerubbabel
Cainan	Eber	Perez	Solomon	Jotham	
Mahalaleel	Peleg	Hezron	Rehoboam	Ahaz	
Jared	Reu	Ram	Abijah	Hezekiah	
Enoch	Serug	Amminadab	Asa	Manasseh	
Methuselah	Nahor	Nahshon	Jehoshaphat	Amon	
Lamech	Terah	Salma	Joram	Josiah	
Noah	Abraham	Boaz	Ahaziah	Jehoiakim	

The following is a composite list of the high priests from Aaron to Jaddua as compiled from 1 Chronicles 6:3-15, Ezra 7:1-5, and Nehemiah 12:10-11.

Priest	Contemporary	Priest	Contemporary	Priest	Contemporary
Aaron	—Moses	Zadok	—David	Azariah III	
Eleazar		Ahimaaz		Seraiah	—Slain by Nebuchadnezzar
Phinehas		Azariah I		Jehozadak	—Brother of Ezra
Abishua		Johanan		Jeshua	—Zerubbabel
Bukki		Azariah II	—Uzziah	Joiakim	
Uzzi		Amariah II		Eliashib	—Nehemiah
Zerahiah		Ahitub II		Joiada	
Meraioth		Zadok II		Jonathan	
Amariah		Shallum		Jaddua	—Alexander the
Ahitub	—Samuel	Hilkiah	—Josiah		Great (noted by Josephus)

5. **THE DANGER OF PROSPERITY.** Chronicles stresses the danger of forsaking the Lord in times of prosperity or power. This is noted in the declines of Rehoboam (2 Chr. 12:1), Asa (16:1-2), Jehoshaphat (18:1), Jehoram (21:3-4), Amaziah (25:11-14), Uzziah (26:16), and Hezekiah (32:23-25). Prosperity and power were divine blessings, but easily tended toward a spirit of independence of the Lord.

6. **JEHOSHAPHAT'S BIBLE CONFERENCES** (2 Chr. 17:7-12). Jehoshaphat distinguished himself by his unique method of revival—that of sending traveling preachers and teachers (princes, Levites, and priests) to teach the Book of the Law in all the cities of Judah. The direct outcome of this revival was peace and good relations with the surrounding nations, favor with God, and national prosperity.

7. **CHRISTOLOGY IN CHRONICLES.** Besides the already noted types of Christ in David and Solomon, christological suggestions are seen in the genealogies of David's line which are also messianic in purpose. As these books conclude the Hebrew Old Testament, Matthew picks up that genealogy immediately in the New Testament to demonstrate Jesus' right to the throne in presenting Him as King of Israel.

The Books
of Ezra–Nehemiah

Introduction

AUTHORSHIP

A. *THE TITLES*

1. The books of Ezra and Nehemiah were regarded as one book in ancient times, as noted by Josephus, the Talmud, and Jerome. This facilitated limiting the number of canonical books to the number of letters in the Hebrew alphabet.
2. The *Greek LXX* also regarded them as one, "Ezra B" (Gr. *Esdras*), which followed "Ezra A," the apocryphal book (which reproduced 2 Chr. 35–36, Ezra, and Nehemiah 7:38–8:12 as a summary of the period).
3. The *Latin Vulgate* divided them into two books, calling Ezra "Ezra A" and Nehemiah "Ezra B."
4. Protestant and Modern Hebrew Bibles divide them into two, naming them after the principal figures, Ezra and Nehemiah.

B. *THE AUTHOR OR COMPILER*

1. Ezra the priest is generally considered the author or compiler of the four historical

---

Outline of Ezra

THEME: Israel's Return from Exile to Rebuild the Temple for Worship.

books of this period, 1 and 2 Chronicles, Ezra, and Nehemiah. In the section involving Nehemiah, it is probable that Ezra used the memoirs of Nehemiah, inasmuch as Nehemiah speaks in the first person on occasion.

2. Assuming Ezra to be the author-compiler, the following source materials were used in the writing:

   a. The *Memoirs of Ezra* (since both first and third persons are used).

   b. The *Memoirs of Nehemiah* (first person being used).

   c. Other official documents and catalogues were also used as evident in the sections, Ezra 4:7–6:18 and 7:12-26, being written in Aramaic, the official language of international correspondence of the time.

3. Ezra was the son of Seraiah the high priest who was slain by Nebuchadnezzar in 586 B.C. (Ezra 7:1; 2 Kin. 25:18-22), and the brother of Jehozadak the high priest who was taken captive (1 Chr. 6:15). His greatness as the Law-teacher

Outline of Nehemiah

THEME: Rebuilding the Broken Wall and Renewing the Broken Covenant.

who concluded the Old Testament is often likened to Moses the Law-giver who began the writing of the Old Testament. Both also were Levites. As Moses wrote the first five, Ezra wrote or compiled the last four.

4. Ezra's functions with the returned remnant included several monumental tasks:

    a. Re-instituting proper worship in the rebuilt temple in 457.

    b. Writing or compiling 1 and 2 Chronicles, Ezra, Nehemiah, and Psalm 119.

    c. Presiding over the "Great Synagogue" which presumably determined and arranged the Hebrew canon of Scripture.

    d. Instituting local synagogues in Judah for Torah study, similar to those begun in Babylon (which became the regular gathering place of the dispersed Jews, as in Ezek. 20).

Chronology of Events in the Persian Period

DATE	EVENT	SIGNIFICANCE
559 B.C.	Cyrus the Great took Persian throne (559–330).	Cyrus conquered and organized Persian Empire, taking Media, 550, and Asia Minor, 546.
538	Babylon fell to Persia as Darius the Mede took city.	This ended the Babylonian Empire, the first of the Gentile kingdoms of Daniel's vision.
538	Cyrus released captives, decreeing temple rebuilding.	Fulfilled Isaiah's prophecy of "Cyrus" and Jeremiah's prophecies of "seventy years" in Babylon.
537	Return of Jews under Zerubbabel to rebuild temple.	Worship of God in the temple was first sought before protection of a rebuilt wall.
530	Cambyses decreed temple-building to halt.	This followed a period of struggle with Samaritans after altar and offerings re-instituted.
525	Cambyses conquered Egypt.	This made Persia the largest empire of history. But Cambyses died enroute home by suicide.
522	Darius took throne from usurper, Pseudo-Smerdis.	This returned throne to house of Cyrus the Great. Divided Empire into 127 satrapies. He was defeated by Greeks at Marathon, 490.
520	Temple building resumed at urging of Haggai and Zachariah.	Further Samaritan complaints brought decree from Darius to rebuild and enemies to help subsidize.
516	Zerubbabel's temple completed.	It was completed seventy years after destruction, 586.

HISTORICAL SETTING

A. *DATE OF WRITING*—c. 430–425 B.C.

Since the ministries of Ezra and Nehemiah took place during the reign of Artaxerxes I (465–424 B.C.), it is probable the writing was completed near the close of this period, after the last prophet, Malachi, had spoken and written.

B. *THE TIME-SPAN INVOLVED IN EZRA–NEHEMIAH*—538–430 B.C.

This history covers a period of over 100 years, from the first return of the temple-builder, Zerubbabel (537), to the last return of the wall-builder, Nehemiah (after 432). Four returns from Babylon are actually involved, Zerubbabel's in 537, Ezra's in 457, and Nehemiah's in 444 and 432.

DATE	EVENT	SIGNIFICANCE
486	Xerxes I began reign at death of Darius. Reigned 486–465.	His reign brought goodwill to Jews in empire.
480	Xerxes' army defeated at Salamis Isle, near Greece.	This second attempt to add Greece to Persian Empire was the western turning point for Persia.
479	Esther made queen of Persia.	This was four years after Vashti was deposed and just after the Persian defeat in Greece.
473	Esther saves Jews of empire. Mordecai made prime minister.	This established Jewish Feast of Purim, March 13-14, after the infamous "pur" (lot) of Haman was cast to destroy the Jews (Esth. 3:7; 9:26). These two exerted immense influence for Jews in the Empire.
465	Artaxerxes Longimanus began reign of forty years (465–425).	He followed his father in showing Jews goodwill in Empire through Ezra and Nehemiah.
457	Ezra the priest returns to Jerusalem to set up worship.	The Persian king (a polytheist) was greatly exercised to aid Ezra and Nehemiah.
444	Nehemiah returns to Jerusalem to rebuild wall in fifty-two days.	This wall enabled separation to maintain proper worship and restore covenant practices.
432	Malachi denounces indifference and amalgamation with heathen.	This shows a spiritual stagnation process setting in and a questioning of covenant promises.
430	Nehemiah returned second time after brief stay in Persia.	This was final effort of reform in Old Testament period.
430–425	Ezra completed history books of Old Testament and arranged canon.	This completed Israel's first 1000 years history from Moses to Ezra, and provided the remnant and those in dispersion with a record of that history as they lived under Gentile rule awaiting messianic times.

C. *THE POLITICAL SETTING*

1. These books introduce a new period of Israel's history on both the national and international scenes. Nationally, it began the post-exilic era of Israel's return to the land. Her seventy years of exile was over. Internationally, it introduced the era of the Persian Empire with its many new policies that affected Israel and the world.

2. The most significant effect of these policies for Israel was the new Persian practice of returning exiles. Instead of deporting and transporting captured people, as Assyria and Babylon had done, they returned them to their native soil to help promote peaceful relations in the empire. Not only did they release them, they often subsidized their return to help them get resettled and reinstitute their religious system in their homelands.

3. In viewing the politics of the time, it should not be forgotten that several Jews had risen to high posts in the Persian government and doubtless had great influence in the Persian court for the Jews in the empire. Daniel, Esther, and Mordecai were in crucial places of political influence during both the Babylonian and Persian periods.

C. *THE RELIGIOUS SETTING*

1. Internationally, a new religious climate was ushered in by the Persians. The decrees of Cyrus and Darius were partially inspired by their religious faith which was a mixture of the traditional view of a pantheon of gods and the recently developed Zoroastrianism with its two hierarchies of good and evil. The effect was that they returned peoples to their homelands to seek to appease the local gods and promote peace in the empire. This, of course, beautifully effected the return of Israel to Palestine with their temple vessels to reinstitute their religious system.

2. For many in Israel, the exile in Babylon had produced a great spiritual revolution. Though there was an almost universal defection at the time of the captivity (as noted by Jeremiah and Ezekiel), the return in 537 found an aroused group of godly Jews eager to return to the covenant land. Though many chose to remain in the fertile valley of Babylon, a large contingent of nearly 50,000 men (besides women and children) responded to this invitation to endure the hardship of returning to the destroyed cities and overgrown hills of Judah. Their synagogue studies of Torah and the Prophets, Isaiah, Jeremiah, Ezekiel, and Daniel, no doubt played a part in inspiring this godly faith.

3. This period was a time of much religious and philosophical thinking and upheavals in the world. This can be seen by the outstanding thinkers and movements that arose during this time:

    a. Socrates (c. 469), Plato (427), and Aristotle (384) developed much of the Grecian or Hellenistic thought which later affected the world.

    b. Zoroaster (Zarathustra, 628–551) quickly spread over the Persian world.

    c. Buddha (Gautama, 563–486) developed his "four noble truths" of Buddhism rejecting ancient Hinduism with its "castes," spreading over India.

d. Confucius (Kung Fu-tse, c. 551–479) taught in China during a time of great internal strife and rejection of religious traditions.

This world-wide religious activity and unrest emphasizes the importance of Ezra's work to preserve the true religion of the covenant fathers.

THE PURPOSE OF THE BOOKS OF EZRA AND NEHEMIAH

A. *The unified purpose of Ezra–Nehemiah.* Historically, they were written to complete the history of Israel which Chronicles had begun to the time of the 586 captivity. The history of Israel's return from exile was necessary to demonstrate the Lord's continuing covenant relations with them in fulfilling His promise of return.

B. *The unique purpose of Ezra.* The specific purpose of this book was to document the return to rebuild the temple at the specific time the Lord had said it would take place through Jeremiah (Jer. 29:10ff.; Ezra 1:1). As Chronicles adverted to this fulfillment in its final two verses, Ezra returned to this statement and gave the details of the building of the temple and restoring the temple worship.

C. *The unique purpose of Nehemiah.* Ezra used the extended personal records of Nehemiah (Ezra 1:1–7:73) to document the rebuilding of Jerusalem's wall. This included the precise date of the king's decree, "the month of Nisan, in the twentieth year of King Artaxerxes." He shows how God used a concerned layman to lay the building blocks of Jerusalem's wall to give a measure of protection to the remnant and the rebuilt temple, and to provide a bulwark against the inroads of heathen commercialism and culture that tended to dilute their godly purity. The date of this command to rebuild the wall also provided the precise date at which the "seventy weeks" (heptads) of Daniel were to begin (Dan. 9:24ff.) Thus, the datings of these two books provide encouragement concerning past prophecy (fulfillment of Jeremiah's seventy years) and the point of beginning for future prophecy (the fulfillment of Daniel's "seventy weeks").

Unique Contributions of Ezra–Nehemiah

1. *ISRAEL'S POST-EXILIC HISTORY.* With some help from the prophetic books of Haggai and Zechariah, these books tell of that historic return from captivity. Ezra describes how the prophecy of Jeremiah 25:12 and 29:10 was fulfilled in two ways: 1) a period of seventy years bondage took place from the first captivity in 606 to the release and return in 536. 2) An overlapping period of seventy years also occurred from the destruction of the temple in 586 to its completion in 516. Though their total bondage lasted only fifty

years, the seventy years of shame was emphasized in both their captivity and place of worship.

The returned remnant were mostly Jews, but they evidently represented all Israel as suggested by the following: 1) The edict of Cyrus was given to all Israel, including the northern ten tribes taken to Assyria (Ezra 1:3). 2) The twelve tribes are represented by the twelve leaders (Neh. 7:7; cf. Ezra 2:2). 3) Twelve male goats offered at the temple dedication were for the twelve tribes (Ezra 6:17; 8:35). 4) Whereas "Judah" is referred to twenty-six times in Ezra–Nehemiah, the inclusive term "Israel," is used over sixty times, as though all tribes were represented.

2. *CONFIRMATIONS OF THE PROPHETIC WORD.* Ezra's great emphasis was on the "Word," as noted in Psalm 119 (ascribed to him). Likewise, the Book of Ezra begins

International Rulers Effecting Israel's Captivity and Returns

LATE ASSYRIAN KINGS—745–626 B.C.

Tiglath-Pileser III (Pul)	745–727	Invaded Israel; exiled Galilee and Trans-Jordan.	2 Kings 15:29
Shalmaneser V	727–722	Subjugated Israel, besieged revolting Samaria, 725.	2 Kings 17:5-6; 18:9
Sargon II	722–705	Exiled Israel in Assyria. Invaded Philistia and Judah.	2 Kings 18:11; Is. 20:1
Sennacherib	705–681	Invaded Philistia, Tyre, and Judah. Besieged Jerusalem and army destroyed in 701.	2 Kings 18:13ff.
Esarhaddon	681–669		
Ashurbanipal	669–626	Invaded Judah, taking Manasseh captive to Babylon, c. 650.	2 Chr. 33:11

After 626, the Assyrian Empire disintegrated under three last kings. Babylon destroyed Nineveh in 612, took Haran in 610, and Carchemish in 605.

NEO-BABYLONIAN KINGS—626–539 B.C.

Nabopolassar	626–605	Took Babylon in 626 and began rise.	
Nebuchadnezzar	605–562	Took Palestine in 606; destroyed Jerusalem and temple and exiled remnant in 586.	2 Kings 24–25; Dan. 1–4
Evil-Merodach (Amel-Marduk)	562–560	Released and elevated Jehoiachin.	2 Kings 25:27; Jer. 52:31ff.
Nergal-Sharezer	560–556	Murdered brother-in-law to reign.	
Labashi-Marduk	556		
Nabonidus	556–539	Murdered king and took throne.	
Belshazzar (co-regent)	553–539	Made Daniel third ruler the night before he himself was slain by Darius.	Dan. 5:29-31

Under Nabonidus the Babylonian Empire disintegrated after serving to destroy violent Assyria and to bring rebellious Judah into Babylonian exile.

with an affirmation of the fulfillment of God's word through Jeremiah, but also alluding to the fulfillment of Isaiah 44:28. Over 150 years before, Isaiah had named Cyrus as the one whom the Lord would use to subdue nations, release captives, rebuild the temple, and proclaim the name of Yahweh "from the rising of the sun to its setting" (Is. 45:1, 6). This return was an auspicious event in Israel to which all four of the major prophets had looked forward.

3. **THE PERSIAN EMPIRE IN GOD'S PLAN.** The inclusive history of Ezra–Nehemiah begins with Cyrus the first Persian king, and extends its scope to the naming of Jaddua the high priest when the Persian Empire ended in 333. This empire was the second of the Gentile kingdoms in Daniel's prophecies (Dan. 2:39; 7:5), all of which were to discipline the people of Israel while ruling them. Persia's radically different policies toward captive peoples, seeking their repatriation and goodwill rather than their bondage (as Assyria and Babylon had), nicely fit God's program of restoring His people. That goodwill continued through Old Testament times, aided of course by such leaders as Daniel, Esther, and Mordecai.

4. **TRAVEL TIME FROM BABYLON** (Ezra 7:9; 8:31). Ezra gives a clue as to the travel time from Babylon to Jerusalem (c. 900 miles). It took three months and eighteen days, "according to the good hand of his God upon him" (7:9). They purposely moved quite quickly, not having asked for a military escort to protect them. This also supplies an answer to how long it might have taken the Magi to arrive at Bethlehem after they saw the star "in the east" and hurried west.

PERSIAN KINGS (first non-Semitic world rulers)—539–333 B.C.

Cyrus the Great	559–530	Conquered Media, 550, Asia Minor, 546, and Babylon, 538; released exiles and decreed rebuilding of temple.	Ezra 1:1ff.
Darius (Gobryas) (co regent)		Made Daniel first commissioner.	Dan. 6:2, 28
Cambyses (Ahasuerus)	530–522	Conquered Egypt. Halted rebuilding of temple to appease Samaritans.	Ezra 4:6, 21
Guamata (Pseudo-Smerdis)	522		
Darius Hystapis I (Of house of Cyrus)	521–486	Divided empire into satrapies. Re-decreed building of temple.	Ezra 6:3ff.
Xerxes (Ahasuerus)	486–465	Made Esther queen and Mordecai prime minister.	Esther 1:1ff.
Artaxerxes I Longimanus	465–424	Encouraged the returns of Ezra and Nehemiah to establish Jerusalem.	Ezra 7:1ff. Neh. 1ff.
Darius II (Nothus)	424–404		

Royal rivalries followed death of Darius II, bringing weak rules of Artaxerxes II and III and Darius III. Darius III was finally defeated by Alexander as he swept across Asia Minor, Palestine, Egypt, and Mesopotamia, conquering to India.

5. **THE SAMARITAN CONTROVERSY** (Ezra 4). The refusal of Israel to accept the Samaritan help in rebuilding the temple seems trivial, but it issued in a rift that extended into New Testament times. The two peoples came to regard each other as their worst enemies, refusing any association. Why were the builders so independent, inasmuch as David welcomed the help of the Phoenicians? They probably reasoned that to accept their help in building would bring also their demand for a voice in establishing worship in the temple. Their eclectic religious background might have compromised the ancient basis of Israel's worship and religious system. Interestingly, the Samaritans were the first to speak of the remnant as the "Jews" (Ezra 4:12). That time called for separation and purity to jealously preserve true religion.

6. **ZERUBBABEL AND SHESHBAZZAR** (Ezra 1:8, 11; 2:2). Shall we identify or distinguish these two men, both of whom are said to have "laid the foundation" of the temple (Ezra 3:8, 10; 5:16; Zech. 4:9)? Though the names could refer to the same person, the texts seem to distinguish them. An attractive theory is that "Sheshbazzar" is another spelling of the "Shenazzar" of 1 Chronicles 3:18, who is a son of Jeconiah and therefore an uncle of Zerubbabel. If so, Sheshbazzar was commissioned by Cyrus to lead the group and be governor in Jerusalem (5:14), but perhaps died before the foundation was completed. Zerubbabel, the leading royal son of the next generation then took over to complete the temple and become governor. Thus both "laid the foundation" of the temple, but the messianic line came through Zerubbabel.

7. **ZERUBBABEL'S TEMPLE** (Ezra 6:3-4). How does it compare with Solomon's? The text does not furnish the elaborate details given for Solomon's (1 Kin. 6; 2 Chr. 3), but it does give the basic, outside dimensions. It was 90 feet wide, 90 feet high, and 150 feet long, having three stories. This was one-third larger than Solomon's, though it was much more simple and less ornate. Its furniture also was much more limited, being the pieces included in Moses' tabernacle, not the multiple pieces of Solomon's (e.g., one lampstand rather than ten). The Talmud lists five things of the Solomonic temple that were missing in Zerubbabel's: the ark, the sacred fire, the Shekinah, the Holy Spirit, and the Urim and Thummin. In the place of the ark of the covenant was placed a large stone.

8. **EZRA'S COMMAND TO DIVORCE** (Ezra 9:1ff. 10:3, 11). This unique command that the remnant divorce their heathen wives appears to contradict Moses (Deut. 21:10-14; 24:1-4). Moses simply required heathen wives to go through a purification ritual. The problem Ezra dealt with might well have been similar to what Malachi confronted in Malachi 2:11-16, that of marrying foreign wives in addition to their first or covenant wives. Divorcing the "wife of your youth" was the sin Malachi said God hated (3:15-16). Just as God had commanded Abraham to divorce his additional and foreign wife, Hagar (Gen. 21:12), it is likely that Ezra commanded a similar separation of the remnant who were tending to amalgamate with the heathen about them. The long counseling sessions

for these 113 offenders suggests they were required to make proper provisions for the bereft wives and children.

9. **CHRISTOLOGY IN EZRA–NEHEMIAH.** The two leading figures of Zerubbabel and Joshua are seen in the two prophetic books of this period, Haggai and Zechariah, to pre-figure Christ as a King-Priest (Zech. 6:13). ''The Man whose name is the BRANCH! . . . shall build the temple of the LORD. He shall bear the glory, and shall sit and rule on His throne. So He shall be a priest on His throne, and the counsel of peace shall be between them both.''

Haggai portrays Zerubbabel as the outstanding type of Christ who receives God's ''signet ring'' or authority to overthrow all kingdoms and rule the nations for God. (Hag. 2:23). Zerubbabel, of course, was also in the messianic line (Matt. 1:12). Ezra and Nehemiah portray the great need of the remnant for such a Governor who would lead and direct His people in the midst of the growing opposition of post-exilic times.

The Book of Esther

Introduction

AUTHORSHIP

A. *THE TITLE*
1. Its title derives from the central figure rather than from the author. ''Ester'' ('ester) was her Persian name, meaning ''star,'' and ''Hadassah'' was her Jewish name, meaning ''myrtle.''
2. The book is one of two Old Testament books named after women:
   a. Ruth was a Gentile who married a wealthy Jew of royal promise, Boaz.
   b. Esther was a Jewess who married a wealthy Gentile of royal power, Ahasuerus.

B. *THE AUTHOR*
1. Mordecai has been the leading candidate for author from ancient times, and Ezra and Nehemiah have also been suggested. The last chapter appears to disqualify Mordecai (though it could have been added by an editor, as Ezra). Linguistic evidence appears to be against Ezra or Nehemiah.
2. Though the author is unknown, he or she was well acquainted with Persian customs and the Persian court and had a genius for discerning and constructing the dramatic. The Talmud ascribed it to the ''Great Synagogue,'' of which Ezra was supposedly president and might well have collaborated in its writing.

HISTORICAL SETTING

A. *DATE OF WRITING*—c. 460 B.C.
   1. It was probably written soon after the death of Ahasuerus (Xerxes) (465) when the royal records of Ahasuerus were completed in the royal Chronicles (Esth. 10:2).
   2. It was then written as an encouragement to Jews dispersed in the Empire and perhaps constituted an encouragement to those returning in 457 and 444.

B. *THE TIME-SPAN INVOLVED*—483–473 B.C.
   1. In 483, Queen Vashti was deposed (Ahasuerus' third year).
   2. In 479, Queen Esther was crowned (Ahasuerus' seventh year).
   3. In 473, the Jewish deliverance of Purim took place (Ahasuerus' thirteenth year).
   4. The events of this book fit chronologically between Ezra 6 and 7.

C. *THE POLITICAL SETTING*
   1. The Persian ruler. Under Ahasuerus, the Persian Empire came to the zenith of its power. This king was the Persian ruler who made a gigantic expedition against Greece in 480, seeking to accomplish what his father Darius failed to do in 490, to conquer and add the Grecian Peninsula to the Persian Empire. Though he took Athens (pillaging the city and destroying the Acropolis), his fleet was defeated off the Island of Salamis, and he retreated to Persia. The Grecian debacle occurred between Esther 1 and 2.
   2. The capital cities. Shushan (Gr. *Susa,* "lillies") was one of three capitals maintained by Persia, the others being Babylon in Mesopotamia and Persepolis in southeast Persia. Shushan was considered the summer palace, located about 250 miles east of Babylon on the highlands of Elam. Daniel had also lived there for a time under Belshazzar (Dan. 8:2).
   3. Jews in the Empire. Though a large contingent of Jews had returned to Palestine nearly sixty years earlier with Sheshbazzar (and Zerubbabel), many still remained in dispersion throughout the Empire. Under the Persians they received good treatment, learned Aramaic and economics, and had few restrictions. The anti-Semitism noted in Esther was not Persian, but Agagite.
   4. Persian changes in the Empire. Several changes in the Empire took place in the transition from Babylonian to Persian rule:
      a. A more compassionate attitude toward conquered peoples was practiced. An interesting concomitant was that this began a period of relative peace in the empire which lasted nearly 200 years.
      b. The Empire was vastly larger, reaching from India to Europe.
      c. This introduced an Aryan (Caucasian) rule over the world, since the Persians were of European stock, the first such world empire.
      d. The Persians made Aramaic the official language of the Empire for commerce and politics, as it had already become the lingua franca.
      e. Old boundaries among nations were changed and a new division of satrapies

or provinces was instituted to break up old alliances, allowing local rule, however, under Persian supervision.

5. The Grecian challenge. The Persian attempts by both Darius and Xerxes to invade Europe by assaulting Greece in 490 and 480 became a bench mark of the east in seeking world dominance. The massive defeat of Xerxes at Salamis and Plataea by the Spartans after he had successfully bridged the Hellespont and destroyed Athen's Acropolis, turned the tide of empires. The Greeks never forgot the Persians' pillage of Athens until Alexander avenged the atrocity by pillaging and burning Persepolis in 331, the ceremonial capital of Darius and Xerxes. The Greek and Aegean cities strengthened themselves for 150 years to thrust their

Outline of Esther

THEME: The Lord's Continued Care for Israel—Even in Dispersion.

champion, Alexander, across the Hellespont and to claim all the Persian Empire and much more.

D. *THE RELIGIOUS SETTING*
1. Religion in Israel. For a note on the state of Israel's religion in the post-exilic period, see Introduction to Ezra–Nehemiah. It was a time of little spiritual progress, much tendency to amalgamate with the surrounding culture, and general indifference, though they were quite cured of wood and stone idolatry.
2. Religion of the Jews in dispersion. Zoroastrianism was the religion promoted by the Persian rulers, named after Zoroaster ("camel handler") who began the religion and supposedly converted Hystaspes, the father of Darius I. This was a quasi-dualistic religion that was tolerant toward the "beneficent and true" deities, but not the "malevolent and false." Thus, while expressing great favor and kindness toward worshipers of the good deities, they could be most vicious toward those in the other camp. The Jews in the Empire came to be regarded as worshipers of the good spirits, and thus were not only tolerated, but aided and subsidized in the rebuilding of their worship system.

THE PURPOSE OF THE BOOK OF ESTHER

A. The *historic purpose* of this book was evidently to encourage the Jews scattered throughout the Empire with this story of the Lord's continued concern and presence with them, though He is not seen and though they are far from His temple in Jerusalem. Though His name is not mentioned in the book, His divine guidance is seen everywhere.

B. A *further religious purpose* was to supply the authentic explanation of the origin of the Jewish Feast of Purim, a festival that was to be especially dear to the Jews of world dispersion.

Unique Contributions of Esther

1. *THE SEEDS OF ANTI-SEMITISM.* Anti-Semitism is a form of prejudice against the Jews, ranging from antipathy to violent hatred. Though the term was first used in 1879, (see Max Dimont, *Jews, God and History,* pp. 313ff.), the phenomena of anti-Semitism was first expressed in the Book of Esther. Being anti-Semitic differs from being anti-Jewish in that it is an irrational prejudice against the race, not just against what they do or think. Anti-Semitism judges the Jews for the "crime" of being Jewish; anti-Jewish people condemn the Jews for what they do or for their "crime" of having crucified Jesus. While the second can be atoned for (by conversion or other acts), the first, anti-Semitism, cannot.

The Book of Esther introduces us to both. Haman was anti-Semitic with a race hatred against the Jews (3:6), but he induced the king's edict to destroy the Jews in the empire because of their laws or practices. Dimont describes the Arabs' problem with the Jews as anti-Jewish (invading their land), but the Nazi problem of the Third Reich as anti-Semitism. Like Hitler, Haman's problem was a deep-seated prejudice against the Israelite nation, probably found in his background as an Agagite. (Agag being the royal name for Amalekite kings, Esth. 3:1; 1 Sam. 15:2-9; 32-33).

2. *ESTHER'S PLACE IN HISTORY.* This book has been held in two extremes of esteem in history: 1) World Jewry have traditionally held it in the highest esteem, second only to the books of Moses. Besides reading it annually at the Feast of Purim, they have read and revered it in their world-wide dispersions through countless times of similar oppression and threats of annihilation. 2) Others, like Martin Luther, have held it in the lowest esteem. Luther said he wished the book did not exist. This reflects the attitude of the church in Luther's time, and the Catholic Church in general, that the Jews were an accursed race for having crucified Jesus, and therefore had no future place in God's program. In response, the Jews have considered the church as their traditional enemy, and the person of Jesus as the focal point of their problem and reason for persecution.

3. *THE BIBLE BOOK "WITHOUT GOD."* Esther is one of two Bible books that have no mention of the name of God. Song of Solomon refers to Yahweh only once in the Hebrew (Song 8:6). Yet the divine hand of providence overshadows the whole story of Esther. This silence about God is quite inexplicable, but it symbolizes the feelings of many of the Jews in dispersion who felt abandoned by the Almighty. The book shows that though His Name is not mentioned (in either covenant or universal form), His hand of care is still with them, working "within the shadows." Several commentaries have noted the interesting acrostics of the name "Yahweh" (four Hebrew consonants) in the book. The Tetragrammaton is mystically drawn from the first or last letters of consecutive words of Esther 1:20, 5:4, 13, and 7:7, both forward and backwards. A. T. Pierson, *Knowing the Scriptures,* has illustrated this phenomena by using the English name "LORD":

    1:20   "Due Respect, Our Ladies all,
            shall give their husbands, great and small."

    5:4   "Let Our Royal Dinner bring
            Haman feasting with the king."

    5:13 "GranD foR nO avaiL my state,
            While this Jew sits at my gate."

    7:7   "IlL tO feaR decreeD I find,
            Toward me in the monarch's mind."

Though God is incognito in this book, His hand is everywhere evident.

4. **THE JEWS IN THE STRUGGLE OF EMPIRES.** Esther gives some unique insights into the struggles of the Persian court, as well as those of the Jews. The Persian Empire was the second of the Gentile kingdoms of Daniel's vision in Daniel 7:1-7 (cf. Dan. 8:19ff.), the first being Babylon that came and went in less than ninety years. During the reign of Ahasuerus, portents of a great western power from Greece began to develop. The failure of Ahasuerus to annex the Grecian cities after sacking Athens and destroying the Acropolis ignited an unquenchable desire for retaliation by the Grecians. That retaliation finally came 150 years later when Alexander, fulfilling the plan of his father Philip of Macedonia, crossed the Hellespont, defeated the Persians at Granicus, and swept all the way to the Persian capitals of Susa and Persepolis, burning the latter city as Ahasuerus had done to Athens. As the Persians had fostered Zoroastrianism, Alexander was to all but destroy that polytheistic dualism, as he spread the philosophy of Aristotle and Hellenism with its "pagan joy, freedom, and love of life" all the way to the Indus River. This new western philosophy of life was to challenge Israel through intertestamental times, and it became a part of the world setting when Messiah came.

The point is that the struggle of empires was not areligious or merely military. This conflict of cultures and philosophies should really be seen on the higher level of spiritual forces, as Daniel was informed in Daniel 10:13-21. The "prince of . . . Persia" (a satanic angel) withstood Daniel's counseling angel, and the "prince of Greece" was waiting in the wings to oppose him also. He encouraged him with the fact that Michael the archangel was on his side. Daniel 11:1-3 then describes the coming invasion of Ahasuerus and final conquest of Alexander. The story of Esther illustrates how Israel's struggle in the fray will not be won by physical forces or schemes, but spiritual exercises and trust in the covenant Lord who overrules all.

5. **THE GREATNESS OF MORDECAI.** Though Joseph and Daniel ruled world empires as vice-regents, no Jewish leader ever ruled such a vast empire as did Mordecai. These three rulers from Israel, however, had a number of unique things in common:
   a. All were Jewish exiles who lived godly lives in foreign lands.
   b. All endured suffering at the hands of jealous enemies who schemed to kill them.
   c. All rose from positions of lowly service to become world rulers.
   d. Each came to power suddenly after faithfully serving at lowly tasks.
   e. Each was used to preserve God's people in times of oppression or slavery.
   f. Each was used to save or benefit the king he served.
   g. Each exemplified the way God blesses Abraham's children when cursed by enemies—not by retaliatory schemes, but by trust and faithful service.

6. **THE CAPTIVATING DRAMA OF ESTHER.** This story is one of the most captivating dramas of all literature. It has all the elements of high drama, suspense, and intrigue. Two ancient foes suddenly confront each other. One is a crafty villain who worms his way to power; the other is a lowly peasant who righteously ingratiates himself to the king. A Cinderella story unfolds that builds up in the middle chapter to a perfect plot of suspense. A hanging is planned and a racial holocaust is to immediately follow. But two

cases of insomnia bring about a complete reversal, as the villain becomes impatient and inadvertently condemns himself before the king and thus justifies his being hung on his own gallows. Far from being mere brilliant drama, however, the story is a true portrayal of events that changed the course of history for a whole race of people. It really had repercussions for the whole race, since the progenitors of Messiah himself were in jeopardy.

7. *CHRISTOLOGY IN THE BOOK OF ESTHER.* This book has no specific prophecies or types of Christ, except as Christ is part of the Jewish race that faced extinction. The lesson is certainly highlighted that, no matter how fierce the adversary, no Haman, Herod, or Hitler can destroy the seed of Abraham whom God has vowed to bless. On the contrary, God has often preserved His people through great persecution for even greater blessing through leaders He has raised up: Joseph in Egypt; Moses in Egypt; Mordecai in Persia; and Jesus in Galilee of the Gentiles. In this way the three might be considered types of Christ, the final Deliverer of His people.

Select Commentaries on the Historical Books *

JOSHUA

Armerding, Carl. *Conquest and Victory.* Chicago: Moody Press, 1949.
*Blaikie, W. G. *The Book of Joshua* (Expositor's Bible) New York: Armstrong, 1905.
*Davis, John J. and J. C. Whitcomb. *A History of Israel From Conquest to Exile.* Grand Rapids: Baker, 1980.
*Garstang, John. *Joshua and Judges.* London: Constable and Co., 1931.
Gettys, John. *Surveying the Historical Books.* Richmond, Va.: John Knox Press, 1961.
Jensen, Irving L. *Joshua: Rest-Land Won.* Chicago: Moody Press, 1966.
Pink, Arthur W. *Gleanings in Joshua.* Chicago: Moody Press, 1964.
*Redpath, Alan. *Victorious Christian Living.* New York: Revell, 1955.
Schaeffer, Francis A. *Joshua and the Flow of Biblical History.* Chicago: InterVarsity Press, 1975.
*Woudstra, M. H. *The Book of Joshua* (NICOT) Grand Rapids: Eerdmans, 1981.

JUDGES

Aharoni, Y. and M. Avi-Yonah, ed. *Macmillan Bible Atlas.* New York: Macmillan, 1977.
Burney, C. F. *The Book of Judges.* Reprint. New York: Ktav, 1970.
*Cundall, A. E. and Leon Morris. *Judges and Ruth.* (Tyndale series) Chicago: InterVarsity Press, 1968.
Faussett, A. R. *A Critical and Expository Commentary on the Book of Judges.* Minneapolis: James and Klock, 1977.
*Hunter, John. *Judges and a Permissive Society.* Grand Rapids: Zondervan, 1975.
Martin, J. D. *The Book of Judges* (Cambridge series) Cambridge: Cambridge Press, 1975.
Ridout, S. *Lectures on the Book of Judges.* New York: Loizeaux, 1912.
*Wood, Leon. *Distressing Days of the Judges.* Grand Rapids: Zondervan, 1975.

RUTH

*Cundall, A. E. (See under Judges) Treatment of Ruth by Leon Morris.
DeHaan, M. R. *The Romance of Redemption.* Grand Rapids: Zondervan, 1958.

Hals, Ronald. *The Theology of the Book of Ruth*. Philadelphia: Fortress Press, 1969.

Leggett, D. A. *The Levirate and Goel Institutions in the Old Testament with Special Attention to the Book of Ruth*. Cherry Hill, N. J.: Mach, 1974.

*Mauro, Philip. *Ruth: The Satisfied Stranger*. New York: Revell, 1920.

*McGee, J. Vernon. *In a Barley Field*. Glendale, Ca.: Regal, 1968.

Rowley, H. H. "The Marriage of Ruth" in *The Servant of the Lord and Other Essays on the Old Testament*. Naperville, Ill.: Alec R. Allenson, 1952.

1 and 2 SAMUEL

*Barber, Cyril and J. D. Carter. *Always a Winner: A Commentary For Laymen on I Samuel*. Glendale: Regal, 1977.

*Blaikie, W. G. *The First Book of Samuel* (Expositor's Bible) London: Hodder, 1898.

Carlson, R. A. *David, the Chosen King*. Stockholm: Almquist and Wiksell, 1964.

*Crocket, William D. *A Harmony of the Books of Samuel, Kings, and Chronicles*. Grand Rapids: Baker, 1951.

*David, John J. *The Birth of a Kingdom*. Grand Rapids: Baker, 1970.

Hertzberg, H. W. *I and II Samuel*. Philidelphia: Westminster Press, 1964.

*Laney, J. Carl. *First and Second Samuel* (Everyman's Bible Commentary) Chicago: Moody Press, 1982.

Mauchlin, John. *I and II Samuel*. Greenwood, S.C.: Attic Press, 1971.

McNeely, Richard. *First and Second Samuel*. Chicago: Moody Press, 1978.

Meyer, F. B. *Samuel the Prophet*. Chicago: Revell, n.d.

Winter, Willard. *Studies in Samuel*. Joplin, Mo.: College Press, 1967.

1 and 2 KINGS

Bright, John. *A History of Israel*. Philadelphia: Westminster Press, 1952.

Bronner, Leah. *The Stories of Elijah and Elisha*. Leiden: E. J. Brill, 1968.

*Ellul, Jacques. *The Politics of God and the Politics of Man*. Grand Rapids: Eerdmans, 1972.

Gordon, C. H. *Introduction to Old Testament Times*. Ventnor, N. J.: Ventnor, 1953.

Heaton, E. W. *The Hebrew Kingdoms*. London: Oxford University Press, 1968.

Meyer, F. B. *Elijah and the Secret of His Power*. Grand Rapids: Zondervan 1955.

Payne, J. Barton. *An Outline of Hebrew History*. Grand Rapids: Baker, 1954.

*Robinson, J. *The First Book of Kings* (Cambridge series) Cambridge: Cambridge Press, 1972.

*Thiele, E. R. *Chronology of the Hebrew Kings*. Grand Rapids: Baker, 1977.

*Whitcomb, J. C. *Solomon to the Exile: Kings and Chronicles*. Grand Rapids: Baker, 1971.

*Wood, Leon. *A Survey of Israel's History*. Grand Rapids: Zondervan, 1970.

1 and 2 CHRONICLES

Anderson, Hugh. *Historians of Israel*. New York: Abingdon Press, 1962.

Bennett, W. H. *The Books of Chronicles* (Expositor's Bible) New York: Hodder and Stoughton, n.d.

Ellison H. L. "*I and II Chronicles*" in The NBC. Grand Rapids: Eerdmans, 1953.

*Heading, John. *Understanding I and II Chronicles*. Kansas City: Walterick Press, 1980.

*Meyers, J. M. *I and II Chronicles* (Anchor Bible) 2 vols. Garden City: Doubleday, 1965, 1973.

*Murphy, J. G. *The Books of Chronicles*. Minneapolis: James and Klock, 1976.

EZRA and NEHEMIAH

Adeney, Walter F. *Ezra and Nehemiah*. Minneapolis: James and Klock, 1980.

*Barber, Cyril J. *Nehemiah and the Dynamics of Effective Leadership*. Neptune, N. J.: Loizeaux, 1976.

Fensham, F. C. *The Books of Ezra and Nehemiah* (NICOT) Grand Rapids: Eerdmans, 1982.
Kidner, F. Derek. *Ezra and Nehemiah* (Tyndale series) Madison, Wis.: InterVarsity Press, 1979.
*Laney, J. Carl. *Ezra–Nehemiah*. Chicago: Moody Press, 1982.
Meyers, J. M. *Ezra and Nehemiah* (Anchor Bible) Garden City, N. Y.: Doubleday, 1965.
Pfeiffer, Charles. *The Exile and Return*. Grand Rapids: Baker, 1962.
*Rawlinson, George. *Ezra and Nehemiah* (Men of the Bible series) New York: Anson and Randolph, 1980.
*Redpath, Alan. *Victorious Christian Service*. Westbook, N. J.: Revell, 1959.
*Swindoll, C. R. *Hand Me Another Brick*. Nashville: Nelson, 1978.

ESTHER

Armerding, Carl. *Esther: For Such a Time as This*. Chicago: Moody Press, 1955.
*Carson, Alex. *God's Providence Unfolded in Esther*. Evansville, Ind.: Sovereign Grace, 1960.
*McGee, J. Vernon. *Exposition in the Book of Esther*. Wheaton: Van Kampen Press, 1951.
Raleigh, Alex. *Book of Esther: Its Practical Lessons and Dramatic Scenes*. Minneapolis: Klock, 1980.
*Whitcomb, J. C. *Esther: The Triumph of God's Sovereignty*. Chicago: Moody Press, 1979.

*Though all entries are recommended, the asterisks identify those of first priority.

Introduction to the Poetic Books

To understand and appreciate the Poetic Books, it is essential to first recognize the basic characteristics, purposes, and distinctives of poetry itself Hebrew poetry, however, has a special distinction of its own which must be understood as well.

I Defining the Poetic Area

A. A poem is a literary composition, arranged in some form of verse, to express a thought with feeling and creative imagination.

B. Although many sections of the Bible contain bits of poetry (cf. the Prophets), the Hebrews especially recognized three great poetic books: Job, Psalms, and Proverbs.

C. In our English arrangement (taken from Jerome's Vulgate) the didactic books of Ecclesiastes and Song of Solomon are also included, making five books commonly called "The Poetic Books."

D. These five are further divided into two groups of books called "Wisdom" and "Hymnic" literature:
   Three Wisdom Books—Job, Proverbs, and Ecclesiastes.
   Two Hymnic Books—Psalms and Song of Solomon.

II   Distinctives of Poetry

A. *RHYME* (Rime)

Rhyme is the literary devise of *harmonizing sounds,* developing rhythm by the regular occurrence of similar sounds. Alliteration and various forms of consonance accomplish this, but the most prominent is the recurrence of terminal sounds.

B. *RHYTHM* (Metre)

Rhythm is the *regularity of movement* in literary composition, developed by the recurrence of beat, pause, or accent. This rhythm or metre is determined by the frequency of accents (the "foot" being a group of syllables with one accent), whether regular or irregular. Rhythm creates a mood or pattern that demands fulfillment or completed symmetry.

C. *FIGURATIVE EXPRESSION* (Imagery)

Figurative language is a third prominent characteristic of poetry. This is the device of *making analogies* or comparisons by thought pictures. In contrast to common prose, figures of speech make their point by challenging the mind to discover obvious relationships, thereby stirring the emotions and the will. Most prominent are the basic forms of *simile, metaphor, personification, apostrophe, hyperbole,* etc. Economy of language or "pointedness" is also a feature of poetry often used to eloquently emphasize a profound truth by combining exclamation and ellipsis.

III   Distinctives of Hebrew Poetry—"Parallelism"

A. *THE ESSENCE OF PARALLELISM*

Hebrew poetry emphasizes "thought rhythm" rather than "sound rhythm," or rhyme, the eastern mind being more concerned with thought content than mere literary mechanics. This feature is called "parallelism" by which the first line of a poem is paralleled or balanced in the second or succeeding lines by building on it in one of a variety of ways. This may be done in distichs (two-line verses), tristichs, tetrastichs, or even pentastichs. Longer verses simply combine one or several of the previous.

B. *THE ADVANTAGE OF HEBREW PARALLELISMS*

Besides challenging the reader to think relationally, this feature of Hebrew poetry has a special translation advantage. Its rhythmic effect and flow are not lost when translated into another language, as is often the case when translating mere mechanical features. To preserve the feature of rhyme in translation, for instance, a translator might have to compromise the exact thought to achieve the proper sound effect. The genius of parallelism is that it allows translation into other languages without altering the precise thought, since it is not restricted to an imposed sound pattern of syllables.

C. *TYPES OF HEBREW PARALLELISMS*

Many types of parallelism are used, the most prominent being "synonomous," "antithetic," and "synthetic" (as analyzed by Bishop R. Lowth in 1753).

1. *Synonomous.* The second line repeats or echoes the first in similar words.
   Psalm 19:1 "The heavens declare the glory of God;
   And the firmament shows His handiwork."

2. *Antithetic.* The second line expresses the opposite for contrast.
   Psalm 1:6 "For the LORD knows the way of the righteous,
   But the way of the ungodly shall perish."
   This is especially prominent in Proverbs 10–15.

3. *Synthetic.* The second line completes or amplifies the first.
   Psalm 19:7 "The law of the LORD *is* perfect, converting the soul.
   The testimony of the LORD *is* sure, making wise the simple."
   Three types of synthetic are: "completion" (Ps. 2:6); "comparison" (Ps. 118:9); and "reason" (Ps. 2:12).

4. *Several less prominent types should also be noted:*

   a. *Analytic.* The second line gives a consequence of the first.
      Psalm 23:1 "The LORD *is* my shepherd;
      I shall not want."

   b. *Climactic.* The second line repeats the first and brings it to a climax.
      Psalm 29:1 "Give unto the LORD, O you mighty ones,
      Give unto the LORD glory and strength."

   c. *Emblematic.* The second line illustrates the figure presented in the first.
      Psalm 103:11 "For as the heavens are high above the earth,
      So great is His mercy toward those who fear Him."

   d. *Chiastic.* The second repeats the first, but in reverse order. (Inverted)
      (Called "chiastic" from the Greek letter *chi*, forming an X.)
      Psalm 51:1: "Have mercy upon me, O God,
      According to Your lovingkindness;
      According to the multitude of Your tender mercies,
      Blot out my transgressions."

IV *Distinctive Classes of Hebrew Poetry* ("Creative Literature" of the Hebrews)

A. *POETIC DRAMA*—A series of acted scenes presented mainly in verse form.
The Book of Job—"No element of dramatic effect is wanting" (Richard Moulton, *The Literary Study of the Bible*).

B. *POETIC LYRICS*—Verse set to music for singing or chanting, mediating between the "description" of epic and the "presentation" of drama.
The Psalms—The Psalms include most types of lyric poetry: Odes, Songs, Elegies, Mediations, Monologues, Visions, and Rituals.

C. *POETIC DIDACTICS*—Poetic verse designed to instruct.
1. Practical Didactics—*The Book of Proverbs*
2. Philosophical Didactics—*The Book of Ecclesiastes*

D. *POETIC IDYLLS*—An arrangement of pastoral or rustic scenes in verse form.
The Song of Solomon

E. *POETIC ELEGY*—An arrangement of verse expressing sorrow or lamentation.
The Book of Lamentations

Introduction
to the Wisdom Books

The Book of Job introduces us to a different kind of literature. Job is not only the first Poetic Book but also the first of the "Wisdom Books." These books are more interpretive than historic in their emphases. Moving from Esther to Job is like moving from Acts to Romans in the New Testament. The "travelogue" of events has ended and we find ourselves in a classroom atmosphere, challenged to think as well as observe. Several clarifications concerning "Wisdom Literature" should be made to properly appreciate this "change of pace" in the biblical presentation.

I   The Background of Wisdom Literature

There appears to have been a prominent class or school of literary men in ancient Israel known as "wise men." Solomon, of course, was the most prominent, but was preceded and followed by many others. His father David referred to the wisdom of the ancients (1 Sam. 24:13), and the schools of Samuel no doubt studied these in conjunction with Torah. Other contemporary nations such as Egypt, Mesopotamia, Edom, and Phoenicia also had wise men who sought to produce guides to the "good life." Examples of

Socrates, Confucius, and Buddha might be cited also. The background of Hebrew wisdom was unique, however, in being based on "the fear of the LORD."

II The Character of Wisdom Literature

A. *PRACTICAL PURPOSE.* The concern of these wise men of Israel was not so much philosophical as practical wisdom. Metaphysics or the search for ultimate reality was not their problem; that was assumed as axiomatic in the Hebrew faith as revealed in Torah. Their concern was rather for ethics or the application of divine truth to human experience. They observed human character, conduct, and the consequences of actions, so as to establish refined principles for moral action. They were "buttonhole philosophers' with the man in the field or woman in the home, gathering wisdom tested by experience, ministering to individuals, and exerting influence where they might.

B. *DIVINE HUMANISM.* Old Testament Wisdom Literature has been called the "documents of Hebrew Humanism" (O. S. Rankin, *Israel's Wisdom Literature*). It is sharply contrasted, however, with classical humanism which conceives of man as the measure of all things. It is rather grounded in the belief that man is created by God in His image and likeness and that God's command, word, and will constitute the only true standard of truth and actions. It is concerned with the human personality, moral action, and social responsibility in the light of this theological foundation. Wisdom for them was "nothing less than God Himself in communication with spiritual creation" (A. Robert and A. Feuilet, *Introduction to the Old Testament*). Thus the wise men of Israel sought to apply divine principles for the common man, not only for his better enjoyment of life, but for his better perspective of life in terms of finalities.

C. *PHILOSOPHER'S OUTLOOK.* In contrast to the priest and prophet of Israel, the wise man had the outlook of a philosopher. His calling was not by inheritance or special appointment, but by a moral concern for behavioral response to truth. As the priest was concerned with ritual and the prophet with proclamation, the sage's forte was counsel. As the priest would say of sin, "It is defilement" and the prophet, "It is sin," the wise man would say, "It is folly." He saw God's commands as having a moral consequence which inevitably issues in happiness or sorrow.

III The Biblical Books of Wisdom Literature

A. *JOB: "Wisdom for Understanding the Trials of Life."*
The first wisdom book deals with one of the strangest enigmas of life: Why do the righteous suffer, or why doesn't righteous living always result in happiness

and inner peace? This irony of life is catastrophic to most moral systems and challenges the Bible believer to some of his most profound thinking concerning God and His ways with man. This book is a cosmic drama in which God sovereignly rules all spheres, and yet leads Job, a man of perfection and religious orthodoxy, through the crucible of suffering to a plane of higher knowledge and greater faith in God. On trial is a stalemated religious system with a distorted view of both God and man, that only reluctantly bows to the deeper truths of God's person. The book is a call for all those in distress to reach higher in their faith in God and to trust Him "even when the heavens are silent" and justice seems to go begging. True faith can serve God in cosmic ways which He is not able to reveal to us now.

B. *PROVERBS: "Wisdom for Growth and Discipline in Life."*
Proverbs is a classical collection of divinely selected sayings on the subject of building godly character. The purpose throughout is to contrast the two ways of life—wisdom and folly—showing the utter idiocy of following the easy road of living by the passions. It stresses the need to start early with God, to employ discipline for the higher and lasting values of life, and to recognize the power and potential one can acquire through strong character and spiritual living. The book is not a hodgepodge of unrelated proverbs. It is rather a carefully selected group that gives "wisdom" a grand introduction, elaborates on its benefits, and concludes with a classical portrait of one who has applied this wisdom—the virtuous and vivacious lady of charm in the last chapter.

C. *ECCLESIASTES: "Wisdom for Finding True Meaning in Life."*
Ecclesiastes is a unique book of wisdom on the need to enjoy life in light of God's sovereignty, not to succumb to the pessimism of life's seeming incongruities. Its underlying trust is not futility or pessimism, but joyful optimism. The purpose of the book is to show the futility of building a life philosophy without God, "under the sun." The author or compiler conducts a tour through the laboratory of life, examining various ways of pursuing satisfaction and meaning. Led by Solomon, the tour is authentic, for he was especially well-equipped with wisdom, riches, wives, passions, etc. to pursue the search with supreme vigor. His findings and conclusions are herein declared for all to profit who will learn from instruction rather than through the "fool's school of hard knocks." Life is to be enjoyed with sobriety, keeping in mind all the while, that final rendezvous of each person with his Creator.

The Book
of Job

Introduction

AUTHORSHIP

A. *THE TITLE*

Like Esther, Job is another book named after its hero rather than its author, though the man Job may have recorded much of the details. The etymology of the name Job (Heb. *'Iyyob*) is quite uncertain. The Hebrew could mean "to be at enmity," or the "object of enmity." The Arabic spelling (*'Awwabun*) suggests the meaning, "repent," "turn back," or "be restored." William F. Albright, *The Archaeology of Palestine* derives the meaning, "Where is Father" (*'aba*) from Egyptian Amarna Letters. Being a story related to north Arabia, it is most plausible to assume the Arabic meaning of "restoration" or "repent."

B. *THE AUTHOR*

1. The book is anonymous with few indications of who might have written it. Several names have been assigned as possible authors: Job, Elihu, Moses, Solomon, or Jeremiah.
2. The names of Moses and Solomon have had the most proponents. The Jewish Talmud ascribed it to Moses, assuming that he acquired the story while in Midian and edited or composed the book under divine inspiration. Solomon is also held as the author by the rabbis and others on the basis of the composition and wisdom content.
3. The patriarchal flavor and the absence of any mention of the Mosaic Law or the divine interventions of the exodus argues for one who lived in patriarchal times. Were Moses the author, the Arabic style and background could be accounted for by his having received the authentic story while in Midian for forty years and composed the book during Israel's great difficulties in the wilderness. A later revision of it could explain the more recent linguistics.

HISTORICAL SETTING

A. *DATE OF EVENTS RECORDED*—Patriarchal Period

1. Since the events of Job are sometimes questioned as to their historical base, the basic reasons for maintaining its historicity should be noted:
   a. Job is identified as a man living in Uz, not a fictional place (1:1).
   b. The Lord's word through Ezekiel 14:14-20 argues four times over for the historicity of Job and for the historicity of Noah and Daniel.
   c. James 5:10-11 appeals to the historicity of Job's suffering and endurance as he likewise appeals to the historicity of the prophets.

d. The heavenly scenes of the prologue and epilogue are obviously historical only by virtue of their being divinely revealed.

2. The patriarchal setting of the events (between Abraham and Moses) is quite generally conceded because of the following considerations:

a. The patriarchal pattern of life and religion in which Job acts as the father-priest in his house.

b. The great age of Job (perhaps double 140, 42:15) accords best with the earlier age of the patriarchs (Abraham was 175 at death).

c. Lack of reference to the Mosaic Law in the argument of righteousness or of the miracles of the exodus strongly argues for an earlier date.

d. The name Eliphaz the Temanite could refer to a near descendant of Teman, grandson of Esau, whose father also was named Eliphaz (Gen. 36:15).

B. *DATE OF COMPOSITION*

1. To appreciate the varied views on its date of composition, E. J. Young has given a brief survey of critical opinions held (*An Introduction to the Old Testament*, p. 340):

a. The age of Solomon—Keil, Delitzsch, Haevernick.

b. The eighth century (before Amos)—Hengstenberg.

c. The beginning of the seventh century—Ewald Riehm.

d. The first half of the seventh century—Staehelin, Pfeiffer.

e. The time of Jeremiah—Koenig, Gunkel, Pfeiffer.

f. The exile—Cheyne, Dillmann (1891).

g. The fifth century—Moor, Driver and Gray, Dhorme.

h. The fourth century—Eissfeldt, Volz.

i. The third century—Cornill (later held more indefinite date).

Young himself favored the Solomonic authorship and date.

2. On the basis of the arguments given for the authorship by either Moses or Solomon, and recognizing the possibility of a later linguistic revision, the best dating options would be the early fifteenth or middle tenth century B.C.

C. *THE GEOGRAPHICAL LOCATION*

The biblical references to Uz suggest a location just east of Edom (Gen. 10:23; 36:28; Jer. 25:20; and Lam. 4:21). Thus, the probable location of these events would be northwest Arabia in the desert highlands, perhaps 150 miles east of the Dead Sea (though tradition has generally placed them further north, somewhere east of Galilee).

D. *THE RELIGIOUS SETTING*

1. A father-priest religion. Job's offerings for his family suggest a time like that of Abraham when domestic religious rites were carried out apart from an organization of corporate religion. Job's piety is demonstrated in that he fulfilled this even in times of social pleasure. Before the advent of Mosaic Law personal piety was pursued, yet with joy and prosperity.

2. A legalistic theology. The three friends' legalistic view of sin and suffering was evidently the espoused orthodoxy of the time, held also by Job. God was con-

Outline of Job

THEME: God's Sovereign Use of Satan and Suffering to Mature His People.

ceived as a "cause and effect" deity who immediately rewarded or punished in a rather automatic, reflex manner. Having a wrong view of God gave them a wrong view of Job in his suffering, and fostered a wrong view of themselves. It also produced a wrong view of how God saves and matures individuals. They were strangers to God's way of extending mercy and grace to the undeserving. Therefore, they saw Job's refusal to bow to their mechanical solution to his suffering as sheer blasphemy. This debate and its outcome was a shattering blow to their mistaken orthodoxy, allowing for a reconstruction of their faith around a true conception of God.

THE PURPOSE OF THE BOOK OF JOB

A. The *central purpose* of this book is to show how God often uses adversity as well as prosperity to lead His people to maturity.

B. A *related purpose* was to show God's great sovereignty over Satan and how He can use the devil's worst attacks for His own purposes and His people's good.

C. *Another purpose* showed the dynamic of God's person as He deals with His people, not with mechanical, legalistic rules, but with infinite variety and love.

D. An *additional purpose* demonstrates to all the universe God's great ability to so reproduce His love in people that their every response is worship, even when they don't understand.

Unique Contributions of Job

1. *ITS RELATION TO THE BOOK OF ESTHER.* Several striking relations and contrasts may be noted between the last Historical book and the first Poetic book:
   a. Both books are dramas, Esther a narrative drama and Job a poetic drama:
      In Esther the hero goes "from rags to riches" to serve God and His people.
      In Job the hero goes "from riches to rags" to serve God and His people.
   b. Both books highlight the sovereignty of God in special ways:
      Esther highlights God's sovereign protection in times of distress.
      Job highlights God's sovereign purpose in times of distress.
   c. Both have underlying plots, God and Satan doing battle within the shadows:
      In Esther the battle is on the international or political scene.
      In Job the battle is in the interpersonal and religious scene.
   d. Both portray the devil's subtle ways of seeking to destroy God's people:
      In Esther God's people are preserved from the devil's disasters.
      In Job the man Job is preserved through the devil's disasters.
   e. Both describe cosmic defeats of Satan at the hands of God:

In Esther he is defeated trying to destroy God's chosen people.

In Job he is defeated trying to destroy Job's faith in God by showing he is basically selfish and not a true worshiper of God.

2. **ITS INTRODUCTORY CHARACTER.** The Book of Job is introductory in at least three ways:

    a. It is the first of three Wisdom Books (Job, Proverbs, and Ecclesiastes).

    b. It is the first of five Poetic Books (Job through Song of Solomon).

    c. It is the first of twenty-two Interpretive Books (Job through Malachi).

    The Book of Job is a classic in all three of these areas.

3. **THE GREATNESS OF GOD.** The Book of Job is filled with the greatness of God from the prologue through the epilogue. The following are several aspects of that greatness:

    a. The Greatness of God's Person (42:1-5). This greatness is seen not only in His sovereignty over all things but in the dynamism of His ways. Not a whimsical tyrant or mechanical deity, responding to mere outward conformity as the worldly wise might expect, He works with infinite variety with individuals to accomplish His purposes.

    b. The Greatness of His Power (1:6; 38:1ff.; 41:10-11). The power of His law commands the whole spiritual and physical world, and the power of His love is able to command the love and devotion of persons without mere material rewards.

    c. The Greatness of His Program (1:6-7; 19:26-27). His program is universe-wide and eternal, not a mere response to sudden problems. He directly commands all spiritual and physical intelligences, holding each to give an account at a coming day of reckoning.

    d. The Greatness of His Purposes (1:8-12; 2:3). His purpose for humans is not just to pamper them with an easy life here and now, but to perfect them for eternity. In the process He may even use Satan, thereby fulfilling another purpose of demonstrating to all spiritual intelligences the greatness of His wisdom and grace.

    e. The Greatness of His People (1:20-22; 13:15; 23:10). True children of God are those who love and serve Him by faith, not because of what He gives. As they recognize the greatness of His person, power, program and purposes, they are available to God for service, allowing Him to refine them through trial if need be, to come forth as "gold."

4. **WHY THE RIGHTEOUS SUFFER.** This early revelation from God supplies the answer to one of man's greatest problems, why God allows the righteous to suffer if He is both loving and sovereign. Various answers to this question are propounded throughout the book:

    a. Satan: Suffering is a tool with which he can force anyone to renounce God (1:11; 2:4-5).

    b. Three Friends: Suffering is always a punishment for sin (4:7-9; 8:3-6; 11:13-15).

    c. Elihu: Suffering is used by God to correct or discipline (33:13-17, 29).

    d. Job:

        1) At first—Suffering is for the wicked, not the righteous (6:24; 7:20).

        2) Later—Suffering is God's refining process to produce gold (23:10).

    e. The Lord:

        1) Suffering is a privilege God gives His people to help Him fulfill some great purpose, such as refuting the devil (1:8, 12).

        2) Suffering is a call to trust when we do not understand, because to know the purpose might destroy the effect (13:15).

        3) Suffering may be God's tool to bring one to the end of himself and his protective defenses so that God may become his defender (42:3-7).

5. *THE RARE SCENE OF GOD'S THRONE* (1–2). As the last book of the Bible emphasizes God's throne in times of trial (Rev. 4–5; 21), so this earliest book (possibly before Genesis) pulls back the heavenly curtain for a brief view of God's throne room (cf. 1 Kin. 22:19-23; 2 Chr. 18:18-22). His complete sovereignty and great concern for the plight and affairs of men is stressed on each of these rare occasions.

6. *MAN'S GREAT ADVERSARY THE DEVIL INTRODUCED* (1:6). Assuming the Book of Job to be the most ancient Bible book, it is significant that its first chapter introduces man's great adversary, the devil. He is described here in simple, unmistakable terms, not as an evil force, but as a real person challenging God, having immense power over nature and harboring great enmity toward those that serve God. His enmity toward them, however, is always under the close scrutiny of God and restricted only to fulfilling God's purpose. Of this believers are not to be ignorant (2 Cor. 2:11).

7. *THE COLLAPSE OF "DEAD ORTHODOXY"* (42:5-6). The three friends' basic error was assuming they were righteous because rich, and holy because healthy. That was probably Job's previous position also, as the current orthodoxy of the day, but his suffering shattered that view. He found his "fat-cat" theology comfortable until he became a castaway; then he saw his own hypocrisy in his three friends. Recalling the prosperity of the wicked, he began to discern that health or wealth in this life do not indicate one's standing with God. The book shows how that whole system of "dead orthodoxy" came crashing down as that meritorious principle was shattered by Job's experience. True religion is described as trusting God regardless of rewards in this life, with a view to the final day of resurrection and reckoning (19:25).

8. *CHRISTOLOGY IN JOB* (16:19; 19:25). In his despair Job longed for a mediator to plead his cause before God and men (9:32-33). As he expressed his bafflement in the following exchange with the three friends, Job also expressed several "reaches of faith" to God. In 16:19, he declared he had an "Advocate" on high, and in 19:25, a living "Redeemer," who would finally bring him vindication before God. Not yet aware of the Redeemer God would send, he groped after Him and by faith laid hold on Him.

The suffering of Job in a sense also portrays the sufferings of Christ who was declared perfect by the Father, fiercely attacked by Satan, wrongly accused by His people, and came to experience the lot of a castaway. He became a castaway that He might reach castaways and bring mediation and redemption for His people (Phil. 2).

The Book of Psalms

Introduction

AUTHORSHIP

One of the great distinctions of this book is its character as a hymnbook, for which it served Israel and the church almost exclusively until recent centuries. As such it has been one of the greatest sources of inspiration for prayer and praise to God. The Psalms have been placed at the heart of the Bible, Psalm 117 being the central chapter, and Psalm 118:8 being the central verse of the Bible: "*It is* better to trust in the LORD Than to put confidence in man." This attitude especially reflects the character of David after whom the book has been traditionally called, "The Psalms of David."

A. *THE TITLES*

    1. Book Title. The Hebrews called it "The Book of Praises" (*Sefer Tehillim*) or simply "Praises," designating its main purpose, to praise the Lord. The Greek translators named it "Psalms" (*Psalmoi*) which translates the Hebrew title (*Mizmor*) affixed to fifty-seven Psalms, meaning songs sung to the accompaniment of stringed instruments. The New Testament also used this title in Luke 20:42 and Acts 1:20. From this came the title, "Psaltery."

    2. Chapter Titles. A unique feature of the Psalms is that many have individual titles prefixed to them (134 in Hebrew text; 148 in Greek, counting "Alleluiah" as a title for several). Though these titles are not part of the original text (Hebrew Bibles accept them as verse 1 in each chapter), they do date to antiquity, antedating the Septuagint version (second century B.C.)

Seven such titles are used, mainly to suggest how they were used.

       a. Mizmor   (57 times)   — A song with stringed accompaniment.
       b. Shir   (30)   — Any song of sacred or secular nature.
       c. Maschil   (13)   — A meditative or didactic poem.
       d. Mikhtam   (6)   — Uncertain meaning, perhaps "atoning."
       e. Tephillah   (5)   — A prayer.
       f. Tehillah   (1, Ps. 145) — A song of praise. From this came the Hebrew title of the whole book.

g. Shiggayon (1, Ps. 7) — Uncertain, perhaps a penitential psalm.

3. Other Functions of Inscription Titles. To appreciate the prefixed inscriptions, it is helpful to note their fivefold functions:

The Five Books of Psalms Distinguished

	BOOK 1 1–41	BOOK 2 42–72	BOOK 3 73–89	BOOK 4 90–106	BOOK 5 107–150
AUTHORSHIP	David = 37(+ 3)* Anonymous = 44	David = 18 Korah = 7 Asaph = 1 Solomon = 1 Anonymous = 4	David = 1 Korah = 3 Asaph = 11 Heman = 1 Ethan = 1	David = 2 (+ 1)* Moses = 1(+ 1)** Anonymous = 14	David = 15 Solomon = 1 Anonymous = 28
TOTAL	= 41	= 31	= 17	= 17	= 44
PENTATEUCH RELATION BOOK	Genesis	Exodus	Leviticus	Numbers	Deuteronomy
THEME	The righteous man and his ways	Israel's ruin and redemption	Israel's sanctuary and assembly	Israel's relapse and recovery	God's Word and universal praise
BOOK INTRODUCTION	Psalm 1 The righteous man	Psalm 42:5 In despair, hope in God	Psalm 73:17 The sanctuary of God	Psalm 90:7 Consumed by Your anger	Psalm 107:2 Let the redeemed say so
CONCLUDING DOXOLOGY	Psalm 41:13 "Amen and Amen"	Psalm 72:19 "Amen and Amen"	Psalm 89:52 "Amen and Amen"	Psalm 106:48 "Amen! Praise the LORD!"	Psalm 150:6 "Praise the LORD. Praise the LORD!"
TYPICAL CHAPTER	Psalm 8 Man made to rule	Psalm 68 The Lord among them at Sinai	Psalm 84 Long for the sanctuary	Psalm 90 Teach us to number our days	Psalm 119 I shall not forget Your word
NAMES OF GOD LORD (Yah or YHWH)	273	29	43	111	262
Lord (Adonai)	14	18	15	3	11
GOD (El or Elohim)	67	216	82	27	40

*Psalms 2 and 95 are identified as Davidic in Acts 4:25 and Hebrews 4:7, and Psalms 10 and 33 are continuations of 9 and 32 respectively (9 and 10 by acrostic, 32 and 33 by content).

**Psalm 91 is often attributed to Moses as well as 90 because of its many associations.

a. Titles describing the character of the Psalm (as noted above).
b. Titles giving musical instruction, e.g., "To the Chief Musician." (4)
c. Titles indicating liturgical use, e.g., "Song for the Sabbath." (92)
d. Titles relating authorship (all but 50).
e. Titles describing its original setting (only 14, all related to David—3, 7, 18, 30, 34, 51, 52, 54, 56, 57, 59, 60, 63, and 143).

B. *THE AUTHORS*

1. The whole collection of Psalms has been called "The Psalms of David," inasmuch as his name is prefixed to nearly half and he no doubt inspired many others. As the books of Samuel record David's history, the Psalms reveal his heart and theology. His immense personality uniquely prepared him for the writing of these Psalms in several ways:
   a. He was a man with a big heart, a keen mind, a dedicated and disciplined life, sensitive throbbing emotions, a strong will, and a vital relationship with God (2 Sam. 23:1).
   b. He had wide experience as a shepherd, musician, poet, warrior, fugitive, lover, theologian, and statesman in many vicissitudes of life.

2. Twelve authors have been identified by the title inscriptions and by the Septuagint translators (100 by inscriptions):
   a. Moses   (1) — Psalm 90.
   b. David   (73) — 3–9; 11–32; 34–41; 51–65; 68–70; 86; 101; 103; 108–110; 122; 124; 131; 133; 138–145.
                   (2) — 2, (identified by Acts 4:25); Psalm 95 (by Heb. 4:7).
   c. Solomon   (2) — 72; 127.
   d. Asaph   (12) — 50; 73–83.
   e. Korah sons (10) — 42; 44–45; 47–49; 84–85; 87–88.
   f. Heman   (1) — 88 (Also a son of Korah).
   g. Ethan   (1) — 89.

   By Septuagint translators' identifications (19):
   h. Hezekiah (15) — 120–134 (cf. Isa. 38:20).
   i. Jeremiah (1) — 137.
   j. Haggai   (1) — 146.
   k. Zachariah (1) — 147.
   l. Ezra   (1) — 119.
   The rest are called "orphaned Psalms," unidentified (though the New Testament identification of ninety-five as Davidic could include the group, 95–100).

3. Ezra has been recognized traditionally as the compiler of the Psalms in their present arrangement, though David, Solomon, the Men of Hezekiah (Isaiah and Micah), and Jeremiah may have been compilers in their times.

HISTORICAL SETTING

A. *DATES OF WRITING THE PSALMS*

    1. Assuming Moses was the earliest writer of Psalms (c. 1430) and Ezra was the latest (c. 430), the time span of the Psalms covered c. 1000 years. During the past century, critical scholars assigned Maccabean dates to some of the Psalms, but have generally abandoned those late dates in favor of a pre-Hellenistic dating (Encyclopedia Judaica, p. 1312).

    2. The designated authors suggest several periods of concentration in which Psalms were written, the time of David (1020–970), Solomon (970–931), the sons of

---

Classification of Psalms

The study of Psalms has recently shifted from the almost impossible search for the original time and setting of each psalm to classifying them by their use in public worship and private devotions, as noted in the forms of their contents. The following is a fivefold arrangement modified and adapted from Leopold Sabourin, *The Psalms: Their Origin and Meaning,* p. 124:

I HYMNS OF PRAISE. (31 Psalms)
    1. *Hymns Proper:* 8, 19, 29, 33, 100, 103-104, 111, 113-114, 117, 135, 136, 145-150.
        Contains responsories, "Amen," "Hallelujah," etc.
    2. *Psalms of the Lord's Enthronement or Kingship:* 47, 93, 96-99.
    3. *Songs of Zion:* 46, 48, 76, 84, 122, 132, (extolling Zion or Jerusalem).
    Characteristic Elements:
        a. Introduction, or Call to Worship, e.g., "Praise the LORD."
        b. Body of hymn describing God's acts or attributes.
        c. Conclusion, calling for renewed praise or obedience.

II INDIVIDUAL LAMENTS, EXPRESSIONS OF CONFIDENCE IN GOD, OR THANKSGIVING. (58)
    1. *Individual Laments:* 5-7, 13, 17, 22, 25-26, 28, 31, 35-36, 38-39, 42-43, 51, 54-57, 59, 61, 63-64, 69-71, 86, 88, 120, 130, 140-143.
    2. *Individual Confidences Expressed:* 3-4, 11, 16, 23, 27, 62, 121, 131.
    3. *Individual Thanksgiving:* 9-10, 30, 32, 34, 40-41, 92, 107, 116, 138.
    Characteristic Elements of Laments:
        a. Address to God and cry for help.
        b. Complaint often expressed in figures.
        c. Confession of trust.
        d. Petition for the Lord's help.
        e. Appeal to God's special care or covenant promise.
        f. Vow of praise and thanksgiving.
        g. Confidence of God's answer.

Asaph and of Korah may be anytime before the exile, and the time of the "Men of Hezekiah," about 700 B.C.

B. *THE RELIGIOUS SETTING*

1. Religion is, of course, the native soil of the Psalms. Leland Ryken has noted that "virtually every poem in the Psalter contributes in some way to the overall plot conflict between good and evil" (*The Literature of the Bible,* p. 125). In the world of the Psalms, there are two categories of people, the good and evil, the godly and ungodly. The psalmist is often in the midst of the battle, aligning himself with the cause of God and giving praise for His intervention which has already occurred in history or is about to occur prophetically.

2. The title inscriptions show that many of the Psalms were used by the congregation for liturgical purposes. Leopold Sabourin shows that they often accompanied sacrificial worship (*The Psalms: Their Origin and Meaning,* p. 18). It is also evident that the Hezekiah group (120–134) were used by the pilgrims as they ascended to Jerusalem for the feasts, and the Hallel group were sung at the Passover celebration, as noted in Matthew 26:30, and at Pentecost and Tabernacles.

C. *THE NATIONAL SETTING*

1. In Israel religion and politics or military operations were largely of the same cloth. Thus in the Psalms the military battles of Israel are seen as religious crusades

III COMMUNITY LAMENTS, CONFIDENCES, OR THANKSGIVING. (27)
1. *Community Laments:* 12, 44, 58, 60, 74, 77, 79-80, 82-83, 85, 90, 94, 106, 108, 123, 126, 137.
2. *Community Confidence Expressed:* 115, 125, 129.
3. *Community Thanksgiving:* 65-68, 118, 124.
Characteristic elements or form similar to the individual groupings.

IV ROYAL PSALMS (Of Israel's Temporal King, looking to the Eternal King) (11)
1. *Royal Marriage:* 45.
2. *Coronations:* 2, 72, 101, 110.
3. *Battle Songs* of prayer or praise: 18, 20-21, 89, 144.
Presented in various forms.

V. INSTRUCTION OR DIDACTIC PSALMS. (23)
1. *Wisdom Psalms:* 1, 37, 49, 73, 91, 112, 119, 127-128, 133, 139.
2. *Historical Psalms:* 78, 105.
3. *Prophetic Exhortation:* 14, 50, 52-53, 75, 81, 95.
4. *Liturgies:* 15, 24, 134.
Characteristic elements of teaching such as proverbs, exhortations, historical reflections, contrasts of the righteous and the wicked, and reminders of the "blessed."

Outline and Descriptive Titles of Psalms

THEME: Expressions of Prayer and Praise to God in all the Range of Human Experience.

DESCRIPTIVE TITLE	UNIQUE FEATURE OR USE
BOOK 1	
1. Psalm of the Two Ways of Life.	Begins with beatitude on godly living.
2. God's Anointed Son to Reign, After Rejected.	*Introduces Messiah's* coming as God's Son.
3. David's Refuge from His Many Adversaries.	A morning prayer.
4. Retiring at Night with Peace and Confidence.	An evening hymn.
5. Walking Courageously Among the Wicked.	
6. Despondency Overwhelmed by Godly Trust.	
7. The Reaction of the Godly to Slander.	
8. Man's Dignity as God's Viceroy on Earth.	*Messiah* to rule as Son of Man (Heb. 2:6ff.).
9. God's Sovereign Judgment on the Wicked.	Psalms 9–10 form one alphabetic acrostic.
10. The Depraved Haughtiness of the Wicked.	
11. God's Inevitable Judgment on the Wicked.	
12. The Condemnation of Proud Lips.	
13. The Need of Patient Trust When God Delays.	
14. The Tragic End of the Atheistic Fool.	Almost identical to Psalm 53.
15. The Grand Character of Zion's Citizens.	
16. The Delights of Living in God's Presence.	*Messiah's* resurrection foretold (Acts 2:27; 13:35).
17. Our Protection as the "Apple" of God's Eye.	
18. The Lord as our Rock, Fortress, and Deliverer.	Almost identical to 2 Samuel 22.
19. God's Natural and Special Revelation to Men.	The supremacy of the "Law of the LORD."
20. The Righteous Recourse in Times of Trouble.	
21. The Majesty of Kings Who Trust in God.	
22. David's Prophetic Psalm of the Cross.	*Messianic:* Christ on the cross.
23. The Grand Shepherd Psalm of David.	*Messianic:* Christ as the Good Shepherd.
24. The Lord to Enter Zion as King of Glory.	*Messianic:* His coming as King of Glory.
25. Divine Instruction for Times of Trouble.	An irregular acrostic psalm.
26. The Prayer of the Upright Avails Much.	
27. The Strength of the Upright Waiting on God.	
28. David's Thanksgiving for Answered Prayer.	
29. The Majestic Power of the Lord's Voice.	
30. Extolling the Lord for His Healing.	
31. Trusting the Lord in Deepest Despair.	Called the Martyr's Psalm (31:5).
32. The Joy of Forgiveness After Confession.	David's joy of restoration, after Psalm 51.
33. A Song of Praise to God as Creator.	
34. The Nearness of the Lord to the Penitent.	*Messianic:* No bones broken (34:20).
35. A Plea for Divine Help Against Enemies.	
36. The Goodness of God and Wickedness of Men.	
37. Delight Yourself in the Lord, Not People.	
38. Trusting God When Condemned by Friends.	
39. The Comfort of Hope in Times of Chastening.	
40. The Delights of Doing God's Will.	*Messianic:* Christ's obedience to Father.
41. The Lord's Grace to Those Who Help the Poor.	*Messianic:* The betrayal (41:10).

for God. The enemy is viewed as irretrievably evil and imprecations are made for his destruction as one who fights against God. The Psalms depict a strong nationalistic loyalty as tantamount to godliness, and find it so as they cast themselves on the Lord for victory.

2. This national and military backdrop is seen in a large proportion of the Psalms and is noted in most of the fourteen Psalms ascribed to David that give additional details of its writing. In Psalm 3, for instance, he is being chased by Absalom, in 18, he has just escaped from Saul, in 34, he has made an escape from the Philistines, and in 54 he is hiding from Saul.

The point is that the psalmists wrote of their distresses, victories, and praises as they encountered the many difficulties of everyday life. The intensity of their secular problems drove them to God and taught them to sing praise in victory.

DESCRIPTIVE TITLE	UNIQUE FEATURE OR USE
BOOK 2	
42. Thirsting for God When Far from Home.	Chapters 42 and 43 are related by common refrain,
43. Hoping in God, Continued, Far from Home.	"Hope in God."
44. The Mystery of God's Extended Chastening.	
45. A Song of the Divine King's Marital Love.	*Messianic:* Royal Wedding of the Lord as God, King, and Divine Lover.
46. The Believer's Mighty Fortress in Trouble.	
47. Celebrate God as the King of the Earth.	
48. The Majesty of Zion, City of Our God.	
49. The Folly of Trusting in Riches.	
50. God's Silence to be Broken in Judgment.	
51. David's Psalm of Confession and Restoration.	David's penitential prayer (cf. 32).
52. The Treachery of a Deceitful Tongue.	
53. The Inevitable Depravity of the Atheist.	Nearly identical to Psalm 14.
54. The Power of God's Name to Defend Us.	
55. Our Refuge in God in Times of Betrayal.	
56. David's Prayer as a Wanderer in Exile.	
57. David's Refuge in the Shadow of God's Wings.	
58. Unrighteous Human Judges to be Judged by God.	
59. The Tranquility of God's Strength in Trials.	
60. God's Restoring Grace for the Broken.	
61. "Lead me to the rock that is higher than I."	
62. Waiting and Trusting in God Alone.	
63. Finding Continual Satisfaction in God.	
64. The Wisdom of Leaving Vengeance with God.	
65. The Abundant Satisfaction of God's People.	
66. A Song of Praise for God's Mighty Works.	
67. All Nations Called to Sing and Praise The Lord.	
68. The Processional Hymn of God, Mighty Conqueror.	*Messianic:* Christ's ascension.
69. God's Delight in Thanksgiving for Reproach.	*Messianic:* Christ's zeal, reproach.
70. David's Cry for Quick Deliverance.	
71. David's Prayer for God's Grace in Old Age.	
72. Solomon's Prayer for Wisdom to Judge Rightly.	*Messianic:* Solomon's reign typifies the more glorious reign of Christ.

THE LITERARY FEATURES OF THE PSALMS

A. LYRICS

The Psalms are not just poems, but lyric poems. A lyric poem may be defined as "a short poem, originally meant to be sung, expressing the thoughts and especially the feelings of a single speaker" (Leland Ryken, *The Literature of the Bible,* p. 123). Lyric poetry has four notable characteristics:

1. Lyric poetry is musical, originally meant to be sung with stringed instrument accompaniment. For this reason it has versification in some kind of a pattern of "stress accents" (though it does not employ rhyme, and genuine metre is great-

DESCRIPTIVE TITLE	UNIQUE FEATURE OR USE
BOOK 3	
73. The Folly of Envying the Wicked.	
74. The Mystery of God's Inaction to Restore.	
75. God Identified as the Ultimate Judge.	
76. The Majestic Power of Israel's God.	
77. Recalling God's Mighty Acts in Dark Days.	
78. The Marvel of God's Grace and Israel's Rebellion.	*Messianic:* Christ's use of parables.
79. Asaph's Prayer for Jerusalem's Restoration.	
80. Israel's Shepherd Besought for Restoration.	Israel, the vine of God's planting.
81. The Lord's Great Longing to Bless Israel.	
82. God's Stern Judgment on Unjust Judges.	
83. A Prayer for God's Vengeance on Oppressors.	
84. The Great Delights of Dwelling in God's House.	The great sanctuary psalm.
85. Israel's Plea for Complete Revival from God.	
86. The Goodness of God to the Poor and Needy.	
87. The Glories of Zion, City of God.	
88. A Psalm of Continued Unanswered Prayer.	
89. God's Faithfulness to Fulfill His Covenant.	The Davidic Covenant confirmed.
BOOK 4	
90. Moses' Prayer for God's Renewed Favor to Israel.	Most ancient psalm—by Moses.
91. The Peace and Protection of Dwelling in God.	Chapters 90–91 relate to Deuteronomy 33:27.
92. The Great Value of Giving Thanks to the Lord.	Called the "Sabbath Day Psalm."
93. The Majesty of the Lord's Eternal Throne.	
94. The Certainty of God's Coming Vengeance.	
95. A Call for Thanksgiving, Worship, and Obedience.	David's invitation to sing, 95–100.
96. Singing the Lord's Praise in View of His Coming.	
97. The Great Majesty of the Reigning Lord.	
98. The Victorious Lord Brings Salvation and Judgment.	
99. A Call to Worship the Lord for His Holiness.	
100. "Enter into His gates with thanksgiving."	The classic psalm of thanksgiving.
101. David's Commitment to Righteous Ruling.	
102. Clinging to God's Eternal Care When Overwhelmed.	
103. David Summons the Universe to Bless the Lord.	Chapters 103–104 begin and end, "Bless the Lord."
104. The Lord's Splendor And Majesty as Creator.	
105. The Lord's Covenant Mercies to Seed of Abraham.	Chapters 105–106 both treat Israel's history:
106. Israel's Rebellion and God's Covenant Mercies.	105– God's Grace; 106– Israel's Disgrace.

DESCRIPTIVE TITLE	UNIQUE FEATURE OR USE
BOOK 5	
107. A Call to Thank God for His Many Deliverances.	Introduces Book 5 as a book of thanks.
108. A Psalm of David for Military Victory.	Chapter 108 repeats 57:7-11 and 60:5-12.
109. The Lord's Certain Judgment on Evil Accusers.	Called the "Iscariot" psalm (109:8).
110. The Lord to Rule in Zion as Priest-King.	*Messianic:* Also most quoted in New Testament.
111. Hallelujah for the Lord's Wonderful Works.	Chapters 111–112 both have acrostic structures,
112. Hallelujah for the Benefits of Fearing God.	each with 10 verses and 22 lines.
113. God's Unique Delight in Elevating the Poor.	First of "Hallel" Psalms (113–118).
114. The Drama of Nature's Part in the Exodus.	"Exquisite Psalm" of Israel's history.
115. The Impotence of Idols and Omnipotence of God.	Chapters 115–118 were second part of Hallel, sung
116. The Lord's Great Power to Rescue from Death.	at Passover after meal (Matt. 26:30).
117. All Nations Summoned to Praise God's Grace and Truth.	Shortest Psalm and middle chapter of Bible.
118. Israel Called to Give Thanks for God's Grace.	*Messianic:* "Rejected stone" Headstone.
119. The Majestic Psalm in Praise of God's Word.	A perfect alphabet acrostic on the Word.
120. The Warring Character of Slanderers.	First of Pilgrim (ascents) Psalms, 120–134,
121. The Lord as the Traveler's "Guardian Angel."	unnamed ones perhaps by Hezekiah.
122. David's Prayer for the Peace of Jerusalem.	
123. A Psalm of Patient Trusting in Adversity.	
124. David's Thanks for a Great Deliverance by God.	
125. The Lord's Strong Protection of the Upright.	
126. The Joyful Harvest of Those Who "sow in tears."	
127. The Futility of Building a House Without God.	The central Pilgrim psalm by Solomon.
128. The Sure Blessings on a Home That Fears God.	Note the domestic relations of 127–128.
129. The Inevitable Defeat of Israel's Enemies.	
130. The Lord's Forgiving Love, Israel's Only Hope.	Note Hezekiah's final psalm (Is. 38:20).
131. The Quiet Tranquility of Trusting the Lord.	
132. David's Concern for God's House and Vice Versa.	
133. The Eternal Rewards of Harmony in the Home.	
134. The Lord's Added Blessing for Evening Worshipers.	
135. Praising the Lord as the Only Living God.	A mosaic of 113:1; 136:17ff.; 115:4ff.
136. Israel's National Anthem: the Lord's Enduring Mercy.	Called by Jews "The Great Hallel."
137. Israel's Intense Love for Zion While in Exile.	A unique psalm of the exile.
138. David Praises the Faithfulness of God's Word.	The first of last Davidic group, 138–145.
139. The Limitless Reach of God's Searching Power.	Unequaled in its profound theology of God's omnipresence and omniscience.
140. David's Prayer for the Overthrow of the Wicked.	
141. David's Prayer for Guarded Lips and Guided Ways.	
142. David's Prayer as a Forgotten Prisoner.	
143. David Pleads for Deliverance as God's Servant.	
144. "Happy *are* the people whose God *is* the LORD."	
145. David's Final Praise of the Greatness of God.	David's final psalm. Called "Praise."
146. Praise the Lord for His Help to the Helpless.	First of final "Hallelujah" group, 146–150. Called
147. Praise the Lord for His Care of All the Earth.	"Te Deum Laudamas." Note absence of fear,
148. The Psalmist Commands Praise from all Creation.	distress, and laments and stress on joy, peace,
149. Praise the Lord with Joyful Song, Judgment Sword.	etc.
150. The Grand Finale and Prophecy of Universal Praise.	Final psalm summarizes theology of praise: Who? Where? Why? How? and by whom? is praise to be given?

ly doubted in any regular sequence—La Sor, Hubbard, and Bush, *Old Testament Survey,* p. 312ff.).

2. It is subjective or personal, expressing the speaker's own feelings. As the prophet utters the word of God to man, the psalmist expresses the thoughts and feelings of man to God. Though he may use the plural ''we,'' he expresses his own personal feelings as representative of all.

3. It emphasizes emotions as one of its chief identifying traits. To portray intense emotions, it uses such figures as hyperbole and other emotive words and expressions. Its primary purpose is not to describe history or even doctrine (though it certainly does involve these), but to give expression to the emotional side of religion. The Psalms were written to emote.

4. The lyric is also brief. Since emotions cannot be prolonged at great intensity, the Psalms must of necessity be brief. The emotions expressed are sustained just long enough to climax and round out the unifying theme. Psalm 119, of course, is of great length, but makes its total emphasis by completing its cycle throughout the entire Hebrew alphabet.

B. *PARALLELISMS*

Parallelism is the basic poetic technique of Hebrew poetry, which must be recognized if the Psalms are to be properly understood. To interpret poetry as prose and fail to give proper recognition to this Hebrew technique of parallelism tends to either distort the parallels or make them look ridiculous. The various types of parallelism have been noted in the Introduction to the Poetic Books.

C. *IMAGERY OR FIGURES*

As prose makes its point by literal descriptions, poetry uses figurative representations. Most Psalms employ such figures in which two levels of meaning or spheres of life are related. Psalm 1, for instance, portrays the delights of godly living by a single image of a tree planted by a stream of water. The psalmist laminates two or more levels of meaning to vividly portray the truths being declared. The purpose is not entertainment, but emphasis. In Psalm 23, the shepherd and his sheep are described to stress the relationship of believers to the Lord. The commonly known figure helps to teach the unknown. These figures help to instruct and persuade, but their basic appeal is to the instinct for analogy and emotions, impressing the truths to be perceived through different levels of experience. The following are the more prominent figures in Psalms:

1. *Simile* is a figure that makes a comparison by resemblance in one or more points. It is a formal comparison, using the word ''like'' or ''as.''
   Psalm 1:3 ''He shall be like a tree. . . .''

2. *Metaphor* makes its comparison by representation, declaring one thing to be another (not using the formal, ''like,'' ''as,'' etc.).
   Psalm 23:1 ''The LORD *is* my shepherd.''

3. *Allegory* is the figure of extended metaphors around a central theme.

Psalm 80:8ff. Israel is here described in many ways as a "vine out of Egypt."

4. *Metonymy* is a figure that puts one word for another because the two are related in some way.

Psalm 73:9 "Their tongue (words) walks through the earth."

5. *Synecdoche* is a figure in which the whole is put for a part, or vice versa.

Psalm 52:4 "You love all devouring words, *You* deceitful tongue" (the tongue standing for the person).

6. *Hyperbole* is an exaggeration used for emphasis.

Psalm 6:6 "All night I make my bed swim."

7. *Personification* speaks of inanimate objects or abstract ideas as having the attributes of a living being.

Psalm 35:10 "All my bones shall say, 'LORD, who *is* like You.' "

8. *Apostrophe* (similar to personification) addresses absent persons or lifeless objects as though they were living and present.

Psalms 114:5–7 "What ails you, O sea, that you fled?...."

9. *Anthropomorphism* is a figure that speaks of God as having a human body.

Psalm 10:12 "Arise, O LORD! O God, lift up Your hand!"

10. *Anthropopathism* speaks of God as having human passions and feelings.

Psalm 6:1 "O LORD, do not rebuke me in Your anger, Nor chasten me in Your hot displeasure."

D. *ALPHABETIC ACROSTICS*

Nine psalms are called "alphabetic psalms," exhibiting an alphabetic order in the opening letter of their succeeding lines, verses, or stanzas. The evident purpose of this literary device was to aid the memory for learning or reciting, and perhaps to call attention to the order and beauty of the passage. This device is used in various arrangements in 9, 10, 25, 34, 37, 111, 112, 119, and 145.

1. Psalms 25 and 34 are the only ones building the acrostic on 22 letters.
2. Psalms 9 and 10 are joined by an irregular acrostic that runs through both Psalms.
3. Psalms 111 and 112 each have 10 verses with 22 lines on which each builds.
4. Psalm 145 has 21 verses, leaving out the nun (between vv. 13 and 14).
5. Psalm 119 is the most elaborate having 22 stanzas of 8 verses each, all 8 verses of each stanza beginning with the same letter of the alphabet. This structural orderliness stresses its theme, which is the Law of God.

E. *"SELAH" AND "HALLELUJAH"*

1. "Selah." This much debated word is used seventy-one times in the Psalms and three times in Habakkuk 3. It occurs seventeen times in Book 1, thirty in Book 2, twenty in Book 3, and four times in Book 5. It is not used in Book 4 (90–106). It is found at the end of a verse in all cases except four, but J. W. Thirtle sees it as giving notice of the beginning of a new section or stanza of a hymn. Its meaning is not certain. It may derive from "salah," to pause, or "salal," to lift up, or possibly both. Delitzsch saw it as "an interlude played by stringed

instruments''; Aquila understood it as meaning ''always, forever''; Jerome classed it with ''amen'' or ''peace'' (Shalom). Its first occurrence is in Psalm 3, the first psalm ascribed to David, being used there three times. The general view is that it calls for a pause or interlude of some kind, either for the musical instruments or for those reciting to solemnly reflect.

2. ''Hallelujah.'' This term is not found in most versions of the Old Testament. In Revelation 19:1-6 it appears as Alleluia! It is a compound of two words, ''hallel'' and ''Yah'' (the shortened form of Yahweh), meaning ''praise the LORD'' (imperative). As ''praise the LORD,'' it occurs thirty-five times in the Psalms. Three groups of psalms are known as ''Hallel'' or ''Hallelujah'' Psalms:

   a. Psalms 111–113 in which each psalm begins, ''Praise the LORD.''
   b. Psalms 115–117 in which each concludes with ''Praise the LORD'' (plus an extra ''Praise the LORD'' at the beginning of the last one).
   c. Psalms 146–150 in which each begins and ends with ''Praise the LORD.''
   d. Psalms 105–106 also begin and end with ''Praise the LORD'' if the last line of 104 is made the first of 105 (as it apparently should be).

   This phrase is never found in the psalms of David or his singers. Ginsburg saw it as a liturgical phrase for antiphonal use in response to which the congregation repeated the first verse after each consecutive verse repeated by the leader. It called for united worship and praise of the Lord, which is the way it is also used in Revelation 19, the only usages in the New Testament.

THE PURPOSE OF THE PSALMS

A. They were written by the psalmists as their heartfelt responses to God as they experienced the innumerable joys, sorrows, and trials of life.

B. They also provide vehicles of expression for God's people through the whole range of human experience to enable them likewise to clothe their feelings and desires to God in meaningful and vivid terms.

C. They served to voice the yearnings of Israel for the coming of Messiah, expressing by divine inspiration many prophetic details of His first and second comings.

D. The Psalms served as Israel's songbook for many of their rituals and functions such as the religious festivals, temple worship, and local and national gatherings.

Unique Contributions of the Psalms

---

1. *THEIR MINISTRY TO THE HEART.* The language of the Psalms is more the language of the heart than that of the head. Rather than full statements of history or propositional theology, the Psalms often present a tapestry of thoughts on a subject that may include many repetitions, contrasts, and analogies. Its composition is the work of an artist with deft touches and subtle colors that would be unnecessary verbiage to an artisan. The poet is not content to merely convey information, but seeks to give a colorful display of

special truths in stereoscopic dimensions by calling forth memorable or familiar analogies that appeal to the heart, emotions, and aesthetic tastes, as well as the mind. The Psalms are multi-dimensional in their presentations of truth. This recognition is essential for anyone approaching the Psalms, whether for reading or for expositional purposes. Their many figures are carefully selected to effect a proper balance and must be appreciated as such, elucidating the central truth or object. Besides being divinely inspired, the Psalms constitute the finest work of literary art and command the attention of one's whole being in their perusal or study.

2. *ISRAEL'S PENTATEUCH TO GOD.* As the five books of Moses are God's Pentateuch to Israel, the Psalms are often called "Israel's Pentateuch" to God. They constitute the responses of the godly to the Lord in ways that resemble the conditions and problems of the books of Genesis through Deuteronomy. This feature of addressing God, rather than primarily men, is one of the distinguishing traits of the Psalms, found only occasionally in other Bible books. Nearly half the Psalms begin as prayers, very often expressing some dire need or distress. David's psalms were called "the prayers of David" (72:20), and the whole collection has been called the "Prayer Book" of Israel. They became Israel's instruction manual for prayer and worship, the concept of worshiping in prayer being their dominant theme. One of the great practical values in their study is to absorb their spirit of worship which pervades all the expressions of laments, anger, joy, and assurance through the whole range of human experience described.

3. *THE "HALLELUJAH" BOOK OF THE OLD TESTAMENT.* This term is a transliteration of two Hebrew words, meaning "praise the LORD," and is so translated in most Bibles. The New Testament, however, uses the transliteration four times in Revelation 19. In most languages today the term "hallelujah" is used in its transliterated form. This term is a command to praise the Lord, and is used only in Chronicles, Ezra, and Nehemiah, besides the Psalms. Of the eighty-two occurrences, sixty-one are in the Psalms. As previously noted, there are three Hallelujah or Hallel sections, the last of which is the final five chapters (146–150). These bring the Psalter to a dramatic climax by giving specific instruction in the art of praising the Lord. Each chapter begins and ends with "Praise the LORD," building to a staccato crescendo in the final psalm. Each chapter contributes to the theme and the final chapter summarizes the whole:
    146—When to praise the Lord?—"while I live."
    147—Why?—Because it is good, it is pleasant; because of His person and work.
    148—Who?—All creation; all people.
    149—Where?—In the sanctuary, at festivals, in bed, at war, etc.
    150—Summary: Who, where, why, how, and by whom should praise be given.

4. *THE THANKSGIVING PSALMS.* Though only Psalm 100 is entitled "A Psalm of Thanksgiving," the Psalms have more references to thanks than the rest of the Old Testament (50 of 75). Psalms 105, 106, 107, and 118 each begin by calling God's people to thank the Lord. In Psalm 136 this theme of thanks and praise is made into an

antiphonal anthem, lauding the great "lovingkindness" of the Lord. The point of this psalm that became a "National Anthem" is that just as the Lord is characterized by lovingkindness, so His people should be characterized by thankfulness.

5. **PSALMS QUOTED IN THE NEW TESTAMENT.** Of the 360 quotations and allusions of the Old Testament in the New, nearly one-third (112) are from the Psalms. W. Graham Scroggie (*The Psalms*) has noted that these references come from ninety-seven of the Psalms and they are quoted or alluded to in twenty-three of the twenty-seven books of the New Testament. The following is a list of seventy-seven of the most significant quotations from the 112 listed by Leopold Sabourin.

PSALM	NEW TESTAMENT REFERENCE		PSALM	NEW TESTAMENT REFERENCE	
2:1-2	Acts 4:25-26	Nations against Messiah	51:4	Rom. 3:4	You may be justified
7	Heb. 1:5	You are My Son	55:22	1 Pet. 5:7	Cast your burden
8-9	Rev. 2:26ff.	Break with rod	62:12	Rom. 2:6	Render according to deeds
4:4	Eph. 4:26	Angry and sin not	68:18	Eph. 4:8	Ascended on high
5:9	Rom. 3:13	Throat open tomb	69:9	John 2:17	Zeal for Your house
6:8	Matt. 7:23	Depart from me	9	Rom. 15:3	Reproaches fallen
7:9	Rom. 8:27	God tests heart	21	Matt. 27:34	Gave wine with gall
8:2	Matt. 21:16	Praise from infants	22-23	Rom. 11:9-10	Let eyes be dark
4-6	Heb. 2:6-7	Lower than angels	25	Acts 1:20	Habitation be desolate
10:7	Rom. 3:14	Mouth full of curses	28	Rev. 3:5	Blot from book
14:1-3	Rom. 3:10ff.	No one does good	72:10ff.	Matt. 2:11	Gifts of gold
16:8-11	Acts 2:25ff.	Holy One not corrupt	78:2	Matt. 13:35	Parables
18:2	Luke 1:69	Horn of salvation	24	John 6:31	Bread from heaven
19:4	Rom. 10:18	Voice to all earth	82:6	John 10:34	You are gods
9	Rev. 16:7	True and just judgment	89:3-4	Acts 2:30	Sworn to David
22:1	Matt. 27:46	My God, My God, why?	20	Acts 13:22	I found David
7-8	Matt. 27:39	Wagging their heads	91:11-12	Matt. 4:6	Gave angels charge
22:18	John 19:24	Cast lots for garments	94:14	Rom. 11:1	Not reject people
22:22	Heb. 2:12	To My brethren	95:7ff.	Heb. 3:8ff.	Harden not hearts
23:1	John 10:11	The Good Shepherd	97:7	Heb. 1:6	Let angels worship
3-4	Matt. 5:8	Blessed are pure	98:2-3	Acts 28:28	Salvation to Gentiles
31:5	Luke 23:46	Father, into Your hands	102:25-27	Heb. 1:10	They shall perish
32:1-2	Rom. 4:7-8	Not impute sin	103:17	Luke 1:50	Mercy on those who fear
33:6	John 1:3	By word heavens made	104:4	Heb. 1:7	Makes angels spirits
34:8	1 Pet. 2:3	Taste and see that	105:8	Luke 1:72	Remember covenant
12-16	1 Pet. 3:10ff.	Keep tongue from evil	21	Acts 7:10	Made Joseph ruler
14	Heb. 12:14	Strive for peace	106:20	Rom. 1:23	Exchanged glory
20	John 19:36	Not a bone broken	107:9	Luke 1:53	Hungry He filled
35:19	John 15:25	Hated without cause	109:8	Acts 1:20	Another take office
36:1	Rom. 3:8	No fear of God	110:1	Matt. 22:44	Sit at My right hand
37:11	Matt. 5:4	Humble inherit earth	4	Heb. 5:6	Priest forever
38:11	Luke 23:49	All stood at distance	111:9	Luke 1:49	Holy is His Name
40:6-8	Heb. 10:5ff.	To do Your will	118:6	Heb. 13:6	Lord is my helper
41:9	John 13:18	Lifted his heel against	22	Matt. 21:42	Stone builders rejected
44:22	Rom. 8:36	For Your sake killed	26	Matt. 21:9	Blessed is He who
45:6-7	Heb. 1:8-9	Your throne, O God	130:8	Matt. 1:21	Will redeem Israel

PSALM	NEW TESTAMENT REFERENCE		PSALM	NEW TESTAMENT REFERENCE	
135:14	Heb. 10:30	Lord will judge	143:2	Rom. 3:5	No one is righteous
140:3	Rom. 3:13	Poison under lips	146:6	Acts 4:24	Made heaven and earth
141:2	Rev. 5:8	Prayer as incense			

Approximately one-half of these relate to Messiah and His ministry. The many quotes and allusions indicate the importance the New Testament writers attach to the Psalms.

6. *PSALMS OF LAMENT OR COMPLAINT.* Reading the Psalms one quickly discerns a strong note of distress evoking complaints and a cry to God for help. These make up the largest category of psalms (one-third) and are spread throughout the five books. They are called "Laments," individual and community, but are to be distinguished from mere dirges that have no hope. They portray a person in deep distress, often approaching death, who becomes conscious of his sin in the presence of the Lord, casts himself on God's grace alone and vows to serve and praise the Lord anticipating His deliverance. They arise from a wide range of problems: national calamities, personal threats by enemies, unjust accusations, and situations of illness or approaching death. Many are from David who suffered many harrowing experiences that drove him to more implicit trust in God. These psalms are also to be distinguished from mere human complaints in that they move to the higher level of trust in God, appealing to His word and character, and confidently anticipate His deliverance. They exemplify the true struggle of the godly in a world fraught with adversaries, finding solace and deliverance by simple trust in God.

7. *THE IMPRECATORY PSALMS.* A number of psalms are shockingly judgmental of the wicked, invoking God's curse and vengeance on them. The longest imprecations are in Psalms 35, 69, and 109, but strains of vengeance appear in a number of others: 31:17-18; 40:14-16; 54:7; 55:15; 58:6-7; 59:9-13; 83:9-17; 137:8-9; 139:19; 140:11. Several recognitions should be kept in mind in reading these:

a. They express the yearning of the godly for the destruction of the wicked and the triumph of righteousness. The Hebrew mind saw wickedness as personal, identifying the sinner with his sin and the man with his family.

b. The imperative, such as "let them be destroyed," may be translated prophetically as "they shall be destroyed" in some instances.

c. The idea of destroying the wicked, however, was entirely in keeping with the commission of Israel to cleanse the land of Canaan. Moses, Joshua, Samuel, David, and many others actually did it, and Elijah called down fire from heaven upon the wicked.

d. The judgments pronounced by Christ on the rebellious in Matthew 23 were not less invective, being a consequence of the rejection of His grace.

8. *THE MESSIANIC PSALMS.* The Psalms contain many references to the person and coming of Messiah. The descriptions of Christ and His work are sometimes more detailed

than the Gospels, recording, for instance, not only His death, but His thoughts while on the cross. So significant were these references that the Lord rebuked the disciples for their failure to understand how they spoke of Him (Luke 24:25, 44). The following brief outline displays the major references to His person and work:

a. *Messiah's Person*

As Man	(Ps. 8:4-5; Heb. 2:6-8). As Eternal (Ps. 102:25-27; Heb. 1:10).
As God	(Ps. 45:6, 11; Heb. 1:8). As Son of God (Ps. 2:7, 12; Matt. 22:45; Heb. 1:5).

b. *Messiah's Character*

Gracious	(Ps. 72:4, 12-14; Matt. 11:5; 12:20).
Righteous	(Ps. 45:7; Heb. 1:10).
Holy	(Ps. 89:18-19).

c. *Messiah's Work*

In life	(Ps. 40:6-8; Heb. 10:5-7).
In death	(Ps. 22; The Four Gospels).
In resurrection	(Ps. 16:10; Acts 13:33-36).
In ascension	(Ps. 68:18; Eph. 4:8).
In judgment	(Ps. 72:2-14; 86:13; 98:9; 2 Thess. 1:7-9; Rev. 19).
In reigning	(Ps. 72:8; 96:10; 103:19; Rev. 19:16).

d. *Messiah's Offices*

As Prophet	(Ps. 22:22; 40:9-10; Heb. 2:12).
As Priest	(Ps. 110:4; Heb. 5:6).
As Judge	(Ps. 72:2; 96:10-13; Matt. 25:32; Rev. 19:11; 20:11).
As King	(Ps. 2:6; 89:27; Matt. 25:31-34; 27:11; Rev. 19:16).

The Book of Proverbs

Introduction

AUTHORSHIP

A. *THE TITLE*

1. The Hebrew title, "*Mishle Shelomoh*" (Proverbs of Solomon), means the analogies or sententious sayings of Solomon. The term, "Mishle," means a comparison or proverbial saying and probably derives from the verb, "mashal" (meaning "to rule"). It thereby denotes a governing principle of life, expressed by an analogy.

2. The English title, "Proverbs" ("pro" = for; "verba" = words), signifies a short maxim, expressing a truth in few words. The Proverbs have been called "short sentences drawn from long experiences." William Arnot has called them "Laws from Heaven for Life on Earth" in his book by that title.

Outline of Proverbs

THEME: The Great Benefits of Wisdom and Godly Discipline in Personality Growth.

B. *THE AUTHORS*
1. Solomon was the author or collector of chapters 1–24 (1:1; 10:1), and he was the original author of the group in chapters 25–29 (25:1), collected by the "men of Hezekiah."
2. Agur was the author of chapter 30, of whom nothing is known.
3. King Lemuel was the author of chapter 31, recording the counsel of his mother. His identity is also unknown, some seeing him as an Arabian prince and others assuming him to be an alias for Solomon who expresses the counsel of Bathsheba.
4. The book apparently concluded at the end of chapter 24 prior to the time of Hezekiah when he and his scribes (perhaps Isaiah and Micah) collected the additional proverbs of Solomon in chapters 25–29.

HISTORICAL SETTING

A. *DATE OF WRITING—950–700 B.C.*

Though liberal critics date Proverbs as late as post-exilic times, assigning the collection to other compilers, there is no valid reason to reject the traditional view that Solomon either gathered or wrote chapters 1–24. A likely date then would be c. 950 B.C., the middle of his reign, for this group, and c. 725–700 B.C. for the latter chapters, 25–31.

B. *WISDOM LITERATURE*

For an introduction to wisdom literature, see "Introduction to the Wisdom Books." This class of writing was common to most ancient nations as noted in Babylon, Egypt, Edom, and Phoenicia. They each had their "wise men." Israel's wise man, Solomon, was the wisest of them all as acknowledged by the Queen of Sheba (1 Kin. 4:34; 10:6-7), and his students came from all nations. He is said to have spoken 3000 proverbs in many fields of science, many more than the 800 included in the Book of Proverbs.

C. *THE RELIGIOUS SETTING*

The settings of the two compilers, Solomon and Hezekiah, suggest the proverbs came out of times of spiritual concern and revival. Solomon's early reign was characterized by spiritual dedication and Hezekiah's by a time of reawakening in Judah after great idolatry. The proverbs were not mere practical prudence to enjoy the good life, but wisdom to live life in the "fear of the Lord." The terms "righteous" and "righteousness" are used over forty times in Proverbs, more than any book except Psalms. Hezekiah might well have stressed the proverb to his people: "Righteousness exalts a nation, But sin *is* a reproach to *any* people" (14:34).

THE LITERARY STRUCTURE OF PROVERBS

A. *LITERARY FORMS EMPLOYED*

The Book of Proverbs utilizes various literary devices to present practical maxims for life through creative figures, striking analogies, and contrasts. The basic poetic units employed are the following:

1. *Unit Proverbs*. This proverb has two basic forms:
    a. A couplet in which the first line expresses a thought and the second line supplements it by expanding or interpreting it.
        Example: "The fruit of the righteous *is* a tree of life,
        And he who wins souls *is* wise." (Prov. 11:30).
    b. A couplet in which both lines are required to express the thought by the use of some form of parallelism.
        Example: "Hatred stirs up strife, But love covers all sins" (10:12).
2. *Proverb Clusters*. These are groups of proverbs on a common theme, such as those on the King (25:2-7), the Fool (26:1-12), and the Sluggard (26:13-16).
3. *Epigram*. The epigram is an enlarged proverb which has at its heart two lines (not necessarily consecutive) that express its gnomic germ thought, the rest being supplementary or an expansion of it. Example: Shunning Evil (1:8-9). It often makes its point by pithy, witty, or satirical statements.
4. *Sonnet*. Though popularly known as simply a brief poem, the English sonnet is technically a fourteen liner (hexastich and octastich). The distinction of the Hebrew sonnet is not the exact number of lines, but that the poem begins with an opening couplet expressing its theme, then forms two blocks or two emphases of thoughts, one of which expands the first line of the couplet and the other expands the second line. This forms a poetic mold throughout the poem. Example: Evil Company (1:10-19).
5. *Dramatic Monologue*. In this device inanimate objects or abstract ideas are personified to speak in warning or to emphasize their nature or purpose.
    Example: The Call of Wisdom (1:20-33).
6. *Acrostic*. An acrostic on the Hebrew alphabet concludes the book, 31:10-31.

B. *LITERARY ARRANGEMENT OF THE BOOK OF PROVERBS*

1. Chapters 1-9—fifteen clusters, epigrams, sonnets, or monologues.
2. Chapters 10–22:16—375 maxims mainly in unit proverb form.
    Chapters 10–15 are mostly antithetic; 16–22 are mostly synonymous or synthetic.
3. Chapters 22:17–24:34 contains sixteen epigrams with a variety of stichs (lines).
4. Chapters 25-29—Mainly clusters, epigrams, and unit proverbs.
    25–27—seven epigrams on various subjects; 28–29—55 unit proverbs.
5. Chapter 30—thirteen epigrams or unit clusters. (Note the "end stresses").
6. Chapter 31—An acrostic on the Hebrew alphabet, using the beauty of literary structure to emphasize the beauty of wisdom personified as a virtuous woman.

THE PURPOSE OF THE BOOK OF PROVERBS

Its twofold purpose is positively stated and negatively implied in 1:2-4:

1. To teach and highlight the great benefits that accrue to all of life by a disciplined

mind and a God-oriented way of life, and conversely.

2. To warn of the great dangers that inevitably come by following the dictates of the lower nature or passions.

Unique Contributions of Proverbs

1. *CONTRASTING PROVERBS WITH PSALMS.* As the Psalms obviously deal with man's worship and relations with God, Proverbs deals with his walk and relations with men. The Psalms primarily address God while the Proverbs address the sons and daughters of men. Proverbs is uniquely the ethical book of the Old Testament, applying biblical principles of righteous living. It instructs those that would be wise that their actions are to be directed by God's written word in the Law and His spiritual word to the active conscience, which is seen as "the lamp of the LORD" (20:27). The progressive movement from Psalms to Proverbs, as organized in the canon, nicely suggests the right order of godly living—right relations with God are always primary; but right relations with men must always follow. Each is essential to the other.

2. *"WISDOM" IDENTIFIED.* Wisdom has many forms. The Book of Proverbs uses three terms for wisdom to distinguish related but different aspects of this ability:
   a. "Wisdom" (*Chokhmah*). Used forty-seven times—1:2, 7, 20, etc. (cf. 1 Kin. 5:12). This term speaks of a moral discernment between good and evil, right and wrong. It also applies to secular prudence in business matters.
   b. "Understanding" (*Binah*). Used fifty-three times in several forms—1:2, 5; 2:2, 3, etc. This means an intellectual ability to discern between truth and error or between reality and sham. It is the faculty to objectively perceive long-range values as opposed to momentary attractions in ordering one's life.
   c. "Sound wisdom" (*Tushiyyah*). Used only three times—2:7; 3:21; 8:14. Coming from the root "to elevate," this term means a divine or spiritual insight into truth, developed by long acquaintance with God's Word. It is the ability to view life from the divine perspective or to put divine principles into everyday practice.

   These terms for wisdom in Proverbs connote a practical or utilitarian wisdom, not a mere intellectual wisdom or genius. They emphasize the common virtues of hard work, prudent speech, good manners, and a disciplined life. However, they have a distinct religious flavor in relating all one's actions to God and His Law. They are characterized by truth and morality, stressing service to God and each other.

3. *CLUES FOR RECOGNIZING FOOLS.* In contrast to wisdom, a variety of fools are noted in Proverbs to alert us to several stages of folly:
   a. The "simple one" (*pethi*). Used fourteen times—1:4, 22, 32; 7:7; 8:5; etc. This person is the naive one who is rather innocent, but gullible, easily led, and devoid

of understanding. He is morally naive, an easy prey for hucksters, and direly in need of instruction to avoid the pitfalls of life.

b. The "fool" (*euil* and *kesil*). Used fifty-eight times—1:7, 22, 32; 3:35; 7:22; 10:8, 18, 21, 23; 12:15, etc. Both of these "fools" are rejecters of truth, they despise wisdom, hate knowledge, and find evil a rather enjoyable "sport" (10:23).

c. The "scorner" (*lits*). Proverbs 1:22 (NKJ) and 9:7, 8; 13:1 (KJV). The "scoffer" or scorner is a deliberate troublemaker who scoffs at righteousness and derides any kind of correction. His dereliction appears to be more advanced than the fools noted above.

These three kinds of fools are introduced and described in 1:22, representing three stages of idiocy, but none is considered beyond hope in this life while "wisdom" yet calls (1:20). Psalm 1:1 also warns against three stages of unrighteousness.

4. **BUILDING GODLY PERSONALITIES FOR ETERNITY.** This book is a mine of maxims and principles for practical prudence in learning the art of godly living. The main thrust of the book, however, should not be overlooked in this maze of individual principles. That thrust is the theme of "Growing a healthy personality for eternity." All the varied maxims and principles of the book have this as their ultimate goal, which is also the central thrust of the Bible. A healthy, redeemed personality, refined by divine principles, is the supreme product of the sovereign God's creative genius. This book is designed as a manual to help believers to be "workers together *with Him*" (2 Cor. 6:1) in the process. Second Peter 1:3-11 describes the process from the New Testament perspective.

5. **THE CLASSIC PORTRAIT OF AN EXCELLENT WIFE.** The final poem in praise of "a virtuous wife" (31:10-31) is highlighted by both its literary structure and its content. Its structure is an acrostic on the Hebrew alphabet with twenty-two verses. This neatly structured versification was designed as a memory aid for Hebrew readers, but also to highlight the similarly beautiful and organized character of this most excellent wife. In a sense this virtuous woman is a personification of the wisdom extolled throughout the book, especially in 9:1-12. The many mentions of the "foolish woman," "evil woman," "contentious woman," and "immoral woman" are given to warn the young against succumbing to the dictates of the lower passions. But, lest one infer from these that women generally are morally inferior to men, the book several times extolls a virtuous wife (5:15-20; 12:4; 18:22; 19:14). The compiler then crowns this book of instruction on wisdom with this noble portrait of a wife and mother who has ordered her life and home by the principle of wisdom. She brings happiness to her husband and family with a charm that is credited to her fear of the Lord (31:30). It beautifully illustrates the theme of the book stated in 1:7 and 9:10 that "the fear of the LORD *is* the beginning of wisdom." That wisdom is not just intellectual, but a practical wisdom that applies especially to the home.

6. **THE PROVERBS AS GENERAL PRINCIPLES.** The maxims of this book are given as general principles, not as mechanical, "cause and effect" formulae. They declare how

God normally works or responds to persons, what folly generally brings, and the rewards wisdom and righteousness generally lead to in this life. Principles, however, are not inflexible but often involve exceptions in their universal applications. The wise or righteous, for instance, are promised "long life," "peace," "barns filled . . ." and "sleep will be sweet." (Prov. 3); but those results do not invariably follow, as noted in Job. The Lord may withhold the blessings normally promised the righteous in order to accomplish some greater purpose. This re-investment of the promised reward is always to multiply the eternal benefits, as illustrated in the martyrs of Hebrews 11. The veracity of God's promises in the Proverbs is not to be judged by immediate results. They are general principles that spell out the way God normally works and the way cause and effects can normally be anticipated.

7. **CHRISTOLOGY IN PROVERBS.** The references to Christ in Proverbs relate primarily to the characterization of "wisdom" in chapter 8. That passage, however, refers to Christ only obliquely, not directly. The book's purpose is to introduce wisdom and its great benefits, and that introduction is brought to a climax in 8–9 as the benefits are summarized. In dramatic monologue, "wisdom" declares her eternal association with the Lord, especially in the work of creation. The point is not basically christological, but to show that the wisdom extolled in this book is the same as the wisdom by which God works. Acquiring and applying this wisdom can equip one to be used of God in cosmic service. The New Testament reminds us, however, that Christ is the "wisdom of God" (1 Cor. 1:24, 30; Col. 2:3) and the one "in whom all the treasures of wisdom and knowledge" are hidden. Many of the characterizations of wisdom in Proverbs 8:22-31 have striking christological resemblances.

8. **ETHICAL TOPICS OF PROVERBS.** This book is a great source for a wide variety of ethical subjects. Many of these ethical principles can be illustrated from the narrative sections of the Old and New Testaments, as Harry Ironsides has done in his book, *Notes on the Book of Proverbs*. The following is a list of some of the ethical topics of Proverbs in an alphabetic order:

    a. Bad company and its effects   1:10-19; 4:14-19; 13:20; 24:1-2; 29:24.
    b. Contention   3:20; 10:12; 13:10; 15:1-4; 16:27-28; 18:6-8.
    c. Discipline and its rewards   1:8; 6:20; 10:13; 13:24; 15:10; 22:15; 23:13; 29:15.
    d. Fear of the Lord   1:7; 9:10; 15:33; 16:6; 23:17; 24:21-22.
    e. Filial respect   1:8-9; 6:20-21; 13:1; 15:20; 19:26; 30:17.
    f. Recognizing a fool   1:7; 12:15-16, 23; 13:20; 14:9; 17:24; 18:2-7; 19:1; 20:3; 23:9.
    g. Aware of God's omniscience   15:3, 11; 22:12.
    h. Value of good character   22:1; 24:21-22.
    i. Hypocritical religion   15:8; 29; 21:27.
    j. Intemperance and its dangers   20:1; 23:1-3, 20-35; 31:4-6.
    k. Liberality   3:9-10; 11:24-25; 13:7; 19:6, 17; 22:9; 28:27.
    l. Licentiousness (immorality)   2:16-19; 5:3-20; 6:23-35; 7:4-27; 22:14.

m. Lying and deceit   6:16-17; 12:13-14, 19-22; 19:5-9; 26:28.
 n. Pride and its dangers   6:16; 8:13; 11:2; 13:10; 16:18; 20:6; 27:2; 29:23.
 o. Sloth or idleness   6:6-11; 10:4-5; 13:4; 18:9; 20:4; 21:25; 24:30-34.

The Book
of Ecclesiastes

Introduction

AUTHORSHIP

A. *THE TITLE*

   1. The Hebrew title is *Qoheleth,* meaning "Preacher" or "one who addresses an assembly." This term is used seven times in this book, but no place else in the Old Testament.
   2. The Greek translators called it "Ecclesiastes," meaning the "office of a preacher." This title fits the book well, for it contains many features of a sermon, though it does not begin with a biblical text.

B. *THE AUTHOR*

   Though Solomon is the only credible name suggested as the author, conservative scholars are quite divided as to whether he did indeed write the book.

   1. Solomonic authorship denied. Since Luther denied the Solomonic authorship, most Bible scholars have denied it also. The main reasons for this denial:
      a. The historic conditions do not appear to be from Solomon's time.
      b. Solomon's name does not appear in the book, whereas he is named in the Book of Proverbs and the Song of Solomon.
      c. The language, diction, and style are supposedly post-exilic, containing many Aramaisms.
      d. The introduction refers to Solomon as the hero, but not the author, according to Richard Moulton (*The Literary Study of the Bible*). Most commentators acknowledge the figure of Solomon as either the experimenter or the one being impersonated, perhaps to enforce the credibility of the message.
   2. Solomonic authorship confirmed. Many conservative scholars still maintain that Solomon was indeed the author for the following reasons:
      a. The author's self-identifications strongly point to Solomon (1:1, 12; 2:7, 9; 12:9). To have falsely impersonated this greatest of wise men on such crucial issues of life would have been detected long ago by Israel's wise men, denying its inclusion in the canon.
      b. The author identifies himself as one who had gathered and arranged many

proverbs (12:9; cf. 1 Kin. 4:32). No other writer in this class has been identified from the Old Testament period.

c. Jewish traditions ascribed it to Solomon, though some of the later rabbis suggested it may have sustained a refinement later by scribes such as the ''Men of Hezekiah.''

d. If Solomon did not write this book, most would agree he should have. The experiments, arguments, and conclusions presented would require one equipped like Solomon with great wisdom, riches, fame, success in business enterprises, and passion for women. No one was so supremely endowed for this research and writing task as was Solomon.

HISTORICAL SETTING

A. *DATE OF WRITING*—c. 935 B.C.

If Solomon was indeed the author, the book was probably a product of his later years. Tradition attributes three books to him, The Song in his early life, Proverbs in his middle years, and Ecclesiastes in his senior life. The content and conclusions certainly fit well with his more mature years, thus providing all generations the benefit of his wide experiences and wise philosophical thinking concerning the purpose of life. Since he reigned 970–930, a likely date of writing would be c. 935 B.C.

B. *THE POLITICAL AND RELIGIOUS SETTINGS*

1. Politically, the setting of Solomon's reign was an oasis of peace and prosperity between the time of David's conquests and Egypt's resurgence in 926. Solomon's many alliances with the neighboring nations promoted much trade and interchange of ideas throughout the East. Many world figures sought the counsel of Solomon attracted by his wisdom, wealth, splendor, and art. The political setting was ideal for building, travel, and the growth of literature and art. It was a rare time of world peace.

2. Religiously, this period was unique for its evident unity of worship in Israel. Music and literature were given special prominence by David and Solomon, and the construction of the temple served to centralize the worship system. Perhaps no period of Israel's history had greater opportunities for interchange of ideas, study of Torah, and religious reflection than this age. Sometime after the middle of his reign, however, Solomon appears to have developed an ecumenical spirit of religious compromise as he sought to appease his many foreign wives. This so affected his thinking and relations with God that the kingdom itself was influenced and divided immediately after his death. He had built accommodating ''high places'' for all his foreign wives. (1 Kin. 11:7-8). It is presumed that Solomon himself was restored to the Lord after his divine rebuke. This may have been the opportune, reflective period in his life when he composed this philosophical book on the ultimate purpose of life.

C. THE PROMINENCE OF WISDOM LITERATURE

1. The Hebrew people were led by three classes of spiritual leaders, the priests, the prophets, and the wise men (cf. Jer. 18:18). Solomon, of course, was the greatest of the wise men and perhaps a leader of a school of wise men. Whereas the prophet was a spokesman for God, the wise man was an observer of people and events and spoke with the authority of experience. He was often an elderly, father figure, one who collected wisdom from the sages and condensed his reflections into maxims or proverbs. He was thought of as a "button-hole philosopher," ready with an observation from experience for every problem of life.

2. Solomon's time was known as the beginning of the golden age of wisdom literature. Though Zadok, the priest, and Nathan, the prophet, helped put him on the throne, the priests and prophets had little prominence during Solomon's reign. They were far overshadowed by this great "wise man" who was counselor, judge, and preacher to Israel, as well as king (1 Kin. 3:28; 4:29-34; 8:14ff.). Though various prophets counseled David, none is recorded as having counseled or corrected Solomon. He was acclaimed as wiser than all the wise men of the East or of Egypt, not one who sought counsel. The product of that wisdom is

---

Outline of Ecclesiastes

THEME: The Futility of Seeking Meaning in Life Without God.
(Corollary: The Felicity of Life with God.)

preserved in the practical Book of Proverbs and the philosophical Book of Ecclesiastes.

THE PURPOSE OF THE BOOK OF ECCLESIASTES

The writer's purpose was to present a scientific and philosophical display of the inadequacy and futility of life without God, and conversely, to show the satisfaction and joy of living in the realization of God's sovereignty. The book is a dramatic expose of the proud claims of naturalism.

Unique Contributions of Ecclesiastes

1. *ITS CONTRAST WITH PROVERBS.* Whereas Proverbs applies wisdom for the practical benefits of a God-directed life, Ecclesiastes applies wisdom to the philosophical purpose of understanding the meaning of life. Solomon here focuses on the whole of life rather than on the particulars of living. His concern is for the meaning of existence rather than the problems of existence. He stands back as a philosopher to interject the question of "why?" to life. Without an adequate answer to "why?" the questions of what, how, when, etc. become rather meaningless. This Book of Ecclesiastes then is the first book of the Bible to pause and reflect philosophically on the meaning of life itself in light of the seeming futilities everyone faces. God endowed Solomon with special divine wisdom for this task.

2. *REFUTING NATURALISM.* No book of the Bible is more specifically designed to refute naturalism, or the efficacy of mere human wisdom to interpret life, than Ecclesiastes. The term, "under the sun" (used twenty-nine times), refers to the natural man's view of life apart from divine revelation. The author vividly lays bare the futility of a life philosophy built on mere natural wisdom, showing how the greatest wisdom, riches, and pleasures of life will end in total disillusionment if pursued as ends in themselves. He likens that pursuit to "grasping for the wind" (1:14, 17). His final caution is to beware of this naturalistic outlook in the many persuasive writings of men (12:12). In reading them it is essential to be stabilized by "words of truth" (12:10-11).

3. *COMMENDING JOY IN LIFE.* This book has often been regarded as the "saddest book of the Bible," having a prevailing cry of despair. Actually, it is the very opposite. Ecclesiastes is the outstanding book of the Old Testament that commands men and women to rejoice in life. The one with a divine perspective of life is called to rejoice in every aspect of life. These admonitions are given in several key passages:

2:1-10   Rejoicing in mere fleshly pursuits and pleasures is seen as pure idiocy.

2:24-26   With God's perspective, even the prosperity of the wicked is a matter of joy, inasmuch as it eventually becomes the prosperity of the godly.

3:12-13   Rejoicing in the labors of life is seen as a gift of God, and it is not to be reduced by the seeming injustices of life. God will sovereignly attend to those injustices by the wicked in His time.

5:18-20   Though wealth is not itself an object of rejoicing, it is not to be despised. It is to be received as a gift from God and used as He gives power and proper opportunity to use it.

7:3, 14   Even in sorrow (attending a funeral), the godly should be happy in heart. God's wisdom can cheer the heart when the face is sad. Both prosperity and adversity are to be regarded as God's gifts for our good.

8:13-17   When the wicked seem to prevail, the righteous are to rejoice in God's overall sovereignty. God rarely executes sentence against the ungodly immediately, but will thoroughly attend to them in His own time.

9:7-10   Since God is the Author of real joy, life is to be lived cheerfully and to the fullest. The joys of married bliss are to be seen as gifts from God.

11:8-10   Both the young and the old are commanded to rejoice every day of life. This rejoicing, however, is to be done with a view to God's day of judgment when each will give account to God. This is not meant to suppress joy, but to direct and enlarge it.

The point of these exhortations to joy is similar to that of Paul in Philippians 4:4: "Rejoice in the LORD always." God sees no piety in a sad look, but in the smile of faith. His presence brings fullness of joy.

4. *THE STRANGE AGNOSTIC STRAINS* (2:14-16; 3:19-20; 9:2; etc.). No book of the Bible has been so questioned as to its divine inspiration as Ecclesiastes, primarily because of its apparent agnostic statements. It appears to teach the same fate for human and beast, righteous and unrighteous. This follows from a failure to grasp the purpose and point of the book. It is a sermon with text, introduction, thesis, elaboration, illustration, conclusion, and application, and must not be interpreted piecemeal. Its method is dialectical. Two opposing views are presented with negations and affirmations following each other throughout. The view of naturalism ("under the sun") is frankly stated as the various experiments are carried out, declaring the total futility of life from that perspective. The author has a quest motif, leading his class through the maze of life's conundrums as he helps them to discern the true purpose of life. Stating the pessimistic conclusions of naturalism is essential to the emphasis of his final conclusion that the real meaning of life can only be perceived as one fears God and keeps His commandments.

5. *GOD'S SOVEREIGNTY ON THE PERSONAL LEVEL.* As many Bible books teach the sovereignty of God on various levels, Ecclesiastes stresses that sovereignty on the personal level. He is seen to work through all personalities to bring to naught the wisdom and pride of persons and to make even the wicked to serve His purposes. He makes the prosperity of the wicked to eventually accrue to the righteous. They are unwittingly "gathering and collecting" for the righteous (2:26). The irony of His sovereignty is that He makes even the wrath of men to praise Him (Ps. 76:10). This sovereignty is further

stressed by the use of the name "Elohim" (forty times) in this book, the name that stresses His creative power and sovereignty.

6. *STRESSING ETERNITY AND JUDGMENT* (3:11, 17; 11:9; 12:14-15). Ecclesiastes is one of the few books of the Old Testament that stress eternity and judgment after death. The Preacher declares that God has "put eternity in their heart," and that they are heading for their "eternal home" (12:5). He emphasizes that "the days of darkness" (11:8), will be many. Therefore, life is to be enjoyed to the full as a gift of God, but always with a recognition that "God will bring you into judgment," for all these things. Unlike the beasts, humans are made for eternity and are obliged to prepare for the eternal home in this life before the parting of dust and spirit (12:7).

7. *THE FIRST MENTION OF GOD AS "CREATOR"* (12:1). "Remember *now* your Creator," is the first reference to God as Creator in the Bible (cf. Is. 40:28; 43:15; Rom. 1:25; and 1 Pet. 4:19). He is seen here as not only Creator of the universe, but also as the Creator of redeemed and righteous personalities. The exhortation is to let God continue His creative work in our hearts and lives and allow Him to start the work early in life. This need to start early is then dramatized by the old man who is likened to a dilapidated old house, showing how the aging process makes it more and more difficult to make a change. The change must be made before the "silver cord is loosed" (12:6). The New Testament parallel to this is 1 Peter 4:19, where God is seen as a "faithful Creator," even using adversity to perform His creative work in the soul.

8. *ITS STRONG CLAIM OF INSPIRATION AND INERRANCY* (12:10-12). Though this book has been greatly assailed and questioned as to its divine inspiration, it concludes with one of the strongest claims of truth from the "one Shepherd" found in the Bible. This was perhaps made by the wise Preacher anticipating strong opposition to his expose of humanistic naturalism. To master these truths, he declared, is to attain strong stability in facing both the enigmas of life and the challenges of rationalism.

9. *CHRISTOLOGY IN ECCLESIASTES.* Though no messianic prediction or types appear in this book, some oblique references may be seen. Its message is called "words of truth," given by "one Shepherd" (12:11). Christ called Himself the "truth," "the good shepherd" (John 10:71), and "a greater than Solomon" (Luke 11:31), coming to show the true meaning of life. As Solomon experienced these many futilities that we might vicariously share his conclusions without actually experiencing all of them, Christ also experienced vastly more, even being forsaken of God, that we might vicariously share the benefits of His redemptive work and wisdom.

The Song of Solomon

Introduction

AUTHORSHIP

A. *THE TITLE*

1. The Hebrews entitled it "The Song of Songs" (*Shir Hash-shirim*), from the opening words, "The song of songs which *is* Solomon's," thus emphasizing its significance as "the best of songs" from Solomon.
2. The English title, "Canticles," derives from the Latin Vulgate's "Canticum Canticorum," which translates the Greek, *Asma Asmaton*, both of which mean "the best of songs."

B. *THE AUTHOR*

1. Solomonic authorship denied. Many modern scholars believe the Song was written about Solomon, not by him. The contention is that it had to be written several hundred years later because of the presence of various Aramaisms and Persian and Greek loanwords. Solomon's cosmopolitan acquaintance through his commerce, foreign wives, and many visitors, however, might well explain these linguistic phenomena.
2. Solomonic authorship confirmed. The authorship by Solomon is confirmed by several internal and external evidences:
    a. The opening verse ascribes it to Solomon with the normal Hebrew prefix for authorship (*lamedh*). He is referred to five times in the Song, the last one addressing him (8:12).
    b. Solomon did write 1005 songs, this being the only one preserved (1 Kin. 4:32).
    c. The many references to flowers and trees (21 varieties) and animals (15 species) point to Solomon, a specialist in these studies (1 Kin. 4:33).
    d. The geographical references in both North and South Israel speak of the nation still in unity, before the division of 931 B.C.
    e. Jewish tradition has universally held Solomon as the author, the Jewish people reading the Song every year at the Feast of Passover.
    f. The book has many similarities in terminology with Proverbs and Ecclesiastes (neither Ecclesiastes or the Song use the divine name Yahweh).
    g. The objection that a polygamist could not have written this song of marital fidelity is like objecting to Solomon's authorship of Proverbs on the basis that he violated so many of its principles. The Song actually speaks of sixty queens, eighty concubines, and countless virgins from which the Beloved turns in addressing the Shulamite (6:8-9).

HISTORICAL SETTING

A. *DATE OF WRITING*—c. 960 B.C.

1. Assuming Solomon to be the author, the Song was probably written after he became king, had gathered many chariots of horses from Egypt, and had extended his vineyards to the northern valley of Jezreel. His harem of wives and concubines was yet small (60 and 80 compared to his later 700 and 300).
2. As previously noted, this book was probably Solomon's earliest canonical book. It fits well his early years as king, as Proverbs reflects his middle years and Ecclesiastes the later years of his reign. The three books also reflect his great personal gifts as a lover, wise man, and preacher.

B. *THE HISTORICAL SETTING*

1. Solomon's interest in music and song followed naturally as a son of David, the "sweet psalmist of Israel" (2 Sam. 23:1). As David wrote many psalms, Solomon wrote 1005 songs (1 Kin. 4:32). His preoccupation with women might also be traced to his father's many romances. It is certainly obvious that many of Solomon's marriages were for convenience or political reasons, to promote peaceful alliances with neighboring nations. Most of these women were of high standing or royalty in all probability, not generally rural maidens of low estate. This fact sets off his romance and marriage to the Shulamite in the Song as especially unique, dramatizing his genuine love for her because of her native beauty and character, not her political connections.
2. The setting of the Song is primarily pastoral, though flashes of the royal court in Jerusalem are interjected. The speeches and refrains are full of rural images of gardens, trees, flowers, wooded mountains, wild animals, vineyards, valleys, fountains, and streams, the very things of which pastoral portrayals of romantic love are made. The place names run from En Gedi and Jerusalem in the south to Mount Gilead, Mount Hermon, and Lebanon in the north. The majority of scenes describe the rural north rather than south. Weddings in ancient Israel were of great importance to both the family and the rural community. They were usually week-long nuptial festivals in which the groom and bride were treated as king and queen by the local peasantry.

C. *THE RELIGIOUS SETTING*

1. The question arises as to what part religion had in the book, Song of Solomon. To all appearances it is an erotic love song with little relation to religion or faith in God. The name of God is not mentioned, except for the incidental reference to the shortened divine name "Yah," in 8:6. Yet Rabbi Akiba (c. A.D. 135) maintained it was the most holy of the Holy Writings (Hagiographa) of Israel. It was considered sacred as an allegory of the love relation between Israel and her covenant Lord. As such it was read annually by the nation at the Feast of Passover when they commemorated their redemption from Egypt and new cove-

nant relationship with Yahweh as their covenant God. How early the nation conceived it in this way is not known, but that was apparently one of the main reasons it was included in the Hebrew Canon.

2. This Song of Love, however, was also appreciated and deemed sacred by Israel for its beautifully figurative but frank description of marital love. It lifts the marriage relation to the high plane of a sacred duty and spiritual experience, fulfilling the Lord's command of marital intimacy in Genesis 2:24. It also emphasizes the importance to delay such intimacy, "nor awaken love" (8:4), until the day of entering the marriage chamber comes.

THE METHODS OF INTERPRETATION

A. *THE SONG'S UNIQUE KIND OF LITERATURE*

Few books of the Bible have been so misunderstood as the Song. Some see it as crass erotica and others as hopeless allegory. The speeches seem to run together and the movement of the plot is difficult to discern. The many figures are not always easy to distinguish from the literal descriptions. To help clear up these problems it is important to determine what kind of literature is involved. If the book is a drama, it appears to have one interpretation; if it is a series of lyric "idyls," it very likely has another. It is therefore important that the two types of literature be understood and distinguished.

1. Drama. A drama is an acted presentation of a series of events leading to a climax. It is a presentation of actions rather than a description or reflection. In the latter (which are epic and lyric), one can go back parenthetically to describe or recall previous events or background features for clarification; but not in drama. Drama is pure presentation of actions in sequence. Further, drama does not have or need an abstract chorus interrupting, except as that chorus is part of the real scene. All speakers or actors in drama contribute to the movement of the story dramatized. The Book of Job is an example of religious drama.

2. Lyric Idyl. This form of lyric is rather uncommon and needs to be distinguished from epic and drama. The term "idyl" came from Sicily, meaning a "pastoral scene" being described for the city folks of Alexandria. Idyls then are pictures of rural scenes arranged together to tell a story with its background. It differs from drama in that the story may begin at the middle or end and recall the background or introductory events through a series of flashbacks or reminiscences. Another feature of idyls is that the scenes are often interrupted by parenthetic refrains unrelated to the immediate scene, but emphasizing the overall theme. These refrains also serve to separate the various dialogues or pictures. (See Richard Moulton, *The Literary Study of the Bible*, pp. 78, 297ff.).

3. The Significance of Form for Interpretation. Recognizing these two forms of poetry helps to classify the Song of Solomon, which in turn helps to determine its interpretation. The two forms yield different interpretations:

   a. The Shepherd Hypothesis. "Those who consider it a drama are in substantial agreement as to its plot: that the Shulamite is wooed by King Solomon with offers of regal splendour, that she remains faithful to her humbler Shepherd lover, that in the end King Solomon gives way and the faithful lovers are united.'' (*Ibid.*, p. 207). Solomon then is the rejected lover. But, as Leland Ryken notes, ''Drama is based on conflict and an easily grasped sequence of events. We get neither in the Song of Solomon, which is a celebration of happy love instead of a conflict, and which has a fragmented structure that would be confusing if staged. If the poem were a drama in any sense at all, the poet would have inserted names for the various speeches. Far too much—in fact, practically everything—has to be supplied in order to turn the work into a play.'' (Ryken, *The Literature of the Bible,* p. 217).

  b. The Romance and Wedding of Solomon and Shulamite. Those who consider the poem a set of idyls identify Solomon as the lover throughout. This then is the story: ''King Solomon, visiting his vineyard upon Mount Lebanon,

---

Outline of Song of Solomon

THEME: The Delights of Pure Marital Love, Portraying the Lord's Love for His People.

comes by surprise upon the fair Shulamite maiden; she flees from him, and he visits her disguised as a Shepherd and wins her love; then he comes in state to claim her as his queen; they are being wedded in the Royal Palace when the poem opens.'' (*Op. cit.*, p. 207). Interspersed are reminiscences of earlier courtship days and meditations by the lovers, as well as choral refrains that set off the various pictures.

The latter view appears the most plausible for several reasons:

a. The Song is called ''The Song of Songs, which is Solomon's,'' that is, his choicest love song, not his most memorable defeat in love. It is difficult to conceive Israel highly regarding the Song from this view as the melancholy vanquishing of their most famous lover.

b. The literary form of pure drama was extremely rare among the Hebrews. The Song, furthermore, does not fit the literary requirement of drama.

c. The Song does fit nicely into the literary form of idyls with its seven pictures, flashback reminiscences, and parenthetic refrains.

d. Viewing Solomon as the one lover throughout also better comports with the religious flavor—symbolizing the Lord's love for Israel and typifying Christ's love for the church—the triumph of divine love.

B. *THE METHODS OF INTERPRETATION*

Various views have been taken as to how the descriptions in The Canticles should be interpreted as to its basic purpose and how it should be applied. Granting that the plot concerns the most ideal romance in the life of Solomon, why was the Song preserved, or what purpose was it intended to serve for Israel and the church?

1. The Literal (pure naturalist) View. This view construes the poem as a picture of pure, marital love without any higher or spiritual meaning. Theodore of Mosuestia (A.D. 533), for instance, saw it as a song which Solomon wrote on the occasion of his marriage to Pharaoh's daughter. Though the church condemned him for this purely human interpretation, it does have an apparent moral purpose in stressing the dignity and purity of marital love. But if it is just a human love story that does not rise above the moral lesson, its inclusion in the Hebrew canon is difficult to explain.

2. The Allegorical View. Early Jewish traditions viewed the poem as an allegory that portrayed God's love for Israel, and the early church simply baptized that concept as Christ's love for the Church. This became the dominant interpretation through most of church history. It certainly comports well with other biblical passages on those relations. Its problem, however, is that this story is not an allegory, but is a stated and well-validated history in the life of Solomon. To deny its history in order to illustrate a spiritual truth taught elsewhere is to miss its original purpose. The allegorical view also leads itself to great extravagances and embarrassing analogies which are obviously far-fetched.

3. The Typical View. This view is really a combination of the previous interpretations without falling into their pitfalls. It gives proper recognition to the historicity of the story with its essential lesson of pure marital love; but it also discerns a spiritual application concerning the Lord's love relation with His people. This avoids the mere secularism of the strict literal view and the wild extravagances of the allegorical view. It recognizes that a type is to be interpreted in only a few salient points, not to be made to "walk on all four." It thus teaches some essential lessons, long neglected in the church, concerning the "marriage bed" for Christian couples, and impresses also the great truth of God's intimate love for Israel and the Church.

THE PURPOSE OF THE SONG OF SOLOMON

A. *The historical purpose* of the book was to celebrate Solomon's wedding to the beautiful Shulamite and to express the pure delights of human marriage in its most intimate relations as a gift of God. Coupled with this positive emphasis is the constant reminder to the young to patiently maintain sexual virginity and purity for the time of its proper expression in the marriage union.

B. *The religious purpose* of the book builds on the historical lesson of pure marital love to portray the love relation between the Lord and His people, Israel and Yahweh in the Old Testament and the Church and Christ in the New Testament. No book of the Bible is so exclusively given to express this marital intimacy of love as this book. The two purposes nicely complement each other.

Unique Contributions of Song of Solomon

1. *THE "GREAT HONEYMOON BOOK" OF THE BIBLE.* Unsurpassed in its beauty, subtle figures, and deep truths of human life, this Song of Solomon's has been called the "great honeymoon Song of the world" (R. Moulton, p. 221). Written by Israel's most experienced lover, it is the one book of the Bible majoring on matrimonial love. Of the forty-six occurrences of the term "beloved" (dod) in the Old Testament, thirty-three of them are in this Song. Its emphasis is so exclusively on the physical aspects of romance, beauty, and love, that many have seen it as gross erotica and hardly qualified to be in the sacred canon. The primary purpose, however, is to magnify the marital union which was ordained by God in Eden, showing the glory and delights of that high estate which so easily becomes denigrated by the ascetics or vilified by the erotics. Its message may well be the Old Testament base (with Gen. 2:24) for Paul's references to the marriage bed not being defiled (1 Cor. 7:2; 1 Tim. 4:3; Heb. 13:4). The name "Shulamite" (Song 6:13) is thought to be the feminine of "Solomon" (Shelomoh), signifying the vital, complementary role Solomon saw for his bride.

2. *ITS VITAL MESSAGE FOR YOUTH.* Though the Jewish Rabbis of Intertestamental times are said to have forbade those under thirty to read this book, it was especially written for the young. Those most frequently addressed are the young virgins ("daughters of Jerusalem" 2:7; 3:5, 10; 5:8, 16; 8:4). These thematic refrains encourage them to calm their passions and preserve their virginity for the all-important occasion of their honeymoon with their covenant partner, the dream of every maiden. The book provides a bit of frank but delicately figurative sex education, framed in subtle imagery and poetic beauty to present the truths without coarseness. Being read annually by the nation at the Feast of Passover, the Song was a traditional part of their culture. Its sexual message would slowly dawn on the youth as they gained maturity to discern its meaning beneath the story drapery. It thus appealed to one's joy of discovery, impressing the hidden truth of the eminent value of sexual purity as one struggled with the maturing passions and awaited the day of their proper expression in the marriage union.

3. *THE SONG OF THE PASSOVER FEAST.* It may seem strange that this Song of romance with its emphasis on physical love and attraction should be the book of "Holy Writings" chosen to be read at the Feast of Passover. This was the first feast of Israel's religious year, a most solemn occasion. The fact that the book has no mention of God (only "Yah" as a word-ending, "flame of the Lord," 8:6), worship, or religion, also adds to the incongruity. Remembering, however, that Passover was a commemoration of Israel's redemption and rescue from bondage and the beginning of their covenant relationship as a nation, gives a clue as to the appropriateness of this Song at Passover. Israel's covenant relation with the Lord is many times portrayed as a marriage union (Is. 50:1; 54:5; etc.), and the Passover therefore was, in a sense, an anniversary celebration. This subtle portrayal of the divine relationship behind the human romance story of Solomon and his bride also explains the absence of any direct mention of the Lord. His presence permeates the book in the person of Solomon the lover. As Jesus' parables often portray God in the figure of a "king," a "judge," "father," etc., so the Song of Solomon deftly teaches the heavenly truth of the Lord's relation to His people while describing the earthly pattern of a marital union. The presence of God at Passover was everywhere discerned in recalling His mercy, and reading the Canticles gave further emphasis to that spiritual covenant union. No wonder the Jews held it as the "holy of holies" of "Holy Writings!"

4. *THE TWOFOLD CHARACTER OF LOVE EMPHASIZED.* This Song of love stresses two essential features of love—its tenderness and its terror. It is graciously tender in its affectionate care and fiery fierce in its jealous protection. It is seen to be as gentle as the delicate handling of a lily among thorns (2:2-4), and as ferocious as "A most vehement flame," (8:6). This power, tenacity, and immense value of true love is magnificently portrayed in 8:7; "Many waters cannot quench love, Nor can the floods drown it. If a man would give for love All the wealth of his house, It would be utterly despised." These two features of love are seen to be its seal on the heart and the arm, its tender affection and its true affirmation (8:6). They are the commended qualities of all married love, and preeminently the qualities of God's love (Ex. 34:14; Deut. 5:9; Luke 1:78).

5. *A MISUNDERSTOOD AND NEGLECTED BOOK.* Rightly understood, the instruction of this book is essential for every generation, especially for ours with its strong emphasis on liberated passions and permissiveness. Yet the Song of Solomon, like Solomon's previous Book of Ecclesiastes, ranks as one of the most misunderstood and avoided books of the Bible. The two books seek to combat two of the greatest philosophical and moral evils of our time, the evil of a beast philosophy of life that sees one's existence ending at death, and the evil of a permissive view of pre-marital sex. Neglect of the Song of Solomon, however, has been practiced by those who should have welcomed its emphasis, those who take the biblical position of no pre-marital sex. This has largely resulted from a failure to discern its figurative language of cautions to the unmarried and its rather shockingly frank descriptions of marital love. Many well-meaning puritan as-

cetics have viewed human sex as a necessary evil to be discussed only in whispers and thus find the frankness of the Song almost illicit. A proper discernment of the movement and images employed reveals a most delicate handling of the subject, not unlike that of the Prophets and the Lord (Ezek. 23:3, 21; Luke 23:29).

6. *THE CHRISTOLOGY OF THE SONG.* As the Canticles symbolized for Israel the love relation between the covenant Lord and Israel, it likewise typifies the love relation between Christ and the Church. Christ is the "greater" Solomon to whom the Church is betrothed "*as* a chaste virgin" (Matt. 12:42; 2 Cor. 11:2; Eph. 5:27). Perhaps no greater figurative portrayal of that intimate, marital relation is given than that of the Song of Solomon. Though He came as a Shepherd the first time to espouse His bride, He will yet come in royal splendor to receive her to His bridal chamber. In the meantime, His "banner" (protective care) over her is love (Song 2:4).

Select Commentaries on the Poetic and Wisdom Books

GENERAL INTRODUCTION

Bullock, C.H. *An Introduction to the Poetic Books of the Old Testament.* Chicago: Moody, 1979.
Gordis, Robert. *The Word and the Book.* New York: Ktav, 1976.
*Robinson, T. H. *The Poetry of the Old Testament.* London: Duckworth Press, 1947.
*Ryken, Leland. *The Literature of the Bible.* Grand Rapids: Zondervan, 1974.

JOB

Andersen, F. I. *Job: An Introduction and Commentary.* Downers Grove, Ill.: InterVarsity Press, 1976.
Archer, Gleason. *The Book of Job.* Grand Rapids: Baker.
*Dorhme, E. *A Commentary on the Book of Job.* Camden, N. J.: Nelson, 1967.
Gibson, E. C. S. *The Book of Job.* Minneapolis: Klock, 1978.
*Green, Wm. H. *The Argument of the Book of Job.* Reprint. Minneapolis: Klock, 1977.
Johnson, L. D. *Israel's Wisdom: Learn and Live. Introducing the Wisdom Books.* Nashville: Broadman Press, 1975.
*Ellison, H. L. *From Tragedy to Triumph.* Grand Rapids: Eerdmans, 1958.
Robinson, H. Wheeler. *The Cross of Job.* London: SCM, n.d.

PSALMS

Alden, Robert L. *Psalms: Songs of Discipleship.* 3 vols. Chicago: Moody Press, 1975.
*Alexander, J. A. *The Psalms.* Grand Rapids: Zondervan, 1864. (Still excellent)
*Allen, R. B. *When Song Is New.* Nashville: Nelson, 1983.
——. *Praise! A Matter of Life and Breath.* Nashville: Nelson, 1980.
Davis, John J. *The Perfect Shepherd: The Twenty-third Psalm.* Winona Lake: BMH Books 1979.
*Kidner, F. Derek. *Psalms 1–72.* (Tyndale series). Downers Grove, Ill.: InterVarsity Press, 1973.
*Leupold, H. C. *Exposition of the Psalms.* Columbus, Ohio: Wartburg Press, 1959.
*Lewis, C. S. *Reflections on the Psalms.* London: Jeffrey Bles, 1958.

Maclaren, Alex. *The Psalms*. 3 vols. Minneapolis: Klock, 1980.
Sabourin, Leopold. *The Psalms: Their Origin and Meaning*. 2 vols. Staten Island: Alba House, 1969.
*Scroggie, W. Graham. *The Psalms*. Westwood, N. J.: Revell, 1948.
Spurgeon, Charles H. *The Treasury of David*. 5 vols. Grand Rapids: Zondervan, 1957.

PROVERBS

Alden, Robert L. *Proverbs: A Commentary on Ancient Book of Timeless Advice*. Grand Rapids: Baker, n.d.
Arnot, William. *Laws from Heaven for Life on Earth*. London: Nelson, 1859.
Bridges, C. *An Exposition of Proverbs*. Reprint. Evansville, Ill.: Sovereign Grace, 1959.
Greenstone, J. H. *The Holy Scripture with Commentary: Proverbs*. Philadelphia: Jewish Publishing Society, 1950.
*Ironside, Harry A. *Notes on the Book of Proverbs*. New York: Loizeaux, 1908.
*Kidner, F. Derek. *The Proverbs: An Introduction and Commentary* (Tyndale series) Chicago: InterVarsity Press, 1964.
Scott, R. B. Y. *The Way of Wisdom in the Old Testament*. New York: Macmillan, 1971.

ECCLESIASTES

*Cox, Samuel. *The Book of Ecclesiastes* (Expositor's Commentary). New York: Armstrong, 1908.
Gordis, Robert. *Koheleth—Man and His World*. New York: Schocken Books, 1971.
Hubbard, David A. *Beyond Futility*. Grand Rapids: Eerdmans, 1976.
*Kaiser, W. C. *Ecclesiastes: Total Life*. Chicago: Moody Press, 1979.
Kidner, F. Derek. *A Time to Mourn, A Time to Dance: Ecclesiastes and the Way of the World*. Downers Grove, Ill.: InterVarsity Press, 1976.
*Leupold, H. C. *Exposition of Ecclesiastes*. Columbus, Ohio: Wartburg Press, 1952.

SONG OF SOLOMON

*Dillow, J. C. *Solomon on Sex*. Nashville: Nelson, 1977.
*Ironsides, Harry. *The Song of Solomon*. New York: Loizeaux, 1933.
Knight, G. A. *Esther, Song of Solomon, and Lamentations*. London: SCM Press, 1955.
*Glickman, S. C. *A Song for Lovers*. Downers Grove, Ill.: InterVarsity Press, 1976.

---

*Though all entries are recommended, asterisks identify those of first priority.

Introduction
to the Prophetic Books

The Prophetic Books introduce a special kind of Bible literature written for specific purposes in Israel's later history. These seventeen books of prophecy complement the seventeen historic books in many ways. Their emphasis is not so much historic as it is interpretive and hortatory. Their mood also is more intense, as special heralds bringing counsel and warning in times of great national crisis and distress. Besides chiding them for past failures and warning of present dangers, however, the prophets pointed to the future. They spoke of coming judgment and messianic times to promote repentance and their return to righteousness. To properly appreciate the Prophetic Books, one should be aware of their special functions, their times of ministry, and their major themes.

I The Functions of the Prophets

The prophets of Israel were individually called and anointed by God for "emergency" service, in contrast to the regular service of the priests, elders, and kings. Besides being called "prophets" (Heb. *nabi*), they were also called "seers" (*roeh* or *chozeh*), "watchmen" (*tsaphah*), or "shepherds" (*raah*). These terms signified their roles of being called of God to interpret and announce God's special word to His people. Their general functions may be noted in the following three classifications:

A. *"Forthtellers," or special spokesmen for God*. The term "prophet" (Heb., *nabi*, and Gr., *prophetes*) means to "speak for" or represent. Their foremost task was to act as divine ambassadors or messengers, declaring God's will for His people, especially in times of crisis. They were preeminently preachers of righteousness in times of moral and spiritual decay, often standing alone.

B. *"Foretellers," or forecasters of future events*. The credentials of a true prophet of God was his ability to inerrantly pierce and reveal the future (Deut. 18:21-22). This ability authenticated his message as from God, inasmuch as God alone knows the future. Through this prophetic function God called attention to His future program for Israel and the nations, further elaborating what He had already outlined in the covenants to the fathers.

C. *Teachers of the Law and righteousness*. Though the priests and Levites were the normal teachers in Israel, the prophets were also given this function when the priesthood fell into degeneracy (Lev. 10:11; Deut. 33:10; Ezek. 22:26). Their teaching ministry was usually in a context of judgment (Is. 6:8-10; 28:9-10).

II The Relation of the Prophets to the Priests

Though the prophets and priests were both appointed by God for religious service, they had some significant distinctions. These may be seen in several ways:

A. *As to their call,* the prophets were individually called and appointed by God, whereas the priests were appointed by virtue of their descendancy from Aaron.
B. *As to their office,* the prophets were representatives of God before the people; the priests were representatives of people before God. Therefore, the priests' primary place of ministry was the sanctuary, the place of God's Presence, whereas the prophets went to the cities and countryside of the people.
C. *As to their special work,* the prophets were concerned with spiritual righteousness and purification of the heart; the priests were more concerned with religious ritual and purification of outward symbols. Both functions were essential to Israel's covenant system, serving complementary roles.
D. *As to their teaching ministries,* both were expounders of the Law. As previously noted, the priests were the regular teachers, the prophets were the revival preachers.

The Times of the Writing Prophets of Israel*

JUDAH			ISRAEL		
DATE	KING	PROPHET	DATE	KING	PROPHET

CRISIS: In 931, at Solomon's death, the nation divided into two kingdoms, Judah and Israel.

DATE	KING	PROPHET	DATE	KING	PROPHET
931 B.C.	Rehoboam		931 B.C.	Jeroboam I	
913	Abijam				
911	Asa		910	Nadab	
			909	Baasha	
			886	Elah	
			885	Zimri	
			885	Omri	
873	Jehoshaphat		874	Ahab	(Elijah, 870–845)
			853	Ahaziah	
853	Jehoram	*OBADIAH* (845)	852	Jehoram	(Elisha, 845–798)
841	Ahaziah				

CRISIS: In 841 Jehu slew the kings of both kingdoms, took the throne of Israel, and destroyed rampant Baal worship in the Northern Kingdom.

DATE	KING	PROPHET	DATE	KING	PROPHET
841	Queen Athaliah		841	Jehu	
835	Joash	*JOEL* (830–825)			
			814	Jehoahaz	
796	Amaziah		798	Jehoash	
			793	Jeroboam II	*JONAH* (785–760)
792	Uzziah (Azariah)				*AMOS* (760)
			753	Zechariah	*HOSEA* (755–725)
750	Jotham		752	Shallum	
		ISAIAH (740–680)	752	Menahem	
		MICAH (730–720)	742	Pekahiah	
			752*	Pekah	
743	Ahaz				
728	Hezekiah		732	Hoshea	

The priests were the "informers," the prophets were the "reformers." The priests instructed the minds of the people, the prophets challenged the wills. Thus the prophets appeared when the Law had been neglected by the leaders and people, speaking with a strong sense of urgency.

III   The Various Classes of Prophets

The prophets of Israel go back to the founding fathers, Abraham, Moses, and Samuel, each of whom was called a "prophet" (Gen. 20:7; Deut. 18:15; 1 Sam. 3:20). Through them God spoke to the people and established His covenants with the nation. Moses was a kind of prototype of the prophets, adumbrating the final great Prophet Messiah who would arise to speak mighty words, authenticated by mighty works and clear fulfillments (Deut. 18:15-22). Though the offices of priest and king were restricted to men and specific tribes, several prophetesses were called to fill this office in Israel's history, Miriam, Deborah, and Huldah (Ex. 15:20; Judg. 4:4; 2 Kin. 22:14).

Samuel is generally considered to have begun the prophetic order, being the first of a succession during Israel's monarchy (1 Sam. 3:1; Acts 3:24). This succession of course was not unbroken, but sporadically continued as the Lord made appointments for special service. These prophets may be reviewed as "speaking" and "writing" prophets:

A. THE SPEAKING PROPHETS

1. Gad   Counseled David in the wilderness.   (1 Sam. 22:5)
2. Nathan   Counseled David on Covenant and his adultery. (2 Sam. 12:1)

DATE	KING	PROPHET	DATE	KING	PROPHET
CRISIS: In 722 Assyria destroyed Samaria and exiled Northern Israel to Assyria. Judah was spared because of Hezekiah's reformation and purge of idolatry.					
697	Hezekiah	NAHUM (c. 710)			
642	Manasseh				
640	Amon Josiah	JEREMIAH (627–585); ZEPHANIAH (625)			
609	Jehoahaz				
609	Jehoiakim	HABAKKUK (607)			
597	Jehoiachin				
597	Zedekiah	DANIEL (603–536); EZEKIEL (592–570)			
CRISIS: In 586 Babylon destroyed Jerusalem and exiled the Jews to Babylon. In 538 Persia released and dispatched the exiles to rebuild the temple in Jerusalem.					
536	Zerubbabel (Gov.)	HAGGAI (520); ZECHARIAH (520–480)			
CRISIS: In 444 Persia sent Nehemiah to rebuild Jerusalem's wall and to rule as governor.					
444	Nehemiah	MALACHI (430)			
*See "Chronologies of the Kings of the Divided Kingdom" for overlapping regencies.					

3.	Iddo	Wrote the Acts of Solomon.	(2 Chr. 9:29)
4.	Ahijah	Informed Jeroboam he would be king of North.	(1 Kings 11:29)
5.	Shemaiah	Warned Rehoboam not to resist Jeroboam.	(1 Kings 12:22)
6.	"Man of God"	Rebuked Jeroboam for calf worship.	(1 Kings 13:1)
7.	"Old Prophet"	Tested "man of God" to show certainty of word.	(1 Kings 13:11)
8.	Azariah	Encouraged Asa in his early reform movement.	(2 Chr. 15:1)
9.	Hanani	Rebuked Asa for Syrian help; was imprisoned.	(2 Chr. 16:7)
10.	Jehu, son of Hanani	Rebuked Baasha of Israel—"The dogs shall eat whoever belongs to Baasha."	(1 Kings 16:1)
		Rebuked Jehoshaphat for allying with Ahab.	(2 Chr. 19:2)
11.	Jahaziel	Counseled Jehoshaphat to trust God for victory.	(2 Chr. 20:14)
12.	Elijah	Rebuked Ahab and Jezebel for Baal worship.	(1 Kings 17:1ff.)
13.	Unknown Prophet	Counseled Ahab for victory over Syria.	(1 Kings 20:13)
14.	Micaiah	Informed Ahab of the Lord's plan for his death.	(1 Kings 22:14)
15.	Elisha	Rebuked Baal worship in Israel with many miracles.	(2 Kings 2:1ff.)
16.	Young Prophet	Anointed Jehu king and destroyer of Ahab's house.	(2 Kings 9:1ff.)
17.	Zechariah, son of Jehoiada	Rebuked Joash for apostasy and was slain by him.	(2 Chr. 24:20)
18.	Obed	Cautioned Pekah of Israel to release captive Jews.	(2 Chr. 29:9)

B. *THE WRITING PROPHETS*

Nearly all the "writing prophets" spoke and wrote after the "speaking prophets," as noted in the following chart. Beginning around the time of Jehu's purge of Baal worship, their periods of greatest concentration were just before the destruction of the North and just before that of the South. They usually spoke in times of national degeneracy and impending judgment, and were, in a sense, the nagging conscience of the nation. From this context we may note their major themes:

1. *Their Ethical Themes:*
   a. Condemnation of idolatry, immorality, and injustice with a call to repentance and righteous living.
   b. The character of God in requiring justice and mercy and promising judgment for the unrepentant.
   c. The character of true religion as related to the heart, not merely the hands.

2. *Their Eschatological Themes:*
   a. The coming day of the Lord and its impact on Israel and the nations.
   b. The character and coming of Messiah in judgment, salvation, and glory.
   c. The coming of the messianic age and its blessings for Israel and the world.
   d. The Lord's preservation of the faithful remnant of Israel.

The Book
of Isaiah

Introduction

AUTHORSHIP

A. *THE TITLE*

1. The name of this first prophetic book, "Isaiah," means "The Lord (YHWH) is salvation," a name expressive of the theme of the book, as well as of the overall theme of the prophets. Like all the books of The Prophets, Isaiah is named after its author.

2. It should be noted that the title of each prophetic book has a meaning that strikingly suggests its content. This was true also of the names of many individuals in the Old Testament whose names profiled their character, e.g., Abraham (father of nations), Jacob (supplanter), etc. God's covenant name, Yahweh, for instance, means "I Am," the One who everlastingly keeps His word.

B. *THE AUTHOR*

1. The prophet Isaiah is called the "prince of Old Testament prophets" because of the vast sweep, majestic character, theological insights, and messianic content of his prophecy. The text describes him quite briefly as the "son of Amoz," the husband of a prophetess, and the father of two sons who were to be for "signs" to the nation. (1:1; 8:3, 18). Jewish traditions also indicate that he was the cousin of King Uzziah and that he was sawn in half by wicked King Manasseh.

2. Being of the royal family, deeply spiritual, well-educated, and chaplain to the royal courts of four kings of Judah for some fifty years, Isaiah was perhaps the most monumental figure in the middle centuries of Israel's history.

C. *THE AUTHORSHIP DEBATE*

1. Although the Isaianic authorship of the whole book was practically undisputed until 1775, it is almost universally denied today by higher criticism. The basic reason for this denial relates to the very precise prophecies of the book, some of which were fulfilled in great detail 150 years later, even the naming of Cyrus, the Persian king who released the captives (44:28; 45:1). Many arguments have been summoned to support a dual or multiple authorship of the book, the main ones denying chapters 40–66 to the prophet Isaiah.

2. Arguments denying the single authorship by Isaiah:

   a. The exilic background of Isaiah 1–39 differs from that of chapters 40–66. Since 40–66 describe Jerusalem as ruined and the people afflicted by Babylon, these chapters must have been written after Jerusalem's destruction in 586 B.C. This conclusion follows from the usually valid premise that the prophets always spoke to their immediate generation concerning contemporary issues. To apply that premise universally would, of course, practically deny all long-range, predictive prophecy.

b. The literary style of Isaiah 1–39 differs from that of chapters 40–66. The assumption is that a writer would not alter his style over a period of 40–60 years even though he writes on a variety of subjects. (Would you then parcel Shakespeare's work because four different periods of style have been discerned in his productions, as Gleason Archer has noted, *In the Shadow of the Cross*.) It should be observed that numerous similarities in style prevail between the two sections of the book.

c. The theological viewpoints of the two divisions are also said to be different. The emphasis of 40–66 on God's infinitude is seen to differ from that of 1–39 on God's majesty. To deny the unity of any writing on the basis of a more advanced conception towards the end, however, is really so simplistic as to be absurd. The differences are only differences of progression.

3. Arguments for maintaining the single authorship of Isaiah:

a. The superscription of Isaiah 1:1 lists Isaiah as the author and no hint of a break or change is suggested between any of its divisions in any of the ancient manuscripts (confirmed also by the Dead Sea Scrolls and the LXX). The author of each of the other prophetic books identifies himself in an opening superscription (except Daniel who identifies himself numerous times throughout his book).

b. The historic setting of 40–66 better fits Palestine than Babylon in its background color of trees, rocks, hills, etc. Its background of widespread idolatry and the cities of Judah still standing also demands a time prior to the exile in Babylon. The strongest condemnations of idolatry are given in chapters 41, 44, 57, 65, and 66. Such idolatry was no longer a problem in Israel after the 586 captivity.

c. The two sections also have a theological symmetry in their views of God and Messiah. The term "Holy One of Israel" is used twenty-five times in the book, twelve in 1–39, and thirteen in 40–66, but only rarely by other writers. That consistency of theology prevails throughout.

d. Pre-exilic prophets refer to the writings of Isaiah 40–66 (e.g., Nah. 1:15 and Is. 52:7; Zeph. 2:15 and Is. 47:8; Jer. 31:35 and Is. 51:15). The resemblances strongly suggest the priority of Isaiah.

e. Jewish tradition is unbroken in attributing the whole book to Isaiah.

f. New Testament writers quote Isaiah more than all the other prophets together, citing Isaiah as the author of both sections. Note John the Baptist in Matthew 3:3 (Is. 40:3); John in John 12:38-41 (Is. 6:9-10; 53:1); and Paul in Romans 9:27-33 and 10:20 (Is. 10:22; 65:1).

g. The very issue of fulfilled prophecies was made a mark of divine prophecy by Isaiah (41:21-23, 26). To question precise prophecies as being written after the facts is to grossly misunderstand the prophets.

Outline of Isaiah

THEME: Salvation Is of the Lord—Both National and Personal.

h. It is inconceivable that the author of the most majestic literature of the Old Testament should have passed into anonymity, whereas all others are clearly identified.

HISTORICAL SETTING

A. *DATE OF WRITING*—c. 740–680 B.C.

1. Isaiah prophesied over sixty years, from before the death of Uzziah (740) to some time after the death of Sennacherib (681). See Isaiah 1:1; 6:1; 37:38.
2. He appears to have written the bulk of 1–39 during the reigns of Uzziah, Jotham, Ahaz, and Hezekiah and the remainder, 40–66, during the oppressive reign of Manasseh, perhaps between 697 and 680. His sufferings under Manasseh may have contributed background to his poignant passage on the "Sin-Bearing Servant" of 52:13-15. He himself suffered a similar fate.

B. *THE POLITICAL SETTING*

1. Internationally, the setting was that of Assyria's ascendancy to its greatest strength in the Empire. Tiglath-Pileser came west to invade northern Israel and Trans-Jordan in 745 and 734. Sargon and Shalmanezer besieged and destroyed Samaria in 724–722 in their drive through the North. Sennacherib under Sargon invaded Judah and western Palestine in an extended conquest from 714 to 701 that ended with the loss of his army in 701 at Jerusalem about the time of the pinnacle of his success. He never returned.
2. Nationally, it was a time of oppression and chaos. The northern kingdom had quickly deteriorated after Jeroboam II's "golden age," under six chaotic reigns. Judah had likewise deteriorated under idolatrous Ahaz. Many alliances with foreign powers were made to stave off total subjection to the mounting power of Assyria as it sought to engulf the west.

C. *THE SPIRITUAL SETTING*

1. Judah's spiritual condition in the mid-eighth century ran quite parallel with her political condition—both quickly deteriorated under King Ahaz (743–728). The great strength built up by godly Azariah and Jotham dissipated almost immediately as Ahaz (called Jehoahaz by Assyrians) began courting foreign alliances instead of relying on the Lord (Is. 7:12). Under attack by Syria and Israel, Ahaz futilely sought divine appeasement by sacrificing his oldest son on an altar, then invited the help of the Assyrians. The result was that he became a vassal of Tiglath-Pileser of Assyria, he lost the Red Sea access of Elath to the Edomites and much of the western Negeb to the Philistines, and he supplanted Jehovah worship with foreign idolatry in the temple.
2. The coming of Hezekiah to the throne of Judah brought an almost immediate reform movement in Judah. This began in the first month of his reign and included an unprecedented Passover held one month late which the Lord honored because of his good intentions to stem the tide of judgment (2 Chr. 30:1-13).

This hurried reform and zeal for revival by Hezekiah appears to have turned the tide of judgment and saved Judah from a fate similar to Israel's destruction in 722 B.C. Hezekiah's later alliances with Egypt and Babylon, however, brought the renewed aggression of Assyria against Judah which finally hemmed Jerusalem in, threatening its destruction, until the king took Isaiah's advice to rely completely on the Lord for deliverance. That deliverance came in 701 when the Angel of the Lord destroyed Sennacherib's army of 185,000 and ended his western campaign. The recording of this event constitutes the mid-point of Isaiah's prophecy, graphically demonstrating his emphasis in the first half, that the nation's first line of defense is to simply trust and obey their covenant Lord.

D. *CONTEMPORARY PROPHETS WITH ISAIAH*
1. The prophet Micah was Isaiah's rural counterpart in Judah. While Isaiah ministered to the royal court and aristocracy of Jerusalem, Micah preached to the common people of the western countryside of Judah, condemning the social inequities of the time. Like Isaiah, he also proclaimed the coming of Messiah who would be born in Bethlehem and would deliver both kingdoms in His final conquest.
2. The prophet Hosea was Isaiah's northern counterpart in Israel, especially during his early ministry. Hosea followed the fiery prophet, Amos, who had denounced the Samaritan leaders, ringing the changes of God's judgment on the northern kingdom. Complementing that judgment ministry, Hosea appealed to Israel's respect for their covenant relationship with the Lord, reminding them of His covenant love if they would yet respond to Him.

THE PURPOSE OF THE BOOK OF ISAIAH

The many purposes of Isaiah may be summarized by two grand purposes which relate to the divine titles: "the Holy One of Israel," and the "Suffering Servant."
1. To warn the nation of impending judgment because of their idolatry and worldly alliances. The historic interlude (36–39) describes this fulfillment in the invasion of Assyria and the prediction of a later captivity by Babylon. The "Holy One of Israel" required holiness of His people.
2. To remind the nation of God's program of deliverance, especially His redemptive program through Messiah who would come first as the Suffering Servant, and later as Ruler of the whole earth (52:13–53:12). These twofold purposes complement the theme of the book: "Salvation is of the Lord," not from idols or worldly alliances.

Unique Contributions of Isaiah

1. *ISAIAH, A MINIATURE BIBLE.* This book is often called a "miniature Bible" because of its organization and content. It has 66 chapters with two main divisions of 39

and 27 chapters. The first division emphasizes the Lord's judgments, and the last part presents His grace as the "suffering Servant," concluding with the final judgment. As Isaiah lived midway between Moses and Christ (c. 710 B.C.), he highlights both the Law that came by Moses and the grace that would come by Jesus Christ. The second division (40–66) also begins with a "voice" crying in the wilderness with a message of salvation, similar to the voice of John the Baptist who first announced that message in the New Testament. The two sections are bridged by an historic interlude (36–39) in which Israel is threatened by two world empires. The analogies of this book to the Old and New Testaments are quite remarkable.

The Structural Symmetry of Isaiah 40–66

The grandeur of Isaiah 40–66 can be seen in its architectural symmetry as well as in its content. This is suggested by the alerting refrain at the conclusion of each of the three nine-chapter sections: "*There is* no peace, for the wicked," graphically portrayed at the end of the last section in the wickeds' destruction (48:22; 57:21; 66:24). This symmetry may be seen in a pyramidal outline, converging on chapter 53.

I *THE GREATNESS OF GOD IN HIS WORK OF CREATION.* 40—48
40. His greatness as a sovereign Shepherd.
41. His greatness to deliver Israel.
42. His greatness to heal and judge.
43. His greatness to save the undeserving.
44. His greatness contrasted with Israel's idols.
45. His greatness to restore Israel by Cyrus.
46. His greatness over Babylon's gods.
47. His greatness to judge great Babylon.
48. His greatness to purge Israel of idolatry.

II *THE GRACE OF GOD IN HIS WORK OF SALVATION.* 49—57
49. The Lord's Servant as a world-wide Savior.
50. The Lord's Servant deplores Israel's divorce.
51. The Lord's Servant to save in righteousness.
52. The Suffering Servant announces His coming salvation.
AS A "LAMB"   53. The Suffering Servant makes atonement for sin through death.
54. His salvation promised barren Israel in remarriage.
55. His salvation extended to all the world.
56. His salvation made secure to all who respond.
57. His salvation extended to the worst of sinners.

2. **ISAIAH'S COMPREHENSIVE THEOLOGY.** The Book of Isaiah is the most comprehensible of all the Prophets in its theological sweep. Its prophecies range from Israel's immediate situation, the fall of the North and the South, the exile in Babylon and the return by the Persians, the coming of Messiah in humility, His life and atoning death for His people, the final scattering of the nation to all the earth, their regathering in repentance and their kingdom blessing in the messianic age. Its prophecies of the messianic age describe changes in all spheres of human life, e.g., spiritual, national, international, economic, geographic, cosmic, and the animal kingdom. Isaiah's theology of God is the most extensive and thorough of any book of the Old Testament.

3. **THE "HOLY ONE OF ISRAEL"** (1:4; 5:19, etc.). Isaiah referred to the Lord as the "Holy One of Israel" twenty-five times throughout the book, a term rarely used by other writers. This follows from his commission in 6:3 where the Seraphim introduced the Lord of Hosts as "Holy, holy, holy." In the midst of an unclean people he was reminded of the uncompromised holiness of God. With this revelation of His holiness, Isaiah was also reminded of the "Mighty One of Israel" (1:24), and the "Lord of

---

III *THE GLORY OF GOD IN HIS WORK OF RESTORATION.* 58—66
>   58. Israel's religious depravity deplored.
>   59. Israel's social depravity declared.
>   60. Israel's future righteousness and joy.
>   61. Israel's Bridegroom to come with jewels.
>   62. Israel's royal remarriage in righteousness.
>   63. Israel's great deliverance at His return.
>   64. Israel's penitence in great affliction.
>   65. Israel's purging for millennial glory.
>   66. Israel's re-birth in humility and joy.

Notice that the central chapter of each section (44, 53, 62) epitomizes the emphasis of that section, and all the chapters converge on the unbelievable report of 53. The first 13 chapters build up to it by reviewing Israel's great need and the Lord's promises, and the last 13 descend from it by applying its results to Israel and the world. Chapter 53 is central to the whole prophecy of consolation.

It might be noted, incidentally, that the middle four verses of 53 (5-8) constitute the heart of the gospel, Messiah being pierced by men in rejection and then having the sins of the world laid on Him by God. Furthermore, the word "lamb" (53:7) is almost the center word of this central chapter in the Hebrew and Septuagint texts. This is the only direct reference to Messiah as "lamb" in the whole Old Testament (though typified many times from Ex. 12:3 on). John the Baptist introduced Jesus by this designation to the disciples (John 1:29) and it becomes His preponderant name in Rev. 21–22. Messiah's work as Lamb of God is central to Isaiah's theme, as well as to the whole Bible.

hosts'' (used fifty-four times in Isaiah 1–39 and only six times in 40–66). His holiness and His might always complement each other. All the subsequent prophecies of judgment and deliverance relate to these characterizations of God who is mighty to save but never delivers through compromise with evil. This description of the thrice Holy God is not again seen until the similar six-winged creatures of Revelation 4:8 repeat it at the commencement of the tribulation judgments. The supreme focus of that holiness and might, however, is His work of redemption where ''The Lord has made bare His holy arm In the eyes of all the nations'' (52:10).

4. *THE "REDEEMER" OF ISRAEL* (41:14–63:16). This divine name is another unique name used by Isaiah (thirteen times, but only in the second half), occurring in other Old Testament books but five times. It is never used of the Lord in the New Testament, though often implied in the seventeen references to Christ's redemptive work in the Gospels and Epistles. The term derives from the verb ''gaal,'' signifying one that redeems (''goel'') or buys out of a market a person or piece of property (e.g. Lev. 25; 27). Its usage in Isaiah refers primarily to Israel's deliverance as a nation of blind and deaf refugees, captives to foreign enemies (41:14ff.; 44:24ff.; 54:5ff.). It also signifies spiritual redemption for those who ''turn from transgression'' (59:20). The term ''Savior'' (Yasha) is also used by Isaiah eight times (43:3, 11, etc.), a name often used of Christ in the New Testament.

5. *ISAIAH'S STRONG PROPHETIC CONFIRMATIONS.* Though the writing prophets were not miracle-workers, as were Moses, Elijah, and Elisha, the ministry of Isaiah did include some remarkable miracles (e.g., offering any sign to Ahaz, 7:11; destroying the Assyrian army in one night, 37:36; setting the sun back ten degrees, 38:8; healing Hezekiah, 38:21). These strongly confirmed the sovereignty of God over foreign gods. Another feature of Isaiah's long ministry was the many short-range prophecies that were fulfilled in his time or in the following centuries. A few examples would be: northern Israel's captivity by Assyria (7:4); Assyria's destruction (10:12, 25); Babylon's destruction at the hands of the Medes (13:17ff.); the judgment of Philistia, Moab, Damascus, Ethiopia, Egypt, and Tyre (14–23). These were fulfilled in great detail for all to observe. The naming of Cyrus the Persian 150 years before his birth to be the Lord's instrument to subdue nations in order to restore Israel's remnant and rebuild her temple dramatically demonstrates His sovereignty over time and all nations (44:28–45:6). The effects of many of these remain even today, e.g., Babylon, as the Lord predicted, has never been rebuilt (13:20).

These miracles and many fulfilled prophecies give strong validation to the many long-range prophecies that have not yet been fulfilled. Such short-range prophecies were designed to attest a prophet, as noted by Moses (Deut. 18:21-22). The long-range prophecies of the coming Day of the Lord with the Lord's great wrath against all nations (34), the complete restoration of Palestine to holiness, peace, and prosperity (35, 60–62), and the recreating of the heavens and earth with everlasting peace, prosperity, and holiness (65), will likewise be fulfilled with equal detail and certainty (34:16; 40:8;

41:23). The detailed fulfillment of short and long-ranged prophecies is seen by Isaiah to be the test and exclusive right of Israel's covenant God, Yahweh.

6. **THE LORD'S GREAT DISAPPOINTMENTS IN ISRAEL** (1, 5, 54). Isaiah portrays Israel's apostasies as great personal disasters in the Lord's family:
   a. In Isaiah's first vision the Lord announced to heaven and earth that His children had become juvenile delinquents, in spite of His careful rearing (1:2ff.). So corrupt had they become, He called them "Sodom" and "Gomorrah" (1:10).
   b. In chapter 5 the Lord sings a song of lamentation over Israel as a disappointing vineyard. Though He had tenderly planted and cultivated its vines and given them the best in horticulture, it produced "wild grapes." Instead of the fruit of righteousness, He found wickedness.
   c. In chapter 54 the Lord acknowledges His "wife" Israel had been unfaithful and had deserted Him and that He had left her as a youthful widow (54:4-8).

These three tragedies of marital infidelity and forsaking, the Lord's children becoming delinquents, and the crop failure of His choice vineyard, however, will one day be reversed. His faithless wife will be restored "like a woman forsaken" (54:4-8), or as "a young man marries a virgin," (62:5), His children will acknowledge the Lord as "Father" and "Redeemer" (63:16), and the people of Israel will become the Lord's "pleasant vineyard," filling the whole world with fruit (27:2-6 RSV). Besides having eschatological significance, the reversals of these tragedies through the Lord's grace and patience were obviously meant as personal encouragement for those who suffer similar tragedies and with patience trust the working of God's grace to bring about a glorious conclusion (64:4).

7. **ISAIAH'S PLEA FOR RIGHTEOUSNESS AND JUSTICE.** Like Micah, his contemporary, Isaiah strongly emphasizes the need for heart righteousness and social justice (Mic. 6:6-8). The terms "righteousness" (*tsedeq* and *tsedaqah*) and "justice" (*mishpat*) are used some eighty times by Isaiah, more than any other book except the Psalms. The Lord's initial complaint was that Israel had supplanted righteousness with evil, violence, murder, and thievery (1:16-23). Twice the Lord deplores their perfunctory rituals of fasting and "futile sacrifices" because these had become a cover-up for greed and oppression (1:11-15; 58:4-5). The Lord's idea of a "fast" was to give freedom to the oppressed and bread to the hungry (58:6ff.). Isaiah 58 could well have been Jesus' text in His contrast of true and false righteousness in His Sermon on the Mount.

8. **THE VIRGIN BIRTH OF IMMANUEL** (7:14). This prophecy of the virgin birth is the first of the "Immanuel prophecies" (7–12) in which Messiah's coming is elaborated upon. Though this virgin birth prophecy has been much debated, the New Testament settles the fact of Messiah's divine conception and virgin birth in both the grammar and context of Matthew 1:23. The New Testament word, "virgin" (*parthenos*) can have no other meaning than "virgin." But, since Ahaz was promised a "sign" in the prophecy, various attempts have been made to relate the virgin birth to a fulfillment in his time.

Some scholars see the prophecy as having its complete fulfillment in the birth of the son of Isaiah (8:3) or of Ahaz. Some see it as having a near fulfillment (Isaiah's son) and a far fulfillment. Others see it as two prophecies with two distinct fulfillments in the near and far future. To properly view this important prophecy, several factors should be kept in mind concerning the grammar and context:

a. The context requires a near fulfillment to constitute a "sign" (or rebuke) to the "house of David," presumably to Ahaz for refusing the deliverance God offered.

b. The term "virgin" (*almah*), like the New Testament term "*parthenos,*" does not refer to a married woman in either of the Old Testament references (Gen. 24:43; Is. 7:14), (nor does the LXX translate it as such).

c. Since the prophecy was not given as a "type," but as a specific prediction, a double fulfillment would require a genuine virgin birth in both the near and the far fulfillments. To assume Isaiah's wife was a virgin at the time of the prophecy would not make her to be a "virgin with child" when she conceived.

d. No child besides Messiah was ever called "Immanuel" in either Testaments. The name means "God with us," which could be said of no one but Messiah Himself.

e. Isaiah was instructed to bring his son Shear-Jashub with him as he brought this message to Ahaz (7:3), evidently because his name (meaning, "a remnant shall return") was designed as a "sign" or message to Israel (8:18). This name signified first that a judgment would leave few survivors ("Shear," a remnant), and that a small return would follow ("Jashub"). (C. W. E. Nagelsbach, *Langes Commentary of the Bible, Isaiah.*) This judgment was to occur before the "boy" was age 12 (knew to refuse evil and choose good). Those eating "curds and honey" are identified in v. 22 as the remnant.

These considerations suggest that two prophecies were given in 7:14-16, one a prediction of the virgin birth of Immanuel as later noted in 9:6, and the second a prediction that the Assyrian king would defeat the northern confederacy before Isaiah's son Shear-Jashub came to the age of accountability. But, because Ahaz had rejected the deliverance the Lord offered, he and his people Judah would also experience the judgment of the Assyrians who nearly devastated Judah also (7:16-25).

This answers the need for a sign to Ahaz as a near fulfillment and also preserves the single fulfillment of the virgin birth which could obviously be one of a kind. For a similar twofold prophecy with two distinct fulfillments, see the prophecy to Jeroboam I of the distant coming of Josiah and the immediate splitting of the altar as a "sign" to that unbelieving king (1 Kin. 13:1-5).

9. **THE FALL OF LUCIFER** (14:4-20). Though Satan appears many times throughout the Bible (called Satan eighteen times in Old Testament and thirty-five times in New Testament, and the devil "diabolos" thirty-five times in New Testament), only Isaiah 14 and Ezekiel 28 describe his creation, perfection, and great fall. In Isaiah 14:4 he is seen as the "king of Babylon," and in Ezekiel 28:12, as the "king of Tyre," because he was the diabolic power behind them. Daniel also spoke of the "prince of Persia" and the "prince of Greece" (Dan. 10:20), as battling with Michael the archangel, obviously a

reference to the evil spirits behind these heathen nations. The description of this "king of Babylon," presuming to be like the Most High, falling from heaven, and thrust to the recesses of the pit, expands far beyond that of a man such as Nebuchadnezzar (who is last seen in Daniel exalting and honoring the "Most High God" after his judgment for pride, 4:37). It rather relates to the similar taunt over the "king of Tyre" in Ezekiel 28:12ff. who is also described in figurative terms that are superhuman. He is the one who claimed "all the kingdoms of the world" (Matt. 4:8), as he confronted Jesus in the wilderness. Isaiah introduced him here as an outstanding example of the fate of one who vaunted himself against God.

10. *ISAIAH'S CLASSIC SCORN OF IDOLATRY* (44–46). No book has more brilliant satire showing the utter idiocy of idolatry than does Isaiah in 40–48. The classic chapters are 44 and 46, where he contrasts the Lord's omnipotence and omniscience with the lifeless "block of wood" that could neither walk nor talk, let alone deliver them or predict the future (44:19). As Elijah made sport of Ahab's Baal gods when they were introduced to the north, so Isaiah ridiculed this new generation of idolators as Manasseh re-introduced these gods to Judah. Neither Elijah nor Isaiah, however, were successful in effecting any great revival in their generations. Idolatry in any form is strangely unmoved either by the great miracles of Elijah or by the great literature of Isaiah, simply because their problem is not intellectual, but spiritual or willfull.

11. *THE SUFFERING SERVANT* (53). Isaiah 41–53 presents a series of "servant" passages building to a portrayal of the suffering Servant in 52:13–53:12. In this climactic preview of the suffering Servant, a most revealing description of Jesus' person and work in His first coming is given (cf. Mark 10:45). Some of these features are not even given in the Gospels. Isaiah notes that this report is one that will not be believed (53:1). He describes this Servant as having no human beauty, but despised and an embarrassment to men (53:2-3); they regard Him as disapproved and afflicted of God (53:4). In the hands of men he is marred beyond human resemblance (52:14). Though wounded by men, this did not bring salvation, but the fact that the Lord laid on Him the transgressions of all (53:6, 10). Surprisingly, this offering "pleased" the Father in that it made full satisfaction concerning the sin issue. This pleasure is also seen in the fact that His one offering provided full atonement for sin and continual intercession for sinners (53:10-12).

Yet the identity of this "servant" has been greatly debated, inasmuch as similar references are made of Israel. Five basic passages are involved: 42:1-9; 44:1-5; 49:1-6; 50:4-9; and 52:13–53:12. The best harmonization of this servant identity is that suggested by Franz Delitzsch (*The Pentateuch*), which recognizes three levels of servanthood, symbolized in the form of a pyramid:

a. Israel is the first level of servanthood (broad base of pyramid), being called to be the Lord's servant, but failing miserably (41:14; 42:19; 44:21).

b. The faithful remnant of Israel is the second level (narrower mid-section of the pyramid), serving as the Lord's witness to the faithless nation (48:20; 49:3, 5; and 50:10).

c. Messiah Himself is the ultimate Servant (symbolized as the apex of the pyramid), who came as the perfect Servant of the Lord, fulfilling God's will to bring redemption to Israel and the world (42:1-4; 49:1-7; 52:13-53:12; cf. Mark 10:45). As such He became the ultimate offering for sin and the Eternal Priest for sinners, making both propitiation and intercession (53:12).

12. **THE CHRISTOLOGY OF ISAIAH.** No book of the Old Testament is so thoroughly messianic as is Isaiah. It is sometimes called the "Fifth Gospel" or the "Evangelical Prophet," because of its many previews of Messiah. This messianic content may be seen in several categories:

a. The Person of Messiah.
   1) To be truly human, born of a woman (7:14; 9:6; 53:2).
   2) To be virgin born; by supernatural conception (7:14).
   3) To be God in human flesh (9:6).
   4) To be the Son of David (9:7; 11:1, 10).
   5) To be Jehovah (YHWH) the Creator of all things (44:24; 45:11-12).

b. The Character of Messiah.
   1) To be humble and unattractive (7:14-15; 53:2-3).
   2) To be gentle, not loud or rough (40:11; 42:2-3).
   3) To be righteous in all His actions (9:7; 11:5; 32:1).
   4) To be gracious to the weak and afflicted (61:1).
   5) To be angry and vengeful toward the unrepentant wicked (11:4; 63:1-4).

c. The Work of Messiah.
   1) To be introduced by a forerunner in the wilderness (40:3).
   2) To be anointed to work in the power of the Holy Spirit (11:2-4; 61:1).
   3) To preach and give counsel as a prophet (11:2-4).
   4) To perform many miracles, especially at His Second Coming (35:4-6).
   5) To be unbelieved by His own generation (53:1).
   6) To die with the wicked and be buried with the rich (53:9).
   7) To be pierced and crushed for our iniquities (53:5).
   8) To have the iniquities of all persons laid on Him by God (53:6).
   9) To be the conqueror of death (25:8).
   10) To angrily trample the wicked at His Second Coming (34:2-9; 63:1-6).
   11) To be the King of Israel (9:7; 44:6).
   12) To reign as "Lord of Hosts" on Mount Zion in Jerusalem (24:23).

The Book of Jeremiah

Introduction

AUTHORSHIP

A. *THE TITLE*

This prophecy is reflected in the name of its author, Jeremiah, whose name means "The Lord (YHWH) appoints or establishes." His unlikely prophecies were greatly assaulted in his time, but they were firmly established words of the Lord, as his later contemporaries came to realize. The title announces that certainty.

B. *THE AUTHOR*

1. The authorship by Jeremiah is well attested and has not been seriously challenged. Its confirmation may be seen in two general ways:

   a. Internally, the book has numerous biographical and autobiographical references to Jeremiah as the author and Baruch as recorder or secretary. The name of no other prophet is so often repeated as that of Jeremiah (131 times). Baruch is mentioned twenty-three times.

   b. Externally, the book is attributed to Jeremiah in Daniel 9:2 and Ezra 1:1, as well as by unbroken Jewish tradition.

2. The personal background of Jeremiah is intrinsically involved in the prophecy. For this reason more is known about this prophet personally than of any other writing prophet. In many instances his actions became a part of the message. From these notes a personal sketch of the prophet may be drawn:

   a. He was born c. 647 in Anathoth, a priestly town some three miles NE of Jerusalem. He was the son of Hilkiah who was probably the high priest at the time of Josiah's reformation and the great-grandfather to Ezra (Ezra 7:1).

   b. He was ordained a prophet by the Lord before birth (1:5), and was called in Josiah's thirteenth regnal year at about age twenty (1:2).

   c. He was not married, being forbidden of the Lord to marry as a sign to the people of Jerusalem's near destruction (16:2ff.).

   d. Jeremiah ministered in Jerusalem about forty years (627–586) and in Egypt five years (43–44), counseling five kings and one governor of Judah, as well as the mutinous remnant that fled to Egypt.

   e. Though a deeply sensitive, compassionate man, Jeremiah was called to a ministry of pronouncing inexorable judgment on the nation. Regarded as a traitor in giving these judgments, he seems to have had hardly a convert in his long ministry of over forty years.

   f. Though unpopular and despised while prophesying and urging submission to

Babylon, he later became the folk hero of the remnant in Babylon after his predictions of judgment came true and they recalled also his predictions of a future release and return.

HISTORICAL SETTING

A. *DATE OF WRITING*—627–580 B.C.
  1. Jeremiah's ministry began in the reign of Josiah and continued in Jerusalem through eighteen years of reform and twenty-two years of national collapse.

Outline of Jeremiah

THEME: Judah's Final Rebellion and Removal from the Covenant Land.

2. Forced to go to Egypt with the rebellious remnant in 586, he prophesied there for perhaps five years, condemning their idolatry (44:8) and announcing the soon coming of Nebuchadnezzar to conquer Egypt (which occurred in 568).

B. *THE POLITICAL SETTING*

1. Internationally, this was a time of the nations jockeying for preeminence in world power. The three nations especially involved were Assyria, Babylon, and Egypt. In 626, Nabopolassar of Babylon with the help of the Medes took the city of Babylon from Assyria who had been the world power for nearly two centuries. In 612, they destroyed Nineveh, and in 610 took Haran. The mop-up came in 605 when Babylon defeated the Egyptian army at Carchemish and took control of Palestine. This brought Nebuchadnezzar quickly to the zenith of power at the death of his father in 605, though Egypt itself was not conquered till 568. The Middle East then was in turmoil during much of this period, as Jeremiah vainly urged Josiah's sons to submit to Babylon.

2. Nationally, the time of Jeremiah's prophecy was one of the blackest in Jewish history as the sins of the fathers (idolatry) were visited with divine judgment. This judgment was made up of four national tragedies in Israel:

   a. *In 609*, Josiah was slain at Megiddo trying to stop Pharaoh Necho from going to the aid of Assyria in the battle with Babylon. This death, following his great reformation and political expansion, became one of Israel's greatest tragedies, deeply mourned by the whole nation.

   b. *In 606*, Nebuchadnezzar took Jerusalem from Egyptian control and began Judah's deportation by taking some of her royal sons to Babylon, among whom was Daniel. His purpose was to train them for government service.

   c. *In 597*, Nebuchadnezzar had to send his army to Jerusalem on two occasions to quell Judah's rebellion and alignment with Egypt. In the first, King

Jehoiakim was slain and "cast out to the heat of the day and the frost of the night," (36:30); in the second, Jehoiachin was taken by Babylon after a reign of three months. At that time Nebuchadnezzar pillaged the city and temple of their sacred treasures and exiled the higher class of the population to Babylon (2 Kin. 24:11-16).

    d. *In 586,* Jerusalem and the temple were destroyed by Nebuchadnezzar after another rebellion and a two-year siege of the city. This destruction was epochal, even to world history, and almost inconceivable to the Jewish mind who saw Jerusalem as a part of the nation's eternal destiny.

C. *THE RELIGIOUS SETTING*

1. Jeremiah was born during the final years of King Manasseh as he futilely sought to reform the nation that he had led into idolatry, bloodshed, and moral corruption. Though he repented in a Babylon prison and was restored, his long reign of wickedness had exhausted God's patience, dooming the nation to destruction.

2. Following a short, two-year reign by Manasseh's son Amon (also wicked), Josiah came to the throne in 640 at the tender age of eight. This began a glorious period of reform, revival, and political expansion for Judah. Several stages of this time of peace and prosperity should be noted:

    a. *In 632,* Josiah (age 15) began to seek the Lord (2 Chr. 34:3).

    b. *In 628* (at age 19), he began a thorough purge of idolatry in Jerusalem and Judah and enforced it as far north as Naphtali by Galilee (2 Chr. 34:3ff.).

    c. *In 622* (at age 25), after Hilkiah the High Priest found the "Book of the Law" in the temple structure and Huldah the prophetess declared its judgment, Josiah reconvened the elders of the nation to intensify the reform and enforce the commitment of all the people to the purge.

    d. *In 622* at Passover time, Josiah held the greatest Passover Feast in Israel since the time of Samuel, carefully observing every detail.

3. Josiah's revival, though sincerely promoted by the king, was evidently superficially followed by his leaders and people. The nation was divinely pegged for destruction because of the prolonged wickedness of Manasseh and the deeply ingrained decadence of the people. Following Josiah's untimely death in battle at Megiddo, the nation almost immediately reverted to idolatry and corruption.

THE PURPOSE OF THE BOOK OF JEREMIAH

The purpose of this long prophecy (longer even than Isaiah) was to record the Lord's eleventh-hour warnings to the nation as it plunged into spiritual disaster and national destruction. The book portrays not only their rejection of God's Law, but their adamant refusal to be corrected by God's prophets. Unlike Isaiah's plea that they trust the Lord for national deliverance, Jeremiah's message was that the nation should submit to the Lord's judgment of Babylonian captivity and thereby save the city and nation from total destruction. The book shows how his lone cry in the night went almost totally unheeded. His theme text might well have been Proverbs 29:1: "He who is often reproved, *and* hardens *his* neck, Will suddenly be destroyed, and that without remedy."

Unique Contributions of Jeremiah

1. *THE WEEPING PROPHET* (9:1). Jeremiah follows Isaiah as a foreshadowing of the "man of sorrows" prophesied in Isaiah 53:3. Jeremiah, in fact, saw himself as a "docile lamb brought to the slaughter" (11:19). Though most of the prophets brought messages of judgment, none did so with such personal feeling and weeping as did Jeremiah. His words in 9:1 give a classical description of his personal involvement: "O that my head were waters, And my eyes a fountain of tears, That I might weep day and night. . . ." Jesus, likewise, wept over Jerusalem as He spoke of the coming of a second destruction of the city (Luke 19:41).

2. *THE TRAITOR PROPHET* (26:9ff.). Ironically, Jeremiah was considered a traitor to his nation for his insistence that they surrender to Babylon. This was in striking contrast to the preaching of Isaiah who crusaded for faithful resistance to the enemy, trusting God for victory. Jeremiah prophesied during the blackest period of Israel's history, when all hope for the nation's survival had been lost. Judah had "crossed the Rubicon" (because of Manasseh's sins), and surrender to Babylon was the Lord's one option to prevent the complete destruction of Jerusalem. After these prophecies of doom came true, however, Jeremiah was remembered by the remnant in Babylon with great respect. Especially endearing were his prophecies of a regathering after seventy years of captivity in Babylon (25:11; 29:10).

3. *JEREMIAH'S MESSAGE OF HOPE.* Among his prophecies of doom, Jeremiah also had a bright message of ultimate hope for the nation. This optimistic note is struck in four brief passages and in four later chapters (3:16-18; 12:14-15; 23:3-8; and 30–33). These references relate to the covenants the Lord made with the fathers which guaranteed the continuance of the house of Jacob and of the kingly line of David (33:26). Even at a time when righteousness had practically vanished from the nation, the covenant of blessing had been thoroughly broken, and a great heathen power was about to devour the covenant people, the Lord reassured them that His covenants were as inviolable as the fixed order of day following night (31:36-37; 33:20-26). No generation of sinners could cause Him to modify His promises to the fathers. At no time in Israel's history could these reassurances be more significant, theologically.

4. *THE NEW COVENANT* (31:31-34). In addition to the unconditional covenants made with the fathers, Jeremiah announced the fact that a new covenant would be made to replace the Mosaic covenant made at Sinai (31:32). Having broken and forsaken the covenant

made at Sinai, they were about to be evicted from the covenant land (11:3-10). That covenant was a conditional agreement which allowed them the privilege of tenancy in the land. That conditional covenant of blessing, however, would one day be replaced by a new covenant, which would be established with "the house of Israel and with the house of Judah" (31:31). The specific substance of that new covenant is not revealed, but it is to be made with a believing remnant of the whole nation who know the Lord (34). Its nature will be an inward guidance to the heart rather than an outward legal code or script. The writer of Hebrews 8:7-13 and 10:16-17 refers to this promise to demonstrate that the Mosaic covenant was only temporary, ending at the cross (Heb. 7:12), and that it would be replaced by a new and permanent covenant of blessing which would also be made with the "house of Israel and with the house of Judah." The context of Jeremiah 31:31 shows how this new covenant also relates to their restoration to the land, just as their breaking the Mosaic covenant related to their eviction.

5. **THE "CURSE ON CONIAH"** (22:24-30). Jeremiah's reference to Coniah in this passage is commonly interpreted as a curse on his line, nullifying the right of any of his descen-

Chronology of Jeremiah's Prophecies

REIGN	DATES*	CHAPTERS	PROPHECY OR EVENT
Josiah	627–609 B.C.	1–20	Even during Josiah's reformation, Jeremiah announced judgment on Judah because of the sins of Manasseh (15:4). Interspersed are undated, short vignettes from latter prophecies.

The Death of Josiah Terminated Reformation and Began Evil Reigns of Josiah's Sons.

REIGN	DATES*	CHAPTERS	PROPHECY OR EVENT
Jehoiakim	609	26	Jehoiakim, in his first year, sought to slay Jeremiah.
	605	35:11	Judah's disobedience is contrasted with obedient Rechabites.
	605	25	Judah's unrepentance to bring seventy years desolation by Babylon.
	605	36	Jehoiakim disdains and burns Jeremiah's word from the Lord.
	605	45	Jeremiah encourages his faithful secretary, Baruch, concerning his personal safety during the coming judgment by Babylon.
	605	46–49	As Babylon defeated Egypt at Carchemish, Jeremiah announced God's judgment on Egypt and all Palestine (49:34ff. in 597).

The Rebellion of Jehoiakim and Jeconiah Brought the Deportation of 597 to Babylon.

REIGN	DATES*	CHAPTERS	PROPHECY OR EVENT
Zedekiah	597	24	The Lord portrays Zedekiah's administration as "bad figs," compared to Jeconiah's exiled group seen as "very good figs."
	597	27	Jeremiah warns Zedekiah and all nations to submit to Babylon, against the contrary advice of the false prophets.
	594	28	False prophet Hananiah dies for contradicting Jeremiah.
	594	29	False prophet Shemaiah is cursed for contradicting Jeremiah's prophecy of seventy years captivity.
	594	50–51	Jeremiah sends word to Jews in Babylon of the coming total destruction of Babylon for its pride and viciousness.

dants to the throne of David ("Coniah" being short for Jeconiah or Jehoiachin). Inasmuch as Joseph, Jesus' legal father, descended from Coniah, such a curse would jeopardize Jesus' proper claim to being the "King of Israel," sitting on David's throne (Luke 1:32). To avoid this so-called "curse," many interpreters have sought to re-route Jesus' ancestry through a levirate marriage of Coniah's son Shealtiel, or by linking it to the line of Mary (Luke 3:23ff.). Those solutions have two insurmountable problems: 1) The line of Mary had no right to the throne, for her ancestry traced to David through Nathan, not Solomon (through whom the royal line had to come (1 Chr. 22:9-10). 2) Matthew proved Jesus' right to the throne by his genealogy from David through His legal father Joseph who came from Coniah and Solomon (Matt. 1:1-16). Neither Matthew nor the alert genealogists of his time recognized any curse on Coniah's line. Though commentators of church history have almost universally inferred such a curse, the biblical commentators seem to recognize none. In Jeremiah's ten references to this young king who reigned but three months, the prophet recorded nothing for which such a curse should be pronounced on his line. Much is said of the evil of Jehoiakim and Zedekiah, but only passing references to Coniah.

A re-examination of the pronouncement of judgment in 22:30, in fact, gives strong

REIGN	DATES*	CHAPTERS	PROPHECY OR EVENT
Nebuchadnezzar Began Siege of Jerusalem January 10, 588 (39:1; 52:4).			
	Undated	30	Jeremiah announces a future time of restoration of Israel and Judah, to come after the "time of Jacob's trouble" (30:3-9).
	Undated	31	Jeremiah predicts a "new covenant" to be made with Israel and Judah after restoration, replacing the Mosaic (31:31-34).
	588	21–23	As Babylon surrounded Jerusalem, Zedekiah sought Jeremiah for a deliverance miracle, but is refused and given a history lesson on how the Lord judged his wicked brothers.
	588	32–33	Jeremiah purchases a field near Jerusalem, symbolizing a future restoration. That restoration to be brought by a righteous "Branch" of David who will guarantee Israel's continuance.
	587	37	Jeremiah again in prison (as Babylon briefly withdraws to fight Egypt), reaffirms to Zedekiah the certainty of coming captivity.
	587	34	Jeremiah denounces leaders for failure to keep the covenant of releasing slaves, another reason for coming judgment by Babylon.
	587	38	Jeremiah (in prison) repeats counsel to submit to Babylon and avoid destruction of Zedekiah, his family, and Jerusalem.
	586	39, 52	Jerusalem falls to Babylon, Zedekiah's sons and nobles are slain, and Zedekiah is blinded and exiled as Jeremiah is released.
*The Destruction of Jerusalem Occurred August 10, 586 (52:12).***			
Gedaliah	586	40–44	Gedaliah is made governor, is slain by roaming rebels who then take Jeremiah with them to Egypt. There he denounces their idolatry and foretells their destruction when Babylon arrives.

*Most chapters or groups of chapters date themselves in the first verse.
**2 Kings 25:8 gives the "7th" of the fifth month. Since the destruction of the second temple occurred on Aug. 9th, 70, rabbis have settled on the 9th as the commemorating day for both destructions of Jerusalem.

evidence that the curse was administered to Zedekiah, not Coniah. This is seen in the broad context of chapters 21–22 in which Jeremiah responds to Zedekiah's request for a miracle to deliver them from the Babylonians who had surrounded the city. Instead of deliverance, the prophet warned of certain invasion, reminding him of what the Lord had done to his wicked brothers, Shallum and Jehoiakim (21:9; 22:11-19). Because young Coniah had been exiled to Babylon nine years before, Jeremiah asked Zedekiah if he thought that prince was discarded forever. He then addressed all the earth with the pronouncement: "Write this man down as childless . . . none of his descendants shall prosper, Sitting on the throne of David" (22:30). The identity of "this man" was not Coniah (who was in faraway Babylon), but the arrogant king to whom Jeremiah was sending this message (cf. 21:7). As Nebuchadnezzar shortly took the city, the sons of Zedekiah were slain before his eyes and his own eyes were put out before removal to Babylon. Coniah (Jehoiachin), however, was later released and elevated in Babylon (Jeremiah's final note in the book), and his grandson Zerubbabel later returned to Judah as governor (Hag. 2:21). The difficulty in 22:24, "though Coniah . . . were the signet . . . ring," is also cleared up by the alternate reading, "since (ki) Coniah is the signet ring . . . , I will pull you (Zedekiah) off." The only other person called the Lord's "signet ring" in the Old Testament is Zerubbabel, the grandson of Coniah, who returned to rule as governor over Judah (Hag. 2:21-23). As far as the Old and New Testament writers are concerned, the genealogical line of Jesus through Coniah never had a "curse," but was guaranteed inviolable by the Lord's covenant oath (Ps. 89:29-37).

6. **CHRISTOLOGY IN JEREMIAH.** The Book of Jeremiah is the least messianic of the Major Prophets. Only two passages speak directly of Messiah, 23:5-6 and 33:14-17. Both of these refer to Him as a "Branch of righteousness" who will reign on the throne of David and execute judgment and righteousness in the earth. Both also stress the "righteousness" of His people and of His reign, a stark contrast to the people and leaders to whom Jeremiah ministered. In chapter 23, His name is called, "The Lord Our Righteousness," and in chapter 33, His people are called, "The Lord Our Righteousness." His righteousness will be their righteousness.

The Book of Lamentations

Introduction

AUTHORSHIP

A. *THE TITLE*

1. The Hebrews called it *"Ekah"* (How), after the first word in chapters 1, 2, and 4, a characteristic word of lament. Later rabbis called it *"Qinoth"* (cf. Jer. 7:29), meaning "loud cries" or lamentations, as a funeral dirge.

2. "Lamentation" is the Latin translation of the Greek term *"threnoi,"* meaning "loud cries."

B. *THE AUTHOR*
   1. Though the book is anonymous, its authorship is attributed to Jeremiah by both Jewish and Christian traditions. He was one of the leaders in lamenting over Josiah's death, and he was instructed by the Lord in Jeremiah 7:29 to have the people "take up a lamentation on the desolate heights. . . ." Though the literary styles may be somewhat different in the two books, many of the themes and expressions are quite similar. Edward Young notes the following striking similarities: "The oppressed virgin daughter of Zion," Lam. 1:15; Jer. 7:21; "The prophet's eyes flow down with tears," Lam. 1:16; 2:11; Jer. 9:1, 18b; 13:17b; "fear and terrors surround," Lam. 2:22; Jer. 6:25; 20:10; "appeal to God for vengeance," Lam. 3:64-66; Jer. 11:20, among many others.

Outline of Lamentations

THEME: The Human Misery and Divine Meaning of Jerusalem's Destruction.

2. Perhaps no one was better prepared for the writing of these laments than Jeremiah in emotional make-up, spiritual concern, and literary expression. Nor was anyone more historically a part of the scene as an eyewitness to the tragic event. As with the Book of Jeremiah, Baruch may have been the writer as the prophet dictated these expressions of grief (cf. Jer. 36:4).

HISTORICAL SETTING

A. *DATE OF WRITING*—586 B.C.

Two considerations enter into the problem of dating this book, its emotional content and expressions and its exquisite composition. The torrent of grief expressed suggests a time soon after the hallowed city's fall while its memory was still fresh; the exquisite and labored composition done in alphabetic acrostics, on the other hand, suggests a quite long period of reflection and literary construction. To attain these, it is possible that it was composed by the prophet in the immediate wake of the holocaust and then reconstructed with its acrostic refinements for mnemonic purposes some time after. Its initial writing then would have taken place in the summer of 586, in the middle of August.

B. *DATE OF JERUSALEM'S DESTRUCTION*

The ninth of Ab (fifth month) is the commonly accepted date for the yearly commemoration of the destruction of Jerusalem, since its second destruction in A.D. 70. Since other dates are given in the biblical text, the various dates need to be harmonized.

July 9, 586 — City wall broken down, escaped king pursued (Jer. 52:6-11).
Aug. 7, 586 — Temple, city, and houses burned (2 Kin. 25:8-9).
Aug. 10, 586 — Destruction and burning completed (Jer. 52:12-16).
Oct. ? 586 — Gedaliah is slain by Ishmael and dissidents (Jer. 41:1-2).

Since the temple destruction of A.D. 70 occurred on August 9, that date is used to commemorate the destruction of both temples.

C. *THE POLITICAL SETTING*

1. See The Book of Jeremiah Introduction for national and international setting.
2. The flight and capture of Zedekiah brought an end to the Davidic dynasty in its historic movement. This ignominious end came about because of Zedekiah's arrogant rejection of Jeremiah's warning and because of his betrayal and ingratitude to Nebuchadnezzar who had taken the kingdom from Jehoiachin and had given it to Zedekiah. For this he suffered the greatest royal humiliation; the last sight he beheld, before his eyes were torn out, was the slaying of his sons and nobility. He was then taken to Babylon in chains (Jer. 39:6-7).
3. The fall of Jerusalem in the mid-summer of 586 followed a siege of nineteen months that left famine and pestilence in its wake. Though Jerusalem had been threatened and pillaged a number of times, this event of its destruction was almost inconceivable to the Jewish mind who saw it as an eternal city (1 Chr.

17:12; 22:10). With the leveling of the city went any vain presumptions of its divine inviolability. It appeared that the nation was irretrievably finished, if not the race, since their heirs were also being slain.

D. *THE RELIGIOUS SETTING*
1. The time of writing this book of five poems was doubtless the darkest hour of Israel's religion. All the underpinnings of her faith appeared to have been removed. The city chosen by God was leveled, the temple God designed and indwelt was a heap of ashes, and her people were carried off to the idolatrous land of their origin, Babylon. Even the Lord Himself refused to hear their prayers and had become their enemy (Jer. 14:11-12). Jeremiah's forty years of preaching appears to have gone without the least apparent response.
2. The temple's destruction brought on a new era in Israel's religion, the dispersion era of the synagogue. With the passing of the temple, much of the ritual system was suspended, inasmuch as the offerings that accompanied the feasts and sacred events could only be made at the temple altar. In Babylon they learned to worship and study Torah in small gatherings which the rabbis called little "sanctuaries," or synagogues (Ezek. 11:16). Here the faithful were forced to recall and refine their faith to survive as a race in the heathen culture.
3. The one thing remaining of the covenant faith of Israel was their scriptures with the covenant promises of the Lord to their fathers. Stripped of all else, they were made to meditate and rely on these more than ever before.

THE PURPOSE OF THE BOOK OF LAMENTATIONS

The obvious purpose of this "Sea of sobs" was to give literary expression to the great grief of the faithful of Israel over the immense loss of their sacred city and temple. These Lamentations express the depth of Israel's loneliness when the Glory of the Lord departed in shame from her midst. A further purpose was to record how completely and literally the Lord fulfilled His warnings of judgment on this venerated city and sanctuary when they persisted in idolatry and rebellion. Lamentations brilliantly confirms the sovereignty of God, acknowledging Him as the perpetrator of this devastation, not just Babylon (2:17; 3:37-38). The bright ray of hope is that He is not only faithful in judgment, but also in fulfilling His promises of lovingkindness. "Great *is* Your faithfulness," in both judgment and compassion (3:22-23). The covenants also had promises of divine restoration for repentance.

Unique Contributions of Lamentations

1. *THE "JEWISH WAILING WALL."* Jerusalem has suffered several massive destructions in its history, three of which were completed on the calendar day "Ninth of Ab" (August 9, cf. H. H. Ben-Sasson, *History of the Jewish People*, p. 333). These were the Babylonian

destruction in 586 B.C., the Roman destruction in A.D. 70, and the Roman destruction of the messianic movement of Bar Kokhba in A.D. 135 (at Betar near Jerusalem). Each was catastrophic for the nation at its time, and the "Ninth of Ab" became the annual day of commemorating those holocausts by the Jews world-wide. At this annual fast the Book of Lamentations is read in synagogues around the world, and many also read from it every Friday. Throughout their long history of suffering, the Jews in dispersion have been helped by the reading of these lamenting poems to express their sorrow and despair, and also their hope of a future regathering to the "holy city." A relation they have failed to make, however, is the relation both Daniel and Jesus made between the death of Jesus and the destruction of Jerusalem in A.D. 70 (Dan. 9:26; Luke 19:43-44). Jesus described that destruction to be a consequence of the nation's failure to respond to His coming as their Messiah. That annual fast is really a divine reminder to them of that failure.

2. ***THE BOOK OF ARTISTIC STRUCTURE.*** No book of the Bible is so artistically arranged as Lamentations. The five poems present a plaintive "pentateuch of pain," with a symmetrical design to call attention to its content and possibly to serve as a memory device for liturgical service. This symmetry may be seen in the number of verses given each chapter and the consistent number of lines given to each verse in the various chapters. Each chapter has twenty-two verses (as the Hebrew alphabet has twenty-two letters), with the exception of chapter three which has sixty-six verses in twenty-two clusters. The symmetry of the chapters, verses, and lines may be seen in chart form:

Chapter	1	2	3	4	5
Verses per chapter	22	22	66	22	22
Lines per verse	3	3	2	2	1

Another artistic feature that is not apparent in English translations is the use of an acrostic on the Hebrew alphabet in each of the first four chapters. In chapters 1–2 and 4, each verse begins with a succeeding letter of the Hebrew alphabet. In chapter 3 the acrostic is accentuated by forming the acrostic with twenty-two clusters of three verses each, each verse in a cluster beginning with the same Hebrew letter and the clusters advancing through the Hebrew alphabet. Chapter five does not use the acrostic, perhaps by design, to leave the affect of spontaneity in the penitent's prayer and note of confidence.

The immense effort required to achieve this artistic structure suggests the great importance Jeremiah and Baruch saw in this message of judgment and the inviolability of God's Word.

3. ***THE STRONG EMPHASIS ON DIVINE JUDGMENT.*** Lamentations repeatedly attributes the destruction of Jerusalem to the wrath of the Lord, not to the wrath of Babylon. Though the Book of Jeremiah speaks of Babylon 161 times, neither Babylon nor Nebuchadnezzar are even mentioned in Lamentations. This emphasis on divine judgment also emphasizes the point that it was their sins before God that brought their destruction, not the international misfortune of becoming prey to Babylon's conquest. In the same way, their restoration is wholly dependent on their repentance and turning back

to God. The international powers were only God's instruments to accomplish His purposes for His people, as this book reveals.

4. **"GREAT IS YOUR FAITHFULNESS"** (3:23). One would hardly expect this classic theme of confidence in a book of judgment and almost unrelieved despair. It does, however, originate in the heart of the Book of Lamentations. The exclamation is not a jubilant cry of delight from an experience of great blessing and prosperity, but a response to great judgment and discipline. It was while the prophet viewed the charred ashes of Israel's most cherished monument that he exclaimed: "His compassions fail not. *They are* new every morning; Great *is* Your faithfulness" (3:22-23). His point was that God always keeps His word, whether in judging sin or in showing mercy for penitence and faith. In either situation the godly can say, "The Lord *is* my portion" (3:24).

5. **THE EMPATHIZING PROPHET.** Assuming the author to be Jeremiah, no other prophet so thoroughly empathized or entered into the griefs and judgment of his people. For nearly fifty years Jeremiah stood with the recalcitrant nation as it went through its deepest trial, counseling them from the center of the vicious maelstrom. Rather than respected, he was humiliated, denounced, imprisoned in a dungeon, and labeled a traitor. He then endured the siege and famine and watched the roaring breakthrough, pillaging, burning, and slaughter of the city and temple. Taken to Ramah (just north of Jerusalem) he was himself released from chains to witness the further slaughter of most of Jerusalem's population and the departure of the remaining 4600 people to Babylon in chains. Choosing to remain at Mizpah with Gedaliah the appointed governor, however, he endured the further trial of Gedaliah's murder in the rebellion of Ishmael and Johanan, and was then taken to Egypt where he was again reviled (Jer. 41-44). There he is said to have been stoned by his own people for condemning their continued idolatry and unrepentance. Few prophets had more to cry about than Jeremiah, as he expresses in Lamentations 3:48-49.

6. **CHRIST IN LAMENTATIONS.** The single christological feature of this book is that it foreshadows Christ weeping over Jerusalem as he also predicted its early destruction (Luke 19:41-43). In many ways the Book of Lamentations reflects also the grief and sorrow of God for His covenant people in their hour of deepest despair. As Isaiah 63:9 expressed it, "In all their affliction He was afflicted, And the Angel of His Presence saved them." Isaiah and John express the fact that it is God or Christ who will "wipe away" the tears of lamentation from all eyes (Is. 25:8; Rev. 7:17; 21:4).

The Book of Ezekiel

Introduction

AUTHORSHIP

A. *THE TITLE*

The name "Ezekiel" means "God strengthens," an appropriate title for the book and for the prophet who was given a stern message for the Jewish exiles in Babylon.

B. *THE AUTHOR*

1. Ezekiel's authorship of this book is quite universally acknowledged. Though his name is never mentioned in any other Bible book, Ezekiel is identified as the author in several ways in the book:

    a. He identifies himself by name in 1:3 and 24:24, and writes in autobiographical style throughout the book.

    b. He uses a unique, graphic style of visions, parables, allegories, and symbolic actions throughout the book.

    c. The priestly emphasis throughout also points to Ezekiel the priest, e.g., offerings, temple, altar, priests, etc.

2. Ezekiel's background is noted in several ways:

    a. He was born in the family of Buzi the priest in 622 B.C. at the height of Josiah's reformation in Jerusalem. The "thirtieth year" of 1:1 is generally assumed to be Ezekiel's age in 592, the fifth year of Jehoiachin, inasmuch as a priest's ministry began at age thirty (1:1-2).

    b. He was exiled with Jehoiachin in 597 when Nebuchadnezzar took the best of the land to Babylon. There he lived in his own house at a Jewish colony called Tel Abib by the Chebar River (canal to the Euphrates), evidently near Nippur (1:1; 3:15; Louis Finkelstein, *The Jews: Their History, Culture, and Religion,* Vol. I, p. 48).

    c. Ezekiel was married, but his wife died in January 10, 588, the day the siege of Jerusalem began (24:1, 15-18).

    d. Using his own home as a meeting place, he ministered to the elders that gathered for his counsel, perhaps inaugurating the synagogue system. His ministry continued at least twenty-three years, till 570, the latest date given for his prophecies (29:17).

HISTORICAL SETTING

A. *DATE OF WRITING*—592–570 B.C.*

Ezekiel is extremely precise in dating many of his prophecies. The point from which he dates them is 597 B.C., the year of Jehoiachin's captivity.**

The following are the dated prophecies in their biblical order:

1:1	July 5, 592	(5th year)	Ezekiel's first vision of "the glory."
8:1	Sept. 5, 591	(6th year)	His transport in vision to Jerusalem.

Outline of Ezekiel

THEME: Jerusalem's Destruction as the Glory Departs and Restoration as the Glory Returns.

20:1	Aug. 10, 590	(7th year)	His instruction given to the elders.
24:1	Jan. 10, 588	(9th year)	The day the siege of Jerusalem began.
26:1	Apr. 1, 586	(11th year)	The prophecy of Tyre's devastation.
29:1	Jan. 12, 587	(10th year)	The first prophecy against Pharaoh.
29:17	Apr. 1, 570	(27th year)	The sixth prophecy against Pharaoh.
30:20	Apr. 7, 586	(11th year)	The second prophecy against Pharaoh.
31:1	June 1, 586	(11th year)	The third prophecy against Pharaoh.
32:1	Mar. 1, 585	(12th year)	The fourth prophecy against Pharaoh.
32:17	Apr. 15, 585	(12th year)	The fifth prophecy against Pharaoh.
33:21	Jan. 5, 585	(12th year)	The report of Jerusalem's fall arrives, having occurred five months earlier.
40:1	Apr. 10, 572	(25th year)	The vision of the new temple received.

*For correlation of Hebrew and Gregorian calendars, see p. 00.

**Some chronologists advance some of these dates one year, adjusting to the "accession-year" system (postdating), or the "Tishri new year" dating system of kings. (See Edwin R. Thiele, *The Mysterious Numbers of the Hebrew Kings*, pp. 16ff.).

B. *THE GEOGRAPHICAL LOCATION OF EZEKIEL*

1. Ezekiel and Daniel are distinguished from all other prophets in that they ministered primarily outside Palestine. Daniel, a royal son of Judah, served at the royal Gentile court of Babylon, and Ezekiel, a priest, served as counselor to the Jewish exiles. They were also about the same age, Daniel being exiled in 605, and Ezekiel in 597 B.C.

2. The place of Ezekiel's exile was the Jewish colony of Tel Abib near Nippur, about 50 miles southeast of Babylon by the great canal Chebar. This canal ran around Babylon between the Euphrates and Tigris rivers and was located about 150 miles south of modern Baghdad and about 125 miles north of Ur, Abraham's native city. The name Tel Abib means "mound of grain," suggesting the fertility of the well-irrigated plain. Their settling in this fertile area may have been arranged by Daniel who ruled with Nebuchadnezzar over the province of Babylon from 603 B.C. (Dan. 2:48).

C. *THE POLITICAL SETTING*

1. This book moved from the time of Judah's vassalage under Babylon to the time of her captivity in Babylon. As noted, Daniel had providentially risen to be "ruler over the whole province of Babylon," as well as chief of Nebuchadnezzar's "wise men" or counselors. Since this occurred five years before Ezekiel's deportation and sixteen years before the final exile in 586, the Jewish exiles in Babylon were in good care politically. This was also the time of Babylon's zenith of power and glory.

2. Ezekiel had little to say of Judah's politics, not even mentioning Zedekiah, the current vassal king of Judah. His prophecy speaks of no other king of Israel or Judah by name, except David (Jehoiachin noted in 1:2 only for dating purposes).

Concerning the politics of the heathen nations, however, Ezekiel pronounced judgment on many of them surrounding Israel because of their violence against the Jewish nation and God's sanctuary (25–32). Unlike Jeremiah, Ezekiel did not dwell on the political history of the time. The end-time politics of 38–39 relate to Israel's restoration, but the great battle fought is primarily a Gentile one, serving a spiritual purpose.

D. *THE RELIGIOUS SETTING*

1. In this book Israel is not only without a king and country, but without a temple and the facilities to carry on her religious rituals enjoined by Moses. The only place of religious gathering in Babylon noted by Ezekiel is his own house where he counseled the elders. These elders were evidently the prototypes of the synagogue leaders who later became the rulers of the synagogues and the people. Without a temple, of course, their ritual system of slain animals, feasts, and all priestly functions related to the temple were inoperative.
2. The spiritual character of the exiles to whom Ezekiel ministered was hardly better than that of those to whom Jeremiah ministered in Jerusalem. His characteristic phrase to describe them was "rebellious house" (used sixteen times by Ezekiel, rarely by others). The significance is that the change of location did not change their hearts or dispositions toward the Lord, as yet.
3. Ezekiel's viewpoint was especially religious or spiritual, evaluating all political or physical affairs in this light. This is seen in his visions of the "glory" (1:28; 8–11), the six "executioners" of Jerusalem (9:1-2), the supernatural taking of Judah's "prince" to Babylon (12:12-13), the description of the superhuman "king of Tyre" (28:12-19), etc. Ezekiel's view is always priestly or heavenly, rather than merely political.

THE PURPOSE OF THE BOOK OF EZEKIEL

Ezekiel's purpose was twofold, as noted in the two main divisions of the book:

A. *To promote repentance and faith* by warning of God's imminent judgment on Jerusalem and the nations.

B. *To stimulate hope and trust* by his later message of reassurance that the nation would eventually be regathered, the city restored, and a new temple built.

The first message was stressed during the first six years of his ministry (592–586), verifying that Jerusalem and the temple would be destroyed, Babylon would not quickly fall (as the false prophets claimed), and that Egypt was a false hope to trust in for help, inasmuch as she also would fall to Babylon.

After the fall of Jerusalem, however, Ezekiel became the prophet of hope and cheer as he prophesied Israel's final restoration. He gave them this detailed picture of Israel's future glory and holiness, lest they settle down in the prosperous ways of Babylon and forget Jerusalem.

Unique Contributions of Ezekiel

---

1. **THE PROPHET WITH MANY VISUAL AIDS.** No other prophet made such liberal use of pictorial language or visual aids. These abound in the book in such forms as proverbs, allegories, symbolic actions, miniature portrayals, and apocalyptic visions. These were especially used to get the attention and impress truths to the hardened and rebellious remnant in Babylon. They occur throughout the book:

1:4-28	Vision of the Glory of the Lord as "four living creatures" out of cloud.
2:9–3:3	Ezekiel eats the scroll of lamentations for Israel's judgment.
3:16-27	Ezekiel is made speechless except for special messages from the Lord.
4:1-17	Ezekiel acts out siege on Jerusalem and coming famine.
5:1-17	He shaves with sharp sword, dividing hair to signify judgment by sword.
6:1ff.	He prophesies in the direction of the mountains of Jerusalem.
8:2ff.	In vision he is carried to Jerusalem's temple to observe idolatry.
9:1-2	Wrecking crew prepares to destroy Jerusalem as the righteous remnant are marked for preservation.
10:2ff.	The cherubim scatter coals over Jerusalem, indicating conflagration.
4-22	The Glory departs the city and temple on whirling wheels of cherubim.
12:3ff.	Ezekiel acts out Jerusalem's fall by packing bags and sneaking through the wall of the city.
13:10-16	Jerusalem likened to white-washed wall about to wash away.
14:13-23	Inevitability of judgment seen by futility of even prayers of Noah, Daniel, and Job.
15:2-6	Jerusalem is likened to a burning vine.
16:2-63	Jerusalem is likened to a harlot wife.
17:2-10	Allegory of Israel as cedar, and Babylon and Egypt as two great eagles.
22-24	Allegory of the new cedar sprig to be planted in Israel.
18:2-3	Proverb of the fathers eating sour grapes.
19:1-9	Allegory of Israel as a lioness and her cubs captured.
10-14	Allegory of Israel as an uprooted vine.
21:3-22	Parable of the Lord's sharpened sword unsheathed.
22:18-22	Israel likened to the dross of a smelter's pot.
23:2-49	Likening of Jerusalem and Samaria to a pair of adulterous sisters.
24:2-14	Allegory of the boiling pot and the rejected stew meat.
16-27	Ezekiel is not allowed to mourn his wife's death as a sign to Israel.
27:1-36	Allegory of the pride and the "sinking of the S.S. Tyre."
28:12-20	Portrayal of the creation and casting out of the cherubic "king of Tyre."
29:2ff.	Likening of Egypt to a dragon in the Nile. Ensnared in 32:2-10.
31:2-18	Allegory of the felling of two cedars, Assyria and Egypt.
34:2-10	Likening Israel's leaders to murderous shepherds in contrast to the Lord as their true Shepherd.
37:1-14	Parable of the "dry bones" arising, yet without life, the house of Israel.

16-22	Parable of the "two sticks" united, symbolizing Judah and Israel.
40–42	Vision of the surveyor measuring Jerusalem and the temple for building.
43:2-7	Vision of the return of the Glory of the Lord to the new temple.

These portrayals announce and explain the Lord's coming judgments on Israel and the nations through Babylon and the future restoration of Israel as her destroyers are destroyed. The figures are not mysterious, but explained in the contexts. Many of these were borrowed by John in the writing of Revelation.

2. **THE DEPARTURE OF "THE GLORY"** (10:18). The Lord's "Glory," many times referred to in Psalms and Isaiah, is portrayed in Ezekiel as the visible presence of God (the late Hebrew word "*shechinah*" used to designate this). This cloud of "Glory" resided over the mercy seat between the cherubim in the temple. Ezekiel the priest characteristically describes Jerusalem's judgment by the departure of the glory. In chapters 9–11, the Glory is seen reluctantly departing, first from the two cherubim in the holy place, then from the door of the temple on the east, third from the city after hovering over the eastern gate, and finally from the Mount of Olives, as if writing "Ichabod" over the temple and city (8:3; 10:4, 18-19; 11:22-24). Its return is described in 43:2-7, after the new temple is constructed. This coming of the Glory to the millennial temple relates to Exodus 40:34 and 2 Chronicles 5:13-14, where the great cloud descended first on the completed tabernacle and later on the newly completed temple of Solomon. That visible glory was always absent from the temples of Zerubbabel and Herod. The greater glory of the future temple will be the presence of the Lord or Messiah Himself (Zech. 2:5; Ezek. 48:35).

3. **"YOU SHALL KNOW THAT I AM THE LORD"** (6:7, etc.). This refrain is repeated over sixty times in Ezekiel, especially with regard to idolators. It relates well with the similar statement by Elijah as he proved who the true God was in Israel (1 Kin. 18:36-39). The declaration did not mean that they would "know salvation," but that they would know that the Lord (YHWH) was God and able to keep His word (cf. 6:14). He is a covenant-keeping God, whether for judgment or blessing. When He warned of judgment for sin or promised future restoration, He would not fail to keep His word.

4. **ISRAEL'S IDOLATRY IN EGYPT** (20:5-9). Ezekiel makes a significant contribution to the story of Israel's affliction in Egypt, a detail omitted by Moses in Exodus. In reprimanding the idolatrous elders in Ezekiel 20, the prophet reminded them that their history of idolatry as a nation went all the way back to Egypt. The great affliction of the Israelites in Egypt by Pharaoh and the taskmasters is seen by Ezekiel to have had a spiritual cause, as well. That cause was their deep idolatry for which the Lord was about to discard them. "For His Name's sake," however, He wrought with them to salvage them as His people. This tendency to idolatry was now to be cured by a stay in Babylon, and he here makes sure they get the point.

5. **EZEKIEL AS "SON OF MAN"** (2:1, etc.). The Lord addressed Ezekiel as "son of man"

ninety-three times, a title used elsewhere only of Daniel (Dan. 8:17) and of Jesus over eighty times. The title appears to emphasize the prophet's oneness with his people, especially as he pronounced judgment on them. Jesus also used this title of Himself, more than any other title, and explained His authority to judge mankind "because He is the Son of Man" (John 5:27).

6. *ISRAEL'S REGATHERING AND THE CONFLICT WITH GOG AND MAGOG* (36–39). This is a classic passage on the final regathering of Israel and her great conflict with a northern confederacy. The prophet reveals several significant truths of that future return:

   a. The Lord Himself will return them to the land, their enemies notwithstanding, where they will be cleansed and given a "new heart" (36:26).

   b. The nation will arise as "dry bones" (long dead and still dead), but will at a later point receive spiritual life (37:1-14), and be united (37:16-23).

   c. Following her partial regathering, a great northern power (Gog and Magog) will invade Israel and then be challenged by a large southern and western alliance (38).

   d. By supernatural and natural means, "Gog and Magog" will be destroyed to give a demonstration to the world of the Lord's sovereignty (39:1-8; 21:24).

   e. The latter day house of Israel will experience spiritual rebirth when the Spirit is poured out on them at a time subsequent to this battle (39:25-29).

7. *EZEKIEL'S RESTORED TEMPLE* (40–46). Understanding this temple has been one of the most difficult problems of the book. Since it bears little resemblance to the rebuilt temples of Zerubbabel or Herod, interpreters have generally divided by seeing it as either: 1) a symbolic portrayal of the New Testament Church; or 2) a literal description of the restored temple to be built when Christ returns for the millennial age. Though the first interpretation has been the most popular since the Church began to assume the Jews were a cursed people and all their promises were given to the Church, the latter view of a literally restored temple is the most exegetically sound for the following reasons:

   a. In the context, the rebuilding of this new temple is described directly after the explanation of Israel's regathering and her enemies destruction (36–39).

   b. Inasmuch as most of Ezekiel's already fulfilled prophecies (Jerusalem's destruction, Tyre's being scraped clean, etc., 6:3-5; 14:21; 26:4, 12) were fulfilled so literally (as one would normally expect), there is little ground for interpreting these last chapters in a strained, allegorical way. The first thirty-three chapters evidence the prophet's literal intentions in his prophecies.

   c. Interpreting this temple as being fulfilled in the Church, when it was specifically given as a hope for Israel, makes the prophecy a gross deception and a vain hope for the people to whom it was given (43:7, 10).

   d. The detailed dimensions of this temple are almost devoid of real significance if applied figuratively to the Church. Taken literally, they relate consistently to the Lord's method of giving specific dimensions for Noah's ark, Moses' tabernacle, and Solomon's temple (Gen. 6:14-17; Ex. 25-28; 1 Kin. 6:1–7:51). The careful dimensions suggest this temple will be as literal as the others.

e. Ezekiel's temple has some glaring omissions which make sense only in the messianic age. The missing articles are: 1) the ark; 2) mercyseat; 3) cherubim; 4) altar of incense; 5) candlestick; 6) table of showbread; 7) veil; and 8) high priest. With the careful description and dimensions of all the other parts, including the wooden altar that will be prominently used, these omissions especially stand out. Were this temple intended to be a figurative portrayal of the church, it is inconceivable that these important parts should be left out, since they symbolize the heart of the ritual. Recognizing these descriptions in the normal way as literal parts of a literal temple to be set up in the millennial age, the mystery disappears, for Messiah, the fulfillment of these types will then be present in Person. Those shadows will then be obsolete and are therefore omitted in this picture.

8. *THE SACRIFICIAL SYSTEM REINSTATED* (40:39; 45–46). These passages startle us with the prophecy that the Old Testament system of blood offerings will be reinstituted in this temple. The crux of the problem is that Hebrews 8–10 shows that Jesus' one offering for sin made obsolete all further animal sacrifices (Heb. 9:26; 10:18). It should be recalled, however, that the point of Hebrews 8–10 was not that animal offerings were once redemptive and are now obsolete, but that they never did take away sin. They were only pointing forward to Christ's once-for-all offering. To emphasize that point, Jesus gave the Church the ordinances of communion and baptism to symbolize His death, burial, and resurrection until He comes (Matt. 26:26-29; 28:19). They provide a constant reminder of these redemptive truths, pointing back to the cross. Since these were to be remembrances of His death "until He comes" (1 Cor. 11:26), a further memorial would not be out of place for those who are born and redeemed in the messianic age. This is evidently the purpose of the renewed system of animal sacrifices in Ezekiel's temple. They will serve an important memorial function, certainly not a redemptive one.

9. *CHRISTOLOGY IN EZEKIEL.* The messianic references in Ezekiel, as in Jeremiah, are quite limited as far as specific statements are concerned. There are, however, several oblique references adverting to Messiah as Shepherd, King, and Priest.
   a. His work as the "Good Shepherd" is suggested in chapter 34:11-16, following the denunciation of the selfish shepherds of Israel. In verse 11 the Lord declares: "Indeed, I Myself will search for My sheep and seek them out." The following passages then elucidates His work as a "Good Shepherd," caring, delivering, gathering, feeding, leading to rest, seeking the lost, and healing and strengthening the sick. This is undoubtedly the passage Jesus related to when He declared in John 10:11, 14: "I am the good shepherd," distinguishing Himself from the false shepherds of His time.
   b. His kingship is adverted to in 21:27 and 37:22. Following the prediction of Israel's regathering from all nations, the Lord says: "I will make them one nation . . . , and one king shall be king over them all" (37:22). This is patently messianic, relating to Isaiah 9:7 and Luke 1:32. The later statement in 37:24, "David My servant *shall be* king over them," could of course, be a designation of Messiah as the

"Son of David." It could also, however, be a reference to the fact that David after resurrection will serve as king over Israel under Messiah who will be King of Kings (Ezek. 34:24; Hos. 3:5; Rev. 19:16).

c. The priesthood of Messiah is not mentioned in this book, but it is conspicuous by its absence in the detailed description of the temple without a high priest. Since it would be inconceivable to have a temple without a high priest, the non-mention perhaps assumes that all know that a priest like Melchizedek would arise who would be "a priest on His throne" (Ps. 110:4; Zech. 6:13; Heb. 5:6).

The Book of Daniel

Introduction

AUTHORSHIP

A. *THE TITLE*

The name Daniel means "God is Judge" (or "my Judge"), a name that again suggests the theme of the book, God's sovereignty over the nations.

B. *THE AUTHOR*

1. Daniel was born in Jerusalem, evidently in the royal family, about 623 B.C., during the reformation of Josiah and the early ministry of Jeremiah.
2. Taken to Babylon in the first exile (605), he was selected for royal service after a period of three years special studies, being renamed "Belteshazzar" by the officials. This name related him to one of the Babylonian deities.
3. In 603 at the age of c. 20, Daniel was made ruler over the province of Babylon and head of the college of "wise men." He then served as chief advisor to Nebuchadnezzar during the period of Jerusalem's destruction and the exile to Babylon, doubtless exerting influence for the Jewish captives arriving.
4. Over a period of nearly seventy years, Daniel served under six Babylonian and two Persian rulers. Under three of them (Nebuchadnezzar, Belshazzar, and Darius I) he was elevated to prime minister. He served in this capacity during both Judah's final captivity and her return to Judah.

C. *THE AUTHORSHIP QUESTION*

Like Isaiah, this book is hotly disputed by critics as to its author and date of writing. The Danielic authorship was first challenged by Porphyry in A.D. 275 and is universally challenged by modern critics. The following is a brief summary of the arguments denying and those confirming the authorship by Daniel:

1. Arguments denying the Danielic authorship:
   a. Its place in the Hebrew canon with the "Writings" suggests a later date. This argument assume the canon of the Prophets was closed c. 425 B.C., and the Writings, c. 165 B.C. This is an erroneous assumption, for many books of the Writings patently precede the time of Daniel (e.g., Psalms, Proverbs, Job, etc., to note only the obvious).
   b. Its historical "inaccuracies" imply a later author writing of Daniel. Though many such discrepancies have been charged, further research and discoveries of archaeology have furnished adequate answers to them. (See J. C. Whitcomb, *Darius The Mede;* E. J. Young, *An Introduction to the Old Testament,* pp. 380ff.; Gleason Archer, *In The Shadow of the Cross*, pp. 367ff.).
   c. Its literary features, especially the use of Persian and Greek terms, indicate a later writer. Daniel, however, lived into the Persian era, and Greek trade was brisk long before Daniel (Joel 3:6).
   d. Its late theological concepts, such as Messiah, its emphasis on angels, the resurrection, and judgment are seen to be anachronistic, better related to the apocryphal literature of the second and third centuries B.C. This argument appears to be blind to the introduction of many of these as early as Genesis and their mention throughout the Old Testament (Gen. 3:15; 18:1ff.; Judg. 13:17-18; Job 1–2; Ps. 16:10; Eccl. 12:14; Is. 2:4-22).
   e. Its detailed prophecies of the Maccabean age (chapter 11) could not have been written before 165 B.C., when many of them were fulfilled. This is the heart of the humanist's problem with Daniel, his denial of predictive prophecy. The effect of that view is to deny also God's sovereignty in the affairs of men, the very purpose for which the book was written.
2. Arguments confirming the Danielic authorship:
   a. As did Moses, Samuel, Ezra, and other acknowledged authors in the Old Testament, Daniel recorded his historical chapters (1–6) in the third person. In relating his four visions (7–12), he consistently wrote in the first person, identifying himself, "I, Daniel," many times.
   b. Ezekiel acknowledged the historicity of Daniel in his time, noting his outstanding wisdom and righteous character to already be legendary, like unto that of Noah and Job (Ezek. 14:14, 20; 28:3).
   c. The author shows a thorough knowledge of the manners, customs, histories, and religions of the sixth century B.C. (1:5, 10; 2:2; 3:3, 10, etc.).
   d. Jesus acknowledged Daniel as the author of the visions of Daniel 9:27, 11:31, and 12:11, the latest sections of the book (Matt. 24:15).
   e. Josephus (c. A.D. 75) noted that Alexander the Great was shown the Book of Daniel and its prophecy about the rising power of Greece and its first king who would conquer Persia (8:21; 11:3). This was long before the Maccabean age in which the critics would date the writing (Josephus, *Antiquities,* Book XI, VIII, sec. 5).
   f. Jewish and Christian traditions have universally acknowledged Daniel as the

author (until recent rationalists and deists have resurrected the view of Neo-Platonic philosopher Porphyry that it was written by an unknown Jew in Palestine at the time of the Maccabees after 165 B.C.).

HISTORICAL SETTING

A. *DATE OF WRITING*—c. 535 B.C.

1. Note the dates of the histories and visions (either stated or related):

Daniel	1:1	606 B.C.	Daniel's deportation and three years training.
	2:1	603	Daniel's interpretation of the dream and elevation.
	5:31	539	Daniel interprets "handwriting on wall" for Belshazzar.
	6:1	538	Daniel in lion's den, as Darius I (Gobryas) began rule.
	7:1	553	Daniel's earlier vision of "four great beasts."
	8:1	551	Daniel's earlier vision of ram and male goat.
	9:1	539	Daniel's vision of "seventy weeks" for Israel.
	10–12	536	Daniel's vision of Persia, Greece, and the end times.

2. The completion of the book would likely be shortly after the last vision, 535.

B. *THE POLITICAL SETTING*

1. World politics, the rise and fall of great empires, and the relation of these world powers to Israel constitute the main concerns of this book. During Daniel's life span, the Assyrian Empire breathed its last at the fall of Nineveh in 612 and the battle of Carchemish in 605, the Jewish nation was destroyed in 586, the Egyptian Empire was invaded by Babylon in 568, the Median Empire fell to Cyrus in c. 550, and finally Babylon fell to Cyrus the Persian in 539. During much of this time Daniel was in high position to closely observe the international changes and how God overruled all.
2. For a listing of the kings of Babylon and Persia involved, see International Rulers Effecting Israel's Captivity and Returns, p. 108
3. The most significant international event involved in Daniel is the inception of the four-world-kingdom era known as the "times of the Gentiles" (Dan. 2:36-45; 7:2-18; Luke 21:24). This period began with Nebuchadnezzar, the "head of gold," and is characterized by Gentile lordship over Jerusalem. It will only be terminated when "the God of heaven will set up a kingdom which shall never be destroyed" (2:44), the messianic kingdom (Matt. 25:31-34).

C. *THE RELIGIOUS SETTING*

1. For the religious setting in Judah, see "Introduction to Jeremiah"; for the religious setting of the exiles in Babylon, see "Introduction to Ezekiel."
2. The religion of Babylonia at this time centered in the worship of Bel Merodach (Marduk) (Jer. 50:2), at their one great temple, Esagila with its huge tower.

This religion developed from the practice in ancient Mesopotamia of each city having its own god, and Enlil, the patron god of Nippur (40 miles SE of Babylon)

Outline of Daniel

THEME: God's Sovereign Care of Israel Through the Times of the Gentiles.

finally coming to supremacy as "lord of the world" (Charles Boutflower, *In and Around the Book of Daniel,* pp. 92ff., quoting "The India House Inscription" of Nebuchadnezzar). With the later rise of Babylon, however, its patron god, Merodach, was given pre-eminence over Enlil, and it became the lord or "Bel" (cognate of Baal) of the Babylonian pantheon of gods. To its temple, all gods or statues were brought by the priests each year for the Nisan festival, where supposedly the fates of all men were fixed for the coming year. To the Neo-Babylonians, Merodach was the supreme god.

3. Nebuchadnezzar was not only a military genius, a lover of splendor, a builder of monuments, gardens, and canals, and a smart administrator; he was also a very religious man. His religious passion was to enrich the temple of Merodach in Babylon with gold and other jewels or precious stones (Boutflower, *Ibid.,* pp. 24ff.) He also had a tendency to montheism, as the development of the religion shows. The Babylonians believed in several gods: Enlil, the storm god of Nippur; Shamash, the sun god of Sippar; Sin, the moon god of Ur and Harran; Nebo, the god of wisdom and writing (and astrology) of Borsippa (Is. 46:1). But Merodach was exalted far above these and given almost monotheistic stature. "If then," says Boutflower, "Nabopolassar could include Shamash in the Enlilship along with Merodach, and if Nabonidus could bestow the title at one time on Merodach, at another on Sin, it is no matter of surprise to us to find Nebuchadnezzar, under the influence of the mighty miracles wrought before his eyes, bestowing on the God of the Jews the titles "the Most High" and the "Most High God" (*Ibid.,* p. 101). This is especially significant in Daniel 2–4 where Nebuchadnezzar acclaims Daniel's God to be "Most High" after shown that He is the source of wisdom to reveal dreams (2), the source of power to protect in the fiery furnace (3), and the One who sets up and deposes earthly rulers (4).

4. Daniel and his three friends were given Babylonian names relating them to the gods of the Babylonian pantheon. Friedrich Delitszch interprets these as:
   For Daniel, "Belteshazzar"—meaning, "Bel protects his life."
   For Hananiah, "Shadrach"—meaning, "servant of Aku," the moon-god Sin.
   For Mishael, "Meshach"—meaning, "who is like Aku" ("Mishael"—"who is like God").
   For Azariah, "Abed-Nego"—meaning, "servant of Nebo."

THE PURPOSE OF THE BOOK OF DANIEL

The primary purpose of this book is to declare the sovereignty of God over all nations, as demonstrated through Daniel and his friends to two Babylonian and two Persian monarchs. In the process Daniel reveals a time schedule of four Gentile world kingdoms and of "seventy weeks" for Israel that must run their course before God Himself will set up an everlasting kingdom on earth. His purpose throughout is not to emphasize God's redemptive program, but His kingdom program until He establishes His permanent kingdom under Messiah.

1. *DANIEL'S GENTILE EMPHASIS.* In contrast to the prophets, Daniel stressed the future of Gentile kingdoms, rather than of Israel. He mentions Israel or Judah only twelve times, rather incidentally (compared to Ezekiel's 201 and Hosea's 59). Daniel was uniquely prepared for this ministry to Gentile courts, being himself of the nobility of Judah (Dan. 1:3, 6). Even Daniel's name fitted his testimony to Gentiles, having the suffix "El," God's universal name for the Gentiles (Gen. 14:18; Dan. 2:18). Ezekiel, the other prophet in Babylon, also had the suffix "El," as the other two major prophets, Isaiah and Jeremiah, had the suffix "Yah," fitting their ministry in the covenant land of Israel.

    Consonant with this Gentile emphasis, more than half of Daniel is written in Aramaic, the Gentile "lingua franca" of the Middle East of that time (from seventh century B.C. to seventh century A.D.). These chapters (2:4–7:28) introduce the "times of the Gentiles" by two dreams or visions in chapters 2 and 7. The role of Gentile world kingdoms is a major theme of the book.

2. *DANIEL'S PROPHETIC CONTRIBUTION.* His main contribution to predictive prophecy is that he put God's prophetic program on a time schedule. Rather than adding much to the program itself, as already declared by the covenants to the fathers and the earlier prophets, Daniel provided the Gentile calendar of the "times of the Gentiles" and the Jewish clock of the "seventy weeks of Israel" (2:37-44; 7:3ff.; 9:24-27). This provided international pinpoints by which the movement of God's program can be discerned on the world scene and in the Jewish capital of Jerusalem. He carefully designated specific nations and key events (8:20-22; 9:24-27; 12:1, 7-13). These events, of course, relate to Israel and her future as the movement of empires takes place, showing God's sovereignty over both time and the events.

3. *DANIEL'S SUPERNATURAL CONTENT AND APOCALYPTIC LANGUAGE.* Whereas other prophets note no miracles in their ministries (Isaiah and Jonah the exceptions), Daniel records much of the miraculous or supernatural. In each of his first six chapters, events of supernatural wisdom or power are noted (1:17-20; 2:28; 3:25-27; 4:33-34; 5:5; 6:22). In his four visions of chapters 7–12, he describes supernatural events of the throne of God (7:9ff.), Gabriel revealing visions of the future (8:16; 9:21), Michael standing guard over Israel (10:21; 12:1), spiritual powers over heathen nations challenging them (10:13, 20), and a figurative description of the Lord Himself (10). This graphically displays God's sovereignty over all realms.

    Daniel is often classed with that genre of writing called "apocalyptic" literature. That is a branch of prophetic literature that flourished from 200 B.C. to A.D. 140, featuring visions of symbolic imagery of human and spiritual beings with vague meanings. Prominent also were expectations of imminent cosmic catastrophe in which the forces of good defeat those of evil and bring about the establishing of universal messianic rule. The prophets Isaiah, Ezekiel, Daniel, and Zechariah certainly describe supernatural events of cosmic character that issue in the establishing of the messianic age, since forecasting is part of prophecy. However, they are not to be classed with the many "apocalypses" that pseudo writers hatched in that later period. Most of the later writings were pseudepigraphous, adopting heroic names to gain a hearing, and quite deterministic. The apocalyptic elements in Daniel are not left as vague imagery, but explained in terms of the real world; neither are they mere decrees of determinism, but reminders of God's prophesied program to inspire His people to godly action as well as hopeful trust. It is "apocalyptic" in the true sense of "apocalypse," a "revelation" from God.

4. ***DANIEL'S PRACTICAL PURPOSE.*** Though this book is full of predictive content, it is also charged with many challenges to practical, godly living. The prophecies were not given to promote mysticism, but mettle; not curiosity, but courage. The writer is careful to record how purified living, Bible study, and persistent prayer constituted the matrix out of which his visions from the Lord were given (1:8-9; 9:2-20). In the grand prophecy of the "seventy weeks" for Israel in 9:24-27, for instance, the practical principles are first highlighted. This four verse prophecy is preceded by a long account of his studying Jeremiah, prayer, and confession of sin, appealing to God on the basis of His covenants and compassion. It is also to be noted that this far-reaching revelation was given shortly after Daniel's experience in the lion's den (6:1; 9:1). A basic purpose of predictive prophecy is to promote godly living. In the difficult times of the Maccabees, the Book of Daniel was undoubtedly a strong factor in inspiring their godly courage to be strong and perform great exploits (11:32).

5. ***DANIEL'S INTRODUCTION OF THE ANTICHRIST.*** Though Daniel says comparatively little about Messiah, he has much to say of the Antichrist. This sinister personage emerges more and more throughout the book from vague symbols as the "little horn" to his specific title of "king" and "desolator" in later visions. The progress of this revelation may be seen in the following sequence of passages:
   a. Daniel 7:8-11—He is introduced as a "little horn" (power) whose boasts are judged by the "Ancient of Days" as he is finally cast into the burning fire.
   b. Daniel 8:9-25—He is again seen as a "little horn" who even opposes the "Prince of princes," and is "broken without *human* hand" in the latter days of Israel's indignation (v.19).
   c. Daniel 11:36-45—He is now seen as "the king" (in the "end time") who exalts himself above all gods, wins a decisive victory in "the Glorious Land," and sets "the tents of his palace" in the "holy mountain" of Jerusalem (v. 45).
   d. Daniel 12:1, 11—His time of desecrating the sanctuary and "the power of the holy people" is designated as 1260 days or three and one-half years (12:7, 11; cf. Rev. 11:2; 13:5).
This unveiling of the future Antichrist is part of his revelation of the times of the Gentiles, which was introduced in chapter 2. The first king of this period was Nebuchadnezzar, and the last will be Antichrist who will trample Jerusalem (Luke 21:24). Nebuchadnezzar,

however, came to acknowledge the "King of heaven," whereas Antichrist will more and more magnify himself (4:37; 11:36).

6. **CHRIST IN DANIEL.** Dealing more with the "drumbeat" of Gentile world kingdoms, Daniel presents messianic content in only several rare passages:

   a. In 2:34-35, 44-45, the "stone . . . cut out without hands" that falls on the statue of Gentile kingdoms symbolizes Christ's final coming to destroy the world's anti-god system and to set up His everlasting kingdom.

   b. In 7:13-14, the "Son of Man" coming "with the clouds of heaven" to destroy the "beast" kingdoms and receive "everlasting dominion" describes His coming as the God-Man, finally taking His rightful position as the God-appointed King of the earth.

   c. In 9:25-26, the most specific reference to Christ is given as the Messiah. In the course of the seventy week prophecy, He is seen coming and being cut off without receiving what was rightly His. Linked with His cutting off, however, would be another destruction of the city and sanctuary (fulfilled in A.D. 70).

   d. In 10:5-6, an awesome picture is given of the Lord as a "certain man" whose appearance is similar in figure to a "man" above the Glory in Ezekiel 1:26 and the "*One like the Son of Man*" in Revelation 1:13-17. Each of these portrayals was given as judgment was about to be pronounced. In all these references in Daniel, Christ is seen as God's appointed Judge of the nations.

7. **THE "SEVENTY WEEKS" PROPHECY FOR ISRAEL** (9:24-27). Besides a Gentile "time-clock," Daniel also received a Jewish time-clock of prophetic events for Israel. This was given in much more precise measurements of years and days, pin-pointing pivotal events of Israel's redemption and restoration. At its conclusion, Jerusalem's transgression would be finished, atonement would be made, "everlasting righteousness" would be ushered in, and her prophecies would be fulfilled (9:24). The timetable of "seventy weeks" has four points of observation:

   a. Seven "sevens" (49 years)—The rebuilding of Jerusalem in troubled times.

   b. Sixty-two "sevens" (434 years)—After which Messiah is cut off, Jerusalem destroyed.

   c. One "seven" (7 years)—End-time pact between Roman "prince" and Israel.

   d. Half "seven" (3½ years)—Period of abomination and desolation on Jerusalem.

This prophecy has been variously understood because of several interpretive problems:

   a. What is meant by "weeks"?

      The term is a translation of the Hebrew, "*shabua*" (Gr. *heptad*), meaning a period of "seven," whether days or years determined by context (cf. Gen. 29:28-29). In Daniel 9, Daniel had just studied Jeremiah's prophecy of Israel's seventy years captivity, a punishment for failing to keep sabbatical years for 490 years (2 Chr. 36:21). This additional period of 490 years of trial under Gentiles fits symmetrically with the previous similar period.

   b. When did this period of "seventy weeks" begin?

      Though several decrees were issued by the Persian kings to allow Israel to return to Palestine, only one was given to rebuild Jerusalem (Neh. 2:1-8). The previous decrees of 538, 520, and 457 were given to rebuild the temple and restore its worship (Ezra 1:1-2; 6:3; 7:11-28). The decree to rebuild the city wall was given by Artaxerxes to Nehemiah on Nisan 1, 444 B.C. Artaxerxes' twentieth year. (The first of the month was always assumed by Jewish custom when only the month was given, Neh. 2:1-8.) This carefully recorded date gives a firm and easily established point at which the "seventy weeks" count-down was to begin.

   c. When did the "sixty-nine weeks" end?

      Total days: 69 × 7 = 483 years or 173,880 days (Bible year = 360 days as seen in Gen. 7:11, 24; 8:4; Rev. 11:3; 12:6; 13:5).

      Time span: Nisan 1, 444 B.C. (Mar. 5) plus 173,880 days = March 30, A.D. 33. (Check: Add 444 B.C. + A.D. 33 (with no year "0") = 476 years. 476 × 365.2421 (solar year days) = 173,855 days or Mar. 5, A.D. 33. Adding the remaining 25 days to 173,880 brings us to March 30, A.D. 33).

      March 30, A.D. 33 was Palm Sunday when Jesus entered Jerusalem and wept as He rebuked them for not knowing "this your day" of visitation (Luke 19:41-44). (See Harold Hoehner, *Chronological Aspects of the Life of Christ,* p. 138.)

   d. Did the "70th" week directly follow the 69th, or did a gap occur after the 69th? Several observations indicate a rather long gap between the sixty-ninth and seventieth:

      1) An obvious gap did occur between Messiah's cutting off and Jerusalem's destruction (A.D. 33-70). If a short gap was involved, why not a long one?

      2) Jesus noted that the seventieth week is future, for the mid-point "abomination of desolation" of which Daniel spoke will occur prior to His second coming. (Matt. 24:15, 21).

      3) The fact that "everlasting righteousness" and other purposes of this prophecy were not fulfilled historically just after the sixty-ninth week makes it clear that the events of the seventieth week are yet future. They give the basic framework of the events of Revelation 4-19, prior to Christ's return.

8. *DANIEL'S TWO PROPHETIC TIME-CLOCKS.*

   a. *The first time-clock,* "The Times of the Gentiles," is introduced in Daniel 2 as a great metallic statue of a man, and further explained in chapter 7 in symbols of four wild beasts. The first view (Nebuchadnezzar's dream) is from man's perspective, showing its deterioration from gold to clay; the second (Daniel's dream) gives the divine view as four wild beasts that destroy. Many clues are given for its clear interpretation: 1) Since Nebuchadnezzar is identified as the "head of gold" (2:38), his kingdom began the time of the Gentiles. 2) This also suggests the "Times of the Gentiles" to be the period of time during which Israel is ruled over by Gentile powers until the messianic kingdom rules the earth. 3) The third beast had four wings and heads (7:6), so it is easily interpreted as Alexander's empire that was divided into four parts. 4) Since the fourth beast is seen to have ten horns followed by a little horn that conquers all, the kingdom that followed the Grecian empire was Rome, but it also has some relation to the final ten-king confederacy. 5) Inasmuch as the little horn will finally be slain by the coming of the "Son of Man" (7:11) and the whole structure of world kingdoms will be crushed by the "stone cut out without hands" who sets up an everlasting kingdom, this ten-nation confederacy is yet future and will be ruled by the "little horn," Antichrist, just before Christ comes to establish His everlasting Kingdom on earth. This necessitates a hiatus or gap between the ancient Roman Empire and the future revived Roman Empire, or between the legs of iron and the feat and toes of iron and clay. The obvious gap appears to be the Church Age during which Israel's kingdom is nonexistent and Jews and Gentiles are not differentiated in the divine view (until the "little horn" makes a treaty with Israel).

  b. *The second time-clock,* "The Seventy Weeks For Israel," has just been discussed, and is graphed below to show its relation to the Gentile time-clock.

THE TIMES OF THE GENTILES

606 B.C.   538   332   63   A.D. 33

BIBLE REF.	BABYLON	PERSIA	GREECE	ROME	CHURCH AGE	TEN-NATION CONFEDERACY	MESSIANIC KINGDOM
Dan. 2	Head of Gold	Breast of Silver	Belly of Bronze	Legs of Iron	(Timeless	Feet and Toes Iron and Clay	Stone and Mountain
Dan. 7	Lion	Bear	Leopard	Dreadful Beast		Ten Horns and Little Horn	Saints to Rule Earth
Dan. 8		Ram	Male Goat; Large Horn; Four Horns		Inter-Advent	Little Horn	
Dan. 10–12		Persia	Greece Divided; Syria and Egypt		Period)	Willful King (Antichrist)	Judgment and Resurrection

THE SEVENTY WEEKS FOR ISRAEL

444 B.C.   A.D. 33

Dan. 9:24-27		69 Sevens (483 years)	Messiah cut-off; Jerusalem destroyed	One Seven three and one-half years	three and one-half years	Everlasting righteous-ness

Select Commentaries on the Major Prophets*

THE MAJOR PROPHETS

Ellison, H. L. *Men Spake from God*. Grand Rapids: Eerdmans, 1958.
*Freeman, H. *An Introduction to the Old Testament Prophets*. Chicago: Moody Press, 1968.
Rowley, H. H., ed. *Studies in Old Testament Prophecy*. Naperville, Ill.: Alec R. Allenson, 1957.
Schultz, Samuel J. *The Prophets Speak*. New York: Harper and Row, 1968.
Scott, R. B. Y. *The Relevance of the Prophets*. New York: Macmillan, 1951.
*Wood, Leon. *The Prophets of Israel*. Grand Rapids: Baker, 1979.
Yates, Kyle. *Preaching from the Prophets*. New York: Harper and Row, 1942.
*Young, E. J. *My Servants the Prophets*. Grand Rapids: Eerdmans, 1952.

ISAIAH

*Alexander, J. A. *Commentary on the Prophecies of Isaiah*. Grand Rapids: Zondervan, 1953.
*Allis, O. T. *The Unity of Isaiah*. Philadelphia: Presbyterian and Reformed, 1950.
Archer, Gleason. *In the Shadow of the Cross*. Grand Rapids: Zondervan, 1957.
Brown, John. *The Sufferings and Glories of the Messiah*. Evansville, Ill.: Sovereign Grace, 1959.
*Kelley, William. *An Exposition of the Book of Isaiah*. Minneapolis: Klock, 1979.
*Leupold, H. C. *Exposition of Isaiah*. 2 vols. Grand Rapids: Baker, 1968 and 1971.
*MacRae, Allan A. *The Gospel of Isaiah*. Chicago: Moody Press, 1977.
Martin, Alfred. *Isaiah: The Salvation of Jehovah*. Chicago: Moody Press, 1956.
*Young, E. J. *The Book of Isaiah*. 3 vols. Grand Rapids: Eerdmans, 1965.

JEREMIAH and LAMENTATIONS

*Bright, John. *Jeremiah: Introduction, Translation, and Notes*. (Anchor Bible) Garden City, N.Y.: Doubleday, 1965.
*Harrison, R. K. *Jeremiah and Lamentations: An Introduction and Commentary*. (Tyndale series) Downers Grove, Ill.: InterVarsity Press, 1973.
*Ironsides, H. A. *Notes on Prophecies and Lamentations of Jeremiah*. New York: Loizeaux, 1906.
Jensen, Irving L. *Jeremiah and Lamentations*. Chicago: Moody Press, 1974.
Laetsch. T. F. K. *Jeremiah*. St. Louis: Concordia, 1953.
Morgan, G. C. *Studies in the Prophecy of Jeremiah*. Westwood, N. J.: Revell, 1955.
*Thompson, J. A. *The Book of Jeremiah* (NICOT). Grand Rapids: Eerdmans, 1980.

EZEKIEL

*Alexander, Ralph. *Ezekiel*. Chicago: Moody Press, 1976.
Ellison, H. L. *Ezekiel: The Man and His Message*. Grand Rapids: Eerdmans, 1956.
*Fairbairn, Patrick. *An Exposition of Ezekiel*. Minneapolis: Klock, 1979.
*Fienberg, C. L. *The Prophecy of Ezekiel*. Chicago: Moody Press, 1969.
Fisch, Solomon. *Ezekiel*. London: Soncino Press. 1950.

DANIEL

*Anderson, Robert. *The Coming Prince*. Reprint. Grand Rapids: Kregel, 1963.
*Boutflower, Charles. *In and Around the Book of Daniel*. London: SPCK, 1923.

*Culver, Robert D. *Daniel and the Latter Days*. Chicago: Moody Press, 1954.
Leupold, H. C. *Expositions of Daniel*. Reprint. Grand Rapids: Baker, 1969.
Tatford, F. A. *Daniel and His Prophecy: Studies in Daniel*. Minneapolis: Klock, 1980.
*Walvoord, J. F. *Daniel: The Key to Prophetic Revelation*. Chicago: Moody Press, 1971.
Wilson, R. D. *Studies in the Book of Daniel*. Chicago: Revell, 1938.
*Wood, Leon. *A Commentary on Daniel*. Grand Rapids: Zondervan, 1973.

*Entries marked with an asterisk should be consulted first.

Introduction to the Minor Prophets

I   The Names of the Minor Prophets

A. *SIGNIFICANCE OF THE TERM, "MINOR PROPHETS."* The designations, "Major Prophets" and "Minor Prophets," were coined by Augustine in the early fifth century, A.D. "Minor" refers to the brevity of the second group, certainly not to their relative importance. The Hebrews called them, "The Book of The Twelve." They were probably grouped together in this way by Ezra and the "Great Synagogue," c. 425 B.C., perhaps to accommodate their inclusion on one scroll. The whole group is shorter than either Isaiah, Jeremiah, or Ezekiel, individually.

B. *SIGNIFICANCE OF THE NAMES OF INDIVIDUAL PROPHETS.* Almost invariably, the name of each prophet has a meaning which comports strikingly with his message. This providential "coincidence" had real meaning to the ancient Hebrews for whom names were quite significant. God often used names to convey messages.

II   The Arrangement of the Minor Prophets

A. *THEIR ARRANGEMENT ACCORDING TO CHRONOLOGY.* Though the Majors are arranged in a basic chronological order, the Minors are not necessarily so arranged. No concensus exists among expositors (Talmudic or modern) as to the real purpose in the canonical order. The first six are chronologically prior to the last six, and the last six are in general chronological order. But the first six are a bit of an enigma as to their order, except that they all deal with the period preceding the northern captivity. Hosea may have been put first because of its length, but the order of the rest has nothing to do with length.

B. *THEIR ARRANGEMENT ACCORDING TO SUBSTANCE.* Genre often takes precedence to chronology (e.g., New Testament Epistles), especially for the Hebrews who had a thorough knowledge of their national history from the History Books. They were a covenant people and the covenant motif figured largely in all their literature. We might then trace a rational for the order of the books from the substance of the books in emphasizing God's character and this covenant motif. They may be grouped in three crisis periods as the nation moved toward judgment.

1. *Prior to the Northern Captivity* (722 B.C.)

Prophet	Date	Character of God	Covenant Message
Hosea	740	God's Love	Israel's broken covenant relations.
Joel	835	God's Judgment	Judah's warning of judgment for sin.
Amos	760	God's Righteousness	Israel's warning of ripened judgment.
Obadiah	845	God's Vengeance	Judah's reminder of covenant protection.
Jonah	765	God's Mercy to world	Israel's rebuke for national selfishness.
Micah	735	God's Pardon	Judah's rebuke for social injustices.

2. *Prior to the Southern Captivity* (606–586)

Prophet	Date	Character of God	Covenant Message
Nahum	c. 710	God's Jealousy	God's terror on Judah's attackers.
Habakkuk	608	God's Holiness	God's use of foreigners to discipline.
Zephaniah	625	God's Indignation	Covenant fulfillments in Day of Lord.

3. *After the Return from Captivity* (536–425)

Prophet	Date	Character of God	Covenant Message
Haggai	520	God's Glory	Their real glory in God's Presence.
Zechariah	520	God's Deliverance	Covenant fulfillments through Messiah.
Malachi	430	God's Greatness	Covenant obligations until Messiah comes.

The Book of Hosea

Introduction

AUTHORSHIP

A. *THE TITLE*

"Hosea" means "salvation" or deliverance. The name is identical in Hebrew form to "Hoshea" (the last king of Israel). It is also of the same root as "Joshua," which adds the prefix "yod" for "Yah" or Lord ("Yahweh is salvation").

B. *THE AUTHOR*

1. Little is known of Hosea except that he was the "son of Beeri" and that he prophesied to northern Israel in her final thirty years before captivity. He evidently moved south to Judah before the captivity in 722.

2. Like Isaiah, his contemporary in Judah, Hosea had a family whom the Lord used as "signs" to the nation of God's coming judgment and later restoration. His sad marital relations became the plot around which the Lord built His final message to the northern kingdom.

HISTORICAL SETTING

A. *DATE OF WRITING*—c. 740 B.C.
1. During the reigns of four kings of Judah, Uzziah to Hezekiah, c. 767–697, and during the reign of Jeroboam II of Israel, 793–752.
2. The minimum termini—Jeroboam died 752; Hezekiah began 728. Adding several years to this minimum span suggests c. 755–725.

B. *ADDRESSES*

Though Judah's kings are used for dating and Judah is mentioned in this book, the prophecy is addressed to northern Israel (1:4, 6, 10; 3:1; 4:1; 15; etc.). He addresses her as "Ephraim" thirty-seven times, after the central, powerful tribe that came from Joseph's specially blessed son, meaning "fruitful."

C. *THE POLITICAL SETTING*
1. Nationally, the monarchy had been divided into two kingdoms for c. 200 years. Both kingdoms had just passed through their most prosperous periods, known as the golden age. The Lord had also given Israel great national expansion under Jeroboam II all the way to Damascus. This was given as a special gift of the Lord's grace (2 Kin. 14:25-28), His goodness meant to lead them to repentance.
2. Internationally, a great eastern cloud was forming as the Assyrian power rose and began its forages west.

D. *THE RELIGIOUS SETTING*
1. Both religiously and morally, Israel was at its lowest point. The priests had joined the robbers and murderers on the highways (6:9). Their moral depravity had sunk to child sacrifices and prostitution in worship.
2. Jonah and Amos had previously spoken to that generation. Amos was sent from Judah to denounce Israel in blistering terms for moral corruption, religious indifference, and non-response to correction. Though Amos' ministry was short and explosive, Hosea's was long and patient as a pastor weeping and beseeching a flock floundering toward destruction.

THE PURPOSE OF THE BOOK OF HOSEA

The purpose of this book is to record God's final call to the indifferent northern kingdom as it plummeted toward disaster. The prophet describes the abominable condition of the nation who, like his wife, had sold itself into prostitution, and the unquenchable love of the

Lord who wept over Israel's estrangement and stood ready to receive her back into covenant relations through repentance.

Unique Contributions of Hosea

1. **THE BOOK STRESSING GOD'S MARITAL LOVE.** Hosea reveals one of the most profound pictures of God's love found in the Old Testament. Though forced to divorce and judge Israel because of her harlotries (2:2-5), the Lord yet confirmed His love for her and His intention to woo and win her back in righteousness (2:14-16, 20). He likened His covenant relationship with Israel to that of a deep, intimate marital union. Kyle Yates (*Preaching from the Prophets*) says of this great outpouring of divine love: "Nothing equals it in all literature. We find ourselves swept by its rushing torrent of eloquence until we weep our way through its amazing lines to see the great heart of love winning the ultimate victory." Deep, divine marital love is the first note of the Minor Prophets.

2. **THE SECRET POWER OF DIVINE LOVE** (14:9). This final verse is a challenge to the wisest and most discerning to fathom the unique power of God's love. Though His love for Israel appeared to be futile and unproductive in Hosea's time, it would not be so in the long run, for "the ways of the LORD *are* right" (9). His love for Israel would continue in spite of their waywardness, and in the end, vindicate itself in a harvest of righteousness in the nation. God does not make bad investments (2:19).

3. **THE PROPHET WITH A BROKEN MARRIAGE** (1:2; 3:1-3). The Lord's command of Hosea the prophet to marry a harlot comes as something of a shock, presenting a dilemma (1:2). According to Moses' Law, Gomer should have been stoned as a harlot (Lev. 20:10; Deut. 22:21-24). There is, of course, a question as to whether she was a harlot before they were married or became one after. Whichever the case, the times of Hosea were certainly not normal, for the land was filled with harlotry and the priests had become a band of murderers (4:12-14; 6:9). Gomer's adultery, however, was so bad she became a prostitute slave (3:1-2). The grace Hosea then showed in reclaiming and purchasing her out of the prostitution market was not a violation of the Law, however, for the Lord commanded it; it was a special dispensation of grace (similar to the grace shown David when he sinned in a similar way). The Lord used this suspension of judgment to display His own great grace to Israel who deserved total destruction for their prostitution in leaving the Lord for heathen gods (3:1-4).

    The divine analogy made here with human marriage is divinely intended and stated, and should not be overlooked. The truth presented is that sexual unfaithfulness is devastating to a marriage, invites God's judgment, and requires true repentance and genuine renewal of the marriage vows for restoration. Though the letter of the Law called for permanent separation by death or allowing remarriage (Deut. 24:1-4; Matt. 19:8-9), it is the part of grace to extend mercy for reconciliation in a genuine renewal of the union.

The practical message of Hosea is the dividends such grace repays (14:4-7), as demonstrated prophetically in this book.

4. **HOSEA'S RELATION TO JEREMIAH** (11:7-9; Jer. 9:1-2). What Jeremiah was to Judah, Hosea was to Israel 140 years earlier. Each pled with his nation as it plunged to destruction, entreating with God's love. Each ministered after a time of great national prosperity followed by spiritual indifference and moral corruption. Both expressed the Lord's sorrow as He was forced to divorce His people for adultery and allow their destruction by an eastern empire (Jer. 3:8; Hos. 2:2-7). Both also spoke of a renewed covenant relationship between the Lord and His people in the future messianic age (Jer. 31:31ff.; Hos. 1:11; 14:1ff.).

Outline of Hosea

THEME: God's Unfailing Love for Israel to Bring Judgment and Final Restoration.

5. *ISRAEL'S DEGENERATE RELIGION* (6:6-10; 9:15–10:2). Hosea describes one of the lowest points in Israel's religious history. Though they kept their rituals religiously, they were completely turned to idolatry. Banditry had become common among the people, and even the priests banded together to raid and murder pilgrims on the way to Shechem (4:11-13, 18; 6:9). The whole land was given to harlotry (4:11-14, 18; 6:10). Their hypocrisy was blatant. For this the Lord promised to come to them as a lion, leopard, bear, and wild beast to tear and devour them (5:14; 13:7-8). This northern kingdom had degenerated to the place of Judah one hundred and fifty years later in Daniel's time when the Lord described His plan to discipline the nation by four "wild beast" empires (Dan. 7). Amos, the southern prophet, had already been to Samaria to excoriate the northern leaders for their arrogant pride and lack of mercy and justice. As Amos denounced the degenerate system, Hosea pled with them on the basis of God's covenant love for them. Having rejected correction, they were being destroyed for "lack of knowledge" (4:6), and were due for extinction as a nation less than twenty years later.

6. *CHRISTOLOGY IN HOSEA.* The references to Messiah in Hosea are rare and rather oblique. 1) The love of God for Israel stressed in these chapters obviously includes Christ's love for both Israel and the Church (John 13:1). The Lord of the Old Testament (YHWH) was the Trinity, and the "husband-wife" relationship was a covenant relationship between that covenant Lord and His covenant people. The New Testament love relation of Christ and His Church is another expression of that divine love, even for those outside that covenant union (Eph. 2:11-14). 2) The reference in 3:5 that "Israel shall return, seek the LORD their God and David their king," is probably messianic. It could refer to the time of David's resurrection to be king under Christ who will be King of Kings (as noted in Ezek. 34:23-24), or to Messiah Himself as the "Son of David" (Mark 12:35). To Him will the sons of Israel come trembling "in the latter days" (3:5). 3) "Out of Egypt have I called My son" (11:1) is quoted by Matthew (2:15) as an Old Testament prophecy that Jesus would be taken to Egypt and called out by the Lord's angel. Matthew evidently uses this passage as a "type prophecy" of Christ, showing the close relationship of Messiah with Israel, even having similar experiences of Gentile affliction and escape from murderous monarchs.

The Book
of Joel

Introduction

AUTHORSHIP

A. *THE TITLE*

"Joel" means "Jehovah is God," being a compound of YHWH and El. The prophet's name again admirably fits the burden of his prophecy: "You shall know that I *am* the LORD your God" (2:27; 3:17).

B. *THE AUTHOR*

Like Hosea, little is known of Joel but his father's name which was Pethuel. The content indicates he lived and prophesied in Judah and Jerusalem and may have been a priest, as suggested from the frequent references to priests. Fourteen other Joels are found in the Bible.

HISTORICAL SETTING

A. *DATE OF WRITING*—c. 825 B.C.
   1. Joel is one of six Minor Prophets not specifically dated in the text (with Obadiah, Jonah, Nahum, Habakkuk, and Malachi).
   2. Joel's dating is generally agreed to be quite early, c. 825, though some critical scholars date it c. 350. Several considerations require either an early date or a quite late date after the captivity:
      a. The prominence of priests and elders and the absence of any reference to Judah's kings.
      b. The absence of any reference to idolatry when speaking of their sins.
      c. The denouncing of local enemies and the absence of any reference to Assyria, Babylon, or Persia.
   3. The early date of c. 825, when King Jehoash was sixteen and Jehoiada the priest still was the greatest influence, is best confirmed as noted below:
      a. During the early part of Jehoash's reign Jehoiada the high priest actually ruled, having set up Jehoash as king when he was six.
      b. At this time their enemies were local rather than eastern (2 Kin. 12).
      c. The position of Joel before Amos in the canon suggests an early date.
      d. Joel is much quoted by pre-exilic prophets such as Amos, Isaiah, and Micah. The reverse is highly unlikely (compare Joel 3:10 with Isaiah 2:4 and Micah 4:3; Joel 3:16 with Amos 1:2; Joel 3:18 with Amos 9:13).
      e. The language and thought are similar to Amos, and the mention of the Greeks (3:6) is consistent with archaeological findings.
      f. The reference to the Valley of Jehoshaphat, mentioned only here, is most fitting here, for he was the last good king at this time, winning great victories around Jerusalem by calling on the Lord.

B. *THE POLITICAL SETTING*
   1. On the national scene, Judah was in a period of rebuilding following the wicked reign of Queen Athaliah (841–835). This rebuilding was mainly under the leadership of the old high priest, Jehoiada, who had had the queen slain and the heir apparent Joash made king at age six (2 Kin. 11-12).
   2. On the international scene, no great empires were prominent. Judah, however,

was being harrassed by various local enemies such as Tyre, Sidon, Philistia, Edom, and Egypt (3:4, 19).

C. *THE RELIGIOUS SETTING*
1. The period of Baal worship had come to an end with the purge of Jehu in 841 and that of Jehoiada in Judah in 835. Following that purge, however, true godliness did not suddenly characterize the nation, but a spirit of indifference set in. The temple itself was not repaired properly until 813, the twenty-third year of Jehoash (2 Kin. 12:6).
2. These failures on the part of the people could well have brought the corrective judgment from the Lord of locusts, drought, and harassment from local enemies.

D. *THE CANONICAL SETTING*
Joel's prophecy followed about twenty years after that of Obadiah in Judah, who

---

Outline of Joel

THEME: The Lord's Judgment and Salvation in the Day of the Lord.

prophesied the doom of Edom. It also preceded chronologically the ministries of Jonah and Amos to Israel in the North, who spoke about sixty years later. While Joel prophesied to Judah, Elisha was ministering to Israel in a long ministry that lasted from c. 850 to 798.

Joel follows Hosea in the canon as God's judgment follows the spurning of His love. The name Joel ("Jehovah is God") also fits well in the early part of the canon when, historically, the battle with the Baal system had just been concluded. Jehovah was indeed the God of nature and of judgment.

THE PURPOSE OF THE BOOK OF JOEL

The Book of Joel has a twofold purpose, historic and prophetic. The historic purpose was to call the nation of Judah to national repentance as a proper response to the Lord's judgments of locusts and drought, lest a more devastating scourge come upon them. The prophetic purpose was to introduce the future Day of the Lord in which the Lord will bring the heathen into subjection, deliver His people, and take up His dwelling in their midst. The unprecedented locust plague was only a foretaste of that future Day of the Lord.

Unique Contributions of Joel

1. **THE DAY OF THE LORD EMPHASIS.** Joel is popularly known as the prophet of the day of the Lord, supposedly having coined the phrase for the Lord's great judgment day for the nations. He may, however, have borrowed the term from Obadiah who used it in this way some twenty years earlier in reference to Edom's coming judgment. The significance of this term has already been noted in the previous discussion.

2. **THE PROPHET OF THE SPIRIT'S OUT-POURING AT PENTECOST** (2:28-32). Both Peter and Paul use this passage as a prophecy of the Christian dispensation (Acts 2:16-21; Rom. 10:13). Peter used it to confirm the validity of the tongues gift at Pentecost, and Paul used it to confirm the validity of the offer of salvation by faith to all the world. Neither claim the prophecy was "fulfilled" completely at Pentecost, but that it related. The first part was evidently fulfilled at Pentecost, that is, the Spirit was poured out for the world-wide proclamation of salvation by simply calling upon the name of the Lord. The last part, concerning the heavenly signs of physical disturbances in the sun, moon, and sky, however, did not occur at that time, but will take place just before the "great day of His wrath," as noted in Revelation 6:12-17. Peter evidently quoted the whole prophecy at Pentecost to include the universal offer of salvation at the close (Joel 2:32). Like the prophecy of Messiah's coming in Isaiah 9:6-7, this prophecy of the Holy Spirit's work of grace and work of awesome judgment has two stages, quite widely separated.

3. **THE PROMISE OF MATERIAL PROSPERITY FOR REPENTANCE** (2:18-27). Joel makes a special emphasis on material and physical benefits flowing from repentance and

obedience. Such repentance, he said, would remove the plagues of locusts and drought and restore the blessings of rain, good crops, and protection from enemies (2:19-20). These promises were for Israel, not necessarily for the New Testament Church. Israel was under covenant relations with the Lord and had been promised those benefits for obedience (Lev. 26:14-20; Deut. 11:13-17). The Lord's purpose in this promise to Israel was to demonstrate His sovereignty over all nature as a testimony to both Israel and the nations. No such "material benefits" covenant was made with the church, as such. Having thoroughly demonstrated His sovereignty in previous ages, the Lord appeals to faith in His established Word, apart from material benefits (Matt. 19:21; Luke 14:33). The general principle of rich reaping for generous sowing, of course, is always applicable, but the reaping may be reserved for heaven with its eternal rewards (Prov. 11:24; Luke 6:38; Gal. 6:7-9).

4. *MAKING THE LORD AN ALLY* (2:16-18). Verse 17 is the turning point of the book. It

---

The Prophetic Day of the Lord

The first Writing Prophets, Obadiah and Joel, introduce the concept, "day of the LORD," called by Franz Delitzsch, (*The Pentateuch*) the "watchword of prophecy." Though it is alluded to earlier (Ps. 9:8; 96:13; 98:9) and referred to many times in both Testaments, it is specifically mentioned by half (eight) of the Writing Prophets (see below). To understand its significance, several features of that period should be noted:

1. *Its definition.* The day of the Lord is a biblical concept signifying any time of divine intervention when God assumes command of the world order to bring judgment or blessing in conformity to His stated principles. It is God's day of world rulership in contrast to "man's day." Such was His judgment at the great flood (2 Pet. 3:5-10), the drought of Joel's time (1:15), the destruction of Jerusalem (Zeph. 1:4, 7), and the judgment of Palestine and Egypt under Nebuchadnezzar (Ezek. 30:3ff.). The references indicate, however, a special period entitled "day of the LORD," which figures in the eschatological program of God in the end times. It is not just the time of the "great white throne" (Rev. 20:11) judgment of individuals, but the time of His calling the living nations to account as to how they have responded to His "everlasting covenant" of truth and justice (Is. 24:5; cf. Gen. 9:6-16).

2. *Its time or duration.* In this eschatological sense, the day of the Lord is that future period when Messiah, God's King, begins to deal with nations in judgment to prepare the earth for His millennial reign. The New Testament more precisely delineates its time limits as beginning with the great "departure," following which Antichrist will appear to coalesce the world in rebellion against God (2 Thess. 2:3). After the dark night of the Lord's judgment, the day of the Lord will have a bright period of blessing throughout

contains the Lord's prescribed prayer of repentance for the people that changes the perspective of the book from adversity to blessing. The following verse begins, "Then the LORD will . . . ," and elucidates the various blessings He will be able to give them following repentance. He would turn from His role of adversary to being an ally; He would turn their adversity into prosperity. The point is that true repentance makes God a defender for the penitent and makes the penitent capable of properly receiving His blessings.

5. *CHRISTOLOGY IN JOEL.* Joel, the "prophet of the Holy Spirit," does not have many direct references to Messiah. In many of the Lord's declarations as "Jehovah" (YHWH) however, He speaks as Messiah who will come to deliver and rule His people in the messianic age. Several such passages are, "Then you shall know that I *am* in the midst of Israel," (2:27), "I will pour out My Spirit on all flesh" (2:28), "I will also gather all nations, . . . I will enter into judgment with them" (3:2), "Let the nations be wakened, and come up to the Valley of Jehoshaphat; For there I will sit to judge" (3:12), and "I

the millennial reign of Christ on earth, continuing until the renovation of the earth (2 Pet. 3:10-12). The preponderant emphasis through the Bible is on that time of tribulation judgment described in Revelation 4—20.

3. The *"great and terrible day of the LORD."* This doubly fearsome term is used only by the first and last prophets of Judah (2:31; Mal. 4:5). It appears to describe the last half of the seven-year period of Daniel's "seventieth week," which Jesus referred to as the "great tribulation" (Matt. 24:21; cf. Rev. 7:14). Before it occurs two things must take place, according to Joel and Malachi: 1) the Lord will display great signs in the heavens to alert the earth (3:14-15; Rev. 6:12-17); and 2) the prophet Elijah will return for a restoration ministry to Israel (Mal. 4:5-6; cf. Rev. 12:3ff.). Other prophets describe this awesome time of world judgment by the Lord that will leave few survivors (e.g., Is. 24:1ff.), but it is the first and last prophets to Judah that give it this special designation.

4. *Its chronological development by the Prophets.*
    a. Obadiah—Described as a time of judgment and reprisal for the nations.
    b. Joel 1:15; 2:1, 11, 31; 3:14—Seen as a day of destruction from the Lord.
    c. Amos 5:18, 20—To be a day of great darkness for the world, but also for Israel.
    d. Isaiah 2:12; 13:6, 9—To be a day of reckoning for the proud and a day of cruel destruction from the Almighty.
    e. Zephaniah 1:7, 14—To be a day of great wrath from the Lord, approaching very quickly.
    f. Ezekiel 13:5; 30:3—The day the nations wailed when Nebuchadnezzar wielded the "sword of the Lord" in conquering the West.
    g. Zechariah 14:1—The coming day of the Lord's fierce defense of Jerusalem when all nations will be gathered against it.
    h. Malachi 4:5—The coming day when the Lord treads down the wicked and destroys them as chaff, preceded by the restoration ministry of Elijah (cf. Matt. 17:11).

will acquit them of bloodguilt, whom I had not acquitted'' (3:21; cf. John 5:22). Though oblique these references can be seen as messianic through the lenses of later passages.

The Book of Amos

Introduction

AUTHORSHIP

A. *THE TITLE*

"Amos" means "burden" or "burden-bearer." The book contains many judgment-burdens or woes which the prophet delivered to Israel.

B. *THE AUTHOR*

1. Much is revealed about Amos the person in the book:
   a. He was from Tekoa, a small village 5 miles south of Bethlehem.
   b. He was a businessman-farmer and a preacher, though not a trained prophet of the schools of the prophets. His business involved both sheep ranching and fruit-growing. (1:1; 7:14).
   c. He was a man of fine intellect and outstanding writing ability. His book is classic in both content and artistic expression.
   d. He had both a deep sense of social justice and courage to confront.
   e. Like Jonah (who just preceded him), Amos was a missionary prophet.
   f. He was very knowledgeable of social and national affairs, evidently traveling to the north to market his produce.
2. Concerning the authorship, there is little controversy by critics as to either the authorship by Amos or the early date of its writing. The imprint and style of this unique prophet persist throughout the book.

HISTORICAL SETTING (2 Kin. 14:23-29)

A. *DATE OF WRITING*—c. 760 B.C.

1. The years Jeroboam II and Uzziah reigned simultaneously were 767–752.
2. The great "earthquake" of 1:1 was evidently accompanied by a solar eclipse, as suggested by 8:8-10, which astronomers have dated June 15, 763 B.C. The prophecy to Israel occurred two years before, 765, and the writing of it was done sometime after the earthquake, c. 760. So great was this earthquake that Zechariah remembered it 270 years later. (Zech. 14:15)

B. *THE POLITICAL SETTING*
1. Internationally, the Fertile Crescent had relative peace from 800 to 745. Egypt was rather weak and Assyria did not begin its western penetration until 745, under Tiglath-Pileser III.
2. Nationally, the kingdoms of Israel and Judah had fiercely fought each other. Israel under Joash had nearly destroyed Jerusalem about thirty years before in Amaziah's reign, taking him captive. Under Jeroboam II and Uzziah, however, the two kingdoms were at peace and both enjoyed a period of great prosperity and expansion. Israel occupied Damascus to the north, after having been previously dominated by her. Jeroboam II put most of the surrounding nations to tribute.
3. This period was known as the "golden age" for both kingdoms and they were "at ease in Zion" (6:1). The idea of judgment or national collapse was far from their thinking. No one suspected that within ten years, political chaos and assassinations would shake the nation as it plunged toward destruction.

C. *THE RELIGIOUS SETTING*
1. Israel's calf worship system at Bethel was 170 years old in Amos' time. Though Baal worship was purged from the land by Jehu in 841, calf worship continued for obvious political reasons. The high priest was Amaziah, probably appointed by the king from the laity.
2. Morally, the nation was corrupt both inwardly and outwardly. The upper class was wealthy, but wicked. Prophets and priests served for personal gain. Social injustice to the poor was the norm; might was right. Rich landlords devoured the poor, living in luxury and vice. The nation was heathen in everything but name.
3. Amos attributed this condition of corruption to the king and high priest. For this, he declared, both the house of Jeroboam II and Amaziah the priest would be destroyed by the sword (7:8, 17).
4. The coming of the predicted earthquake (8:8-9) evidently had little effect in reining in the godless life of indulgence and may have been one of the reasons for Amos recording the prophecy after it occurred. The earthquake was centered near Jerusalem (Zech. 14:5), but Bethel was only about 12 miles north of Jerusalem.

D. *THE GEOGRAPHICAL SETTING*
1. Amos lived 10 miles south of Jerusalem in the high hills of Judah near the highway going from Jerusalem to Hebron and Beersheba. This is thought to be the same region in which John the Baptist later grew up.
2. Bethel, the place where Amos spoke this prophecy, was about 22 miles north of Tekoa up the highway. It was just north of Judah's border, about 2 miles. This was Israel's main sanctuary, where the high priest lived, though the royal residence of Jeroboam II was in Samaria, about 25 miles north. Amos addressed the nation from its religious center.

E. THE CANONICAL SETTING

    1. The Book of Amos follows Joel in the canon as an amplification of Joel 3:16, "The LORD also will roar from Zion," linked to Amos 1:2 (Keil, *The Pentateuch*). The book is followed by Obadiah which amplifies Amos 9:12, "That they may possess the remnant of Edom."

    2. The ministry of Amos to Israel occurred during the latter time of Jonah's ministry to Israel (785–760). Amos' ministry, however, was a short, lightning crusade, an announcement of doom with adroit sharpness. Hosea came on the same scene about 5–10 years later (755–725) to dramatize the nation's condition, bemoaning its hopeless corruption for refusing knowledge.

THE PURPOSE OF THE BOOK OF AMOS

The purpose of this prophecy was to sound a trumpet warning to Israel's leadership and upper classes of the impending judgment of God on the nation. His warning was not so much of religious failures as it was of spiritual, moral, and social corruption. The nation was about to be destroyed because of the social injustices of the upper classes against the poor and weak, for God is a God of righteousness. As Hosea was the preacher of God's love, Amos was the preacher of God's justice.

Unique Contributions of Amos

1. **THE EMPHASIS ON SOCIAL JUSTICE.** No prophet more eloquently thundered against social injustice than did Amos. The key verse of his book is a classic on justice (5:24): "Let justice roll down like water, And righteousness like a mighty stream." Though he held his crusade at Bethel the place of the shrine of calf worship, Amos hardly mentioned that national sin as he proclaimed God's outrage at their violation of human rights and exploitation of the poor (e.g., 5:6-20). He emphasized God's great concern for moral issues. Ritual without righteousness is not God's religion, but a horrible distortion of both His character and His careful instruction to men. The prophet strongly stressed in his many judgments that any nation that violates the moral and social concerns of God and engages in the exploitation of the poor is doomed for early destruction (1:5, 8, 10, 12, 15; 2:3, 5, 14-16; etc.).

2. **THE DOOM'S DAY PROPHET** (4:12). "Prepare to meet your God, O Israel," was the clear, unequivocal message of Amos. In the bright sunshine of Israel's peace and prosperity, he came to announce a soon coming judgment. His message was almost unmitigated in its emphasis on the doom of the nation. Though he offered mercy to individuals who would respond (5:4, 6, 14), the prophet declared that the nation itself had passed its day of pardon and judgment was now inevitable. This announcement and summons from the Lord was not given by a local prophet (such as Jonah who also prophesied at that time),

but by an outside prophet who was specifically commissioned for this mission, to suddenly appear at their national citadel of religion to arouse the leaders. His message was pointed and unmistakable: God was calling them to account and "doom's day" was set; the destroying lion had already roared (3:8; 4:12; 5:27).

3. **THE RUSTIC, COUNTRY PROPHET** (7:14). Like Micah, who twenty years later prophesied in Judah, Amos was a rustic prophet from the farm or ranch. Though his style was most elegant and lively, his idiom was genuinely rustic. The metaphors and symbols he

Outline of Amos

THEME: The Coming Judgment of Israel for Moral Corruption and Social Injustice.

used were of the farm, such as plowing, gardening, vine growing, reaping, dealing with locusts, etc. In this country style Amos was like the first great prophet of Israel, Elijah, who came from the hills of Gilead. He also stood at the head of a long line of prophets and preachers who were men of the soil that God commissioned into prophetic service to arouse the self-indulgent elite and arrogant to the reality of an early accounting before God. John the Baptist was the last prophet of that rustic class.

4. *THE CLASSICALLY ORGANIZED PROPHET.* No prophecy is so neatly organized as that of Amos. The movement of his message is nicely developed from the general to the specific, then elaborating the details. He first gives general judgments on all Palestine nations, as if arousing Israel's attention and common agreement as to the need for judgment before "lowering the boom" on Israel herself. In many ways the book almost outlines itself by the various superscripts that are used to introduce its parts. Chapters 1–2 are punctuated by eight "Thus says the LORD," to divide its messages; chapters 3–5 use the introductory phrase, "Hear this word" three times; and chapters 7–8 present their visions with, "the LORD God showed me." Though the prophet dealt with Israel as "summer fruit" (late summer or overripe, 8:1ff.), he was extremely tidy in his pronouncements of judgment.

5. *THE DAY OF THE LORD CLARIFIED* (5:18). Like Joel, sixty years earlier, Amos emphasized the coming day of the Lord. Unlike Joel, however, Amos presented that day as one of "darkness, and not light" (5:18). Not only would that judgment destroy the heathen (which Israel would applaud), but also sinners in Israel. This was an essential clarification for Israel, for they had misconstrued their covenant relation with the Lord to be some kind of immunization against calamity or judgment (Joel 3:12-16). To this citadel of northern religion the prophet Amos came as an outsider to jolt them with the revelation that the Lord is no respecter of persons. He judges inhumanity, social injustice, and religious corruption wherever it may be found. Religious sinners with their greater knowledge will, in fact, be judged much more harshly than those with lesser amounts of light and revelation (5:21-24).

6. *SYMBOLIC VISIONS INTRODUCED* (1:1). Amos was the first prophet to employ symbolic visions in prophetic utterances. Many later prophets spoke from similar revelations such as the Major Prophets and Zechariah. The power of these symbolic visions by Amos may be illustrated by his first one in 1:2, which was the basis for his judgments on the nations of Palestine in chapters 1–2. The essence of that vision was that the Lord was roaring from Zion in Jerusalem and the whole land from Tekoa's pastures to the top of Mount Carmel in the north would shake and mourn. This symbol of the Lord roaring, as a lion roaring over a prey, is carried through much of the book, emphasizing the imminency of the coming judgment. The final vision of the Lord with His wrecking crew at the altar of Bethel completes the cycle, showing where the Lord's demolition will begin and that there will be no place to hide, even at the "top of Carmel" (9:1-3). Each of the symbols described strikingly tells its story for anyone to understand and be awed.

7. **CHRISTOLOGY IN AMOS** (9:11-15). The messianic contributions of this book are reserved for the last four verses that describe the future restoration of Israel.

a. The fallen tabernacle of David will be raised up (11). This is an early recognition that the house of David would fall and would later be raised up to possess all nations. The raising of the "tabernacle of David" signified re-establishing the throne to promote righteousness and lovingkindness (Is. 16:5), suggesting Messiah.

b. In that day the Lord (Messiah) will restore Israel from captivity to permanently rebuild the cities and plant the ground to enjoy their harvests. The emphasis throughout this passage is on the Lord's "I will." As the Lord Himself was to orchestrate the Judgment (9:1-8), He would likewise personally take charge of the reconstruction (9-15).

The Book of Obadiah

Introduction

AUTHORSHIP

A. *THE TITLE*

"Obadiah" means "servant of the Lord." It was a common name in the Old Testament, similar to Onesimus in the New Testament or Abdullah in Arabic.

B. *THE AUTHOR*

Virtually nothing is known of the prophet Obadiah except that he was a prophet in Jerusalem at the time of Edom's violent attacks on the city. As a servant he obscures his person to accentuate his message.

HISTORICAL SETTING (1 Kin. 8:16-22; 2 Chr. 21)

A. *DATE OF WRITING*—c. 845 B.C.

1. This is one of the most difficult prophecies to date. Conservatives are divided as to whether it was early or late, depending on how each views the disaster to Jerusalem referred to in vv. 10-14. Jerusalem was pillaged five times during the monarchy and the prophets:

926—By Egypt when Rehoboam ruled Judah. (1 Kin. 14:25-26)

845—By Philistines and Arabs (after Edom's revolt). (2 Chr. 21)

790—By Israel under Joash. (2 Chr. 24:23-24)

597—By Nebuchadnezzar when Jehoiachin was exiled. (2 Kin. 24:10-16)

586—By Nebuchadnezzar when city and temple were destroyed. (2 Kin. 25)

The Edomites were involved only in the 845 and 586 pillagings.

2. The 845 date is the most probable for the following reasons:

    a. It was placed in the early part of the canon by the Hebrews.

    b. The disaster referred to by Obadiah was not necessarily a complete destruction and exile, but more of a pillaging.

    c. Obadiah is quoted in Jeremiah 49:7-22 almost wholly about 240 years later. The reverse can hardly be true because: 1) a prophet would not quote an earlier prophet almost wholly, putting his name to it. 2) Jeremiah used many quotes in chapter 49 as he summarized the Lord's judgments on the nations. 3) Obadiah's prophecy was a "vision" from the Lord (1:1), not a restatement of a former prophecy.

B. *THE GEOGRAPHICAL SETTING*

Edom was located in the Mount Seir range of mountains and plateaus to the southeast of Judah beyond the Dead Sea. Its territory extended from Moab at the River Arnon to the Gulf of Aqaba, about 100 miles, with Sela (Petra) in the middle. After Judah's captivity in 586, they took southern Judah, making Hebron their chief city.

C. *THE RELIGIOUS SETTING*

1. Judah in 845 was under Jehoram, a wicked king, who, with his wicked queen Athaliah, allowed Baal worship into Judah, as Ahab and Jezebel had introduced it into Israel about 25 years earlier. This provoked the Lord to allow foreign invaders to punish Judah.

2. Contemporary with Obadiah were Elijah and Elisha in the northern kingdom. Elijah wrote his only recorded letter to Jehoram, announcing his special judgment from the Lord.

D. *THE POLITICAL SETTING*

1. Judah's Internal Politics. Following the prosperous, godly reign of King Jehoshaphat, his wicked son Jehoram became the sole ruler of Judah in 848 B.C. at the age of thirty-two. He began his reign by killing all his brothers and reigned eight years with his idolatrous wife, Athaliah, who was the daughter of Ahab and Jezebel. He died a dishonorable and painful death of a horrible bowel disease, as predicted by Elijah in the only recorded letter from that prophet (2 Chr. 21:12-18). Because of his wickedness the Lord allowed Edom's revolt against Judah and the pillaging of the king's house by the Philistines and Arabs (2 Chr. 21:16ff.). This also cost him the loss of all his wives and children except Athaliah and Ahaziah. It was evidently after one such foray, in which the Edomites joined, that this book was written by Obadiah who received a vision from the Lord.

2. Judah's Relations With Edom. Though Israel and Edom originated from twin brothers, Jacob and Esau, they became inveterate enemies. Their relations may be summarized by the following recorded events:

1406 B.C.   Edom refused Israel passage enroute to Jordan (Num. 20:14-21).

992   David conquered Edom, slaying most males (2 Sam. 8:13; 1 Kin. 11:15ff.).

860   Edom (with Moab and Ammon) attacked Judah, but was destroyed by its allies, Moab and Ammon, after Jehoshaphat's call to prayer (2 Chr. 20).

Outline of Obadiah

THEME: God's Judgment on Vengeful Edom and His Final Restoration of Israel.*

*Or, The Final Triumph of Mount Zion Over Mount Seir.

847	Edom revolted from Judah, setting up its own king (2 Chr. 21:8).
845	Edom with Philistia pillaged Judah (2 Chr. 21:16-17). The Book of Obadiah was probably written shortly after this.
785	Amaziah attacked Edom, slaying 20,000 (2 Chr. 25:11-12).
735	Edom again revolted, taking many captives (2 Chr. 28:17).
586	Edom vengefully aided Babylon in destroying Jerusalem, for which they were allowed to settle in southern Judah (Ps. 137:7; Ezek. 25:12).
300	Edom's cities and land were taken by the Nabataean Arabs, forcing the Edomites into middle and southern Judah.
165	Judas Maccabaeus took Hebron which they had made their capital.
126	John Hyrcanus subdued the Edomites (now called Idumaea) and forced them to become circumcised as Jews.
40	Herod the Idumean, following his father Antipater, became king over Palestine, conquering Jerusalem in 37 B.C.
A.D. 70	The Edomites joined the Romans in destroying and ravaging Jerusalem. Following this, they disappeared from the pages of history as a people, assimilating with the Nabataean Arabs of south Judah.

3. Edom's Political Strength. The Edomites were a hardy, proud people, known for their wisdom and strength. Their rugged, mountainous location provided natural seclusion and protection, and the verdant plateaus provided lush pastures. Sela (Gr. *Petra*) their chief city is one of the most colorful cities on earth, cut out of sandstone, and is almost invulnerable. It has few entrances, the main one being the "Sik," a narrow defile about a mile long. In the time of the Nabataens this city became a center of caravan trade with commerce moving in four directions. It survived as a great center until A.D. 630, when it was desolated by the conquering Moslem Arabs. It was lost to the Western World until rediscovered in 1812.

THE PURPOSE OF THE BOOK OF OBADIAH

The prophet's purpose was twofold: 1) to announce the final destruction of Edom for its unquenchable vengeance and violence toward Israel, God's people; and 2) to reassert the ultimate triumph of Mount Zion in the Day of the Lord when Israel will possess the land of Edom. The "invulnerable city" will not be Mount Seir, but Mount Zion.

Unique Contributions of Obadiah

1. *THE SAD FATE OF ISAAC'S FAVORITE SON.* This book concerns the ultimate fate of the children of the twin sons of Isaac and Rebekah, who had one of the most celebrated

marriages of the Bible (Gen. 24). Its special emphasis, however, is on Esau the son to whom Isaac insisted the blessing should go, though God had already selected Jacob (Gen. 25:23). Isaac's choice of Esau admittedly appeared to be the best choice, as the actions of the two boys are observed in Genesis. The following history of independence, idolatry, vengeance, and violence by Esau's children, however, points up the peril of human choices in opposition to God's choice.

2. *A LESSON ON THE DANGER OF FAMILY BITTERNESS* (10-12). Though coming from twin brothers, the nations of Edom and Israel became bitter and implacable enemies. This enmity began early with a "root of bitterness" that grew into a national, mutual hatred that was never reconciled (Heb. 12:15-17). Ironically, it began in a godly home where favoritism was shown by the parents that ignited into intense rivalry by the boys and a bitter feud by their children (Gen. 25:28ff.; 27:41). That family feud still makes international headlines in the Middle East, reminding us of James' principle: "See how great a forest a little fire kindles!" (James 3:5).

3. *A SHORT BOOK WITH A LONG PRELUDE* (Gen. 25:23; Is. 63:1; Mal. 1:4). The message of this book cannot be properly appreciated without some familiarity with its background. It is not only the shortest book in the Old Testament, but it probably has the longest introduction. The following are some of the highlights of Edom's history:
   a. The story began with a quarrel between twin brothers in which Jacob and his mother schemed to get the birthright and blessing away from Esau (Gen. 25, 27).
   b. Their hatred and bitterness of twenty years somewhat subsided when Jacob had a meeting with the Lord, returning from Padan Aram (Gen. 32, 33).
   c. Their hatred became national when Israel returned from Egypt, though the Lord commanded Israel not to retaliate (Num. 20:14-21; Deut. 2:5).
   d. This hatred between Israel and Edom continued for 1000 years, from Moses to Malachi, involving many minor skirmishes.
   e. The Edomites were condemned by many prophets: Num. 24:18-19, Is. 11:14; Jer. 49:7-22; Ezek. 25:12-14; Joel 3:19; Amos 1:11-12; Mal. 1:3-4.
   f. Matthew introduces the story of Jesus in Matthew 1–2 with the record of the intense enmity of Herod the Edomite who had become king of Israel. That enmity is seen in several generations of the Herodian dynasty:
      1) Herod the Great sought to slay Jesus (Matt. 2:16).
      2) Herod Antipas had John the Baptist slain, sought to kill Jesus, and cruelly humiliated Him at His death trial (Matt. 14:10; Luke 13:31; 23:11).
      3) Herod Agrippa I had James killed and tried to kill Peter (Acts 12:1ff.).
   g. The nation of Edom (Idumea), like Israel, became extinct after the Roman invasion and purge of A.D. 70, the Romans making it part of Arabia Petraea.
   h. The Edomites are evidently slated by the prophets for renewed prominence in the latter days, for they will be one of the enemies Messiah will destroy when He comes in judgment (Is. 34:1-8; 63:1-4; Mal. 1:4).

i. This final destruction will be complete and perpetual, though other ancient neighbors of Israel will be restored (Is. 19:23-25; Jer. 49:13; Ezek. 35:9; Obad. 9; Mal. 1:4). Obadiah summarizes the final chapter in this story, as if closing the books on Edom. They were a people who could have become great, being endowed with rare wisdom and strength, but "sold their birthright" by despising God's Word and God's chosen people. They allowed an early jealousy to turn to bitterness and vengeance, incurring God's eternal judgment. Renowned Edomites of history are extremely rare, being such as Doeg who slew the priests of Nob, Hadad the enemy of David, and Herod the attempted slayer of Messiah (1 Sam. 22:18; 1 Kin. 11:14ff.; Matt. 2:16).

The Book of Jonah

Introduction

AUTHORSHIP

A. *THE TITLE*

The name Jonah means "dove." Jonah was sent by the Lord as a "messenger of peace" to Nineveh, though his attitude was more that of a "hawk" than a dove.

B. *THE AUTHOR*

1. Jonah was probably the author, though the book was written in the third person and does leave Jonah in a rather bad light. Perhaps he did this as an indictment of both himself and the nation for their merciless attitude toward the heathen, while the heathen were responding to God's mercy.

2. He is specifically identified with the prophet of 2 Kings 14:25, as the "son of Amittai." His hometown was Gath Hepher, a small village of Zebulon about two miles northeast of Nazareth (now known as Mashhad). Jewish tradition says he was the son of the widow of Zarephath whom Elijah raised from the dead, though the claim has no verification.

3. Jonah prophesied in the early reign of Jeroboam II, announcing to Israel that the Lord would again have mercy on them by granting them a time of great national growth. This mercy was shown in spite of their wickedness, designed as a stimulus to bring repentance (2 Kin. 14:23-28).

HISTORICAL SETTING

A. *DATE OF WRITING*—c. 765 B.C.

The time range of this prophecy was during the reign of Jeroboam II, 793–753, according to 2 Kings 14:25. Jonah's visit to Nineveh was probably toward the end of his long ministry in Israel, c. 765. He then wrote the book after he returned and sought to minister to Israel through it.

B. *THE QUESTION OF HISTORICITY*

1. The historicity of the events of this book has been challenged by modern critics as has that of Genesis 1–11. It has almost become a "proving ground" for one's acceptance of biblical inerrancy. As Isaiah and Daniel are tests of faith because of their prophecies, Jonah has become a test of faith because of its two "unbelievable" miracles.

2. Two basic views are taken of the story of Jonah, the "allegorical" and the "literal" or historical. The first alleges that the story is a myth or a fictional device to convey some grand spiritual truth, similar to the parables. The literal recognizes it as an actual history. That it should be recognized as an authentic history is evident from the following:

   a. The story is presented as an actual history relating to specific ancient places and people and gives no hint of being fictional.

   b. Jonah is identified as "the son of Amittai" in 2 Kings 14:25 and Jonah 1:1.

   c. Jewish tradition in an unbroken line testifies to the literal historicity of Jonah and his experience.

   d. Christ testified to the historicity of Jonah, noting both miracles as being actual events (Matt. 12:40-42; 16:4; Luke 11:29-32). He links the historicity of Jonah with the historicity of Solomon.

   e. The great fish that provided Jonah with accommodations in the sea is specifically said to have been prepared by the Lord, which may or may not have been an ordinary whale. Secular history provides us with similar stories on a lesser scale, though this record is not dependent on such confirmations.

   f. To reject this story as actual history on the basis of its miraculous elements is to call into question the whole supernatural structure of the Bible. The miracles of Moses, Elijah, and Elisha would also have to be rejected by that standard.

C. *THE SITUATION IN NINEVEH*

1. Geographically, Nineveh was located on the east side of the northern Tigris River, nearly 600 miles from Israel, a three-month trip in ancient times. It was one of the most ancient cities, established by Nimrod (Gen. 10:11). Its population is estimated to have been c. 600,000, having Calah the capital and other towns in its close environs. Though the inner wall of the city was only three miles in diameter, its villages and suburbs stretched over twenty miles.

2. Politically, Assyria was in a state of decline at this time, from the death of Adad-nirari III in 782 to the coming of Tiglath-Pileser III in 745. Following Adad-nirari was Shalmaneser IV (782–773) and Ashur-dan III (773–754). Jonah's visit was probably during the reign of Ashur-dan III.

3. Religiously, a trend toward monotheism had begun in Assyria with Adad-nirari by his monolatry. He advocated: "Put thy trust in Nebo; trust not another god." Several cataclysmic events also occurred during these years which may have been used to prepare them. In 765 and 759 great plagues befell the city and in June 15, 763, a total solar eclipse took place.
4. Morally, the people of Nineveh were known as "a sensual, ferocious race." They lived on plunder, taking pride in the mounds of human heads they could bring back from their scavenging forages on other cities. They fortified themselves with an inner and outer wall, the outer being 60 miles around, 100 feet high, and wide enough for three chariots to be driven abreast on it. Spaced around the wall were 50 towers, 200 feet high, to guard the city.

D. *THE SITUATION IN ISRAEL*
1. Assyria had been a threat to Israel since the time of Omri (c. 880), and had forced them to pay tribute for the last fifty years until Jeroboam II became king. Jeroboam threw off this yoke c. 790 and extended the northern kingdom to its largest extent since Solomon. At the time of Jonah, Israel was secure and on the ascendancy while Assyria was on the decline, politically speaking.
2. Religiously, however, Israel was becoming more and more calloused, independent, morally degraded, and selfish. This period was her "golden age" of prosperity. But she was unaware that God had granted her this mercy to bring repentance, not independence (2 Kin. 14:26-27).
3. Jonah's ministry of mercy to Israel probably just preceded the judgment ministry of Amos who came as a special envoy of the Lord from Judah.

THE PURPOSE OF THE BOOK OF JONAH

Its historic and continuing purpose was to declare the universality of both God's judgment and His grace. He judges wickedness in all spheres, and likewise, responds to repentance in all nations. The story also portrays the truth that when God's people lose their concern for the lost, they have lost their vision of God's purpose and program in the world.

Unique Contributions of Jonah

1. *THE RELATION OF JONAH TO OBADIAH.* As Obadiah describes God's wrath on Israel's enemies, the Book of Jonah counterbalances that by a classic illustration of God's mercy shown to another of her ancient enemies. In Obadiah God's judgment is pronounced on the heathen who reject knowledge and persist in their vengeful arrogance. In Jonah God's mercy is proferred to the heathen who repent and respond to Israel's God. Two extreme cases are used to illustrate the points: The Edomites were the closest to Israel (in relation and proximity), but receive God's wrath because of their arrogance.

The Ninevites were both distant and vicious as a militant people, but received God's mercy because of their repentance (Obad. 3; Jon. 3:5-10).

2. **THE BREVITY OF JONAH** (3:4). No prophet was so concise in his message as was Jonah. His prophecy contained only eight words (five in Hebrew): "Yet forty days, and Nineveh shall be overthrown." Unlike other writing prophets, Jonah's message was more in his experience than in his exposition. Even his short prophecy failed to come true (much to his chagrin). His experience, however, constituted an important message to Nineveh, Israel, and even to the Church today (Matt. 12:39-40).

3. **THE MIRACLES IN JONAH** (1:15, 17; 2:10; 3:5-10; 4:6). Whereas the other Minor Prophets record no historical miracles, Jonah records several around which his message is built (stilling the sea, Jonah's preservation in the fish, repentance of Nineveh, and the quick growth of the plant and worm). Jonah has this in common with Isaiah and Daniel that they each record several historical miracles and are also challenged by the critics as to their authenticity and authorship (Is. 37:36; 38:8; Dan. 3:25; 6:22). Since the purpose

Outline of Jonah

THEME: The Wideness of God's Mercy and the Willful Narrowness of Jonah.

of miracles was nearly always to authenticate revelation (Ex. 4:5; 1 Kin. 18:36-39), Jonah's message of God's judgment to Nineveh and His mercy which Israel misunderstood was quite crucial to both. Its further significance as a prophetic type of Christ's resurrection can hardly be overestimated.

4. **THE REPENTANCE OF NINEVEH** (3:5-9). Jonah had the greatest revival recorded in the Bible, the whole city of Nineveh turning to God from their wicked ways. He was even instrumental in the sailors' turning to the Lord after he was cast into the sea and it stopped its raging. He seemed to have more results "by accident" than most of the prophets had on purpose (Isaiah, Jeremiah, and Ezekiel had little immediate results; Is. 6:9-11; Jer. 14:11ff.; 15:1ff.; Ezek. 3:7). The repentance of Nineveh is sometimes questioned as to whether it was genuine. The answer of Jonah is that God evidently considered it genuine, for He withdrew the judgment He had warned them of (3:10). Jesus also testified that "they repented at the preaching of Jonah" (Matt. 12:41), which Israel failed to do at the preaching of Messiah.

5. **THE "REPENTANCE" OF GOD** (3:9-10). This book records the fact that God also "repented," or "relented," as most versions translate it (Heb. *nacham*). That word, however is also used for man's repentance (Job 42:6). Also this word is used interchangeably with the common word for repent (*shub*), "every one turn from his evil way," in 3:8-9. It primarily means a "change of mind" concerning an intended action. It is used here as an anthropomorphic expression to show the conditional aspect of God's judgment, dependent on man's actions. This principle is stated in Jeremiah 18:8. The statement in Numbers 23:19 (cf. 1 Sam. 15:29) that "God *is* not a man, . . . that He should repent," speaks of His truthfulness and unchangeable character. God's judgment is always made dependent on man's actions.

6. **THE REPENTANCE OF JONAH** (Chapters 2, 4). Though the book records the unexpected repentance of one of the great "bullies" of ancient history, its major emphasis is on repentance or change in Jonah. The repentance of Nineveh occupies one chapter, but the story of Jonah's preparation and further training are given three chapters (1–2, 4). God seemed to have more difficulty straightening out Jonah than with all of Nineveh. Once he was brought to a place of obedience, the revival was a matter of course. Jonah's preparation, however, came in stages. The fish experience prepared him for Nineveh, but he needed further training to return to Israel. If the repentance of Nineveh in chapter three is a surprise, the disgruntled prophet in chapter four is a shock. He appears to be more concerned that his prophecy come true, as a credit to his profession, than he was that the city of Nineveh be spared God's judgment. That is the way the story ends, leaving the reader totally disgusted with this prophet of God. He appears hopelessly selfish and bigoted, until it is recalled that he wrote the book—without touching up this "Mr. Scrooge" image of himself at the end. That image was evidently calculated to make an impression on and humiliate Israel, for his attitude was only a reflection of theirs. They were so wrapped up in their own pleasure and prosperity under the golden age of Jeroboam II, they had lost sight of their mission as God's covenant people.

7. *THE PLACE OF JONAH IN JEWISH RITUAL.* Orthodox Jews traditionally use the Book of Jonah as their prescribed reading for the Afternoon Service on the Day of Atonement (A. Cohen, *The Twelve Prophets,* p. 137). On this day of national fasting, mourning, and forgiving one another's sins, they reread this story of the ancient Ninevites who found mercy by calling a time of national repentance and forgiveness of sins. Though there is no evidence the Israelites of Jonah's time responded in this way, Orthodox Jews have long used the Book of Jonah on the major fast day of their year to recall the truth that the Lord is a God of mercy to repentant people, irrespective of what their race may be. Jonah has been given a special place in Jewish ritual and respect.

8. *THE BOOK OF GOD'S UNIVERSAL MERCY* (4:11). No book of the Old Testament so emphatically teaches the extension of God's mercy to Gentile nations as does the Book of Jonah. This world-wide perspective of Israel's mission was previously noted by Joshua and Solomon (Josh. 4:24; 1 Kin. 8:43, 60), but was often forgotten by the nation in the course of their many apostasies. At this mid-point of their history, Jonah was used to call the nation to reflect on God's program of universal judgment on evildoers and His universal offer of mercy for repentance and faith. Frederick Faber, *Voice of Thanksgiving Hymnal,* has expressed it in verse: "For the love of God is broader Than the measure of man's mind, And the heart of the Eternal Is most wonderfully kind."

9. *THE CHRISTOLOGY OF JONAH.* Jonah's central emphasis of God's mercy being extended to all races of men is, of course, supremely exemplified in the ministry of Jesus. He called all people to repentance, coming as "a light to bring revelation to the Gentiles, And the glory of Your people Israel" (Luke 2:32). Following His resurrection, He sent the Twelve to "make disciples of all the nations" (Matt. 28:19).

The more specific christological relation in this book, however, is Jonah's experience in the great fish as a type of Christ (Matt. 12:40). Jonah was the only prophet Jesus saw as a type of Himself. As Jonah was in the belly of the fish (place of death) three days and three nights, so the Son of Man would be in the heart of the earth. "Day and night" was a Hebrew idiom for any part of a day. As a type has but one point of analogy (like a parable), so Jonah typified Christ in but one point, his experience in the place of death for a period of time that well confirmed death (John 11:17, 39). Jesus used Jonah's experience to typify the greatest truth of the Bible, His own resurrection from the dead.

The Book of Micah

Introduction

AUTHORSHIP

A. *THE TITLE*

The name Micah, an abbreviation of "Micaiah," means "who is like Jehovah (YHWH)?". It is an exclamation that nicely fits the message of this book, emphasizing His great power in the first chapter and His great pardon in the last: "Who *is* a God like You, pardoning iniquity?" (7:18).

B. *THE AUTHOR*

1. The authorship by Micah is quite generally acknowledged, though some modern critics would assign the "hope" sections of 4–7 to some later writer. Jeremiah 26:18 shows Micah was greatly respected in Jeremiah's time (c. 600 B.C.). The content of the book comports well with the time and circumstances of the prophet Micah.
2. Micah was from the western rural comunity of Moresheth Gath, a town located on the border between Judah and Philistia. This was twenty miles southwest of Jerusalem, away from the politics and commerce of the capital.
3. The prophet Micah, was evidently of lowly background, being identified by his humble residence, rather than his lineage. His many allusions to the work of a shepherd suggest this may have been one of his occupations.
4. He is thought to have been one of the "men of Hezekiah" in Proverbs 25:1, who, with Isaiah, transcribed and compiled Solomon's proverbs of chapters 25–29. He is not to be confused with the earlier prophet Micaiah of 1 Kings 22:8.

HISTORICAL SETTING

A. *DATE OF WRITING*—c. 730 B.C.

His prophecy occurred during the reigns of Jotham, Ahaz, and Hezekiah who reigned consecutively from 740 to 697. His main thrust, however, appears to have been during the reigns of Ahaz and Hezekiah prior to the fall of Samaria in 722. The central time period then would be 730–720.

B. *THE POLITICAL SETTING*

1. As contemporary with Isaiah, Micah faced a similar setting as far as the politics and religion of the time was concerned. Micah was the rural counterpart of Isaiah, speaking to the countryside.
2. Micah is distinguished as being the only prophet whose ministry was directed to both Israel and Judah (1:1). Isaiah also prophesied the destruction of Samaria, but his prophecy was "concerning Judah and Jerusalem" (Is. 1:1).

C. *THE SIMILARITIES AND CONTRASTS WITH ISAIAH*

Micah and Isaiah worked together perhaps more than any pair of Old Testament writing prophets, except Haggai and Zechariah. Aside from the difference in length, their books have both similarities and contrasts:

1. The similarities of Micah and Isaiah.

    a. Both prophesied of the early invasion by Assyria.

    b. Both spoke of Judah's deliverance, but later captivity in Babylon.

Outline of Micah

THEME: The Lord's Character as a Righteous Judge and a Caring Shepherd of Israel.

     c. Both emphasized the futility of mere ritual religion.

     d. Both prophesied Messiah's coming; Isaiah spoke of His virgin birth, Micah spoke of His village birth.

     e. Both prophesied Israel's final deliverance which had to be preceded by repentance.

  2. The contrasts between Micah and Isaiah.

     a. Isaiah primarily addressed the aristocracy of urban Jerusalem; Micah spoke to the common people of the rural countryside.

     b. Isaiah dealt largely with the international scene and Judah's false political alliances; Micah focused more on the personal and social sins of injustice that were prevalent in Judah.

     c. Whereas Isaiah extended his judgment to the surrounding nations, Micah limited his condemnations to Judah and Israel.

     d. Whereas Isaiah centered his messianic vision around the Servant concept, emphasizing atonement and personal salvation, Micah portrayed Messiah's national deliverance made possible by God's pardoning grace as promised to Abraham.

THE PURPOSE OF THE BOOK OF MICAH

The historic purpose of this book was to emphasize the greatness of God's coming wrath on the nation for their sins of social injustice and violence while pretending to be religious. Micah's further purpose was to remind them of the eventual coming of Messiah Who would rise to rule out of humble beginnings and bring truth and justice as promised in the Abrahamic covenant.

Unique Contributions of Micah

1. *THE LORD'S TERRIFYING DESCENT TO EARTH* (1:3-4). Micah begins by introducing one of the most awesome pictures of the Lord, His descending to the earth with terrifying wrath. As with Jonah, he proclaims God's judgment before declaring His pardoning mercy. The following three books, in fact, continue this theme of the Lord coming as a mighty warrior under whom the "mountains quake" (Nah. 1:2-6), the "perpetual hills bowed" (Hab. 3:6), and "the whole land shall be devoured" (Zeph. 1:18). Isaiah presents this fearful portrait also in chapters 24 and 63 as he describes the devastations of the Day of the Lord. The prophets saw man's sin as meaning nothing less than a cataclysmic reduction of the earth to chaos (Jer. 4:23-26). Micah introduces this picture of the Lord to emphasize His great wrath on those who practice violence and injustice against the poor. To take advantage of the poor, he warned, is to incur the wrath of the Almighty (cf. Deut. 15:10; Ps. 109:31; 140:12; Prov. 14:31; 19:17).

2. *THE POOR MAN'S PROPHET.* Micah is known as the prophet of the common man. Having come from lowly circumstances himself, he knew the plight of the poor and took up their cause against the self-serving, devouring leaders of the nation (3:1-3). Throughout the book he denounces oppression of the weak, the taking of bribes by the leaders, evicting women from their homes, and practicing all kinds of legal thievery, much of it in the name of religion (2:1-2, 8-11; 3:1-3, 9-11; 6:10-12; 7:1-6). Though he does not exonerate the poor just for their poverty, he stoutly condemns the upper classes for bleeding the poor and helpless. In describing their hope of restoration he surprises the nation with the announcement that the coming "ruler in Israel," Messiah, will come from the small and insignificant town of Bethlehem, rather than from the affluent capital of Jerusalem (5:2-4). He even portrays Him as a "Shepherd" like David, but greater than David, He will become "great to the ends of the earth" (5:4). Micah was the last to mention Bethlehem in the Old Testament, but he focused the attention of the nation on it for over 700 years.

3. *MICAH'S GOSPEL OF SOCIAL JUSTICE* (6:6-8). No more simple and yet profound summarization of the Law can be found in the Old Testament than that of Micah 6:6–8. His requirements are simple and plain: to do justice, to love kindness by showing it, and to walk in humility with God. As Jesus summarized the Law as "love" to the loveless leaders of His time, so Micah summarized it as justice, mercy, and modesty to a people quite devoid of these, though they were deeply engaged in religion (3:11). Their "thousands of rams" and "ten thousand rivers of oil" (6:7), could not bribe God to overlook their lack of these essentials of justice and mercy in their walk with men.

4. *ISRAEL'S TOTAL DEPRAVITY* (7:2-6). As Isaiah noted in 1:5-6 and 57:1, Micah also notes that Israel was so far gone they had "no one upright among men" (7:2). All were wicked and self-serving in that idolatrous society. Having departed from God's truth, they were reaping the social effects in which "A man's enemies *are* the men of his own house," including his wife, children and parents (7:5-6). Jesus quoted this passage from Micah in Matthew 10:21, 35 to show that rejection of truth in His time would bring that same condition. Paul also referred to this in Romans 1:28-32, noting that social depravity is always tied to rejection of truth.

5. *CHRISTOLOGY IN MICAH* (4:1-8; 5:2-5). Two passages in Micah speak of Messiah's kingdom and His coming. In the "last days" He will reign in Mount Zion where truth, justice, prosperity, and peace will prevail. There the lame, outcasts, and afflicted will be gathered to form the nucleus of His "strong nation" (4:1-7).

In 5:2, however, he reveals that His kingdom will not begin great, for Messiah Himself will be born in the small village of Bethlehem, a place of sheep raising. He who is of eternity will come forth from God as Israel's Shepherd. But before He becomes great to the ends of the earth, the nation will be abandoned by the Lord for a time, after which He will arise to shepherd His people in great majesty (5:3-4).

The Book of Nahum

Introduction

AUTHORSHIP

A. *THE TITLE*

The name Nahum means "consolation." As the name suggests, the Book of Nahum is unique among the Prophets in that it has no judgment for Israel, only consolation, predicting the destruction of her great eastern enemy.

B. *THE AUTHOR*

1. That Nahum was the sole author of this book is quite generally agreed (apart from some critics), though little is known about him. His name is mentioned only once in the Bible (Nah. 1:1).

2. His hometown was Elkosh which may be identified as one of the following:
   a. Alkush, a town north of Mosul and Nineveh, east of the Tigris.
   b. El-kauzeh, a small village in north Galilee, identified by Jerome.
   c. Elkesei, a small town in south Palestine. (Kaush was an Edomite god.) The Septuagint speaks of Nahum as "the Elkesite."
   d. The town of Capernaum in north Galilee means "city of Nahum" from the Arabic, "Kefr-Nahum."

3. The best conjecture is that he was born near Capernaum in north Galilee, escaped or migrated to Elkosh in southern Judah after the North fell, and prophesied to Judah in a time of needed consolation concerning their Assyrian enemy.

HISTORICAL SETTING

A. *DATE OF WRITING*—c. 710 B.C.

1. Nahum is one of six Minor Prophets not dated by the text and therefore must be dated by extrapolations from the context. Conservatives generally assign one of two dates to the book, c. 710, during reign of Hezekiah, or c. 650, during the reign of Manasseh.

2. Four facts must be considered in determining the date of writing:
   a. Nineveh was destroyed in 612, which was prophesied by the prophet.
   b. The coming of a "wicked counselor" from Nineveh to Jerusalem was predicted in 1:11, which seems to fit Rabshakeh in 701 B.C. (2 Kin. 18:19-35).
   c. The reference to a previous invasion of No Amon (Thebes), the great southern capital of Egypt. Several such took place:

714 B.C.	Conquest by Ethiopia, establishing the twenty-fifth dynasty.
718	Conquest by Sargon of Assyria, followed by later conquests over the powerful Ethiopian twenty-fifth dynasty.

701	Conquest of Egyptian army by Sennacherib.
671	Conquest of Egypt by Esarhaddon of Assyria.
663	Conquest of Egypt by Ashurbanipal of Assyria.
525	Conquest of Egypt by Persian King Cambyses.

   d. The purpose of the book was to be a consolation to Judah.

3. The 710 date appears more likely than 650 for the following reasons:

   a. In 710 the Assyrians appeared a great threat to Judah as the Assyrians were moving west, more so than in 650, when they were beginning to decline in power.

   b. The prophecy of "consolation" best fits 710 in the time of Hezekiah. There was hardly a call for consolation for Judah in 650 during the reign of Manasseh, the most wicked, depraved king of Judah. His reign brought God's judgment of inescapable doom.

B. *THE HISTORY OF NINEVEH*

1. Nineveh was one of the earliest cities, founded by Nimrod (Gen. 10:11).

2. The city followed Ashur as the capital of Assyria, though the capital moved at times to other locations near Nineveh.

3. Assyria was named after its chief god, Ashur, a god of war.

4. Assyria assumed independence from Babylon sometime before 1500 B.C., but had only sporadic periods of greatness. These were under Ashur-uballit I (1363–1328), Tukulti-Ninurta I (1243–1207), Tiglath-Pileser I (1112–1074), Adad-nirari II (909–889), Shalmaneser III (858–824), and Adad-nirari III (809–782).

5. The "Second Assyrian Empire" had the most relevance to Bible history:

   Tiglath-Pileser III (745–727) — Invaded Syria and North Israel, 734.

   Shalmaneser V (727–722) — Besieged Samaria; took Hoshea captive.

   Sargon III (721–705) — Destroyed Samaria; subjected Babylon.

   Sennacherib (704–681) — Conquered Palestine; destroyed Babylon.

   Esarhaddon (681–669) — Conquered Egypt in 671.

   Ashur-banipal (669–626) — Took Babylon from his brother Samas-sumu-kin in 648; took Manasseh captive to Babylon; established the greatest library of ancient times.

6. The Assyrian Empire began disintegration in 626, Nineveh was destroyed in 612, and their army was finally destroyed at Carchemish in 605 B.C.

7. So complete was the destruction of Nineveh that the city was almost a myth for two millennia until rediscovered in 1842 by Layard and Botta. Alexander marched by it in 331 with no evidence of its existence. No trace of the city and its mighty past remained.

8. Assyria and Nineveh were known for their military power and cruelty. Most of their gods were gods of war. They were a nation of hunters and warriors, not students. Most of their art, culture, and science were derived from Babylon with whom they felt inferior. Their one great student was their last great king, Ashur-banipal, who built a great library at Nineveh of 20,000 volumes.

9. This cruel nation was the instrument God used to destroy the northern kingdom of Israel for their idolatry and violence, carrying them into Babylon and replacing them with mongrel Babylonians.

C. *THE POLITICAL SETTING OF JUDAH*

In 710 B.C., Judah had survived the Assyrian invasion by Sargon because of the great revival of Hezekiah. But Assyria was continuing its movement west, while holding Babylon down in the east. As Assyria came west, it was a great temptation for Hezekiah to strengthen his fortress by seeking the help of Egypt and Babylon (2 Kin. 18:21; 20:12ff.). The Assyrian Empire was at this time coming to the pinnacle of its power and was threatening to swallow up Judah and all the Middle East in its westward plunge. Judah in a time of reformation needed divine consolation concerning this violent horde from Nineveh, the ancient citadel of savagery.

Outline of Nahum

THEME: God's Great Judgment on Nineveh the Violent Queen of the East.

D. *THE RELIGIOUS SETTING* (See The Book of Jonah Introduction)

THE PURPOSE OF THE BOOK OF NAHUM

The primary purpose of Nahum was to console Judah concerning her vicious enemy, Assyria. The prophet announced God's detailed plan to destroy and completely devastate Nineveh. This message was given Judah to remind them of the Lord's sovereignty over all nations and that He does not long tolerate those that rule by plunder and violence, disregarding His warnings of judgment.

Unique Contributions of Nahum

1. *THE RETRIBUTIVE CHARACTER OF GOD* (1:2, 6). Similar to Micah, Nahum begins by stressing the Lord's great wrath against sin and His coming to bring judgment on the earth. The direction of His anger here, however, is to Israel's enemies, rather than Israel. Nahum describes God as a jealous and avenging God who will come with burning anger toward His enemies. This jealous character of God was introduced in Exodus 20:5 and further elaborated in Deuteronomy 32:21ff. Many passages describe the Lord as "slow to anger," but great in power and wrath toward those who refuse His grace (Ex. 22:24; 32:12; Num. 14:18; Josh. 7:1; Ezra 9:15; Job 20:23). In the New Testament Jesus' pronouncements of eight woes on the hypocritical leaders of His day showed the same fiery wrath toward those who deliberately reject both His Law and His grace (Matt. 23). These are climaxed in the ominous portrayal of the Lord's coming in Revelation 14:10, 19 and 19:15 to judge His enemies as He delivers His people.

2. *THE BOOK OF UNRELIEVED JUDGMENT.* No book of the Bible is so incessant in its message of judgment and unavailing mercy as is Nahum. Its only "good tidings" is the predicted announcement that wicked Nineveh was destroyed (1:15). So compelling and emphatic was this message of judgment on Nineveh that the sins of Israel or Judah were not even alluded to. The Lord devoted one complete book to colorfully portray His great wrath against a people that lived in violence, plunder, and bloodshed, and failed to continue in His mercy when it was shown through God's prophet Jonah.

3. *THE GREAT QUEEN CITY OF NINEVEH DESTROYED.* This is no doubt the book Jonah would like to have written (Jon. 4:2), failing to realize that the Lord had a harvest to reap there first. His short prophecy of Nineveh's destruction is amplified here, without the execution date of "forty days." Though Nineveh's repentance postponed her judgment, her later resumption of that wickedness and violence only intensified her judgment as contempt for God's mercy. The ancient city of Nineveh was a classic symbol of the world in its power, violence, and defiance against God since the time of Nimrod (Gen. 10:9-11). But when God commanded her destruction, she was so thoroughly

annihilated that the ancient queen of cities was forgotten for many centuries, covered over with sand to become a desert.

4. **NAHUM'S INTERNATIONAL WARNING TO ALL NATIONS.** The outstanding lesson of Nahum for the nations is that the "law of the jungles" is not the Law of God. Though sin and violence may go unpunished for a time in the outworking of God's program, it will not be forgotten. Not only is the outworking of His program at stake, but also the vindication of His character (Ex. 34:6-7; Num. 14:18). Though He is "slow to anger," in the interest of showing mercy, He is not the least immune from anger when His Law has been impugned and His grace spurned. Nahum's description of the avenging God is one of the most terrifying pictures of the Bible. Whereas the Book of Jonah portrays God's mercy extended to the Gentiles without the Mosaic Law, so Nahum portrays God's wrath and judgment to the nations, whether they have the Mosaic Law or not.

5. **CHRISTOLOGY IN NAHUM** (1:15). Though there are no specific references to Messiah in Nahum, the announcement of "good tidings" in 1:15 has an indirect reference to Christ and His gospel. This is referred to in Isaiah 52:7 and further applied by Paul in Romans 10:15 to the deliverance aspect of the gospel. This is a reminder that the original purpose of Nahum was primarily consolation for Israel concerning her national threat by this wicked bully from the East. Likewise, the good news of the gospel is that Christ brings deliverance from one's enemies as well as the positive benefits of salvation (Luke 1:71). The God envisioned by Nahum is not different from the Christ of the New Testament.

The Book of Habakkuk

Introduction

AUTHORSHIP

A. *THE TITLE*

"Habakkuk" means "to embrace." As many have observed, the prophet earnestly embraced God in prayer for the nation and then warmly embraced Him in praise for His greatness in resolving the prophet's great dilemma concerning holiness.

B. *THE AUTHOR*

1. As with most Minor Prophets, practically nothing is known about Habukkuk. He

is never mentioned elsewhere in the Bible, but twice in his inscriptions, 1:1 and 3:1.

2. He is sometimes assumed to have been a Levite because of his liturgical psalm (chapter 3), but the psalmist David was certainly not a Levite.
3. Habakkuk became the subject of a legend in the apocryphal book, Bel And The Dragon (Or Apocryphal Dan 14:28–42), in which he was supposedly brought to Babylon by an angel to feed Daniel who had been in the lion's den for six days.
4. Although the unity of this book has been challenged by the critics, especially the psalm of chapter 3, there is no real reason to doubt its genuineness. Its authenticity is confirmed in the inscriptions of both parts (1:1; 3:1).

Outline of Habakkuk

THEME: The Just Shall Live by Faith in God's Holiness and Righteous Judgment.

HISTORICAL SETTING

A. *DATE OF WRITING*—c. 607 B.C.
1. Though the book is not dated, several references help to date it:
   a. The reference to the Chaldeans coming in unbelievable ferocity (1:6) suggests a date prior to 605 and after their initial conquests.
   b. The lack of any reference to Nineveh suggests a date following the destruction of Nineveh in 612.
   c. The prophet's great concern for violence in Judah suggests a time after the death of Josiah (609), in the wicked reign of Jehoiakim.
2. The most likely date would then be c. 607, when Jehoiakim's wicked reign was well under way, and before Judah was subjugated to Nebuchadnezzar in 606.

B. *THE POLITICAL SETTING*
1. Internationally, the power struggle between Assyria, Babylon, and Egypt was turning in favor of Babylon. Nineveh fell in 612 and Egypt's army would be routed in 605 at Carchemish. Nebuchadnezzar was in the ascendancy.
2. Habakkuk was a contemporary of Jeremiah, prophesying with him to the southern kingdom as it plunged toward national collapse. Josiah's reformation had ended abruptly with the death of Josiah in 609, and the seeds of corruption planted by Manasseh quickly came to fruition under Jehoiakim.

C. *THE RELIGIOUS SETTING*
As shown by the fleeting reformation of Josiah, Judah was incorrigibly corrupt and ripe for judgment. Not having learned from God's judgment on Samaria, No Amon, or Nineveh, Jerusalem was about to suffer a like fate and at the hands of a similarly vicious adversary whom the Lord had hired for divine service.

THE PURPOSE OF THE BOOK OF HABAKKUK

The purpose of Habakkuk was to emphasize God's holiness in judging violent Judah for her sins, even though He used a more wicked nation to accomplish it, whom He would later destroy for their greater wickedness and idolatry.

Unique Contributions of Habakkuk

1. *BABYLON'S JUDGMENT BY GOD* (3:12). The Book of Habakkuk logically follows Nahum in describing God's judgment on Israel's second great enemy and destroyer from the East. Though both Nineveh and Babylon were used of the Lord to destroy Israel in the north and Judah in the south (Is. 7:18-20; Jer. 27:6), both also were judged for their violence. These two books castigate them for this vengeful violence which God did not

condone or sanction. Both books also reveal the great wrath and terror of the Lord as He was to come in judgment to personally attend to their destruction.

2. **THE HOLINESS OF GOD** (1:12; 2:20; 3:3). Habakkuk's major concern is for the holiness of God with respect to both Israel's wickedness and Babylon's greater wickedness. He fretted over God allowing sin to go unpunished in Judah, then worried about His using more wicked Babylon with seeming approval. This problem and answer are immortalized in two classic verses. "You are of purer eyes than to behold evil" (1:13); "But the Lord is in His holy temple. Let all the earth keep silence before Him" (2:20). If God is longsuffering with sinful men and even chooses to use "vessels of wrath" (Rom. 9:22), to accomplish His purposes, He has not compromised His holiness. He often allows sin to run its course and even to destroy its own kind in the out-working of His program, thereby demonstrating the sovereignty and grandeur of His holiness and justice.

3. **"THE JUST SHALL LIVE BY HIS FAITH"** (2:4). Habakkuk has been called the book that started the Reformation. Paul quoted Habakkuk 2:4 in developing his doctrine of justification by faith in Romans 1:17 and Galatians 3:11, and this became the watchword of Luther and the Reformers. This phrase is also quoted in Hebrews 10:38, and the three New Testament quotes have an interesting progression in emphases: In Romans 1:17, the emphasis is *"The just"*; in Galatians 3:11, on *"shall live"*; and in Hebrews 10:38, on *"by faith."* All three points were emphasized by Habakkuk. Few verses of the Bible have had such a profound effect in the development of theology and the proclamation of the faith.

4. **OFTEN QUOTED PHRASES.** The small book of Habakkuk is noted for its many quoted passages:
    a. "You would not believe though it were told *you*" (1:5).
    b. "You *are* of purer eyes than to behold evil" (1:13).
    c. "But the just shall live by his faith" (2:4).
    d. "For the earth will be filled With the knowledge of the glory of the LORD, As the waters cover the sea" (2:14).
    e. "Woe to him who gives drink to his neighbor" (2:15).
    f. "But the LORD is in His holy temple. Let all the earth keep silence before Him" (2:20).
    g. "O LORD, revive Your work in the midst of the years" (3:2).
    h. "I will joy in the God of my salvation" (3:18).

5. **HABAKKUK'S DARING DIALOGUE WITH GOD.** Unlike other prophetic books, Habakkuk is more of a prayer than a prophecy. The concerned prophet dares to dialogue with God, confronting Him with questions that seem to challenge both His holiness and His love. This prayer continues throughout the book as the prophet inquires and awaits God's answer. This also constitutes his very effective teaching method, posing difficult ques-

tions and elaborating on the answers with divine authority. This was later called the "rabbinic" or "Socratic" method, but it was also very effectively used by Jesus (e.g., Matt. 22:42ff.). Habakkuk's faith in God is so vigorous and deep-seated, he can honestly express his doubts and find satisfaction as the Lord answers with new appeals to faith.

6. **CHRISTOLOGY IN HABAKKUK** (2:14, 20). This book also has no specific references to Messiah, but several implications of the messianic age. In 2:14, the prophet declares the knowledge of His glory will be universal. This is an obvious quote and advance over Isaiah 11:9 in which that earlier prophet described certain aspects of messianic times. Habakkuk specifies that universal knowledge to be of the Lord's glory. His contrast is with those who futilely labor, even to bloodshed, for the brief, passing glory of worldly kingdoms. The knowledge of His glory, which is today practically hidden, will then cover and fill the earth.

A second messianic implication is the exhortation to "Let all the earth be silent before Him," inasmuch as "the LORD is in His holy temple" (2:20). Similar statements are made in Zephaniah 1:7 and Zechariah 2:13, as they announce the Lord's coming in the Day of the Lord. Likewise, Revelation 8:1 speaks of a period of silence in heaven just before the unleashing of God's wrath in the last half of the tribulation period. Those judgments in Revelation are continually seen to proceed from the Lord in His holy temple, emphasizing the holiness of God and the righteousness of the wrath being poured out (Rev. 8:4; 14:15, 17; 15:8; 16:1, 17). That appears also to be the point of Habakkuk as he introduces his psalm of God's wrath on the nations in the portrayal of the majestic, militant theophany (3:3–16).

The Book of Zephaniah

Introduction

AUTHORSHIP

A. *THE TITLE*

The name Zephaniah means, "the Lord hides," or protects. This protective motif for the righteous in the Day of the Lord is seen in 2:3 and 3:8-12.

B. *THE AUTHOR*

1. The prophet is identified in the superscription as the great-great-grandson of Hezekiah (doubtless the king who reigned seventy-five years before). Zephaniah was thus the only Minor Prophet of the royal family.
2. Being a distant cousin of King Josiah, Zephaniah evidently had access to the royal court and knew well the religious climate around Jerusalem.

HISTORICAL SETTING

A. *DATE OF WRITING*—c. 630 or 625 B.C.
1. His ministry occurred during the reign of Josiah, 640–609, and before the fall of Nineveh in 612 (1:1; 2:13).
2. His strong condemnation of idolatry and lawlessness suggests he prophesied before 621, if not before 628, when Josiah pursued his great reformation. If his prophecy preceded the first purge, a likely date would be c. 630 B.C. If it preceded the later purge, c. 625 B.C.

B. *THE POLITICAL SETTING*

Zephaniah was contemporary with the early ministry of Jeremiah. The world scene was changing both on the international and national fronts. Assyria was on the decline, Babylon was growing under Nabopolassar, and Egypt was probing Palestine, but not effectively. Judah had been weakened under the long reign of Manasseh and was practically a vassal of Assyria. Josiah began his thirty-one year reign in 640 at the age of eight with the nation greatly weakened both politically and morally.

Outline of Zephaniah

THEME: The Lord's Great Wrath and Redemption in the Day of the Lord.

C. *THE RELIGIOUS SETTING*
    1. The reign of Josiah followed over fifty-five years of bloodshed and moral corruption under Manasseh and Amon. His reign may be divided into several periods as noted in 2 Chronicles 34.
        a. 640–632—His early reign until he sought the Lord at age sixteen.
        b. 632–628—His reign after seeking the Lord, before reformation.
        c. 628–621—His early purge of idolatry in Jerusalem and all Israel.
        d. 621–609—His later purge after finding the Book of the Law in the temple and gathering the people for covenant renewal.
    2. Zephaniah may have been the influential prophet who turned Josiah to the Lord and helped each stage of this reformation, presenting to the people one of the most terrifying pictures of judgment in the Bible.

THE PURPOSE OF THE BOOK OF ZEPHANIAH

The purpose of this prophecy was to issue an eleventh hour call to the nation, condemning their idolatry and warning them of the great day of God's wrath on the world. Beyond this judgment, however, Zephaniah emphasized again the final results of Israel's judgment, which would be a purified and humble people whom the Lord would restore and dwell in the midst of.

Unique Contributions of Zephaniah

1. *THE "GREAT DAY OF THE LORD"* (1:14). Zephaniah's unmitigated emphasis is the Day of the Lord, stressing its fury. Three of the prophets spoke of the "great" day of the Lord, Joel 2:31 (c. 835 B.C.), Zephaniah 1:14 (c. 630), and Malachi 4:5 (c. 430), spaced about two hundred years apart. Each of these prophets spoke to Judah in a time of apostasy, warning of fiery judgment from the Lord, and each also pointed to the Lord as a place of refuge for the repentant.

2. *ZEPHANIAH'S TERRIFYING PICTURE OF GOD* (1:18). Though Micah, Nahum, and Habakkuk also introduced the Lord as a God of great judgment, the portrait of God's wrath given by Zephaniah is probably the most awesome to be found in the Bible. The description of 1:18 and 3:8 is like the "final crash of the universe." The Almighty is seen devouring the whole earth in the fire of His indigation because of the sin and intransigence of men. No more stern and somber message ever came from a prophet. As Rabbi Lehrman says: "Where Zephaniah differs from other prophets is that he makes denunciation and threat, and not positive moral teaching, the main theme of his preaching" (A. Cohen, *The Twelve Prophets* (Soncino), p. 233). He solemnly confronts men with the harsh reality of their imminent meeting with an outraged God who is about to give short shrift to rebellious and idolatrous men. This is not popular "footage" of the divine scenario and is often watered down as an imaginary "Dante's Inferno," but these later

prophets describe the day of His wrath in the most specific terms. Zephaniah also stressed the availability of God's mercy for those who seek Him, but allows no diminishing of His anger that will make a terrifying end of the earth for its willful rejection of Him.

3. ***THE MOST SWEEPING SUMMARY OF OLD TESTAMENT PROPHECIES.*** It has been observed that "if anyone desires to see all the secret oracles of the Old Testament prophets reduced to one short summary, he has only to read the Book of Zephaniah." His central theme concerns the Day of the Lord, showing its relation to both Israel and the nations. He portrays the judgments issuing from the nature of God and the rebellion and corruption of men. Like most of the other prophets, Zephaniah concludes with a prophecy of Israel's restoration after repentance, as the Lord comes to them as a victorious Warrior to lead His people into renewal and triumph. Though Zephaniah does not present much original content, he summarizes the broad features of prophecy in striking pronouncements of finality. He was especially the prophet of the emphatic and definitive.

4. ***HIS CATALOG OF RELIGIOUS SINS*** (1:4-6; 3:1-5). The Lord's judgment is seen to cut a wide swath across all types of idolatrous systems and superficial religious experiences. The prophet's list includes: 1) worshipers of Baal and other Canaanite deities; 2) worshipers of nature, the sun, moon, and stars; 3) syncretic religions who presume to worship the Lord, but others as well; 4) those willfully abandoning worship of God; and 5) the indifferent who have not concerned themselves with God's demands to obey them (1:4-6). Added to this are those who have deistic ideas, supposing the Lord is busy and indifferent to the plights of men (1:12). But he reserved special denunciation for Jerusalem's corrupt leaders, both religious and civil, who had grown impervious to the Lord's instruction (3:1-5). With consummate disdain for the proud, Zephaniah saw hope only for the humble, who, though lame and outcast, trusted in the name of the Lord (2:3, 3:12).

5. ***CHRISTOLOGY IN ZEPHANIAH*** (3:15, 17). In describing the outcome of the day of the Lord, Zephaniah declares that the "King of Israel" who will be in their midst, will be none other than the Lord (YHWH) Himself (3:15). This One will come to them as a victorious warrior as He clears away their last enemies. His coming to them will be with great joy and exultation to restore their fortunes from reproach to "praise and fame in every land" (19). Till then He offered Himself as their hiding place (2:3).

The Book of Haggai

Introduction

AUTHORSHIP

A. *THE TITLE*

The name Haggai means "festive" or "My Feast" (shortened form of Haggaiah). The prophet may have been born on a feast day. His name complements the major concern of his prophecy which was to complete the temple to resume the religious feasts.

B. *THE AUTHOR*

1. Though Haggai is also mentioned in Ezra 5:1 and 6:14, little is known of him except for his being "the prophet," perhaps a title of recognized distinction.
2. Though some believe he saw the first temple before destruction (2:3), Jewish tradition holds that he was born in Babylon and studied under Ezekiel. He evidently came to Jerusalem after the first return in 537, inasmuch as he is not listed with that group of returnees (Ezra 2:2).
3. Contemporary with Haggai was the younger prophet Zechariah. These two became the prime movers in urging the depressed remnant to resume temple construction.

HISTORICAL SETTING

A. *DATE OF WRITING*—September 1 to December 24, 520 B.C.

The prophecy of Haggai is one of the most precisely dated books of the Bible (Ezekiel and Zechariah also provide exact datings for many passages). Dated in the second year of Darius Hystaspis (521–486), king of Persia, Haggai is the first prophetic book to be dated by Gentile kings (aside from Daniel), reminding readers of the fact that the "times of the Gentiles" was in its second stage.

B. *DATES OF RELATED EVENTS*

538 B.C.	Edict of Cyrus for the Jews to return to rebuild the temple (Ezra 1:1).
537	Return of the first captives under Sheshbazzar (Ezra 2:1).
537	Altar set up and offerings resumed in Jerusalem (Ezra 3:6).
536	Reconstruction of the temple foundation begun (Ezra 3:10).
534	Reconstruction halted by threat of Samaritans (Ezra 4:4-5).
530	Official halting of reconstruction by Artaxerxes (Ezra 4:6, 21).
521	Accession of Darius Hystaspis to the Persian throne (Ezra 4:5).
520	Resumption of temple building after the urging of Haggai and Zechariah (Ezra 5:1-2; Hag. 1:14-15).
520	Edict of Darius I to resume temple building, with guarantees of subsidies and protection to insure its completion (Ezra 4:24; 6:8ff.).

Temple completed on March 3 (Adar), enabling observance of Passover on the 14th of April (Ezra 6:19).

C. *THE POLITICAL SETTING*

1. Following the seventy years captivity in Babylon, the Jews returned under the new Persian policy which encouraged the return of captives, and were given a new status as a district in the province of Trans-Euphrates. This favorable treatment by Cyrus may also have been because of Daniel's influence.

2. Opposition to their rebuilding the temple arose from the neighboring Samaritans who sought to integrate with them and to amalgamate their religions. This opposition resulted in their resorting to personal pursuits of home building while temple construction was idled for some fourteen years.

D. *THE RELIGIOUS SETTING*

1. In 537 a great new era had begun for the Jews in their return from captivity and resumption of the covenant offerings at Jerusalem. But the halt to reconstruction had cooled their ardor as they turned attention to more secular interests. This

Outline of Haggai

THEME: The Lord's Blessing Related to the Rebuilding of the Temple.

resort to secular activities did not prove profitable and may have been a judgment for their less than enthusiastic appraisal of the new temple foundation (Ezra 3:12-13; Hag. 2:3).

2. Following approximately fourteen years of temple negligence, the Lord sent the people drought and crop failure to alert them to their failure. Then He sent the prophets Haggai and Zechariah to show them the cause of that economic problem and to urge them to attend to their first responsibility of rebuilding the temple of the Lord.

THE PURPOSE OF THE BOOK OF HAGGAI

Haggai's one purpose was to urge the leaders and people to get on with the rebuilding of the destroyed temple, showing their failures in other aspects of life to be the result of neglecting the work of the Lord.

Unique Contributions of Haggai

1. *THE TEMPLE-BUILDING PROPHET.* More than anyone else, Haggai was the one responsible for getting the building resumed and completed. He came on the scene when a great start had been made but died aborning; the leaders were frightened and checkmated; their enemies surrounded them; and drought and depression had made further temple building anything but opportune. In the face of this opposition, Haggai urged the leaders and people to attend to this first priorty to enable God's blessing to flow to all their enterprises. This he evidently did before there was any indication that the new Persian king, Darius I, would respond with the favor he later showed (Ezra 5:1; 6:1). The temple that was then constructed stood longer than any of Israel's temples, a real tribute to both Zerubbabel the governor and Haggai the prophet (Ezra 5:1-2).

2. *HAGGAI RELATED TO ZEPHANIAH.* The prophecy of Haggai follows Zephaniah in the canon as a partial fulfillment of it in the post-exilic age. The Lord had promised in Zephaniah 3:18 to regather the outcasts who grieved over the cessation of the feasts and to restore their joys and fortunes. To resume those feasts and fortunes and to provide a place for the Lord's dwelling required the temple to be rebuilt. This was Haggai's immediate burden. Before the final fulfillment of Zephaniah's prophecy, however, the Lord will yet again shake heaven and earth and all nations (2:6-7, 22). This reminded the prophet that the great prosperity of messianic times was yet future, but that His hand of blessing would follow their obedience. If Zephaniah had a cataclysmic message to alert all nations of the Lord's impending judgment, Haggai had an encouraging message of the Lord's immediate presence to bless those who build His house and do His work now (Zeph. 3:8; Hag. 2:4-5).

3. **HAGGAI'S PROMISE OF ECONOMIC PROSPERITY** (1:6, 10). Three prophets especially related economic prosperity to spiritual obedience, Joel, Haggai, and Malachi (Joel 2:18ff.; Hag. 1:6-11; Mal. 3:10). This is true as a general principle of cause and effect (Prov. 11:24), but is especially related to the Mosaic covenant of blessing for obedience (Lev. 26:14-20). Its application by Haggai shows the continuance of this covenant relationship between Israel and the Lord even after the exile. Many exceptions to this principle for general application are noted in both testaments as God uses both adversity and prosperity to mature His people. (See Unique Contributions of Joel for further explication.)

4. **HAGGAI'S BREVITY AND POWER.** Haggai not only wrote one of the shortest books of the Old Testament (next to Obadiah), but delivered some of the shortest sermons (1:13, seven words, or four in Hebrew). Though his messages were brief, they were pointed and powerful. Their power related to the authority by which he spoke, constantly "footnoting" his messages with "thus says the Lord" (26 times in 38 verses). His emphasis was obviously on divine authority, not mere eloquence or argumentation. Yet Haggai was one of the most successful of the prophets in terms of immediate results. He recognized the power of the Lord's authority even in the face of overwhelming opposition.

5. **CHRISTOLOGY IN HAGGAI** (2:7-9). The book contains two references to Messiah, as Priest and King. "I will fill this temple with glory," is stated in a messianic kingdom context, likely referring to the return of the glory in the person of Messiah, as explained in Ezekiel 43:4-7. To the remnant who had seen the former glory of Solomon's temple and now wept over the paltriness of the new, the Lord declared, "The glory of this latter temple shall be greater than the former" (2:9). Its real glory would not be its silver and gold, but the Lord's personal presence among them. This would be Messiah's throne "where I will dwell in the midst of the children of Israel forever" (Ezek. 43:7). A second messianic reference is the choosing of Zerubbabel as the Lord's "signet ring," a symbol of Messiah's royal authority in the kingdom. (For the significance of this related to Coniah and David, see The Unique Contributions of Jeremiah.)

The Book
of Zechariah

Introduction

AUTHORSHIP

A. THE TITLE

The name Zechariah means "The Lord (Yah) remembers." The names of his father and illustrious grandfather, who were priests, are also noted with interesting relations in meaning: Iddo means, "the appointed time"; Berechiah means, "the Lord blesses." Even the names suggest the message of the book: The Lord will not forget His covenant promises to bless Israel at the appointed time.

B. *THE AUTHOR*
1. Zechariah was a priest who returned with his father and grandfather when they joined Zerubbabel in the first return from Babylon (Neh. 12:4, 16). Possibly his father had died prior to this and he was raised by his grandfather (C. F. Keil, *The Twelve Minor Prophets*). Iddo was one of the leading priests in the return.
2. It is possible he was the Zechariah Jesus referred to in Matthew 23:35 as slain in the temple. That reference, however, may be to 2 Chronicles 24:21 ("Berechiah" being a scribal error in Matthew 23:35), Chronicles being last in Hebrew Canon.
3. Zechariah is the only Minor Prophet identified as being a priest. Two Major Prophets were also priests, Jeremiah and Ezekiel.

C. *THE AUTHORSHIP PROBLEM*
The unity of Zechariah was uncontested until the advent of modern higher criticism (Joseph Mede, 1653). Since then the last six chapters have been assigned to one or several other writers, though all acknowledge chapters 1–8 as written by Zechariah. As with Isaiah, Zechariah has been divided into proto and deutero-Zechariah. Some assign 9–14 to pre-exilic times (Jeremiah or before), and some assign them to the Grecian times of Alexander or the Maccabees. The bases for these positions may be noted:
1. Reasons for denying the unity of Zechariah:
   a. Matthew 27:9-10 appears to assign Zechariah 11:12-13 to Jeremiah.
   b. The reference to Assyria (Zech. 10:10-11) seems to suggest a time prior to 612 when Nineveh fell.
   c. The reference to Greece in 9:13 suggests a date after Alexander.
   d. The apocalyptic content of 9–14 requires a date after the third century.
   e. The difference in literary style indicates different authors.
2. Reasons for maintaining the unity of Zechariah:
   a. Jewish and Christian tradition universally acknowledge its unity.
   b. The Matthew 27:9-10 passage combines two prophecies from Jeremiah 32:6-9 and Zechariah 11:12-13, acknowledging only the older prophet, Jeremiah, who spoke of purchasing a field. Zechariah was only part of "The Twelve."
   c. The reference to Assyria was only representative of Israel's enemies.
   d. The reference to Greece (9:13) was obviously prophetic, but was spoken after Greece had become a great power (c. 490 B.C.).
   e. The apocalyptic content of 9–14 was not dependent on later apocalyptic literature, but was (with Daniel and Ezekiel) the divine vanguard of such writing. Many prophets, in fact, employed apocalyptic content.
   f. The stylistic differences are not nearly as great as the similarities, and really to be expected in a period of some forty years of writing (520–480 B.C.)

HISTORICAL SETTING

A. *DATE OF WRITING—520–c. 480* B.C.

Three sections of Zechariah are precisely dated and the last six chapters undated.

1:1-6   November 1, 520 (two months after Haggai's first message, Hag. 1:1).

1:7–6:15   February 24, 519 (two months after Haggai's last message, Hag. 2:18).

7–8   December 4, 518.

9–14   c. 480. Undated, but probably given in Zechariah's later years, after Greece came to world prominence by repelling Darius I in 490 and Ahasuerus in 480 (Zech. 9:13).

Outline of Zechariah

THEME: The Need to Complete the Temple and Prepare for Messiah's Coming.

B. *CONTEMPORARY EVENTS*

1. For the political and religious settings, see Historical Setting of Haggai which covers the same period.

2. Zechariah followed Haggai as his younger contemporary, giving his first message two months after Haggai began. The two were instrumental in springing the remnant into action to complete the temple construction which had lain dormant for fourteen years. Both stressed the relation between their obedience in rebuilding the temple and the Lord's blessing on their lives (Hag. 1:9; Zech. 1:16-17).

3. The historical setting of the first eight chapters involved the problems of rebuilding the temple with local opposition mounting and the people becoming discouraged. This was accomplished, however, "through the prophesying of Haggai the prophet and Zechariah the son of Iddo," being completed on March 3, 516 B.C., the sixth year of King Darius (Ezra 6:14-15). A great celebration with many offerings followed as a dedication for the twelve tribes of Israel (Ezra 6:17). Their first Passover in over seventy years was held the next month, the fourteenth of Nisan.

4. The setting of the last six chapters appears to be markedly different. No longer are dates given; no more mention is made of the leaders Zerubbabel or Joshua; the visions with interpreting angels are past, and two extended burdens are presented (9–11; 12–14). The temple is no longer his concern. Assuming this section was written c. 480, in the later years of Zechariah, the international setting had changed and the area of military concern for the Persians was in the far West. Seeking to extend Persian rule into Europe, Darius met initial success but was defeated by the Greek city-states in the battle of Marathon in 490. His son Ahasuerus (future husband of Esther) in a massive plunge in 480 met an even greater defeat at Salamis, which turned the tide of Persian advance in the West. Thus the Grecians had shown their potential as another Gentile power to be reckoned with.

   This was the setting in which Zechariah wrote chapters 9–14, beginning with the detailed description of a Grecian invasion that would inundate all of Palestine except Jerusalem, which the Lord would miraculously spare and protect (9:1-8). The exiled remnant still in Babylon were urged to return in view of the Lord's promise to defend and empower them, looking to the victorious struggle of the Maccabees. Beyond this he foresaw the two comings of Messiah in His work of delivering from sin and from their enemies.

THE PURPOSE OF THE BOOK OF ZECHARIAH

Zechariah's purpose was twofold: To urge the immediate completion of the temple, and to further instruct the nation as to its future in messianic times. In the swirl of mighty empires around Palestine in the times of the Gentiles, the small remnant of Israel would be caught in the vortex of international struggles and godly challenges. But their King Messiah would come first in lowliness and rejection, and later in great power, to bring spiritual salvation and international prominence to His people in fulfillment of His covenant promises.

Unique Contributions of Zechariah

1. *THE OLD TESTAMENT BOOK OF "REVELATION."* As the New Testament concludes with a grand apocalyptic vision of the end times, the Old Testament does likewise in the Book of Zechariah. Each of these books summarizes and elucidates previously given prophecies in terms of their consummations. In Zechariah the two comings of Messiah are telescoped to present a broad preview of Israel's future; in Revelation the many details leading to His second coming are correlated and highlighted to show the culmination of God's program on earth (Zech. 9:9-10; Rev. 12:6; 13:5; 14:14ff.; 16:18ff.; 19:9ff.). The Book of Zechariah, with Malachi, accentuates and almost outlines the coming work of Messiah to bring spiritual salvation at His first coming and national deliverance for Israel at His second coming (12–14).

2. *A "MOST MYSTERIOUS" BOOK.* Many interpreters, both Jewish and Christian, regard this book as "most obscure and difficult of exposition" (Eli Cashdan, *The Twelve Prophets,* p. 267). For some, beyond the fact that "Yahweh wishes to have the temple rebuilt. . . , all certainty vanishes" (Steven Harris, *Understanding the Bible,* p. 123). The prophecy was not written, however, to mystify, but to clarify the truths concerning Israel's future. When the central truths of the parabolic visions are noted and all the visions related to previous prophecies, the messianic motif becomes central in the progress of Israel's struggles and development. This prophecy supplied some most significant truths for Israel about her redemption and national future as the remnant entered another stage of the Times of the Gentiles with her unfulfilled yearnings for the coming of Messiah (e.g., 8:7-8; 9:9-10; 11:9, 13; 12:10).

3. *ZECHARIAH'S RELATION TO DANIEL.* Though the prophecies of Daniel and Zechariah are both full of predictive content, their prophetic emphases are different:
   a. Daniel mixed prophetic visions and predictions with historic content, Zechariah presented his visions and predictions in a hortatory context (Dan. 2; Zech. 2).
   b. Daniel emphasized the prophetic future of the Times of the Gentiles as they related to Israel; Zechariah dealt almost exclusively with the future of Israel, noting Gentile relations only incidentally (Dan. 2, 7; Zech. 12:3).
   c. Daniel focused on Gentile kings and the coming of Antichrist, mentioning Messiah but once, almost incidentally (Dan. 9:26); Zechariah constantly points to the coming of Messiah, mentioning the coming of Antichrist only incidentally (11:16).
   d. Daniel was a statesman from the royal line of Judah and unveiled the progress of Gentile kingdoms until the setting up of Messiah's kingdom on earth (Dan. 2:44). Zechariah was a priest and characteristically urged the rebuilding of the temple, cleansing of the nation, and restoring of righteousness and holiness in the land (1:4, 16; 3:4; 12:10).

4. *THE LORD'S GREAT DAY OF BATTLE* (14:3). Zechariah concludes his prophecy with a description of the climactic battle of earth when the Lord Himself joins the fray. This "man of war" characteristic of the Lord was alluded to in Exodus 15:3, dramatized in Nahum 1:2, Habakkuk 2:8-15, and Zephaniah 3:8, and is developed full-blown in this vision of consummation. As the Lord goes forth to battle, He will be confronted by all nations gathering against Jerusalem (14:2; cf. Rev. 16:14; 19:19). His weapons are not revealed but their effects are: His enemies "flesh shall dissolve while they stand on their feet, Their eyes shall dissolve in their sockets, And their tongues shall dissolve in their mouths" (14:12), a strong suggestion of nuclear fission. Earthquakes will create great topographical changes in the earth, preparing it for the messianic age in which "the LORD shall be King over all the earth" (14:5-10).

5. *THE TRUE VALUE OF FASTING* (7–8). These two chapters of Zechariah make two clarifications concerning the fasts of Israel. Though Israel had no divinely ordained fast days in her calendar year, she had four self-imposed days of fasting to commemorate various calamities involved in the destruction of Jerusalem in 586 B.C. These were: (7:5; 8:19).

Tenth month (January 10)   —The day the siege of Jerusalem began, 588 (Jer. 52:4).
Fourth month (July 9)   —Babylon breached Jerusalem's wall, 586 (Jer. 52:6).
Fifth month (August 10)   —Jerusalem destroyed and burned, 586 (Jer. 52:12).
Seventh month (October 1)   —Gedaliah, the new governor, also slain, 586 (Jer. 41:1).

The question raised in Zechariah 7–8 was whether those fasts should be continued, inasmuch as they had returned to rebuild the temple. The Lord's answer provided two clarifications concerning fasting (cf. Is. 58:4-8):

a. Fasting was designed for God's glory, not for man's merit. Self-abnegation easily becomes self-pity and an empty ritual of self-worship. (7:5-6).

b. Fasting is worthless unless it is accompanied with acts of justice, kindness, and compassion toward one's neighbors (7:9-10). Israel's lack of these brought the Lord's judgment of destruction and desolation (7:11-14).

6. *CHRISTOLOGY IN ZECHARIAH*. This book is the most messianic of the Minor Prophets and ranks with the Psalms and Isaiah in messianic content. Messiah is either central or in the periphery of each of the visions. The failure or refusal of Jewish commentaries to accept this messianism as fulfilled in Jesus' first and second comings (e.g., Matt. 21:5), contributes to their admitted confusion in understanding the book (Rashi in H. H. Ben-Sasson, *History of The Jewish People,* p. 461). In explaining "they will look on Me whom they have pierced" (12:10), for instance, the Talmud identifies it as a reference to "the Messiah the son of Joseph who will fall in battle" (Eli Cashdan, *The Twelve Prophets,* p. 322). They see him as "one whom God gave to the restored Jewish community, . . . but they rejected him and put him to death." This "martyr" to them is unknown, certainly not Jesus. The messianic content of Zechariah, however, may be seen in the following references with corroborations from other books:

1:8, 11	—Man on red horse as "Angel of the LORD" is the pre-incarnate Christ guarding Israel.	—Exodus 23:23; Isaiah 63:1-6
2:8-11	—Messiah sent by the Lord to dwell in Zion.	—Isaiah 61:1-3; Mal. 3:1-3
3:8	—"My Servant the BRANCH" is Messiah coming in humility (stem) and power (stone).	—Isaiah 4:2; 11:1; Jeremiah 23:5
6:12-13	—"Man whose name *is* the BRANCH" as Priest-King.	—Psalm 2:6; 110:4
9:9-10	—"Behold, your King" coming in humility.	—Matthew 21:5; John 12:15
10:3	—The Lord to visit His flock as Shepherd.	—Ezekiel 34:11-19
11:4-14	—"Feed the flock for slaughter," He breaks the staves of grace and brotherhood.	—Ezekiel 34:3
12:10	—"Will look on Me whom they have pierced."	—Isaiah 53:5; John 19:37
13:6-7	—"I was wounded in the house of my friends."	—John 20:25; Revelation 1:7
14:3-4	—His feet to stand on Mount of Olives after which the mountain splits.	—Acts 1:11-12; Revelation 16:18-20
14:5	—The Lord comes with all His holy ones.	—Daniel 7:10; Matthew 16:27; Jude 14; Revelation 19:11-14
14:9	—"The Lord shall be King over all the earth."	—Psalm 2:6; 72:8-11; Revelation 19:16

The Book of Malachi

Introduction

AUTHORSHIP

A. *THE TITLE*

The name Malachi means "My messenger" (some scholars see it as a contraction of

Malak Yah, "Messenger of the Lord"). Besides the author, three other "messengers" of the Lord are noted in the book: the priest (2:7), the forerunner (3:1), and "Messenger of the covenant," the Lord Himself (3:1). The name implies a strong authority for this final prophetic message of the Old Testament.

B. *THE AUTHOR*
1. Nothing is known of the prophet Malachi but his name, given only in the superscription. He is identified by neither his parents, hometown, office, or date of ministry. Many interpreters regard "Malachi" as a title, rather than a name; the Talmud and Targums list Ezra as the real author. There is, however, no valid reason to deny this as the author's name, since no other Bible book gives only the office of the author. Nor is the parentage of many others given (e.g., Daniel, Amos, Obadiah, Micah, Nahum, Habakkuk, and Haggai).
2. Malachi was the final prophetic voice, contemporary with Ezra who was both priest and historian, writing both before and after Malachi. He was God's final messenger to the covenant people in the Old Testament, ministering about 1000 years after Moses the first prophet and Bible writer.

HISTORICAL SETTING

A. *DATE OF WRITING*—c. 430 B.C.
1. The prophecy is undated, being the last of six such undated prophetic books. These are: All books focusing on heathen nations, plus Joel and Malachi.
2. The date may be approximated by several historical notes in the text:
   a. The Edomites had been driven from Mount Seir, but had not returned, necessitating a date after 585 B.C. (1:3-4).
   b. The remnant had returned, had rebuilt the temple, and had become stagnant and formalistic in their religious experience (1:6ff.).
   c. A Persian governor other than Nehemiah ruled over them, one who might be bribed (1:8).
   d. The moral and religious problems are similar to those faced by Ezra and Nehemiah, e.g., materialism (Neh. 13:15; Mal. 3:5, 9); intermarriage with heathen (Ezra 10:2ff.; Mal. 2:11ff.).
3. These notes suggest a date about 430 B.C.—after Nehemiah's return to Persia in 432 and very likely in connection with his return and new reform in about 430 (Neh. 13:6-31).

B. *THE POLITICAL SETTING*
1. The world of Malachi was like that noted in Nehemiah. The Persian king was Artaxerxes I who reigned (465–424) over an empire that was vast and difficult to control. Their westward advance was stopped in 490 and 480 by the Athenians at Marathon and Salamis. Internal uprisings by the Egyptians were crushed by Artaxerxes (Xerxes) in 454 and by the Syrian satrap, Megabyzus, in 450, creat-

ing a period of nearly twenty-five years of unbroken peace in the empire (A. T. Olmstead, *History of Palestine and Syria,* pp. 582, 588). Palestine was part of the fifth satrapy, Trans-Euphrates, and Israel was a small part of that province. Though Zerubbabel had been appointed governor of Judah in 537 and the time of his death is uncertain, none of his sons were appointed to follow him. Nehemiah the Jewish official in the court of Artaxerxes I was appointed governor in 444 and ruled until returning to Persia in 432 B.C. (Neh. 5:14).

C. *THE RELIGIOUS SETTING*
1. Though the temple had been rebuilt (516), the worship system had been properly restored by Ezra (457), and the city wall had been reconstructed (444), the spiritual state of the Jewish remnant was at a new low point. Both the priests and people were affected. The people had discontinued tithing and crop failure was the result; the priests were uncared for and they became careless and indifferent in their temple service; morals were lax and integration with the heathen around them had become prevalent.
2. This spirit of religious indifference was in stark contrast to their fathers who had braved the dangers of returning to these hills, expecting Messiah's return to set up the new Davidic kingdom (Deut. 30:1-5; Ezek. 37:21-22). The response of the remnant to these frustrations was to become self-righteous, arrogant and oppressive towards others, and impatient and skeptical toward the Lord. This attitude of spiritual stagnation showed itself in several ways:
   a. Religious indifference toward the Law and the offerings, while accusing God of being indifferent to good and evil (1:6-10; 2:17).
   b. Moral indifference to their marriage vows, marrying heathen women and divorcing their Jewish wives (2:11-16).
   c. Social sins of perjury, fraud, and oppressing the weak (3:5).
   d. Material selfishness in robbing God of His tithes (3:8-10).
3. The first problem addressed by Malachi, however, was their failure to remember the Lord's covenant love for them (1:2ff.). This led to their nearsightedness, lack of appreciation, and all the sins of complaints and indifference that followed. His last word to them was to "Remember the Law of Moses" with its promises and warnings (4:4) and to wait for the coming of Elijah who would apply that Law in his restoration judgment (4:5-6).

THE PURPOSE OF THE BOOK OF MALACHI

The purpose of Malachi was to arouse the calloused remnant of Israel from their spiritual stagnation to enable the Lord to bless their lives. This he did by emphasizing the greatness of their God who always responds to obedience to His word and is planning a final day of judgment. It is then that the wicked will be judged and the righteous rewarded (4:1-3).

In writing these last words to the remnant, the prophet also pointed to Messiah's work of cleansing the nation before they could receive His kingdom and blessings (Matt. 4:17; 21:43).

1. ***THE GREATNESS OF GOD.*** No prophet so emphasized the greatness of God to Israel as did Malachi in this final prophetic book of the Old Testament. Three times in 1:11-14

Outline of Malachi

THEME: The Lord's Goodness Toward Israel and Their Haughty Ingratitude.

the Lord calls attention to His own "greatness." Throughout the book He calls attention to the honor due His name ten times (1:6, 11, 14; 2:2, 5; 3:16; 4:2). As the small, tattered remnant of Israel was about to enter four hundred years of prophetic silence, with Gentile conquerors and cultures swirling about them, they needed to remember the greatness of the God who called them. Though their days of greatness all seemed to be past, their claim to greatness was still the greatness of the God who had called them into a covenant relationship with Himself.

2. *MALACHI'S MANY DIVINE QUOTATIONS.* This prophecy consists almost exclusively of quotations from the Lord. Similar to Haggai in his brief message, Malachi continually used the phrase, "Says the LORD of hosts," or its equivalent. No wonder he mentioned his own name but once! He was simply a mouthpiece or messenger for the Lord. That generation, especially, needed a strong, authoritative word from the Lord, for many abuses needed correction. In quoting the Lord, the prophet identified Him as the "Lord of hosts" (twenty-four times). This name emphasized His power as the God of armies, an apt designation for this book of judgment and promise when the small remnant of Israel was virtually without power in themselves.

3. *MALACHI'S QUESTION AND ANSWER METHOD* (1:2, etc.). Malachi's dialectical style is rather unique among the prophets, most of whom used a kind of lecture or narrative style. Malachi records nine such dialectical exchanges of the Lord with Israel, their questions always having an air of hostility or defiance (1:2, 6, 7; 2:10, 14, 17; 3:7, 8, 13). In this provocative format (later called the "Rabbinic" or "Socratic" method), the prophet presented the Lord's major grievances against the remnant and their haughty responses. This style proved quite effective in commanding attention and getting quickly to the central issues. Jesus also resorted to a similar kind of exchange in confronting the hostile leaders of His time (Matt. 21:25, 31, 40; 22:42).

4. *ISRAEL'S DEGENERATING RELIGION.* Strong symptoms of degeneracy were showing in the fabric of Israel's faith, as Malachi addressed them. Their view of God was almost deistic: They questioned His love (1:2), His honor and greatness (1:14; 2:2), His justice (2:17), and His character (3:13-15). This low view of God spawned an arrogant attitude and wearisome service in the temple that insulted the Lord rather than worshiped Him (1:7-10; 3:14). Tithing was half-hearted and the offerings they made were sick and worthless animals that would outrage a human governor if offered as a present (1:8). The Lord's response was that He would spread refuse on the priests' faces (2:3), and curse the seeds they planted for harvest (3:11). The moral effects of this contemptible religion was that they were turning to sorcery, adultery, lying, cheating, and oppressing the poor (3:5). Family discord was prevalent leading to divorcing Jewish wives to marry heathen women (2:10ff.; 4:6). So bad were these conditions an Elijah was needed to restore family peace and prevent another destruction from the Lord (4:5).

5. *ISRAEL'S SIN OF ROBBING GOD* (3:8-10). One of Israel's most persistent sins was that of robbing God of tithes and offerings. It showed up first in the sin of Achan when they entered the land (Josh. 6:17-19; 7:11), and was one of the sins for which they were taken to Babylon in 586 (2 Chr. 36:21). The first mistake many of the kings made when under attack was to strip the treasures from the temple to try to appease the enemy which invariably invited further attacks (e.g., 2 Kin. 18:14-16). The Lord here reminds them that such robbery was really robbing themselves, for it resulted in crop failures. The further peril of the practice was that the more they did it, the less it bothered them (2:17; 3:15).

6. *THE PROMISE OF ELIJAH'S RETURN* (4:5-6). The final promise of the Old Testament was the return of the prophet Elijah prior to the "great and dreadful day of the LORD." Elijah was one of two men (with Enoch) who were translated to heaven without death (Gen. 5:24; 2 Kin. 2:11; Heb. 11:5). Enoch was the first to announce the coming of the Lord in great judgment (Jude 14-15), and Elijah will be the last (perhaps with Moses, Matt. 17:11; Rev. 11:3ff.). Though John the Baptist was like Elijah in his work of preparing Israel for Messiah, he was not actually Elijah (Matt. 11:14; 17:11-12; John 1:21). John was the forerunner prophesied in Isaiah 40:3 and Matthew 3:3 and the messenger of Malachi 3:1. Elijah will come to finish the work he began in the time of Ahab of rebuking national idolatry and restoring the families of Israel in the time just prior to the great Day of the Lord (4:5-6).

In Hebrew tradition, Elijah is "the grandest and the most romantic character that Israel ever produced. . . . it is Elijah who opens secret doors through which the martyred escape, who provides dowries for the unfortunate daughters of the poor, . . . There is a chair for him at every circumcision, and a cup of wine on every Passover table. He is stationed at the crossroads of paradise to welcome every worthy person. He will be the precursor of the Messiah, ushering in the new world in which the sufferings of Israel and of all peoples will be no more" (Abram Leon Sachar, *A History of the Jews,* pp. 50ff.). He seemingly came out of nowhere in 1 Kings 17 and vanished in a similar way in 2 Kings 2; but his austere figure is still held in awe by the nation as they await the meeting with him, as announced by Malachi. His work, however, will first be judgment in order to bring peace.

7. *MALACHI'S FINAL WORDS* (4:4-6). These last three verses are regarded by some as an appendix to "The Prophets" of the Bible. They encompass the Law and Prophets in Moses and Elijah. However, their outlook is not backward, but forward, looking with anticipation to the judgment of Elijah and the joy of the messianic age. In Hebrew Bibles, verse 5 is repeated after verse 6 so as not to end the book on a note of doom (this also occurs in Isaiah, Lamentations, and Ecclesiastes). It might be noted that Hebrew Bibles have no chapter four for Malachi, but continue chapter three to make twenty-four verses. The prominent note of the last six verses is anticipatory, pointing to 400 years of prophetic silence before another "angel" appeared to announce the coming of

the forerunner and the long awaited Messiah (Luke 1:11, 26ff.). Malachi's last word was not the last word.

8. **CHRISTOLOGY IN MALACHI** (1:14; 3:1; 4:2). Though the Lord again assured them of His unchangeable love in the introduction, the basic thrust of the book is judgment. In keeping with this motif, several suggestions of Messiah may be discerned:

a. In 1:14, the Lord declares Himself "a great King," far greater than the "governor" whom they would not think of offending with a blemished offering (1:8). As such He will not fail to judge the "deceiver" who vows magnanimously and is miserly. Zechariah 14:9 saw this kingship in a messianic light, when His Name will be feared among all nations.

b. In 3:1, the Lord declared Himself to be the "Messenger of the covenant" whom they sought. Contrary to their proud thinking, however, His coming would be in judgment for the wicked in Israel, beginning with the sons of Levi at the temple. His first coming to the temple in John 2:14-16 and Matthew 21:12 was a foretaste of that future coming to cleanse the people and land.

c. For those who fear His name, He will come as the "Sun of Righteousness" to bring healing and great joy (4:2; cf. Is. 60:19). The same "Sun" that burns the wicked (4:1) will heal those that fear His name. With this promise of heavenly sunshine to cleanse and heal the nation as it destroys the wicked at an unknown future day, the prophetic voice fell silent. The dark days of the intertestamental period would test their faith in the prophetic word as given in the Law and the Prophets.

Select Commentaries on the Minor Prophets*

THE TWELVE MINOR PROPHETS

*Feinberg, C. L. *The Minor Prophets*. Reprint. Chicago: Moody Press, 1976.
*Gaebelein, Frank E. *Four Minor Prophets*. Chicago: Moody Press, 1970.
Keil, C. F. *The Twelve Minor Prophets*. 2 vols. Grand Rapids: Eerdmans, 1954.
Laetsch, Theodore. *The Minor Prophets*. St. Louis: Concordia, 1956.
Morgan, G. C. *The Minor Prophets*. Westwood, N. J.: Revell, 1960.
*Pusey, E. B. *The Minor Prophets*. 2 vols. Reprint. Grand Rapids: Baker, 1950.
*Robinson, G. L. *The Twelve Minor Prophets*. Grand Rapids: Baker, 1962.

HOSEA

Feinberg, C. L. *Hosea: God's Love for Israel*. New York: American Board of Missions to the Jews, 1947.
Hubbard, David A. *With Bands of Love*. Grand Rapids: Eerdmans, 1967.
Ellison, H. L. *The Prophets of Israel*. Grand Rapids: Eerdmans, 1969.
*Mays, J. L. *Hosea: A Commentary*. Philadelphia: Westminster Press, 1969.
*Morgan, G. C. *Hosea: The Heart and Holiness of God*. New York: Revell, 1934.
*Tatford, F. A. *Prophet of a Broken Home*. Sussex, England: Prophetic Witness, 1974.

JOEL

Allen, Leslie C. *The Books of Joel, Obadiah, Jonah, and Micah* (NICOT). Grand Rapids: Eerdmans, 1976.
*Feinberg, C. L. *Joel, Amos, and Obadiah.* New York: American Board of Missions to the Jews, 1948.
Wolff, H. W. *Joel and Amos.* (Hermeneia series) Philadelphia: Fortress Press, 1977.
*Tatford, F. A. *Prophet of Judgment Day.* Sussex, England: Prophetic Witness, 1974.

AMOS

Cripps, Richard S. *A Critical and Exegetical Commentary on Amos.* Reprint. Minneapolis: Klock, 1981.
Feinberg, C. L. (See under Joel)
McFadyen, J. E. *A Cry for Justice.* New York: Scribner's, 1912.
*Mays, J. L. *Amos.* Philadelphia: Westminster Press, 1969.
*Motyer, J. A. *The Day of the Lion: The Message of Amos.* Downers Grove, Ill.: InterVarsity Press, 1974.
*Tatford, F. A. *Prophet of Social Injustice.* Sussex, England: Prophetic Witness, 1974.
Watts, J. D. W. *Studying the Book of Amos.* Nashville: Broadman Press, 1966.

OBADIAH

Allen, Leslie C. *Joel, Obadiah, Jonah, and Micah* (NICOT). Grand Rapids: Eerdmans, 1976.
Eaton, J. H. *Obadiah, Nahum, Habakkuk, and Zephaniah.* (TB) Chicago: InterVarsity Press, 1961.
*Gaebelein, Frank E. *The Servant and the Dove.* New York: Our Hope Press, 1946.
*Feinberg, C. L. (See under Joel)
Hillis, Don W. *The Book of Obadiah.* Grand Rapids: Baker, 1968.
*Watts, J. D. W. *Obadiah: A Critical Exegetical Commentary.* Grand Rapids: Eerdmans, 1969.

JONAH

*Aalders, G. C. *The Problem of the Book of Jonah.* London: Tyndale Press, 1948.
*Banks, W. L. *Jonah: The Reluctant Prophet.* Chicago: Moody Press, 1966.
Bull, Geoffrey. *The City and the Sign.* Grand Rapids: Baker, 1972.
Ellul, Jacques. *The Judgment of Jonah.* Grand Rapids: Eerdmans, 1971.
*Feinberg, C. L. *Jonah, Micah, and Nahum.* New York: American Board of Missions to the Jews, 1951.
Gaebelein, Frank E. (See under Obadiah)
*Martin, Hugh. *The Prophet Jonah.* London: Banner of Truth, 1870.

MICAH

Allen, Leslie C. (See under Jonah)
Bennett. T. M. *The Book of Micah.* (Shield's Bible series). Grand Rapids: Baker, 1968.
Copass, B. A. and E. L. Carlson. *A Study of the Prophet Micah.* Grand Rapids: Baker, 1950.
*Feinberg, C. L. (See under Jonah)
*Mays, J. L. *Micah: A Commentary.* Philadelphia: Westminster Press, 1976.
*Tatford, F. A. *Prophet of Messiah's Advent.* Sussex, England: Prophetic Witness, 1974.

NAHUM

Davidson, A. B. *Nahum, Habakkuk, and Zephaniah.* (CB) Cambridge: Cambridge Press, 1905.

Eaton, J. H. (See under Obadiah)
*Feinberg, C. L. (See under Jonah)
*Maier, Walter A. *The Book of Nahum*. St. Louis: Concordia, 1959.

HABAKKUK

Davidson, A. B. (See under Nahum)
Eaton, J. H. (See under Obadiah)
*Feinberg, C. L. *Habakkuk, Zephaniah, Haggai, and Malachi*. New York: American Board of Missions to the Jews, 1951.
*Gaebelein, Frank E. *Four Minor Prophets* (Obadiah, Jonah, Habakkuk, and Haggai). Chicago: Moody Press, 1970.
Gowan, D. E. *The Triumph of Faith in Habakkuk*. Atlanta: John Knox Press, 1976.
*Lloyd-Jones, D. M. *From Fear to Faith*. London: InterVarsity Press, 1953.

ZEPHANIAH

Davidson, A. B. (See under Nahum)
Eaton, J. H. (See under Obadiah)
*Feinberg, C. L. (See under Habakkuk)
Kapelrud, Arvid S. *The Message of Zephaniah*. Oslo: University Press, 1975.
*Tatford, F. A. *Prophet of Royal Blood*. Sussex, England: Prophetic Witness, 1973.

HAGGAI

*Baldwin, Joyce. *Haggai, Zechariah, Malachi: An Introduction and Commentary*. (Tyndale series). Downers Grove, Ill.: InterVarsity Press, 1972.
*Gaebelein, Frank E. (See under Obadiah)
Moore, T. V. *A Commentary on Haggai and Malachi*. 2 vols. Reprint. London: Banner of Truth Trust, 1960.
*Wolff, Richard. *The Book of Haggai*. Grand Rapids: Baker, 1967.
Tatford, F. A. *Prophet of the Restoration*. Sussex, England: Prophetic Witness, 1972.

ZECHARIAH

Baldwin, Joyce. (See under Haggai)
*Baron, David. *The Visions and Prophecies of Zechariah*. London: Morgan-Scott, 1951.
*Feinberg, C. L. *God Remembers*. Wheaton: Van Kampen Press, 1959.
Leupold, H. C. *Exposition of Zechariah*. Columbus, Ohio: Wartburg Press, 1956.
*Unger, Merrill F. *Commentary on Zechariah*. Grand Rapids: Zondervan, 1963.

MALACHI

*Baldwin, Joyce. (see under Haggai)
Logsdon, S. F. *Malachi: Will a Man Rob God?* Chicago: Moody Press, 1961.
*Feinberg, C. L. (See under Habakkuk)
Moore, T. V. (See under Haggai)
*Morgan, G. Campbell. *Wherein?* New York: Revell, 1898.
Tatford, F. A. *Prophet of the Reformation*. Sussex, England: Prophetic Witness, 1974.

---

*Though all entries are recommended, asterisks identify those of first priority.

Highlights of the
Intertestamental Period

Persian Rule	430 —Malachi's prophecy ends Old Testament era.
Grecian Rule	332 —Alexander the Great conquers Palestine and Egypt.
Ptolemaic Rule 323—198	323 —Death of Alexander divides empire into four parts. 301 —Ptolemy I (Soter) secures Palestine and Egypt. 284 —Ptolemy II (Philadelphus) succeeds his father, continuing his father's art and cultural interests, building a great library. c. 275 —Translation of Old Testament into Greek, calling it the Septuagint (LXX).
Seleucid Rule 198—166	198 —Antiochus III of Syria defeats Ptolemy V at Panias, taking Palestine. 175 —Antiochus IV Epiphanes takes Syrian throne, begins vigorous Hellenization. 167 —Antiochus IV outlaws Judaism, profanes the temple with swine sacrifices, and sets up Zeus worship in the temple on December 25, 167.
Jewish Hasmonean Rule 166—63	166 —Mattathias the priest of Modin begins the Maccabean revolt. 164 —Judas Maccabeus recaptures Jerusalem, rededicates the temple on December 25, 164, and regains Jewish religious freedom (commemorated by Hanukkah). 160 —Jonathan takes command as Judas is slain in battle. In 152 Jonathan becomes the first Hasmonean high priest ruler. 142 —Simon succeeds brother Jonathan. He gained complete Jewish independence from Syria, making a peace treaty with Rome. In 140 the Great Assembly in Jerusalem confirmed him as Ethnarch and high priest, making the high priesthood hereditary in the Hasmonean line. 135 —John Hyrcanus succeeds his father as ruler and high priest. In alliance with Rome, enlarged the kingdom to the seacoast and to Idumaea, forcing the Idumaeans to adopt Judaism. He minted Jewish coins for the first time. First great rift of Sadducees and Pharisees developed over the high priesthood becoming worldly and Hellenized in 110. 104 —Aristobulus I follows his father for a year of riotous rule. 103 —Alexander Jannaeus succeeds brother, marrying his widow. He greatly enlarged the kingdom to equal that of David and Solomon. His violence and impiety brought outrage by Pharisees, civil war, and much slaughter. 76 —Salome Alexandra, widow of Jannaeus, succeeded him as ruler and appointed son Hyrcanus II as high priest. She re-established peaceful relations between the Sadducees and Pharisees and throughout the kingdom. 67 —Civil war between two sons of Alexandra and Jannaeus, Hyrcanus II and Aristobulus II, contesting the throne and high priesthood.

Roman Rule 63—	63	—Roman General Pompey takes Jerusalem, assigns high priesthood to Hyrcanus and terminates the Jewish independence era of the Hasmoneans.
	62	—Decapolis League of Trans-Jordan cities formed by Pompey to counterbalance the Jewish power of Judea in Palestine.
	60	—First Triumvirate of Caesar, Pompey, and Crassus formed as an unofficial alliance to rule Rome.
	48	—Julius Caesar defeats Pompey and unites empire for first time in a century, Hyrcanus II continued as high priest but Antipater and Idumaean was procurator.
	44	—Caesar is slain on "Ides of March." Second Triumvirate of Octavian, Antony, and Lepidus formed in 43.
	40	—Herod acquires kingship of Judea and finally captures Jerusalem in 37. The Hasmonean heirs to the priesthood are gradually destroyed.
	31	—Octavian (later called "Augustus") gained sole rulership of empire after Agrippa I defeated Antony and Cleopatra in battle of Actium.
	19	—Rebuilding of Jerusalem temple is begun by Herod to mollify the Jews for his many slaughters and his building gymnastic facilities in Jerusalem.
	5	—Birth of John the Baptist (c. June) and of Jesus (c. December).

Sources for dating the Highlights of the Intertestamental Period

Ben-Jacob, A. *Encyclopaedia Judaica,* v. 8, Jerusalem, Israel: Keter Publishing House Jerusalem Ltd., 1972. pp. 766ff.

Bruce, F. F. *Israel and the Nations,* Grand Rapids: Eerdmans, 1963. pp. 120–240.

DeVries, S. J. "Chronology of the Old Testament," *Interpreters Dictionary of the Bible,* Nashville: Abingdon, 1962. pp. 597–596.

Hoehner, H. "Between the Testaments," *Expositor's Biblical Commentary,* Frank E. Gaebelein, ed. v. 1. Grand Rapids: Zondervan, pp. 179–191.

Unger, Merrill. *Unger's Bible Handbook.* Chicago: Moody, 1966. pp. 451–455.

A Glossary of Terms for Bible Introduction

ACCESSION YEAR SYSTEM—That system of dating the accession of kings in the Old Testament by reckoning it as beginning with the month Nisan following the particular king's accession (as employed by Judah).

ACROSTIC—A form of Hebrew poetry in which the initial letters of each line form a word or sequence (as in the alphabetic arrangements of Psalm 119 or Song of Solomon).

AKKADIAN—Pertaining to the Mesopotamian Valley between the Tigris and Euphrates Rivers and between the kingdom of Aram in the north and the kingdom of Sumer in the south.

ALLEGORICAL INTERPRETATION—That method of Bible interpretation, innovated by the Alexandrian Fathers from the Greeks, which sees the histories and statements of the Bible as allegories which must be interpreted as having a primary meaning deeper than the obvious literal sense, with perhaps several levels of meaning.

ANACHRONISMS—A chronological error or the recording of an event out of its chronological order.

ANCIENT MANUSCRIPTS—The most ancient texts of the books of the Bible extant today, not the original autographs themselves.

ANGELOLOGY—The doctrine of the Bible concerning angels and the non-god spirit world.

ANIMISM—The belief in a spirit world distinct from matter, and the concept that inanimate objects possess life and personality.

ANTHROPOLOGY—The scientific study of the origin, makeup, and development of man in his various relationships in the world.

ANTICHRIST—Adjectivally the word signifies that which is opposed to Christ, and nominally or specifically, the term designates that prophesied person in the end-time who will fulfill the place of a counterfeit Christ in presuming to take the kingdom under the power of Satan.

ANTILEGOMENA—Those books of the Bible which were contested as being canonical by some of the early church Fathers: Five in the Old Testament, Esther, Song of Solomon, Proverbs, Ecclesiastes, and Ezekiel; and seven in the New Testament, Hebrews, James, 2 Peter, 2 and 3 John, Jude, and Revelation.

ANTINOMIANISM—A term meaning "opponents of the Law," it came to describe certain Christian groups or cults who saw faith in Christ as absolving a believer from the moral law, a heresy refuted by Paul in Galatians 5.

APOCALYPTIC—Apocalyptic literature is largely visionary and concerns a bright messianic future in which the problems of sins and suffering will be resolved in triumph for the saints and destruction for the wicked.

APOCRYPHA—The non-canonical books later added to the Bible after the canon was established as complete and which do not measure up to the canonical standard, about fourteen concerning Old Testament and intertestamental times, and an unnumbered group concerning the New Testament times. The term signifies "hidden" or spurious.

APOLOGETICS—That branch of biblical science which deals with the defense and confirmation of the claims of the Bible.

APOSTASY—The term signifies a "departure," and has come to mean a defection from the faith generally, although not exclusively.

ARAMAIC—The northern class of Semitic people of Aram or Syria; the language of Chaldea and of the Palestine Jews after the captivity to the time of Christ.

ARCHAEOLOGY—That branch of science which seeks to recover and analyze the remains of ancient civilizations for the purpose of reconstructing their history.

ATONEMENT—An Old Testament term meaning to "cover," which is used theologically to designate the overall sacrificial work of Christ on the cross. The term itself is quite inadequate as such and is used biblically only in the Old Testament.

AUTHENTICITY—The quality of a writing which suggests it to be genuine and therefore authoritative concerning that of which it speaks.

BAAL—The Phoenician and Canaanite term of god or lord and the name of the chief male god of the Phoenicians, son of El the father of the Canaanite pantheon of gods.

BALAAMISM—Balaamism was the philosophy pursued by the pagan prophet Balaam of exploiting his prophetic gift for selfish ends and of seeking to corrupt the people of God whom he could not curse.

BAPTISM—The act of dipping or immersing by which a re-identification is accomplished, utilized in intertestamental times for proselyting, and adopted by John and Jesus as a mark of identification.

Taken from the word *baptidzo* in the dyers' trade and used metaphorically to signify a change of identification.

BEHISTUN STONE—An inscription on a Persian mountain from the time of Darius of the sixth century B.C. which, because it was given in three languages, enabled Sir Henry Rawlinson to decipher the Babylonian language.

BIBLE—The term designation for the whole Scriptures derived from *biblios* a papyrus writing material which came to signify a book. The first word of the New Testament, is *biblos*. Scripture began to be called *Biblia* in the second century A.D.

BIBLE INTRODUCTION—That area of Bible science which deals with the introductory matters of determining the canon, true texts, and the historical features of authorship, dating, and settings.

BIBLICAL THEOLOGY—The theological science of the Scriptures which seeks to organize the various phrases of revelation according to their progressive setting forth by author or historical setting; i.e., the theology of Moses and the Pentateuch.

BRONZE AGE—The age in which bronze came into use for metallurgy, being about 3200 to 2200 B.C. (Albright, *The Archaeology of Palestine*).

CANON—That group of books contained in the Bible which are accepted as Scripture because they conform to the standards of divine inspiration. The term comes from the Gr. *kanon,* meaning a measuring rule, and metaphorically a standard or rule of conduct or judgment. The canonical books are not such because designated so by men, but because they bear the marks of divine authority or inspiration.

CHRISTOLOGY—The docrine of the Bible concerning the Person and Work of Christ.

CODE OF HAMMURABI—A code of laws developed or collected by Hammurabi (king of Babylonia about 1700 B.C.) on a stone pillar, many of which laws dated a millenium earlier. The code contained 282 laws many of which parallel Moses' laws as given by God.

COSMOGONY—The science which studies the creation or development of the world and the universe.

COVENANT—A working agreement or contract between two parties by which certain provisions are guaranteed upon conditions either already met or yet required. The Old and New Testaments are so called because they constitute, generally, God's working agreement with men in the old and new dispensations. The Old Testament includes several covenants all of which have a general relationship to the Abrahamic covenant.

CRITICISM—The term (from Gr. *Krino,* to judge) means to discriminate between two or more things to arrive at a correct appreciation of any one thing. BIBLICAL CRITICISM is that theological science which seeks to determine the exact original text and to recover exactitude in authorship, dates, and historical settings. TEXTUAL CRITICISM deals with the problem of determining the exact text (lower criticism), and HISTORICAL CRITICISM (higher criticism) concerns itself with ascertaining the historical relationships and the validity of the claims the documents make for themselves. DE-STRUCTIVE CRITICISM operates in the area of higher criticism but proceeds on the assumptions of naturalism and evolution in dealing with the development of the text.

CUNEIFORM A wedge-shaped script engraved on clay tablets by the ancient Babylonians and Canaanites.

DAGON—An early Babylonian and Canaanite god, the father of Baal, in the form of a fish with a human body, which became the national god of the Philistines.

DEAD SEA SCROLLS—Manuscripts of the Old Testament and intertestamental period found in 1947 in caves near Qumran off the northeast shore of the Dead Sea, dating to the first century B.C.

DEISM—A belief in God emphasizing His transcendence and which grounds itself in the testimony of reason rather than that of Scripture. While recognizing the obligation to worship God, it denies supernaturalism as well as the deity and atoning work of Christ.

DELPHI INSCRIPTION—An inscription found at Delphi across from Corinth which dates the arrival of Gallio in Corinth as A.D. 51

DIATESSARON—A so-called Harmony of the Gospels assembled by Tatian about A.D. 170 in Syriac, giving a compendium of the four Gospels in a single narrative without striving for completeness in including all the details.

DIDACHE—A document from about the turn of the first century, called *The Teaching of the Twelve,* which emphasized the teachings of Jesus as opposed to the actions of Jesus, as such.

DISPENSATION—A divine administration or economy, usually involving a time period, during which God deals with people in a particular way in the outworking of His sovereign purposes.

DISPENSATIONALISM—A premillennial interpretation of the whole body of Scripture which bases itself on a consistent grammatical historical interpretation of the Scripture and thereby takes seriously the distinction between God's program for Israel and the Church. It distinguishes itself from covenant theology also in claiming to be theologically-centered rather than primarily soteriologically-centered.

DOCETISM—An early heretical belief that Christ was only a phantom who seemed to have a human body, as taught by Marcion and some of the Gnostics. They stressed the evil of matter and the impossibility of Christ actually becoming flesh, using the ''appearance'' theory to explain the life of Christ.

DOCUMENTARY HYPOTHESIS—The theory that seeks to explain the original composition of the biblical texts by assuming that the texts are a composite of two or more documents which were used in its composition, based on a naturalistic and evolutionary concept of development.

ECCLESIOLOGY—The doctrine of the Bible concerning the church.

EPICUREANS—The ancient adherents of the philosophy of Epicurus who sought meaning and fulfillment in life through pleasure and fleshly satisfaction.

EPISTEMOLOGY—The science of knowledge, dealing with its nature, ground, limits, validity, and criteria.

ESSENES—An ascetic religious community of Palestine which existed as a religious order, living monastically and abstaining from marriage. They recruited their members by adoption, maintained a communal society, and held to traditional Judaism, without animal sacrifices.

ETIOLOGY—The science of causes or reasons for experiences or phenomenon.

EVOLUTION—The theory of spontaneous and progressive development of organization from chaos to order and from simplicity to complexity; biologically, the derivation of all forms of life by circumstantial modifications from a simple or rudimentary form.

EXORCISM—The practice of expelling evil spirits or demons.

FATHERS—Early Christian writers and teachers through the first seven centuries who enunciated the great doctrines of the Church and who became a sort of court of appeals for later interpreters.

FIGURE OF SPEECH—A word or expression used in a different sense from that normally belonging to it for the purpose of explaining or emphasizing some particular feature or point by analogy.

FORM CRITICISM—A method of analyzing the biblical texts by seeking the ''forms,'' preliterary moulds, or life settings (G. *sitz-im-laben*) in which they developed, assuming an evolution from oral fragments to written collections.

FUNDAMENTALISM—The doctrinal position often called ''conservative theology'' which takes seriously the doctrine of the verbal, plenary inspiration of the Scriptures. Properly, its fundamentals pertain to Scripture rather than mere creeds, as such.

GEMARA—The second part of the Talmud which is a commentary and explanation of the first part, the Mishna, or oral laws of the Jews. Written in Aramaic and completed in A.D. 500, it contains comments on the law of the sages of many generations.

GILGAMESH EPIC—An early Babylonian document of twelve tablets from the time of Ashurbanipal devoted to the mythical King Gilgamesh of Babylon and depicting much ancient history with parallels to Genesis, albeit polytheistic.

GNOSTICISM—An early Christian heresy which confused the doctrine of the Person of Christ as His being neither true God nor man, and confused the doctrine of salvation through knowledge (or gnosis) which was a mystic knowledge acquired only by initiates.

GREAT SYNAGOGUE—A supposed institution in the early intertestamental period, made up of 120 members including Ezra, which was formed for the purpose of administering the law. It is generally assumed to be the forerunner of the Sanhedrin.

HAGGADAH—The second section of the Midrash which gives an interpretation and explanation of the Old Testament in a popular and homiletical style.

HAGIOGRAPHA—The Greek name to designate the third section of the Hebrew Old Testament (Holy writings, Ketubim) which included eleven books in three sections: three poetical—*Psalms, Proverbs, Job;* five rolls—*Song of Solomon, Ruth, Lamentations, Ecclesiastes, Esther;* and three historical —*Daniel, Ezra–Nehemiah,* and *Chronicles.*

HALAKAH—The first section of the Midrash which gives an exposition of the Hebrew law including judgments of the Rabbis on cases not covered by the law.

HAMARTIOLOGY—The doctrine of the Bible concerning sin.

HAMMURABI, Code of—(see Code of Hammurabi).

HASIDIM—A group of dedicated religious Jews called "The pious" in the time of Antiochus Epiphanes (c. 168 B.C.) who preferred death to the violation of their religious laws and who were perhaps the predecessors of the Pharisees (separatists).

HEBRAISTS—The Jewish people of intertestamental and apostolic times who retained not only their Judaism in religion but also the use of the Hebrew or Aramaic in language and customs, resenting the growth of Hellenism.

HELLENISTS—The Jewish people of intertestamental and apostolic times who embraced the Graeco-Roman culture but retained the Jewish faith.

HERMENEUTICS—The science or art of interpretation, especially of the Scriptures, involving the development and application of proper principles of interpretation.

HERODIANS—A party of the Jews who gave strong allegiance to Herod, politically, and became opposed to Christ religiously, as well as to the Pharisees.

HIEROGLYPHICS—Picture writing (sacred carving) (characters or words) which carry hidden meanings.

HITTITES—A people of Palestine during and after the Joshua invasion who had migrated from Asia Minor where a powerful kingdom existed from c. 1600–1200 (which conquered Babylon in 1550), of Aryan stock.

HOMILETICS—The science and art of sermon building and delivery.

HOMOLOGOUMENA—The designation for those books of the canon which were undisputed as being canonical, numbering thirty-four in the Old Testament and twenty in the New Testament.

HUMANISM—A study of the humanities or the works of men in literature, art, and society as opposed to mere scholastics. It also came to designate a philosophy of life and thinking that is person-centered both in its basis of logic and its desired objectives.

HURRIANS—Known in the Bible as the "Horites" (Gen. 14:6) they were a dominant ethnic group of about 2400–1800 B.C. in the Middle East, which civilization was uncovered in the recently discovered Nuzi tablets. Of Non-Semitic origin, they lived in the region south of the Caucasus, east of the Tigris.

HYKSOS—The term, meaning "foreign rulers", designated the shepherd kings of Egypt from dynasties 13 to 17 (c. 1750 to 1550 B.C.) of predominantly Semitic origin, distinguished for their horses, chariots and implements of war.

IDEALISM—That philosophical system of thinking which seeks to explain life and the universe as the realization of a progressive evolution of an ideal (as opposed to realism or mechanism).

IDUMEAN—The Greek name for the Edomites in intertestamental and apostolic times when the mixed race of Edomites occupied southern Judea around Hebron. They ceased to exist after the fall of Jerusalem in A.D. 70.

IMPRECATORY PSALMS—Psalms invoking a curse upon sinners.

INCARNATION—A term designating the hypostatic union of the divine and human natures of Christ by which the Son of God was manifested in human flesh, without the diminution of either His Godhood or His Manhood.

INERRANCY—The quality of inspiration of the Bible which constitutes the sacred writings inerrant in all areas of truth on which they touch by virtue of an inerrant Divine Author who superintended the writing of the whole. ("Your word is Truth," John 17:17).

INSCRIPTIONS—A writing or engraving in a public place or object (such as on monuments, pillars, coins, etc.) for preservation or public inspection.

INSPIRATION—Signifies the "in-breathing" of God into men by which they were prepared and qualified to receive and communicate God's word, and the quality of the Scriptures themselves as being "God-breathed" (theopneustos), and thus trustworthy and authoritative.

IRON AGE—The last of the classified ages of man, relating to his stages of progressive use of metal (stone, bronze, iron), beginning c. 1200 B.C.

ISAGOGICS—The biblical science of Bible Introduction dealing with the literary history of the books, their inspiration, authorship, historical settings of the compositions, and related areas.

JOSEPHUS—A Jewish historian of apostolic times (c. A.D. 37–100) who wrote *The Antiquities of the Jews, The Wars of the Jews,* etc.

JUDAISM—A term signifying the religion of the Jews but more specifically designating the Jewish religious system as developed from the intertestamental period by the rabbis and continued through our day as Orthodox Judaism. Their central thrust is the unity, transcendence, and Fatherhood of God.

JUDAIZERS—An early heretical party of the church, stemming from the converted Pharisee group, which maintained the necessity of believers to comply with the Mosaic ritual for genuine salvation.

KENOSIS—A term signifying the "self-emptying" of Christ in His incarnation, not implying the subtraction of deity but the addition of humanity. It signified His self-limitation relative to His glory and divine prerogatives during His earthly sojourn.

KENOSIS THEORY—A heretical doctrine which misconceived the self-emptying of Christ to mean that the human limitation in His knowledge limited Him to the current ideas of His environment and therefore rendered His sayings subject to error in various scientific respects.

KERYGMA—A term signifying the preaching or proclamation of the works of Jesus in the early church as a corollary to the *Didache* which signified His teachings. Often the *kerygma* meant simply the gospel message.

KETHUBIM—Hebrew term for the Holy Writings or Hagiographa (eleven books of the Old Testament).

KINGDOM OF GOD—A term used interchangeably with "kingdom of heaven" in the Gospels as derived from Daniel 2:44, designating the rule, realm, and the authority of God both in its universal or individual application and in its spiritual and physical spheres.

KOINE GREEK—The "common" or Alexandrian Greek developed through the conquests of Alexander from the older classical Greek and used by the common populace of apostolic times.

LIBERALISM—A "modernist" eclectic of Christianity and scientism by which the Bible is interpreted on the basis of the presuppositions of rationalism which rejects its supernatural character and emphasizes its application in terms of social needs and progress.

LITERAL INTERPRETATION—That method of interpretation which interprets the language of Scripture in its grammatical-historical sense, recognizing the normal, usual, customary meanings of words and sentences and interpreting proper figures of speech as they are indicated in their particular settings.

MACCABEES—A Jewish family of valiant patriots (sons of the priest of Modein, Mattathias) who revolted against the Syrian rule of Antiochus Epiphanes and delivered Israel to independence c. 164 B.C.

MARI TABLETS—Tablets found at the town of Mari on the Euphrates (Tell Hariri) dating from 1813 to 1781 B.C. and confirming archaeologically the biblical data concerning Abraham's origin in Haran and Nahor of upper Mesopotamia.

MASORETES—A class of Jewish Old Testament scholars of the fifth to the tenth centuries A.D. who by use of the "Massorah" (handed down notations concerning the Hebrew texts), compiled and arranged the text with fixed vowel signs and accents to preserve proper pronunciations for the Old Testament Hebrew which was becoming a dead language.

MEGILLOTH—Hebrew term for the five scrolls that included *The Song of Solomon* (read at Passover), *Ruth,* (read at Pentecost), *Ecclesiastes* (read at Tabernacles), *Esther* (read at Purim), and *Lamentations* (read at anniversary of the Destruction of Jerusalem).

MIDRASH—A Jewish commentary including the Halakah and the Haggadah (both the law and remainder of Old Testament) giving interpretations with a popular flavor.

MIRACLE—A miracle is an extraordinary event, wrought in the physical realm, by the direct agency of God, for a God-ordained purpose—usually for the authentication of revelation.

MISHNAH—The first part of the Jewish *Talmud* which gives the "oral law," (prior to the *Gemara* which gives the commentaries and interpretations of the rabbis) as compiled by Judah the Prince c. A.D. 200.

MOABITE STONE—An ancient monument found in Trans-Jordan in the land of Moab, written by King Mesha of Moab c. 890 B.C. after his successful revolt from Israel, using an alphabetic language similar to Hebrew.

NATURALISM—The doctrinal position that maintains that the universe and all phonemena can be explained in terms of natural causes; also the position that God's revelation in nature is adequate to the religious needs of man.

NAZIRITE—Signified a person of either sex who separated him or herself by a vow to a peculiar kind of service for God in the levitical economy.

NEO-ORTHODOXY—That modern doctrinal reaction to liberalism which stresses the transcendence of God (as the wholly "Other"), contends for the concept of dialectical theology in rejection of the idea of propositional revelation, and emphasizes an "existential experience" (crisis theology) by which an individual confronts God and the Living Word in a crucial, decisive relationship by a passionate commitment to the truth. While embracing the liberal's naturalistic view of Scripture, it declares the purpose of Scripture to be to provoke an existential encounter and to reveal the immutability of Divine election (almost to the point of universalism). Its return to orthodoxy consists primarily in its return to the Reformers' emphasis on the sovereign grace of God.

NESTORIANISM—The doctrine, initiated by Nestorius, patriarch of Constantinople in the fifth century, that denied the hypostatic union of Christ's human and divine natures and emphasized the humanity of the Man Jesus almost to the point of denying His deity as God.

NICENE—Pertaining to the council of Nicaea of A.D. 325 and the confession of faith there adopted by the church.

NICOLAITANISM—An unscriptural concept of the clergy which violates the priesthood of the believer by positing a clergy-priesthood system.

NUZI TABLETS—Documents of patriarchal times found c. 1925 at Nuzi, a Hurrian center, which sheds much light on the background of Genesis as to historical events.

ORAL GOSPEL—The common narrative of the life and ministry of Christ which circulated during the first twenty years after the resurrection among believers and was committed to memory in a virtually stereotyped form before written down (such as that spoken of by Luke in 1:4).

ORDINANCE—In the Old Testament a statute or ritual prescribed by God, and in the New Testament one of two symbolic Christian ceremonies which were instituted by Christ, viz., baptism, a once-for-all symbolic portrayal of the believer's identification with Christ in death and resurrection, and The Lord's Supper, a symbolic enacting of the believer's daily feeding on Christ and partaking of the virtues of His Death. Theologically, an ordinance is an outward symbol, divinely appointed to represent some great spiritual truth of the gospel, making its obligations universal and perpetual.

ORTHODOXY—That body of normative Christian doctrines as expressed in the Scripture and as generally embraced by the church historically.

PARABLE—A parable is a fictitious story, true to life, designed for the pedagogical purpose of teaching some spiritual truth by analogy, relative to the Kingdom of God.

PARALLELISM—That peculiar feature of Hebrew poetry which emphasizes the rhythm of thought or sense, rather than the rhythm of words or sounds. This is accomplished by repetition, contrast, development, etc.

PAROUSIA—A term signifying the second coming and "presence" of Christ, involving both His coming for His church and His return to the earth generally.

PESHITTA—An early version of the Old Testament in Syriac, dating from the second or third centuries

A.D. and taken from the Hebrew and the Septuagint versions. (A Syrian parallel to the Latin Vulgate.)

PHARISEES—An intertestamental and apostolic period religious sect of Judaism which laid strong emphasis on traditions and ceremonial observances, emphasized separation from the world, and centered their religion around the synagogue (Forebears largely of current Judaism).

PNEUMATOLOGY—The study of spirit beings as expressed in the Scriptures.

PRAGMATISM—The philosophical doctrine that makes practical results the sole test for truth.

PROPHECY—A message from God to men through a prophet of the Lord. It may be either the "foretelling" of the future or simply the "forthtelling" of a specific message from the Lord.

PSEUDEPIGRAPHA—Spurious writings concerning Old and New Testament events written under the guise of a prominent Bible author, mostly between 200 B.C. and A.D. 200.

PTOLEMIES—Rulers of Egypt who descended from Ptolomy Soter and who ruled Egypt from the death of Alexander to the time of Cleopatra, c. 30 B.C.

Q or QUELLE—A term to signify a supposed, Greek document which the documentary hypotheses assume to have been used by the Gospel writers as a common source in their compositions.

QUMRAN DOCUMENTS—The Dead Sea Scrolls and intertestamental literature, found at Qumran in the wilderness cliffs of the Dead Sea in 1947 and which give many confirmations relating to the Old Testament texts and historical references to the time of the Essenes in the time of Christ and John the Baptist.

RAS SHAMRA TABLETS—Ancient documents from the age of Moses discovered c. 1929 at Ugarit on the north Syrian coast, showing the alphabetic dialect of the Canaanites and the sensual paganism of the time.

REDACTION—The process of compiling or editing that was involved in the composing of a piece of literature, working from older written or oral sources, often applied by higher critics to the development of the Bible books. The editor was the redactor.

REMNANT—A term signifying that faithful group of any era of the Old Testament, the "little flock" of the New Testament, and those that will be saved and faithful during the tribulation period of Revelation.

REVELATION—A term designating 1) the act of God in manifesting Himself and His works, and 2) the specific record of His self-revelation as recorded in the Bible. The term signifies an unveiling of that which is otherwise unknown and unknowable apart from revelation.

SADDUCEES—A religious sect of Judaism at the time of Christ of the aristocratic class who rejected the traditions of the elders, which the Pharisees held, as well as the doctrine of resurrection, angels, and future life which they could not find expressly taught by Moses. Their religious sphere was the temple.

SAMARITAN PENTATEUCH—The Hebrew Old Testament Pentateuch, written in Samaritan letters about 430 B.C. and recovered in 1616, in substantial agreement with the Hebrew Masoretic text.

SATRAP—A ruling officer in the Persian Empire who governed a province called a "satrapy." Palestine being the fifth Persian Satrapy.

SCHOLASTICISM—A method of explaining the doctrines of the Bible, as developed in medieval times, by the use of philosophical concepts with a view of reconciling faith and reason.

SCROLLS—See "Hagiographa."

SELEUCIDS—The rulers of Syria from the time of the division of the Alexandrian empire of Greece.

SEMITES—The descendants of Noah's second son, Shem (Gen. 10:21-31), who settled mainly in upper Mesopotamia and spread from Elam to southern Asia Minor. They are identified today as the people of the Near East with the inflectional languages of Akkadian, Aramaic, Hebrew, and Arabic.

SEPTUAGINT—The Greek translation of the Old Testament accomplished in Alexandria, beginning c. 280 B.C. under the patronage of Ptolemy II, supposedly by seventy-two Jewish scribes, and used widely in Palestine during the time of Christ. (Symbolized as "LXX").

SHEKINAH—A term signifying the "dwelling" of God's presence, first localized in the Old Testament in the pillar of cloud and departing the temple in Ezekiel 10:18, and reappearing in the Person of Christ, as God localized.

SOTERIOLOGY—The doctrine of salvation as declared and elucidated in the Bible.

STOICISM—A pantheistic religious system, as initiated by Zeno in the fourth century B.C. and popularized by Senaca in apostolic times, which regarded all events as inevitable, passionate expression futile, pleasure or pain a matter of indifference, and resignation to circumstances the only answer to the problems of life.

SYNAGOGUE—A religious, social, and educational Jewish center which was developed during the time of Babylonian exile as a substitute for temple worship and continued as a place of community gathering for worship and Torah study.

SYNCRETISM—A philosophical method of appropriating and amalgamating useful elements from various systems into a pre-determined pattern to blend and unite them against a common opponent.

SYNERGISM—A term which signifies a "working together," or cooperative effort. Relative to the doctrine of salvation it signified the Pelagian view (opposing Augustine's Monergism) that salvation is achieved by a cooperative effort of God and man.

SYNOPTICS—The first three Gospels, Matthew, Mark, and Luke, called "Synoptics," (which means to "see together" or to take a common view of) because of the similarity of the materials presented.

SYSTEMATIC THEOLOGY—Theology is the study and science of God and His relations with His universe. Systematic theology is a thematic arrangement of the study incorporating into its system all related facts and truths from all credible sources available, nature, Scripture, and logic.

TABLE OF NATIONS—The table of genealogies recorded in Genesis 10 where all the nations of the world are traced from the sons of Noah—Shem, Ham, and Japheth.

TALMUD—A Jewish compendium of Israel's civil and religious laws, which are not treated in the *Pentateuch,* with comments, opinions, and judgments of Jewish teachers from the period c. 300 B.C. to A.D. 500. It is composed of two parts, the *Mishna* (oral laws themselves) and the *Gemara* (the commentaries). Two Talmuds were written, the Babylonian, with its Gemara by Babylonian commentators, and the Jerusalem with its Gemara by Palestinian commentators.

TARGUMS—A group of translations or paraphrases of the Old Testament in Aramaic, preserved orally from about the time of Ezra to Christ, and reduced to writing between the first and tenth centuries.

TATIAN'S DIATESSARON—See "Diatessaron."

TELL EL AMARNA—Clay tablets, discovered at Tel-el-Amarna, Egypt in 1887, of official documents sent from Palestinian governors to Egyptian Pharaohs Amenhotep III and IV around 1400 B.C., requesting aid against foreign invaders, and written in the Akkadian dialect.

TELL—A hill or mound under which an ancient city or civilization has been buried, many of which have been found in Egypt, Mesopotamia, Palestine, and Syria. (Arabic term).

TESTAMENT—A term transliterated from the Latin *testamentum* meaning covenant, and denoting the two sections of the Scriptures (from the time of Tertullian c. A.D. 155), which two testaments are theologically distinguished by the annulling of the Mosaic covenant and the commencing of a new order at the death of Christ and the instituting of a new High Priest in man's relations with God.

TETRAGRAMMATON—The four-consonant name of the Lord (YHWH), pronounced "Yahweh," and translated "Kurios" by the Greek Septuagint and New Testament writers, generally translated into English as "LORD."

TEXTUAL CRITICISM—The science or discipline of theological study which examines the extant ancient biblical texts with a view to determining the most exact original texts (often called "lower criticism"). See Criticism.

TEXTUS RECEPTUS—The "received text," a publication of the Greek New Testament in 1633 in Holland, based mainly on French texts of Stephanus and Beza, and prefaced as "received by all" by the Elzevir Brothers publishers in this second edition.

THEISM—Christian and Judaic theism is that philosophical system which accepts both the transcendency and immanency of God, Creator and Sustainer of the universe, with personality and infinite attributes.

THEOLOGY—An organized science of the facts and truths of God and His relations to His universe.

THEOPHANY—An appearance of God in human form to various individuals in the Old Testament (e.g., Gen. 12:7, 18:1; Judg. 13:6; etc.).

TORAH—The Mosaic Pentateuch transliterated from the Hebrew root *tarah,* meaning "to teach," especially from a divine source (later broadened to include "Oral Traditions").

TRINITY—A designation for the one God, Father, Son, and Holy Spirit, signifying that within the one essence of the Godhead there are three Persons, which are neither three Gods nor three parts of God, but a Trinity in Unity, three personalities in one essence, without human or physical analogy.

TYPE—A type is an Old Testament illustration which, while having a place and purpose in biblical history, also is divinely appointed to foreshadow some New Testament truth, relative to God's Kingdom.

UGARITIC—See "Ras Shamra Tablets."

UNCIAL WRITING—The early method of writing manuscripts with all capital letters, each formed separately, which method was in vogue from the fourth to the tenth centuries A.D.

UNIFORMITARIANISM—The theory of science that the development and growth of the universe to its present state can be explained by natural processes observable and operating today, in contrast to "catastrophism" which recognizes the interposition of certain catastrophes to account in part for present phenomena.

UNIVERSALISM—The doctrine of the ultimate salvation or bliss of all individuals whether following a period of punishment or apart from such.

VERBAL, PLENARY INSPIRATION—The view of inspiration which recognizes that the Bible is divinely inspired (and therefore inerrant and authoritative) in every word (verbal) and in every part (plenary, or completely). It is distinguished from the view of "verbal dictation" in that it recognizes that God spoke to and through individual personalities, utilizing their different backgrounds and styles to express God's word in human language without error.

VICARIOUS—A term transliterated from the Latin, signifying "substitutionary," as in the vicarious sacrifice of Christ for the sins of men.

VULGATE—The name given to Jerome's translation of the Bible (c. 400) by the Council of Trent in 1545. The translation was made at the request of Pope Damascus to supply a unified and reliable text in the language of the common people.

WADI—An oriental term for a riverbed or brookbed which is usually dry except in the rainy season.

WESTERN TEXT—One of four classes of texts, proposed by Wescott and Hort, which class originated in Syria in the second century A.D. and was carried to the West and used by the Latin Fathers. It consists of a group of texts looked on with suspicion because of the evident free departures from the true texts where greater force and definitude were desired.

WISDOM—A term used in the Old Testament to signify human skills, abilities, or judgments, which may or may not be God-given. In the New Testament it is both a human intellectual capacity and a revelation of God's Person, program, or will, incarnated in the Person of Christ.

WISDOM LITERATURE—The books of *Job, Proverbs,* and *Ecclesiastes,* dealing with philosophical and practical wisdom concerning life.

YAHWEH—Pronunciation of Hebrew tetragrammaton name for the triune God (YHWH, Hebrew has no written vowels), traditionally spelled "Jehovah" (using vowel pointings of "Adonai," supposedly to avoid blasphemy of saying sacred name, Lev. 24:16; Amos 6:10). From the root "hayah" ("to be"), the name signified for Israel God's character as covenant-keeping, faithful and immutable ("He who is what He is," Ex. 3:14). Translated "kurios" by the LXX and NT writers, it is often written as "LORD" in English versions.

ZEALOTS—A militant, loyalist party of the Jews in the first century A.D. who considered violence justifiable in the interest of Jewish independence, similar to the Pharisees in doctrinal concepts, but extreme in their nationalistic spirit.

ZIGGURATS—Ancient terraced towers of Babylonia and Syria, erected as sacred shrines, and successors in a sense to the Tower of Babel.

ZOROASTRIANISM—A Persian religion developed from about the sixth century B.C. and named after Zoroaster. Dualistic, it emphasized the need to fight for the good, meek, and noble as against the cruel, in view of a resurrection and judgment.

Index of Charts and Special Features

NOTES

NOTES

NOTES

NOTES

NOTES